AMAZONS TO
FIGHTER PILOTS

AMAZONS TO FIGHTER PILOTS

A Biographical Dictionary of Military Women

Volume Two: R–Z

Reina Pennington, Editor

Robin Higham, Advisory Editor

Foreword by Gerhard Weinberg

Greenwood Press
Westport, Connecticut • London

Library of Congress Cataloging-in-Publication Data

Amazons to fighter pilots : a biographical dictionary of military women / Reina
  Pennington, editor ; Robin Higham, advisory editor ; foreword by Gerhard Weinberg.
    p. cm.
  Includes bibliographical references and index.
  ISBN 0–313–29197–7 (set : alk. paper)—ISBN 0–313–32707–6 (v. 1 : alk. paper)—
    ISBN 0–313–32708–4 (v. 2 : alk. paper)
  1. Women soldiers—Biography—Dictionaries. 2. Women
sailors—Biography—Dictionaries. I. Pennington, Reina, 1956– II. Higham, Robin D. S.
U52.A44 2003
355'.0082—dc21   2002044777

British Library Cataloguing in Publication Data is available.

Library of Congress Catalog Card Number: 2002044777
ISBN: 0–313–29197–7 (set)
      0–313–32707–6 (v.1)
      0–313–32708–4 (v.2)

First published in 2003

Greenwood Press, 88 Post Road West, Westport, CT 06881
An imprint of Greenwood Publishing Group, Inc.
www.greenwood.com

Printed in the United States of America

The paper used in this book complies with the
Permanent Paper Standard issued by the National
Information Standards Organization (Z39.48–1984).

10 9 8 7 6 5 4 3 2 1

Contents

List of Entries by Geographic Region

Note: Some of the individuals listed may not have their own entry but appear in other entries (for example, within a group entry). Others may be mentioned in more than one entry. Check the index for precise locations.

List of Entries by Time Period/Conflict

Note: Some of the individuals listed may not have their own entry but appear in other entries (for example, within a group entry). Others may be mentioned in more than one entry. Check the index for precise locations.

Ancient and Classical Times

Amazons

Arsinoë III

Artemisia I of Halicarnassus

Artemisia II of Halicarnassus

Berenice II Euergetes

Berenice Syra

Boudicca

Candace

Cartimandua

Chi Zhaoping

Chiomara

Cimbrian women

Cleopatra VII

Cloelia

Cynane

Deborah

Eurydice II

Hatchepsut

Judith

Olympias

Phung Thi Chinh

Semiramis

Telesilla of Argos

Teuta

Tomyris

Triaria, Empress

Trung Trac and Trung Nhi

Late Antiquity (3rd–7th Centuries)

Brunehaut

Clotild

Fredegund

Hind bint'Utba

Kāhina

Khawlah, Bint al-Azwar al-Kindiyyah

Leubevére

Li Xiu

List of Entries by Role/ Branch of Service

Note: Some of the individuals listed may not have their own entry but appear in other entries (for example, within a group entry). Others may be mentioned in more than one entry. Check the index for precise locations.

Auxiliary Forces

ATA (Air Transport Auxiliary)

ATS (Auxiliary Territorial Service)

Cochran, Jacqueline

Gower, Pauline

Love, Nancy

OLK (Ochotnicza Legia Kobiet)

Osoaviakhim

WAAAF (Women's Auxiliary Australian Air Force)

WAAC (Women's Auxiliary Army Corps)

WAFS (Women's Auxiliary Ferrying Squadron)

WASP (Women's Airforce Service Pilots)

Women's Land Army

Women's Military Congress

Women's Military Unions

Zagórska, Aleksandra

Aviation Air Forces

122nd Aviation Group

125th Guards Bomber Aviation Regiment

46th Guards Bomber Aviation Regiment

586th Fighter Aviation Regiment

Brasseur, Deanna

Chechneva, Marina

Clay, Wendy

Dolgorukaia, Princess Sofiia Aleksandrovna

Egorova [Timofeeva], Anna Aleksandrovna

Fedutenko, Nadezhda

Fomicheva-Levashova, Klavdiia

Foster, Jane

Grizodubova, Valentina

Hellstrom, Sheila

Holm, Jeanne

Khomiakova, Valeriia

List of Entries by Role/Branch of Service

List of Entries by Prisoner/POW Status

Note: Some of the individuals listed may not have their own entry but appear in other entries (for example, within a group entry). Others may be mentioned in more than one entry. Check the index for precise locations.

List of Entries on Groups and Organizations

Note: Some of the individuals listed may not have their own entry but appear in other entries (for example, within a group entry). Others may be mentioned in more than one entry. Check the index for precise locations.

122nd Aviation Group

125th Guards Bomber Aviation Regiment

46th Guards Bomber Aviation Regiment

586th Fighter Aviation Regiment

Algerian-French War, women in

American Civil War, women in

Armia Krajowa

ATA (Air Transport Auxiliary)

ATS (Auxiliary Territorial Service)

Australian Defence Forces, women in

Central Women's School for Sniper Training

CHEN

Cimbrian women

Crusades, women in

Dahomey, women in army of

Eger, women in siege of

Emilia Plater Independent Women's Battalion

FANY Corps (First Aid Nursing Yeomanry Corps)

French Revolution and Napoleonic era, women soldiers in

Hero of the Soviet Union, women recipients

Hungary, women in 1956 revolution

Hussite wars, women in

Israeli War of Independence, women's military roles

Libya, military women in

"Nancy Harts"

Native American women

OLK (Ochotnicza Legia Kobiet)

Order of Glory, women recipients

Order of St. George, women recipients

Order of the Red Banner, women recipients

Osoaviakhim

Paraguayan women in the War of the Triple Alliance

AMAZONS TO
FIGHTER PILOTS

R

RASKOVA, MARINA MIKHAILOVNA MALININA (born 28 March 1912; died 4 January 1943, Russia). Major, Red Army Air Force. Military pilot and navigator, Regimental commander, Soviet Union, Second World War. Hero of the Soviet Union.

Marina Malinina was born to parents who envisioned a career in music for her. However, her father's death when she was only six years old put the family in a bad financial situation, and Marina decided to pursue chemistry as a more profitable profession than music. She married Sergei Raskov when she was about eighteen years old and divorced him six years later, keeping custody of their daughter Tania.

In 1931 Raskova began working at the Zhukovsky Air Force Engineering Academy in Moscow, where she served as a laboratory assistant for A.V. Beliakov (later famous for his participation in a polar flight from Russia to the United States). Beliakov's specialty was navigation, and Raskova became fascinated with the subject and by 1932 had trained and begun flying as a navigator. Her mother had retired and was able to care for Raskova's daughter, freeing Raskova to pursue a career in teaching and flying. By passing "external examinations," in 1933 Marina Raskova became the first woman to qualify as an air force navigator. She subsequently became an instructor at the Zhukovsky Academy, which sponsored her continued training as both a navigator and a pilot. She also graduated in 1941 from the M.V. Frunze Academy, a prestigious center of military study and research.

In the late 1930s she participated in a series of record-setting flights. Raskova was best known for her role in a 1938 flight in which she and two pilots set

Undated portrait of Marina Mikhailovna Malinina Raskova. (Library of Congress)

a new women's record for distance. The flight was planned by pilot **Valentina Grizodubova,** who brought in Polina Osipenko as copilot and Marina Raskova as navigator. In an aircraft named *Rodina* (Motherland) the three women flew from Moscow to the Far East, nearly 3,700 miles. The route was to be from Moscow to the Far East, a nonstop flight of some twenty-five to thirty hours over the wild terrain of Siberia. Stalin took a personal interest in the planning of the flight. The *Rodina* took off as scheduled on 24 September 1938, but icing, poor visibility near the destination, and low fuel required the crew to make a forced landing in the desolate and swampy Far East. Raskova had to jump out before the landing in order to lighten the plane; she spent ten days wandering in the taiga with little food and no water. A massive air search finally located the *Rodina* and Raskova.

The episode garnered the kind of public attention in the Soviet Union that Charles Lindbergh's crossing of the Atlantic had received in the West. Stalin hosted a Kremlin reception for the *Rodina*'s crew upon their return to Moscow. Raskova, Grizodubova, and Osipenko became the first women to receive the **Hero of the Soviet Union** award and the only women to receive it before the war. One female pilot wrote of Moscow in the late 1930s, "In those years, the names of Grizodubova and Raskova . . . were on everyone's lips."

Raskova wrote that after the flight she and her colleagues received many letters asking them to tell the story of how they became pilots. She decided to write an account of her life, including her ordeal in the taiga, published in 1938 as *Notes of a Navigator*. Raskova's example inspired many Soviet women to learn to fly; young girls pasted her newspaper photographs into their notebooks as if she were a movie star. Raskova was as famous in her native country as was Amelia Earhart or **Jacqueline Cochran** in the United States. It was not only Raskova's fame and flying skill, but her endurance during her trial of survival that won her the love of other women.

When war broke out in 1941, it was Marina Raskova who instigated the creation of all-female combat aviation regiments. All accounts indicate that forming the units was Raskova's idea, and that she persuaded the government to agree. In various reports Raskova went either to the Defense Ministry, "the authorities," or directly to Stalin and convinced them that women's combat aviation regiments should be created. It seems unlikely that these units would have existed if it had not been for Raskova's efforts. Raskova was not, for the most part, enlisting raw recruits, but skilled pilots who could immediately contribute to the war effort. Despite her own influence and the availability of women pilots, Raskova met opposition in getting official approval for the women's regiments. The process took many weeks, from late June or early July 1941 until mid-October.

Raskova was also active early in the war in promoting public support for the war effort. In one famous speech given in Moscow on 8 September 1941, Raskova noted that Soviet women, whether currently working in agriculture, industry, or the professions, were "ready at any moment to sit down in a combat machine and plunge into battle." She urged women to "stand in the ranks of the warriors for freedom!" One month later Raskova received approval to form the **122nd Aviation Group** from which three all-female combat regiments would be created. Raskova created a core staff chosen from women already in the military to assist with personnel selection and training.

Raskova completed the initial organization, formation, and recruitment of the 122nd in an astonishingly short period of time. She received official approval to create women's aviation regiments on 8 October, began interviewing on 10 October, and on 17 October oversaw the evacuation and transfer of her entire organization from Moscow to the city of Engels, several hundred miles east. The journey took nine days by train; Raskova spent time in each of the cars during the course of the journey. Raisa Aronova recalled that Raskova "was always fresh, neat, energetic. Her authority and simply her personal charm in large part contributed to the strengthening of discipline and order in our still motley military unit."

At Engels the female trainees underwent an extremely condensed, intensive course of training. Raskova directly supervised the training of all three regiments, and since one regiment was training for night work, it was a twenty-four-hour-a-day job. She also sat in on many classes and took examinations as she prepared herself to fly the Pe-2 dive bomber. One pilot noted, "It seemed that she never rested. . . . To all of us it seemed that this woman possessed unprecedented energy." Raskova was soft-spoken, though firm, and was beloved by her subordinates to the point of idolization. One of her deputies described her as "gentle and tactful" and said, "I don't remember a single case when she yelled or even raised her voice, or rudely interrupted a subordinate. Her method of education was persuasion."

Raskova made many trips to Moscow and other locations to ensure that equipment was delivered to the 122nd as promised. She was involved in disputes with factory directors. There was a severe shortage of military aircraft in early 1942, and some managers were reluctant to release aircraft to "a bunch of girls" when there were operational regiments also awaiting deliveries.

When training was completed, Raskova took command of the 587th Bomber Aviation Regiment (later the **125th Guards**). Sadly, she never had the chance to fly in combat. On 4 January 1943, en route to the regiment's first operational post near Stalingrad, Raskova was flying the lead aircraft in a three-plane formation of Pe-2 dive bombers when a winter storm closed in. Unable to locate an airfield, with darkness closing in, they had no choice but to try to land. Two of the Pe-2s landed safely in a field, but Raskova's aircraft crashed, killing everyone aboard: Raskova and three men (the regimental navigator, the gunner, and a mechanic who was hitching a ride). At the age of thirty, Raskova was dead; her body was interred at Red Square in Moscow. For ten days the newspapers carried tributes, copies of speeches, and letters signed by people like Stalin and Grizodubova. Raskova's death was a severe blow to the regiments; when she died, many feared that the regiments would be dissolved.

Some later observers have questioned Raskova's flying skills; others have suggested that she should never have been permitted into a command position without having had the usual preliminary military command experience, but should have remained a staff officer, overseeing the women pilots from headquarters. But Raskova, like many Soviet women, wanted to be in combat herself. Other inexperienced women pilots proved themselves quite capable during the war in both flying and leadership positions. Raskova's death is most likely attributable to weather, chance, and perhaps fatigue.

It appears that Raskova was genuinely loved by virtually all who knew her. Many women veterans commented that the impression she made upon them in person was even more profound than when they had idolized her from afar. Raskova is regarded with deep affection and respect and was truly a pioneer in aviation.

Bibliography: Aronova, *Nochnye ved'my*, 1980; Brontman and Khvat, *The Heroic Flight of the Rodina*, 1938; Cottam, *In the Sky above the Front*, 1984, *Women in Air War*, 1997, *Women in War and Resistance*, 1998, and "Soviet Women Soldiers in World War II: Three Biographical Sketches," 2001; Migunova, *Prodolzheniie podviga*, 1976; Pennington, *Wings, Women, and War*, 2001; Raskova, *Zapiski shturmana*, 1976.

—Reina Pennington

RATHBUN-NEALY, MELISSA (born 9 March 1970). Specialist 4th Class United States Army. United States, Gulf War.

During the Gulf War Specialist Melissa Rathbun-Nealy became the first American enlisted woman to be captured as a prisoner of war and the first U.S. woman prisoner of war since the Second World War. Rathbun-Nealy was a twenty-year-old truck driver assigned to the 233rd Transportation Company, 70th Ordnance Battalion, Fort Bliss, Texas, when she was deployed with her unit to Saudi Arabia in October 1990. On 31 January 1991 she and Specialist David Lockett were delivering supplies to troops when her vehicle and one other took a wrong turn near the bor-

> I have absolutely no problem with women in combat units . . . the idea that women can't make good soldiers is a mindset, not an incontrovertible fact.
>
> —William G. Bainbridge, and Dan Cragg, *Top Sergeant: the Life and Times of Sergeant Major of the Army William G. Bainbridge* (New York: Fawcett Books, 1995), 59.

der of Kuwait and Saudi Arabia. The lost soldiers believed that they were headed back to their base, but were in fact moving in the direction of fighting in the Saudi Arabian town of Khafji. When they encountered a disabled Saudi tank in the road and enemy troops ahead, one truck was able to turn around and escape, but Rathbun-Nealy's vehicle became stuck in the sand. She and Specialist Lockett were wounded by enemy gunfire; she received a bullet through her upper arm and shrapnel in her lower arm, and Lockett was shot in the chest.

Rathbun-Nealy was first taken to a prison in Basra, then to Baghdad; she spent thirty-four days as a POW. She later told her father that she was given "excellent care" by her captors, who told her that she was a hero "as brave as Stallone and as beautiful as Brooke Shields." However, Rathbun-Nealy did not consider herself a hero, saying, "I just got stuck in the sand." She was released by the Iraqis on 4 March 1991.

Bibliography: "As Brave as Stallone . . . Beautiful as Brooke Shields," *Washington Post* 6 March 1991: 23A; Francke, *Ground Zero*, 1997; Holm, *Women in the Military*, 1992.

—Vicki L. Friedl

RAZIYA, SULTAN (died 1240, India), also known as Raziyya, Altamsh, Radiyya Bint Shams al-Din Iltutmish. Ruler, Delhi Sultanate (1236–1240).

Sultan Raziya, who ruled in northern India in the thirteenth century, was an unusual figure in many ways. She was the only woman among the thirty-two sultans, or rulers, in the three-century history of the Delhi Sultanate (1206–1526). Raziya was raised and trained to take on a man's role as sultan, and she wore male clothing (including trousers, turban, and sword) and went without the usual woman's veil. She pursued men's activities, such as hunting, and led her army in battle.

The life and career of Raziya have never been adequately reconstructed. The most complete contemporary account of her reign is the *Tabaqat-i-Nasiri*, which was written twenty-one years after Raziya's death by one of her opponents, Minhaj-us-Sinaj. This work is remarkably balanced in its assessment of Raziya, but is unfortunately lacking in detail. Nevertheless, it has formed the basis for all modern studies of the life and career of this remarkable woman.

Raziya's father, Shams-ud-Din Iltutmish, was an elite slave-soldier of the central Asian Ilbari tribe in the service of Muhammad Ghori, the founder of the first lasting Turkish sultanate in South Asia. Granted freedom in 1206, Iltutmish led a faction of nobles opposed to the hereditary succession of Aram Shah, eldest son of Muhammad Ghori. Deposing Aram Shah in 1211, Iltutmish permanently moved the capital of the sultanate from Lahore to Delhi and spent much of the rest of his career consolidating rebellious frontier provinces and adding new territories in Rajputana and Malwa to the empire. Under his governance the Delhi Sultanate benefited from the displacement of numerous central Asian warriors and scholars by the Mongol conqueror Genghis Khan;

these refugees were absorbed into the Indo-Islamic elite, although Iltutmish did not assist the Muslim states of Afghanistan.

Iltutmish determined that his family should found a dynasty, but the death of his eldest son, Nasir-ud-Din, in 1229 endangered his scheme. His most powerful queen, Shah Turkan, put forward her son Rukn-ud-Din Firoz as heir to the throne, but Iltutmish himself favored his daughter, Raziya. She was accordingly raised as a son, permitted to attend court, and instructed in military arts and statecraft. Before Iltutmish died in 1236, Raziya held several major posts in his government, attending mainly to financial matters.

When Iltutmish died, the Turkish nobility, known as "the Forty," joined forces with the queen, Shah Turkan, to proclaim her son Rukn-ud-Din the new sultan. Provincial *iqtadars* (governors) recognized the new ruler's weaknesses and rebelled, marching upon the capital. Within the palace Shah Turkan unleashed a campaign of assassination against Iltutmish's family. Fearing for her life, Raziya raised a rebellion among the Muslim population of Delhi while Rukn-ud-Din's army was marching to meet the rebel *iqtadars* of Lahore and Multan. The congregation of the Jama Masjid, proclaiming Raziya the rightful heir to the throne, attacked the palace and killed Shah Turkan; when Rukn-ud-Din turned back to recapture the capital, the garrison, now under Raziya's command, captured and executed him. Raziya took the title of sultan and was proclaimed as such in the reading of the *khutba* in the Jama Masjid at Friday prayers. One of her first acts was to strike coins in her own name.

Raziya's first challenge as ruler of Delhi was the suppression of the rebel *iqtadars* of the western provinces. With few military forces at her disposal, she relied upon bold tactics and subtle propaganda to strengthen her political position. Unnerving the enemy troops with threats of retribution and using well-placed bribes, Raziya dispersed the rebel coalition and won the allegiance of much of the empire. Within her own government Raziya subsequently elevated a new elite of Indian bureaucrats and warriors, thus minimizing the political influence of the Forty at the court. Keenly aware of the treachery of many of the noblility, Raziya transferred numerous provincial governors and engaged much of the army in a campaign to recover Ranthambhor Fort from the Rajputs.

Unable to oppose Raziya militarily, her enemies sought to undermine her authority by targeting the popular support upon which it rested. Raziya was accused of displaying improper affection for one of her court favorites, an Abyssinian slave-soldier named Jalal-ud-Din Yakut, who held the office of royal stable master and attended Raziya's horse. Such rumors, however, did not sap the loyalty of Raziya's army, which crushed a subsequent attempt by religious fanatics to raise a revolt in the capital. Nevertheless, Raziya's chief advisors were quickly being drawn into a conspiracy against her, and she was forced to become increasingly autocratic and ruthless in order to survive. Raziya responded to a plot against her by several courtiers and *iqtadars* by calling Zia-ud-Din Junaidi, governor of Gwalior, to her presence and sentencing him to death on the spot. Outraged, the governors of Lahore and Multan accused Raziya of adultery and behavior "derogatory to the pride of the Turks"; no sooner had she descended upon Lahore with her troops, however, than word arrived of a fresh revolt in Bathinda.

Raziya marched at once against Altuniah, *iqtadar* of Bathinda, but was defeated and captured. Her unpopular confidant Jalal-ud-Din Yakut was slain by her own officers during the battle. The Forty took advantage of Raziya's imprisonment to proclaim one of her half-brothers, Behram, the new sultan of Delhi and monopolized for themselves the highest state offices. Altuniah, excluded from these latest political maneuvers, changed sides and allied with Raziya; the two married with an agreement to share the sultanate. Together they marched to recapture Delhi, but their dispirited army soon dwindled. The survivors, cornered at Kaithal, were destroyed on 13 October 1240; Altuniah and Raziya were taken prisoner by the Forty and beheaded the following day.

Despite the scandals, disasters, and brevity of her reign, Raziya came to be celebrated by Indo-Islamic historians as one of the most able of the Delhi sultans. Minhaj-us-Siraj remarked in his account written in 1261, "Sultan Raziya was a great monarch. She was wise, just, and generous, a benefactor to her kingdom, a dispenser of justice, the protector of her subjects, and the leader of her armies. She was endowed with all the qualities befitting a king, but she was not born of the right sex, and so in the estimation of men, all these virtues were useless." His analysis of Raziya's character and administration was to set the tone for most future accounts of her career.

Bibliography: Brij Bushan, *Sultan Raziya,* 1990; Mernissi and Lakeland, *The Forgotten Queens of Islam,* 1993; Minhaj-us-Siraj, *Tabaqat-i-Nasiri,* 1984.

—James W. Hoover

REACHY, IGNACIA (born 1816?, Guadalajara; died 1866). Soldier, French intervention in Mexico, nineteenth century.

Ignacia Reachy was born in Guadalajara about 1816 (some sources indicate 1828). During the French intervention in Mexico at the time of the **American Civil War,** Reachy started a women's battalion. Various officers gave her military attire, affirming the right of a "valiant woman patriot" to fight in battles dressed as a soldier: Colonel Antonio Rojas gave her riding boots, Colonel Gonzalez gave her a uniform of a second lieutenant, and General Ignacio Zaragoza put her in the Second Division under General Jose Maria Arteaga. Reachy distinguished herself in the Battle of Acultzingo, 28 April 1862. She was captured by the French while covering the retreat of General Arteaga. After being in prison for a year, she escaped and presented herself to General Arteaga for more combat duty. Her last rank was as a commander of the Lancers of Jalisco until she died in action in 1866.

Bibliography: Kentner, "The Socio-Political Role of Women in the Mexican Wars of Independence," 1974; Romero Aceves, *La mujer en la historia de México*, 1982; Salas, *Soldaderas*, 1990.

—Elizabeth Salas

REISNER, LARISA MIKHAILOVNA (born 1 May 1895, Vilna, Poland; died 1926). Military commissar, Naval Staff Headquarters, Red Fleet. Russia, Russian Civil War.

One of very few women to serve in the navy during the **Russian Civil War,** Larisa Reisner matched her unique military contribution with significant literary activities. Best known in the prewar years as a writer, Reisner demonstrated skill, intelligence, and initiative in her military endeavors. After joining the Communist Party in the spring of 1918, she began a three-year term of service in the naval forces. Her service record included postings as chief of a reconnaissance detachment, political worker in the Volga-Caspian Fleet responsible for mobilizing sailors for special missions, and commissar in Naval Staff Headquarters. During this period Reisner participated in naval operations on the Volga, the Kame, and the Caspian Sea. In the pivotal August 1918 battle for Sviazhsk she served as chief of an intelligence section of the Volga River flotilla. In his description of the operation, War Minister Leon Trotsky wrote: "With her appearance of an Olympian goddess, she combined a subtle and ironical mind and the courage of a warrior" (Trotsky, 139).

Reisner exhibited this courage in her reconnaissance work in particular. Arrested on one mission while disguised as a peasant worker, she was captured but managed to escape in the midst of interrogation by a Japanese intelligence officer. A comrade in arms, the writer V. Vishnevskii, claimed that Reisner's composure under close-range enemy fire instilled confidence among skeptical sailors, as did the "knowledge and strength" she displayed on joint reconnaissance missions (Naumova, 166). Reisner put this knowledge to good use by establishing the first cavalry reconnaissance unit among sailors of the Red Fleet. Throughout her service she continued to make literary contributions to military journals such as the *Red Baltic Fleet, Red Gazette,* and *Voenmor.* After the war she wrote one of the first books on the Civil War; entitled *The Front,* this collection of wartime sketches was popular with the Soviet reading public until 1929, when her work fell into disfavor as a result of its sympathetic treatment of many discredited heroes of the Civil War. On demobilization in 1921 Reisner was assigned to diplomatic work in the newly created republic of Afghanistan. In 1926 she fell victim to typhus.

Bibliography: Baturina, *Pravda stavshaia legendoi,* 1964; Naumova, "Zhenshchina s barrikady," 1968; Reisner, *Svyazhsk,* 1948; Trotsky, *My Life,* 1930; Zeide, "Larisa Reisner," 1992.

—Mary Allen

REITSCH, HANNA (born 29 March 1912, Hirschberg, Silesia; died 24 August 1979, Frankfurt, Germany). Flight captain. Military test pilot, Germany, Second World War; recipient of Military Flying Medal, Iron Cross I and II.

The diminutive Hanna Reitsch, who stood just over five feet tall and weighed less than one hundred pounds, was a gifted pilot and a controversial and exceptional woman. Her biographer Dennis Piszkiewicz describes her as having "the drive of Amelia Earhart, the vision of Charles Lindbergh, and the daring of Chuck Yeager." She became a test pilot of military aircraft; and at a time when most German women were confined to the spheres of "kitchen, children, and church" she never married or had children. She never joined the Nazi Party; however, her loyalty to the Nazi

Wolf Hirth helping Hanna Reitsch out of their experimental glider. (Library of Congress)

regime and her brash attitude evoked widespread antagonism. Virtually all sources agree on her skill, bravery, and boldness.

Her childhood ambition was to become a "flying missionary doctor" in Africa; she seems to have added the "missionary doctor" part mainly to justify flying lessons. When she was a young woman, her increasing involvement in flying quickly eclipsed her medical studies. During the summer of 1933 she became an instructor in a gliding school and became the first woman and one of the first pilots to cross the Alps in a glider. Beginning in 1934, she participated in a number of international competitions and exhibitions, traveling to Brazil, Argentina, Finland, and the United States.

Germany was still operating under the constraints of the Treaty of Versailles, forbidding it to have an active air force, and thus glider schools attained a unique significance in providing a pool of potential pilots and attracted the attention of military leaders. Reitsch became a member of the German Institute for Glider Research in Darmstadt in 1931 and remained associated with this organization until the end of the war in May 1945. She had the freedom to conduct meteorological flights, long-distance flights, and altitude flights with an eye toward setting new records. She was also permitted to attend training at the Civil Airways Training School in Stettin, although women were not allowed to fly as professional pilots. During the 1936 Berlin Olympics Reitsch performed in aerial displays with a gliding team. In 1936, as a reward for her test work, Luftwaffe General-Major Ernst Udet awarded her the honorary title of "flight captain," previously reserved for Lufthansa pilots (although she did not meet all the formal requirements). Hanna Reitsch never held actual military rank, but she often appeared in a uniformlike suit.

In September 1937 Udet sent Reitsch to the Luftwaffe testing station at Rechlin for duty as a test pilot, giving her a quasi-military status. Reitsch notes that "among the staff at Rechlin my appointment aroused not only surprise but the strongest disapproval" (*Flying Is My Life*, 128). Nevertheless, the support of Udet and a few other high-ranking Luftwaffe commanders guaranteed Reitsch the opportunity to fly in a wide variety of military aircraft. When Charles Lindbergh visited Germany in 1937, Reitsch put on a helicopter demonstration for him that so impressed her superiors that she was awarded the Military Flying Medal. Later she tested a prototype troop-carrying glider. After war broke out in 1939, Reitsch says that she wrote to General von Richthofen, whose commands included the Glider Unit, and asked to be accepted as an active military pilot, but was refused.

As fighting intensified, Reitsch noted that her increasing involvement in military test flying generated continued hostility from male military pilots. She writes that "their obstructive attitude was to cost me many battles and would often have delayed the execution of vital work had it not been for the timely help of men like Udet and Ritter von Greim, who were intent on a larger struggle than the battle of the sexes and, thanks to their rank and position, were able to smooth my path" (*Flying Is My Life*, 177). After Udet shot himself in 1941, Reitsch increasingly turned to General Robert Ritter von Greim. He was an important mentor to Reitsch; apparently their relationship included a romantic aspect as well, though in a platonic sense. Reitsch was involved in testing many odd innovations, including a glider tanker, and was invited to visit Göring and Hitler. The Führer rewarded her work with an Iron Cross (second class) in 1941. She tested variants of the Messerschmitt-163 Komet "rocket plane" and was so badly wounded in one crash landing that she spent several months in the hospital in the winter of 1942–1943.

By late 1943 Reitsch became convinced that the war was being lost, and that drastic actions would be required to save Germany. Together with a few friends she proposed an "Operation Self-Sacrifice" unit of pilots who would fly either rockets or "glider bombs" into key enemy facilities. The Luftwaffe rejected the idea, but when Reitsch met with Hitler in February 1944 to receive the Iron Cross (first class), she presented the plan to him. Hitler disliked the idea, but she was given permission to experiment with potential aircraft. The unit never became operational, although Reitsch went on to fly as a test pilot in an experimental piloted V-1 rocket. She derided the "total failure on the part of higher authority to appreciate that the Suicide Group was no stunt, but a collection of brave, clear-headed and intelligent Germans" (*Flying Is My Life*, 219).

In 1945 Reitsch served as a special courier, flying in and out of cities under siege as the Allied armies closed in on Berlin. Her most notorious action was a visit to Hitler's bunker during the final days of the war—an event famously recounted in two books published in 1947, William Shirer's *End of a Berlin Diary* and Hugh Trevor-Roper's *The Last Days of Hitler*. On 25 April 1945 Reitsch accompanied Ritter von Greim on a hazardous flight into besieged Berlin. She claims that she was summoned by Greim due to her recent experience as a courier pilot with low-level "hedge-hopping" flights. It was first planned to use a helicopter to fly into Berlin, and Reitsch was a natural choice as pilot; but when they got to the transfer point at Rechlin, the helicopter had been damaged. They were flown in a Focke-Wulf 190 to Gatow, with Reitsch squeezed into the fuselage. The last leg of the flight was in a single-seat Fieseler Storch; Greim piloted the plane and Reitsch wedged herself in behind his seat, from which position she claims to have landed the aircraft after Greim was wounded and lost consciousness.

Once in Berlin, Greim and Reitsch were taken to Hitler's bunker, where Greim was treated for injuries to his foot sustained during the flight. Greim had been summoned by Hitler to replace Göring as commander in chief of the Luftwaffe. Greim was ordered to leave Berlin, but it took several days before an operational aircraft was successfully sent in. Reitsch says that she was summoned to a private meeting with Hitler, during which he gave her two phials of poison so that she and Greim would have "freedom of choice." Transport became available on 28 April. Shirer reports that Reitsch said that she and Greim both wanted to stay (and die) with the Führer. This is not reflected in her autobiography, however; she says that Hitler insisted that they leave. The flight out was as hazardous as the flight in, and they negotiated a series of brief visits to various bases in their attempt to get to safety and determine whether any effective defense could be organized. During this time Reitsch claims to have met with Himmler and says that she castigated him for his disloyalty to Hitler.

Most of Reitsch's family had left Silesia for Salzburg. Convinced that the Russians would rule their homeland and that such a life would be unbearable, in May 1945 her parents, her sister Heidi, and Heidi's three children all committed suicide. Greim broke the news to her; within the month, while in custody of the Americans, he too died, using the cyanide capsule Hitler had given him. It appears that Reitsch intended to follow him after a decent interval to avoid the scandal of an obvious suicide pact.

Reitsch ended up a prisoner of the American occupying forces. It was known that she was one of the last people to see Hitler alive, and she was interrogated about the possibility that Hitler was in hiding or had escaped. The "interrogations" consisted of discussions and interviews in a house-arrest situation, and she developed a friendly relationship with her American interviewers. She willingly wrote reports on her work as a test pilot. Her interrogation became part of the supporting documents at the Nuremberg war-crimes trials. The interpretation of those interrogations that appeared in Trevor-Roper's book outraged her, but became the standard source on her wartime activities. Trevor-Roper took a negative view of her character and portrays her as self-aggrandizing and hysterical.

Reitsch spent more than a year in an internment camp. Constrained by postwar prohibitions against flying, she spent time writing her memoir, *Flying Is My Life* (first published in Germany in 1951), in an attempt to counter Trevor-Roper's portrayal. She returned to gliding in 1951 and returned to competition and record-setting activities during the 1950s. She once more became an informal ambassador for her country, traveling to India in 1959 (where she took Nehru on a glider flight), Finland in 1960, and the United States in 1961. She met President Kennedy and Wernher von Braun and was warmly received by the American public. Reitsch spent 1962–1966 in Africa, setting up and running a gliding school in Ghana. Unfortunately, her reputation was once again tarnished by her association with a dictator, Kwame Nkrumah, and some Westerners viewed her gliding school as neofascist in its emphasis on discipline. When Nkrumah was ousted from power, she returned to Europe, made more visits to the United States, and became an Austrian citizen. She attained several more world gliding records before dying of heart failure in 1979 at age sixty-seven.

Reitsch's story makes an interesting contrast with that of the other German female test pilot, **Melitta Schiller Stauffenberg**. Lomax characterizes them as "bitter rivals" and says that "Hanna refused to have anything to do with Melitta, who was several years older, or acknowledge her as an equal" (47). In a 1960 interview Reitsch stated that she was the only woman test pilot in wartime Germany and categorized Stauffenberg as "a scientist pilot." However, Stauffenberg appears to have had equivalent status to Reitsch as a test pilot. While their accomplishments were similar, their politics differed. Stauffenberg supported her brother-in-law's plot to kill Hitler, while Reitsch supported the Führer to the very end of the war.

Bibliography: Lomax, *Hanna Reitsch: Flying for the Fatherland*, 1988; Piszkiewicz, *The Fantastic Flights of Hanna Reitsch*, 1997; Reitsch, *Flying Is My Life*, 1954, and USAF Oral

History Interview K146.34-86, by Kenneth Leish, October 1960; Shirer, *End of a Berlin Diary*, 1947; Trevor-Roper, *The Last Days of Hitler*, 1971.

—Reina Pennington

REN, first name unknown (fl. 768, China), also known as Mistress of Wanhua. Commander of a self-organized troop during the Tang dynasty (618–907).

Ren used her family fortune to form a brigade that she led to protect Chengdu from rebels. Tall, robust, valiant, and determined, Ren was very good at archery on horseback. She was the concubine of Cui Ning (ca. 735–796), administrator of Chengdu, the defense commissioner of Shanxi, and military commissioner of Xichuan.

In 768 Cui Ning was called to the capital, leaving his brother Cui Kuan to guard Chengdu. Yang Zilin, the regional inspector of Luzhou, took the opportunity to rebel, leading several thousand cavalry to attack Chengdu, which he took and pillaged, defeating Cui Kuan. At that point Ren used 100,000 taels' worth of family assets to recruit about 1,000 fighters overnight, formed a troop, and led it herself against the rebel. Yang Zilin feared her attack, and inside Chengdu his troops' provisions were short. Yang was said to know some black magic, and that night he invoked a pouring rain that let him escape by boat. Thus Ren succeeded in ousting Yang Zilin and recapturing the city of Chengdu.

Bibliography: Chen Menglei, *Gujin tushu jicheng (Qin ding)*, 1993; Liu Xu, *Jiu Tang shu*, 1975; Ou-yang Xiu, *Xin Tang shu*, 1975.

—Sherry J. Mou

RESISTANCE MOVEMENTS, FRENCH WOMEN (1940–1945). France, Second World War.

During the German occupation of France in the Second World War, French women assisted the Resistance's efforts in significant numbers—higher than their general participation in French society. As in other resistance movements, women's roles have been trivialized or ignored in many histories. Women performed a wide variety of supporting functions such as serving as couriers, transport, clerical work, decoding, and hiding and caring for Resistance members. Most of the early activities of the resistance movement consisted of this sort of planning and organizing work.

In late 1940 Charles de Gaulle authorized the creation of a women's auxiliary corps patterned on the British **ATS** that eventually included 4,000 members. Although the British allowed women to train for clandestine intelligence and sabotage activities, and many were later dropped into occupied France, the French auxiliary under de Gaulle relegated most women to traditional nursing and support duties.

However, women also played military roles. They were rarely allowed to

The telephone operator at Boussoulet, in the Haute Loire, helps members of the Maquis of French Resistence who use a code between telephone operators to report the movements of the German forces, 1944. (Hulton/Archive by Getty Images)

fight due to the combination of male opposition and the scarcity of weapons. Historian Margaret Weitz believes that there was much stronger prejudice against women using weapons in France than in Greece or Italy. As in other resistance movements, it was primarily in Communist cells that women had the widest latitude for action, in keeping with socialist ideals of gender equality (though old attitudes prevailed even here). When paramilitary groups (the maquis) were formed, often in more remote areas, they frequently relied on women to keep them supplied and to deliver weapons, but rarely allowed women to fight.

Some of the better-known women in the resistance movement included Lucie Samuel (who used the pseudonym of Lucie Aubrac) and Berty Albrecht; both helped form cells and worked on their underground newspapers. Lucie Samuel's Jewish husband, an escaped prisoner of war, also served in the Resistance. When he was arrested by the Gestapo in 1943, the pregnant Lucie arranged and participated in his escape (along with a dozen others). They were evacuated to England, where Lucie gave birth to a daughter a few days later. After the war she received the Croix de Guerre and the French Medal of the Resistance. Danielle Casanova, a former dentist, led a Communist group in Paris that was responsible for the assassination of a German soldier; Casanova was arrested and later died in Auschwitz.

Only one woman is known to have led a major Resistance network: Marie-Madeleine Fourcade, who was promoted by British intelligence to lead its 3,000-strong network when the leader was captured. A few women, like Jeanne Bohec, worked in demolitions. Georgette "Claude" Gérard was unusual in heading a maquis. She had been rejected by the Free French but then worked with Allied agents as a scout. After being arrested and released by the Vichy, she relocated and helped organize the "Secret Army" in the Dordogne region. After some eighteen months as a regional leader responsible for some 5,000 people, she was arrested by the Germans in May 1944. Gérard was released during the liberation of France, and when women were integrated into the French army, she attained the rank of major and was assigned to supervise other women.

Women who were trained abroad, such as **Noor Inayat Khan,** seem to have been more likely to play an active role in the French Resistance. Marguerite Petitjean was one of eleven French women trained by the British SOE (Special Operations Executive) and smuggled into occupied France. Petitjean had been trained in sabotage, but was assigned by her French boss primarily as a courier. She helped carry explosives used in derailing trains and escaped to Spain in August 1944 when her network was compromised. Russian partisan Liudmila Kashichkina had been captured in Russia and was transferred in 1944 to a concentration camp in France; she escaped and joined the maquis and was awarded the Croix de Guerre after the war.

Women risked arrest, torture, and execution for their Resistance activities, just as men did. Although women might evade detection more easily since they were seen as less likely to be a threat, there is little evidence that they were treated gently when caught. Early in the war the Germans sometimes commuted women's death sentences although men arrested at the same time were executed. However, many women were subjected to arduous forms of interrogation and torture. Kashichkina described the interrogation she endured: "I was kicked and beaten with whips [until my skin was in ribbons]. I learned what a fascist 'manicure' is. Your hands are put on a table and a device of some kind pushes needles under your nails, all your nails at the same time. The pain is indescribable. You lose consciousness immediately . . . and there was some kind of machine. You heard your bones crunching and dislocating." Fourcade has stated that women endured torture better than men, reporting that none of the female agents in her network who were captured broke under torture, although some of the men did.

Given that resistance movements kept few records, it is impossible to determine the precise number of women and men who participated in the French Resistance. More than 200,000 were officially recognized by the French government after the war. One of the best sources in English on this topic is Margaret C. Weitz's *Sisters in the Resistance: How Women Fought to Free France, 1940–1945*. Weitz based her work on some eighty oral history interviews, as well as written materials.

Bibliography: Alexiyevich, *War's Unwomanly Face*, 1988; Rossiter, *Women in the Resistance*, 1986; Schwartz, "Redefining Resistance: Women's Activism in Wartime France," 1987; Weitz, *Sisters in the Resistance*, 1995, and "Soldiers in the Shadows," 2000.

—Reina Pennington

RESISTANCE MOVEMENTS, ITALIAN WOMEN (1943–1945). Italy, Second World War.

The Italian Resistance that operated between September 1943 and May 1945 was a mass-based and well-organized operation, eventually comprised of some 200,000 partisans, including at least 35,000 women. This movement sought to overthrow the existing Fascist regime, expel the Nazi German occupation forces, and bring an end to the war. After 1943, fourteen of thirty-one German and Fascist divisions in Italy were held down permanently by Resistance forces. Although existing Italian law barred women from employment in any military service, the initially irregular structure and political nature of the Resistance gave some women opportunities to serve in combat and as officers and commanders. Some of the women actually had military rank and command positions and were decorated for their services.

Although not officially a combat position, the *staffetta* or courier was one of the key figures of the Resistance. The functions of a courier were to maintain communication among the units and their command, to transport arms and documents, and occasionally to engage in combat. Most units had between four and ten *staffette* serving them. It was fairly unusual for women to be attached to the formal brigades that engaged enemy units on the largest scale, most closely resembled traditional military organizations, and were quartered in a segregated fashion, often in the mountains. Commanders of these units normally were not anxious to have women in their companies because they feared that women would be a burden or a distraction. Nevertheless, women did join the brigades. Elsa Oliva (born 1921), for example, insisted that she wanted to resist with arms in hand and eventually became a lieutenant in the Second Brigade of the Beltrami Division in Novara.

The experiences of the women who served in these units give evidence of a sort of de facto equality in the face of assault, possible capture, harsh weather, hunger, and even death. When the women engaged in combat, they responded to the demands of warfare much like their male counterparts. One woman who served with a northern ski-patrol band recalled that after serving as a partisan for a year, she had, in fact, forgotten what it meant to be a woman. Others recognized that their nontraditional behavior was perhaps suspect in society's eyes. Irma Marchiani (born 1911) was a vice commander of a battalion in the area of Modena, was captured and shot by the Germans in November 1944, and was posthumously awarded a gold medal. During a period of imprisonment she had written to her brother assuring him that she had served her unit well and had done nothing to tarnish the family reputation.

The majority of women partisans were attached to small attack squads or groups (GAP/SAP). These units were usually detachments of five or six people attached to a larger squad and often operated in an area close to the residences of the participants. The squads had diverse functions, from sabotage and single-strike activity to serving as auxiliaries for the brigades in recruiting, education, and defending the population. Some GAPs had unusually high female participation, and a few of these were all-female and were led by women. In Emilia Romagna the 7th GAP Gianni had 200 members, 80 of them women, led by Novella Albertazzi (born 1925, code name Vanda). Albertazzi had joined the GAP as a *staffetta* in December 1943 after one of her brothers had been shot and another imprisoned. In November 1944 Vanda led the women of her unit in a major battle at their partisan base in the ruins of Ospedal Maggiore, where they fought against cannons, tanks, and armored cars. In the Roman Resistance the GAP units were especially important, and women like Carla Capponi (born 1921), another gold-medal recipient, earned a reputation for courage and calmness under fire. Capponi also notes that initially men resisted having women in the squads and arming them, but eventually the men accepted them.

Women also served in all-female detachments, a number of which were formally recognized by the partisan military command. Their functions were more civilian or political than military, and in some cases the detachments consisted of female relatives of partisans, many of whom had to abandon their homes when Fascist reprisals intensified and they were sought by the Fascist police.

In general, women were crucial participants in all phases of the Resistance. Like their male counterparts, they hoped to defeat an enemy they had come to fear and even despise, and many were willing, even anxious, to take up arms to do so. Some were awarded national and provincial medals for valor and heroism and became national figures after the war. Of the 35,000 women in the resistance, about 5,000 were imprisoned, 3,000 were deported to Germany, and 650 died in combat or were executed. However, the experience of the Resistance did not promote significant rearrangement of gender structures after the war, and in the case of military equity in particular, it would be forty years or more before the first tentative steps were taken to open the armed forces to Italian women.

Bibliography: Alloisio and Beltrami, *Volontarie della Libertà,* 1981; Bortolotti, *Le donne della Resistenza antifascista,* 1978; Bruzzone, "Women in the Italian Resistance," 1982; Franceschi and Gaetá, *L'altra metà della Resistenza,* 1978; Slaughter, *Women and the Italian Resistance,* 1997.

—Jane Slaughter

RESISTANCE MOVEMENTS, SOVIET WOMEN (1941–1944). German-occupied territories of the Soviet Union (Baltic States, Belarus', Moldova, Russia, Ukraine), Second World War.

The Soviet partisan movement was one of the most dramatic aspects of the Second World War. Although the overall effectiveness of the partisan movement has often been exaggerated, the partisan forces helped create chaos and sow panic behind German lines. In addition, the existence of a partisan movement, ostensibly composed of a cross section of the Soviet public, provided crucial political legitimacy for the Soviet regime. According to Soviet secondary sources, women composed approximately 10 percent (between 18,000 and 25,000 women depending on the figures used) of the partisans by 1944. By playing an active part in the partisan movement and, more important, by participating in overt acts of resistance against the German occupiers, Soviet women provided concrete evidence of the "popular" legitimacy of the Soviet

Two Soviet women in the Second World War discuss their attitude toward killing:

[Sniper Klavdiia Krokhina] recalls that she cried after shooting her first German. Afterwards, she saw charred human bones where some Russian prisoners had been burned alive by retreating Germans. "After that," she says, "I never felt pity whenever I killed . . . all I felt was fury and a desire to avenge."

[Partisan Antonina Kondrashova]: "I still have in my ears the cry of a child as it was thrown into a well [by the Germans]. . . . After that, when you went on a mission, your whole spirit urged you to do only one thing: to kill them as soon as possible and as many as possible, destroy them in the cruellest way."

—Svetlana Alexiyevich, *War's Unwomanly Face*, trans. Keith Hammond and Lyudmila Lezhneva (Moscow: Progress Publishers, 1988), 16, 194.

Union. Women partisans not only had to fight the enemy, however, but often had to overcome the hostility of their male counterparts.

Official Soviet policy at the beginning of the war sought to exclude women from the incipient partisan movement. Since central and local officials largely believed that women were incapable of bearing the rigors of military life and combat, women were denied a place in the partisan detachments. However, despite this opposition, some women still participated in the movement, usually as nurses or radio operators. These women included Red Army personnel cut off behind enemy lines and local Party and Komsomol (Young Communist League) officials who helped organize the detachments. Organizing partisan units was extremely dangerous, but as one woman recalled, "I was a Komsomol member and could not remain passive."

Young women also accounted for a substantial number of the saboteurs whom Soviet officials dispatched behind enemy lines in 1941 to attack German infrastructure. Sent out with appallingly little training or equipment, these dedicated women sacrificed themselves in often suicidal efforts. Among them was Zoia Kosmodem'ianskaia, possibly the most famous Soviet heroine of the Second World War (see under "Representative Participants").

By the summer of 1942 Soviet authorities came to believe that the existence of a partisan movement constituted proof that the Soviet people loved the Soviet system and hated their German "liberators." Hence official policy now encouraged all Soviet citizens, regardless of occupation, nationality, political affiliation, or gender, to join the partisans' struggle against the occupiers. Beginning in early 1943, Soviet officials, including the head of the Central Staff of the Partisan Movement (the chief agency overseeing partisan operations), P.K. Ponomarenko, and the first secretary of the Komsomol, N.A. Mikhailov, instructed partisan commanders to allow women to enlist in their detachments. As Ponomarenko warned one local Party official in February 1943, the failure to include women and other traditional noncombatants in the "active struggle" against the Germans would be a serious political mistake that could alienate civilians from the regime. Although many veteran partisan commanders resisted and evaded these directives, the number of women partisans nevertheless increased significantly in 1943. For example, in April 1943 women constituted only 1.9 percent of the personnel of the 3rd Leningrad Partisan Brigade. By November this percentage rose to 6.6 percent even as the unit surged in size from 1,450 to 2,760 partisans during the same period. Such increases gave credence to the official claim that the partisan movement indeed represented a cross section of the Soviet population, thus demonstrating popular support for the Soviet Union.

Although Moscow now encouraged women to join the movement, they still faced significant obstacles in becoming partisans. Many women who wanted to join the detachments were unable to do so because they were often the only ones left to look after their parents and children and could not abandon them. Those women who were able to make their way to a partisan camp were often turned away by commanders on the pretext that they were unarmed or lacked military experience. Many women partisans who were permitted to join a unit faced sexual harassment, particularly from officers and commanders, who used their rank and power to intimidate women; some women were even raped by their own "comrades."

Women partisans were usually relegated to the customary "feminine" duties such as cooking, cleaning, and clothes washing. Although these tasks were essential to maintaining the partisan detachments, they were at the bottom of the partisan hierarchy, which not surprisingly valued combat duties over "civilian" ones. When women attempted to go on missions with men, male partisans often refused them, claiming that women lacked the necessary military skills, conveniently forgetting that many male partisans were also civilians without military training. Women were also denied combat roles because of their alleged physical weakness. This myth of female physical weakness was belied by the fact that many women had to carry extremely heavy burdens when the unit was on the march. "The men carried only a rifle, but I had to carry a rifle, a typewriter and [my two year old daughter]," a woman partisan veteran remembered.

Another traditional but more prestigious "noncombat" role for women was medical service. Women comprised the majority of doctors and nurses in the movement. Nurses accompanied partisans on their missions and risked their own lives attending to the wounded under fire. When units were forced to evacuate their bases and leave their wounded behind, partisan nurses almost always remained with them, despite the certainty of torture and execution if they were captured.

Partly due to pressure from central authorities, but primarily due to their own perseverance and determination, many women partisans succeeded in obtaining combat posts and proved themselves the equals of men in combat. Tatiana Ivanova, a Smolensk partisan, for example, told her commander, "Give me [a weapon], send me, and I will fight." Ivanova was fortunate in that her commander included her in combat operations. She recalled, "When I left the detachment the boys even said, that girl, she was a real partisan." Some detachments organized their women fighters in all-female units, which often were more highly motivated and performed better than their male counterparts. However, even when women went on missions, they still carried the double shift of "work" and household chores. As one male commander recollected, "Upon returning from an action the men would go off to rest, while the girls got down to cooking or washing clothes."

Some women partisans had highly specialized skills as radio operators, snipers, scouts, and saboteurs. Women commanded companies and platoons within the detachments, including both all-women and mixed units. Although no women became detachment or brigade commanders, a few, such as P.N. Lokhmotina, A.N. Zakharova, and V.A. Zolotova, were political commissars, the "executive officers" of their units.

Women also served as couriers between the partisans and the underground networks, carrying crucial information, political materials, and weapons. Women exploited the German gender stereotype that women were less likely to be involved in resistance organizations than men. As one woman explained, "Nobody else could manage the German and police sentries. I alone could do it." In order to smuggle leaflets, women often wrapped them around their children, and one veteran recalled that when she was pregnant, she carried a mine "next to the beating heart of my baby." Women agents infiltrated German administrative offices and headquarters and passed valuable information to the partisans and underground committees. These activities also included political assassination (Elena Mazanik [see under "Representative Participants"] killed Wilhelm Kube, the Reichskommissar of Belorussia).

Soviet women partisans made significant contributions to the partisan movement, far beyond what mere numbers would indicate. Their presence alone indicated that Soviet citizens, both men and women, were willing to risk their lives to resist Nazi occupation. Moreover, they fought under extremely adverse conditions. Not only did women partisans have to battle the Germans, but they did so in the face of opposition from their male comrades. Yet despite these difficulties, Soviet women partisans served their country with honor and distinction. As one women partisan veteran stated, "My only dream was to avenge, to die and to have a book written about me. I was ready to do anything for my homeland."

Representative Participants

Chaikina, Elizaveta Ivanova (1918–1941). Secretary of the underground Komsomol District Committee, Penov District, Kalinin Region, Soviet Union. As secretary of an underground Komsomol committee in Kalinin Oblast, Chaikina organized the local partisan movement there. She was captured and executed by the Germans in late 1941. In 1942 she was posthumously awarded the title **Hero of the Soviet Union,** her country's highest honor.

Kosmodem'ianskaia, Zoia Anatol'evna (1923–1941). At the age of eighteen Kosmodem'ianskaia became a partisan and helped capture the village of Petrishchevo, Moscow Region. Kosmodem'ianskaia was caught by the Germans in the Moscow region in November 1941, where she had been trying to set fire to a German stable. After being tortured, she was executed in a public hanging on 29 November 1941. Soviet propagandists hailed Kosmodem'ianskaia during the war as the supreme example of Soviet youth's patriotism and heroism, and in 1942 she was posthumously honored as a Hero of the Soviet Union. Even today, despite new reports that she may in fact have been killed by Soviet citizens to prevent her from destroying their homes as part of Stalin's scorched-earth policy, Kosmodem'ianskaia remains one of the most recognizable symbols of wartime sacrifice and suffering in post-Soviet Russia.

Mazanik, Elena Grigor'evna (1918–?). Mazanik infiltrated the household of Wilhelm Kube, the Reichskommissar for Belorussia, in the guise of a chambermaid. On the night of 22 September 1943 she assassinated him by placing a time-delayed bomb under his bed. She was evacuated from occupied territory and made a Hero of the Soviet Union on 29 October 1943.

Zverova, Nina Ivanova (1924–?). Commander of an all-women platoon, Second Leningrad Partisan Brigade, Leningrad Region. Zverova joined the partisans in 1942 and soon became a valued member of the unit. Although she was offered command of an all-male platoon, she turned it down. Her women's platoon was regarded as one of the best in the brigade and was often given the most difficult assignments. Zverova served with distinction in the brigade until its disbandment in 1944.

Bibliography: Alexiyevich, *War's Unwomanly Face,* 1988; Cottam, *Women in War and Resistance,* 1998; Ponomarenko, *Vsenarodnaia bor'ba,* 1986; Sartorti, "On the Making of Heroes, Heroines, and Saints," 1995; Slepyan, "The People's Avengers," 1994.

—Kenneth Slepyan

RESISTANCE MOVEMENTS, YUGOSLAVIAN WOMEN (1940–1945). Yugoslavia, Second World War.

Yugoslavia was a unique state, created in the aftermath of the First World War by merging six distinctive but historically related cultures, Serbia, Macedonia, Croatia, Slovenia, Montenegro, and Bosnia-Herzegovina, as well as other smaller groups. These cultures had varying traditions regarding the participation of women in combat. Though all were patriarchal, some allowed women to play a military role in time of need, with the southern regions more prominent than the north-

Lieutenant Colonel Henry Peoples, a recipient of the Distinguished Flying Cross who flew during the war with the Army Air Forces' 332nd Fighter Group, commented on women in combat:

I was shot down over Yugoslavia and spent two months with Tito and his partisans. I went on a couple of their raids and they were exciting, to put it mildly. They were fine people and their women, such women! You talk about amazons; those Yugoslavian female partisans, I swear they could outfight their men. They were strictly f. and f.: fearless and ferocious.

—Mary Penick Motley, ed., *The Invisible Soldier: The Experience of the Black Soldier, World War II* (Detroit: Wayne State University Press, 1975), 234.

ern areas. Montenegrin women fought against the Turks in 1858 and were active in resistance against Austrian domination in the early twentieth century. A few women in all the territories were active supporters of socialist movements in the late nineteenth and early twentieth centuries. Marxist groups advocated equality for women and permitted women to play more active roles than other political movements.

Before the Second World War there had been a political struggle by the Communists under Josip Broz Tito against the military dictatorship then in power. This political struggle continued during the German occupation with the goal of determining the postwar political structure of Yugoslavia. When the Axis powers invaded, some nationalities collaborated, while others resisted. In addition, there were ethnic conflicts between the groups themselves. Political, military, and ethnic issues were intricately intertwined.

There were non-Communist partisan groups, but women's participation was overwhelmingly in Tito's forces. The Yugoslav National Liberation Movement (NOP) claimed nearly six million supporters, 30 percent of whom were women. It was these women who provided essential support to liberation fighters in the form of food and protection.

The Yugoslav National Liberation Army (NOV) grew from 80,000 in 1941 to 800,000 in 1945, including about 100,000 women, or about 12 percent of the total. Women were eager volunteers from the spring of 1941. Training was integrated; it was common for partisans to get about a month of training before being assigned to a unit. The official policy of the Communist Party and its fighting arms was that women were to be considered as equals, but in practice there was significant discrimination.

Records are erratic and focused on the last two years of the war, but analysts have determined some general trends. Women served most often as plain soldiers and medics, although some women worked in radio, artillery, political, and intelligence positions. The average female partisan was a village girl, a teenager or in her twenties. Most women were never promoted above the lowest ranks; only 2,000 (2 percent) became officers. As in other resistance movements, women in the NOV were recorded as performing a variety of heroic acts: throwing bombs under enemy tanks and fighting alongside men in battle. Since most women were regarded as medics, whatever their other functions, they were frequently the ones who rescued wounded partisans from under enemy fire.

Casualty figures for Yugoslavian women are interesting. Overall mortality from all causes for Yugoslavian women, 1941–1945, was 8.5 percent. The death rate for female fighters in NOV was 25 percent. The risk for "civilian" women in the resistance was greater than for those who fought. Women's mortality in combat was twice that of men (about 11 percent in the NOV). There is no definitive explanation for this, but it seems likely that the inexperience of Yugoslavian women was a factor. Many were illiterate and had little or no preparation for fighting, whereas many men were experienced hunters or had served in the military. It has also been suggested that what many women lacked in skill, they made up for in bravado, an often fatal combination. This is a trenchant example of the quandary of war: women are not supposed to fight, and so they are purposely excluded from prewar training and discouraged from learning "masculine" skills like hunting and shooting. When war comes, women in fact do fight, but they are thrown into combat with virtually no training or experience. Most telling is the fact that the mortality rate for women in the broader movement, NOP, was highest of all—31 percent. Female fighters had a better chance of surviving the war than civilian women in the resistance.

In keeping with the worldwide trend, the Yugoslavian military excluded women as soon as the war ended. Women's participation in combat was considered irrelevant to the composition of a peacetime army in a society that valued a return to "normality" as its priority. In a state like Yugoslavia where radical political change was occurring, there were limits to the degree of social change that could be tolerated.

Uncovering the history of these women has been problematic. In addition to the usual difficulties with sources on resistance activities, the movements in Yugoslavia involved diverse national groups, often at odds with one another. Most of the publications that do exist are official publications of the former Yugoslavian government. Some interesting memoirs also mention women in the resistance; Milovan Djilas wrote that they fought more bravely than the men. Only a few scholars have attempted to examine this episode. The most important is Barbara Jancar-Webster, whose 1990 book is the most comprehensive study to date.

Bibliography: Jancar, "Yugoslavia: War of Resistance," 1982; Jancar-Webster, *Women and Revolution in Yugoslavia, 1941–1945*, 1990; Reed, "The Anti-Fascist Front of Women and the Communist Party in Croatia: Conflicts within the Resistance," 1980.

—Reina Pennington

ROCHEJAQUELEIN, THE MARQUISE DE LA (born 1772, Versailles; died 1857, Poitiers, France), née Marie-Louise-Victoire Donnissan. Counterrevolutionary, France, War of the Vendée, 1793–1800.

The Marquise de La Rochejaquelein did not fight in the War of the Vendée, but her experiences as the wife of a soldier were in many ways typical. She documented those experiences in a popular memoir that is one of the best firsthand accounts of the conflict.

A member of the aristocracy, Marie-Louise-Victoire Donnissan was born in 1772 and raised in Versailles. In 1789, at the age of seventeen, she married Henri de Lescure. This was the same year in which the **French Revolution** began, with the goal of overthrowing both the monarchy and the traditional French nobility. A counterrevolutionary movement erupted in western France and was named for the region where it was centered, the Vendée; this movement included both royalists who opposed the new revolutionary government and peasants who revolted against the imposition of a national draft in 1793 (the *levée en masse*). Many peasants and nobility were united in their hatred of the anti-Catholic policies of the revolutionary government and the execution of the king in January 1793. This revolt was a major catalyst in the creation of the Reign of Terror, and many of the executions of the Terror occurred in the Vendée.

By March 1793 Marie-Louise-Victoire and her husband, both eager royalists, were at the headquarters of the *armée catholique et royale* (the so-called Vendéens). Lescure became a royalist general, as did the marquise's own father. During the "Virée de galerne," a long march in Brittany and south Normandy in search of English naval support, Lescure was wounded and died. The revolutionary armies in the region had orders to give no quarter; women, priests, and children who supported the revolt were to be killed. In the midst of this violence Marie-Louise-Victoire was left alone and pregnant; she gave birth to a daughter. She lived for several months hidden in Brittany with the help of peasants, but the baby and another child died during this time.

Amnesty was given in 1795, and during that time she married Louis de La Rochejaquelein, a royalist and relative of her late husband. The marquise began to write her *Memoirs* in 1799–1800. The book gives one of the most impressive descriptions of the war from a woman's point of view. She described with grit and insight the lives of men, women, and children, traveling, hiding, and dying; the atrocities committed during these years by the revolutionary forces were graphically described. The simple life with peasants and the daily dangers due to the republican armies all made for a fascinating story. However, the marquise also had a political agenda: to show that before the French Revolution the nobility lived in relative harmony with the lower classes. Her *Memoirs* stress the excellent relationships between Catholics and royalists, peasants and nobles, during the Vendée.

One other interesting aspect of the *Memoirs* is the story of Jeanne Robin. The marquise wrote that in late 1793, about a month before the Second Battle of Thouars, she was approached by a soldier who confided to her that "he" was a woman. The woman, Jeanne Robin, needed one of the light jackets then being issued, but was afraid to be fitted, since the commander had vowed to have any woman found with the army "shorn and driven away." The marquise agreed on the condition that she would check on the girl's character with her parish priest to ensure that she was not a wanton. The priest confirmed that he knew about the girl and that she had "joined the army from good motives" to fight for God and king despite his objections. The marquise wrote that "I kept the girl's secret as I had promised, only telling M. de Lescure her story, while refusing to disclose her name, what she looked like, or what part of the country she came from." Just before the Battle of Thouars Jeanne came to Lescure's headquarters, where she revealed her identity: " 'General,' she said, 'I am a woman. Madame de Lescure knows my secret; I do not know whether she has revealed it to you, but in any case she was to have made enquiries about me, and the replies will have been favourable. I come to you because I have no shoes and I shall be fighting tomorrow. All I ask of you, if you mean to send me away, is to wait till after the battle, and I will bear myself so well in it that I am sure you will bid me remain with the army.' To prove her words, during the battle she followed M. de Lescure closely, crying, 'General, you shall never outstrip me, I shall always be as near the Blues as you are.' " The marquise never saw her again, but she wrote that "a woman's body was found among the dead; she was always believed to have been killed in the melee, into which she rushed like a madwoman: this was the origin of the fabulous story of Jeanne de Lescure, who never existed." Robin was not the only militant woman mentioned in the memoirs; Rochejaquelein also mentions a Madame de Bruc, a royalist who "went into battle with her husband" in Charette's army, along with a Madame de Fief who was similarly present on the battlefield.

The Napoleonic administration was opposed to any publication about the politically sensitive events of the Vendée. This delayed publication of the *Memoirs* for several years, but in 1814 the return of the Bourbon monarchy finally permitted publication. In the reactionary atmosphere of post-Napoleonic Europe, the book *Memoirs of the Marquise de La Rochejaquelein* immediately became a great success, not just in France, but throughout Europe.

During the period of the Napoleonic Empire the marquise lived in Deux-Sèvres and Bordelais. Her husband, a secret leader of the royalist movement in France, was killed during the royalist insurrection of 1815 against Napoleon. The marquise lived to the age of eighty-five, witnessing further revolutions in France against the power of the upper classes in 1830 and 1848, and died in 1857.

Bibliography: La Rochejaquelein, *Memoirs,* 1933; Martin, *La Vendée et la France,* 1987.

—Jean-Clément Martin

RODIANA, ONORATA (born early 1400s, Castelleone, a stronghold near Cremona, Italy; died August 1452, Castelleone), also known as Rodiani. Fresco painter and mercenary soldier.

The details of the life of the semilegendary Onorata Rodiana are sketchy. She was born near Cremona in the early fifteenth century and trained as an artist. In 1422 she was commissioned by Cabrino Fondulo, the tyrant of Cremona, to decorate his palace. When a courtier tried to rape her, she stabbed him to death. She fled to the mountains, disguised herself in male attire, and joined a company of professional soldiers led by Oldrado Lampugnano, former confidant and eventual betrayer of Cabrino. Some accounts say that she became a captain and held various military offices. Legend has it that after Cabrino's anger cooled, he reinvited her to complete the frescoes. In 1452 the middle-aged Rodiana was still bearing arms, this time under Conrado Sforza, brother of Duke Francesco, to defend her birthplace against the Venetians. She was mortally wounded and died among her friends and compatriots; she was buried in the parish church on 20 August 1452.

Bibliography: Clement, *Women in the Fine Arts*, 1974; Echols and Williams, *An Annotated Index of Medieval Women*, 1992; Grasselli, *Abecedario biografico*, 1827; Petersen and Wilson, *Women Artists: Recognition and Reappraisal*, 1976.

—Gloria Allaire

RODOLFI, CAMILLA (fl. 1449, Italy). Member of the Rodolfi family of merchants, one of the principal governing families of Vigevano. Mercenary soldier.

During Francesco Sforza's siege of Vigevano in April 1449, Camilla Rodolfi led a group of women who took up arms and held the walls, fighting valiantly after many of their husbands and sons had fallen. Sforza sent in fresh troops, forcing the women to retreat momentarily. According to legend, the attacking warlord himself was hit by a spear thrown down from the walls by a woman. This deed struck terror into the hearts of the attackers and encouraged the besieged to fight on. Nevertheless, Sforza captured the city, and on occasion he reportedly liked to have the former women defenders parade in full armor with their commander, mercenary soldier Camilla Rodolfi.

Bibliography: Buccella and Giorgio, *Memorie istoriche della città e contado di Vigevano*, 1810; Collison-Morley, *The Story of the Sforzas*, 1934; Zimonti, *Vicende storiche vigevanesi*, 1983.

—Gloria Allaire

ROSSI, MARIE T. (born 3 January 1959, Oradell, New Jersey, United States; died 1 March 1991, Saudi Arabia). Major, United States Army. United States, Gulf War.

Percentages of American women on active duty, 2001:

Branch of service	Number of women	Percentage of active-duty personnel
Air Force	66,200	19
Army	72,500	15
Navy	50,800	14
Marine Corps	10,300	6
Coast Guard	3,500	10

—United States Army, Defense Manpower Data Center.

Marie Rossi was a 1980 graduate of Dickinson College, where she was active in the ROTC program. After graduation she entered the army as an officer in the field artillery, then became a helicopter pilot, flying Chinook helicopters. She met her husband, Warrant Officer John Cayton, also a helicopter pilot, while she was stationed in Korea. Both Rossi and her husband were deployed to Saudi Arabia with their respective aviation units in late 1990.

In the Persian Gulf War the thirty-two-year-old Rossi served as the commander of B Company, 2nd Battalion, 159th Aviation Regiment, 18th Aviation Brigade, 24th Infantry Division. She was one of the first U.S. helicopter pilots to fly into enemy territory, leading dozens of missions supplying the troops of the 101st and 82nd Airborne Divisions. Rossi came to personify the Gulf War for many after she was interviewed on CNN on 24 February 1991. She spoke of her feelings as a woman flying into a combat zone: "Sometimes you have to disassociate how you feel personally about the prospect of going into war and, you know, possibly see the death that's going to be there. But personally, as an aviator and as a soldier, this is the moment that everybody trains for—that I've trained for—so I feel ready to meet a challenge."

Major Rossi and her three crew members were killed on 1 March 1991, the day after the ground war ended, when, during a flight made at night in bad weather, she flew her Chinook helicopter into an unlighted microwave tower near her base in northern Saudi Arabia. Major Rossi was buried in Arlington National Cemetery on 11 March 1991.

Bibliography: "Female Pilot, 3 Others Die in Crash of Army Helicopter in Saudi Arabia," *Washington Post* 4 March 1991: 17A; "From All Walks, to Death in War: 304 Desert Storm Americans Forever Bound by History," *Washington Post* 10 March 1991: 1A; Francke, *Ground Zero*, 1997; Holm, *Women in the Military*, 1992.

—Vicki L. Friedl

RUIZ, PETRA (fl. early twentieth century), also known as "Pedro," "Echa Balas." A soldier for the Carranza faction of the 1910 Mexican Revolution.

Petra Ruiz disguised herself as a man, calling herself "Pedro" Ruiz, in order to join the revolutionary forces fighting in the Mexican Revolution (1910–1920). Nicknamed "Echa Balas" (Bullets), she distinguished herself in combat. To protect her identity and isolate herself in camp, she affected a ferocious temper. On one occasion other soldiers were persuaded by fear of her bad temper to surrender to her a young woman captive whom they had intended to rape. Ruiz was promoted to the rank of lieutenant. She revealed her true identity to General Carranza only when she asked for her discharge.

Bibliography: *El nacional* 8 November 1959; Salas, *Soldaderas*, 1990; Soto, "The Mexican Woman: A Study of Her Participation in the Revolution, 1910–1940," 1977.

—Elizabeth Salas

RUSSIAN CIVIL WAR, WOMEN IN (1918–1921).

Although the revolution that brought the Bolsheviks to power in 1917 was almost bloodless, the Russian Civil War that followed was one of the most vicious in history. It consisted of a struggle between Communist forces under the direction of the Bolshevik Party, led by the newly-formed Red Army, and various counterrevolutionary White and nationalist forces. The mass mobilization of women into the military during the Russian Civil War was unprecedented. Over a period of two and a half years approximately 70,000 women were enlisted in the Red Army where they performed both support and combat roles. Women had fought for the tsar in the Russian army in the First

World War (see **Mariia Bochkareva, Anna Krasil'nikova,** and index under First World War), with several receiving the **Order of St. George,** and **Women's Battalions of Death** had been organized under the Provisional Government in 1917. However, few if any women took on military roles in the White armies during the civil war.

Bolshevik military ideology, which advocated formation of a militia made up of the whole people, acted as a major catalyst to the inclusion of women in the new armed forces. During the Bolshevik Revolution of 1917 most of the women in military roles provided medical support in sanitary units; other women volunteers appeared as fighters, detachment commanders, guards, or organizational workers in the ranks of the Red Guard (armed workers). Though the proportion of female Red Guards was nominal (approximately 2.25 percent of the total for the central industrial region), the enlistment of women in an organization that formed the ideological and "manpower" nucleus of the Red Army was significant. For many women, service in Red Guard units provided the conduit to service in the army proper: during the early months of 1918 many Red Guard medical and combat units were disbanded and their personnel were attached to sanitary departments and detachments of the Red Army.

Female troops march during the Russian Revolution. (Hulton/Archive by Getty Images)

As revolution turned into civil war, the Bolsheviks offered women increasingly broader spheres of military action. During the war women helped "defend the revolution" by serving in military auxiliary organizations. In addition to those enlisted in partisan and underground groups, many women were mobilized into workers' militias or special detachments composed largely or exclusively of females. While some nonparty volunteers participated, service in these detachments was compulsory for Communist or Komsomol women who were recruited through special military mobilizations carried out by the Party at a local level. Griesse and Stites estimate that there were around 8,000 women serving in these militia units. Operating independently of the army, militia units were generally involved in the construction of defense works and in police, guard, and security duties or were sent on execution missions. These support functions were generally carried out in the rear, however, trained and armed militia forces were used to combat local counterrevolutionaries or were dispatched to the front as reinforcements in emergency situations.

Service legislation passed in the spring of 1918 also placed women in the ranks of the conventional armed forces. The Decree on Compulsory Military Training issued by the Central Executive Committee (CEC) on 22 April stated that females would be offered training on the same footing as males, and on 29 May 1918 a CEC resolution permitted women to join the Red Army as volunteers (female doctors would be subject to conscription) (Chirkov, 106). At the same time, the Party's Women's Department was instructed to train and mobilize women for medical service in the army and to direct "the most active, conscious and battle-worthy women workers and peasants to military authorities for service in the capacity of reconnaissance workers, ammunition transporters, communications/signal workers and other jobs" (*Sbornik Instryktsii*, 16).

While estimates of the number of women involved vary, by the end of the Civil War female enlistment constituted approximately 2 percent of the total (Chirkov, 107; Dmitrieva, 11). Although service regulations did not designate any positions for women only, the majority were trained for and streamed into two areas. Close to 60 percent of enlisted women were assigned to economic-administrative posts where they served as clerical or communications workers in staff headquarters or as communications orderlies, signalers, and telephone and telegraph operators in field headquarters. Approximately 40 percent served in a medical capacity as sanitary workers, nurses, doctors' assistants, or doctors who worked almost exclusively in the field (Chirkov, 107). While medical service in the Red Army was technically a support position, it differed from nursing in the imperial army. Trained in courses offered jointly by the Women's Department, the Ministry of Health, and the military, when circumstances warranted it, Red medical personnel were expected to fight: most were given rifle and small-arms training and carried arms. Many female medical workers reported serving in a combat capacity, and the dispatch of medical personnel to front-line regions resulted in a relatively high casualty rate among this group. Though women were rarely recruited specifically for combat duty, several women did serve as front line fighters. Many of these were assigned to reconnaissance work, which could be readily combined with the duties of medical or political worker. Another common assignment for women fighters was machine gunner. The battle readiness of female gunners in the cavalry forces was immortalized in the classic Civil War film *Chapaev*. Command authority was occasionally conferred on a select group of females who

To the question of women's mandatory military training: The decree of 22 April 1918, paragraph 1, states that military training is required of every citizen of the Russian Soviet Federal Republic, by age: a) those in school, the lower levels of which will be handled by the People's Commissariat for Education, b) preparatory, from 16 to 18 years, and c) conscription, from 18 to 40 years, moreover it declares that "female citizens train, at their agreement, in the fundamentals [na obshchikh ocnovaniyakh]".

The editors of the journal *Voennoe Delo*, standing by their program of far-ranging scientific study of all questions, connected with the matter of forming a battle-worthy army, have formed a special section for the formation of an opinion on women's mandatory military training, not forgetting, that there have already appeared in the military archives, during the current war, materials which completely prove the military fitness of military units, formed from women volunteers. The Editors

—Editors [chief editor D.N. Lebedev], "To the Question of Women's Mandatory Military Training," *Voennoe Delo* (Military Affairs) 10 July 1918: 12.

demonstrated ability and long-term Party commitment. While there is no evidence that women commanded at the regimental or divisional levels, several did command machine-gun detachments, sapper or medical companies, cavalry platoons, special battalions, or armored trains. Women played an especially important role in army political work. Several held the post of military commissar, and Varvara Karparova served as chief of the Agitation and Enlightenment Department of the All-Russian Bureau of Military Commissars. After the establishment of the army's own political administration, many women were recruited to fill agitational, educational, or cultural posts in various army political departments, and several were promoted to political section chief. (See also **A. P. Bogat, Larisa Reisner,** and index under Russian Civil War.)

Over the war years approximately one-fifth of the Red Army's total force was killed, wounded, or captured: of these, women made up only .18 percent (Kotelenets, 93). These casualty figures suggest that women were exposed to situations involving personal risk less often than men. The military's penchant for streaming women into noncombatant roles is also reflected in the proportion of women decorated for bravery displayed in the fight against enemies of the state: while women constituted close to 2 percent of the total military population, they received only .5 percent of all **Orders of the Red Banner**.

Bibliography: Bochkareva and Liubimova, *Svetlyi put'*, 1967; Chirkov, "Zhenshchiny v Krasnoi Armii v gody Grazhdanskoi Voiny," 1975; Dmitrieva, "Rol' zhenshchin Urala," 1985; Griesse and Stites, "Russia: Revolution and War," 1982; Khromov, S.S., ed., "Grazhdanskaia voina i voennaia interventsiia v SSSR," *Sovetskaia Entsiklopediia*, 1983; Kotelenets, *Zhenshchiny Strany Sovetov*, 1977; *Sbornik instryktsii Otdela TsKRKP Po Rabote Sredi Zhenshchin*, 1920; Wade, *Red Guards*, 1984.

—Mary Allen

S

SAINT-BASLEMONT, ALBERTE-BARBE D'ERNECOURT, MADAME DE

(born 14 May 1607; died 22 May 1660), also known as Barbara of Erecourt, "Lady of St. Belmont." Military leader, France, Thirty Years' War.

The aristocrat Madame de Saint-Baslemont became renowned for defending her lands during the **Thirty Years' War**. We know little of her as a girl except that her aunt raised her and that she was both intelligent and athletic. In 1624 she married Jean-Jacques de Haraucourt and bore three children by 1632. She remained on the family estate when her husband left to fight under his prince, the duke of Lorraine (Lorraine was then an independent principality between France and Germany and became a contested battleground as the duke fought against the French).

Madame de Saint-Baslemont's first armed encounter came in the spring of 1636 when 100 French cavalrymen tried to drive off her cattle herd. Without hesitation she rode out to thwart the theft. She displayed great bravery, including riding through the hostile cavalry to take command of a small friendly force, and stymied the marauders. Although she retired to Bar later that year, she returned in 1638 to fight off bands of *cravates*, as the brigands were known. This remarkable woman neither held a formal commission nor marshaled regular troops, but led a small band of retainers, armed peasants, and feudal vassals. Typically she fought in her hunting attire, which was very much in line with current military garb, and with her hair bobbed in a bowl cut to keep it from inhibiting her in action. She did not exercise command from afar, but led from the front, sword in hand.

Madame de Saint-Baslemont enjoyed such a reputation that refugees came to take shelter under her protection. She scored a major victory against the *cravates* in 1643, after which her main military activity consisted of convoy escort. Although she was strong in martial prowess, she was regarded as a model of Catholic piety as well. Not long after her death she was praised as the "Christian Amazon" in a 1678 biography. She is revered today as a Lorraine heroine.

Bibliography: Cuénin, *La dernière des Amazones*, 1992; Lynn, *Giant of the Grand Siècle*, 1997; Romain, *Les guerrières*, 1931; Tranchant and Ladimir, *Les femmes militaires de la France*, 1866.

—John A. Lynn

SAMSON, DEBORAH (born 17 December 1760, Plympton, Massachusetts; died 29 April 1827, Sharon, Massachusetts), also known as Sampson, Robert Shurtleff/Shirtlieff/Shirtliff. Married surname Gannett. Soldier, Continental army, American Revolutionary War.

DEBORAH SAMPSON.
Published by H. Mann, 1797.

Deborah Sampson, 1797. (Hulton/Archive by Getty Images)

Deborah Samson was one of only a handful of women to receive financial recognition from the government for service during the American Revolution. In 1779 the Continental Congress awarded **Margaret Corbin** disability payment for having taken over her husband's post after he was shot; in 1808 **Anna Maria Lane** was pensioned; and in 1822 **Mary Ludwig Hays McCauley** was pensioned by the Pennsylvania Senate. Like Lane, and unlike Hays and Corbin, Samson served in the American Revolution disguised as a man. She enlisted in May 1782 and received an honorable discharge in October 1783.

Deborah Samson had famous ancestors. Her mother, Deborah Samson, was a descendant of Governor William Bradford; her father, Jonathan Samson, Jr., was a descendant of John Alden, Miles Standish, and Peter Hobart. When Samson was five, her father disappeared, leaving the already-impoverished family with no means of survival. Some accounts claim that her father drowned at sea others note that he left for another wife. An early record from the pension file for her brother, Ephraim, refers to their parents' marital problems. Records on other brothers and sisters were not well kept, possibly another indicator of the family's financial or structural instability. These data from court records fit well with the portion of traditional accounts that claim that as a child Samson went to live with relatives and charitable families and spent the bulk of her childhood as an indentured servant for a large family. All sources agree that Samson grew up in poverty, dependent on the generosity of others, and without the privileges and opportunities that money and social status offer.

In November 1780, at the age of nineteen, Samson joined the Third Baptist Church in Middleborough, Massachusetts. Church records dated September 1782 detail her first attempt to enlist in the army; in a matter-of-fact way they refer to Samson, "who last spring was accused of Dressing in mans Clothes and inlisting as a soldier in the army" (original spelling). According to Herman Mann, Samson inadvertently revealed her identity after this first enlistment, after celebrating her new enlistment-bounty wealth with several drinks in a tavern and buying extravagant clothes. Samson was forced to return the enlistment bounty, according to the document, but was not punished. The entry in the church records that refers to this incident documents the withdrawal of her fellowship because she had mysteriously disappeared from town, unbeknownst to church members, having already enlisted a second time.

Samson enlisted again in May 1782 in Worcester and received an enlistment bounty of sixty pounds. The name she assumed, Robert Shurtliff, first appears in muster rolls dated 17 November 1782. Very little is known about her life in the army. One celebrated aspect of Samson's legend is that during her service she was shot in a skirmish in New York. Documents offer no support for Mann's assertions, and there is much to directly challenge the idea that Samson was wounded at all. Samson's drill sergeant, Lieutenant Calvin Munn, was paraphrased by an 1838 biographer as saying, "A novel was written soon after the war of which she was the heroine, not one fourth part of which is true. She was not wounded as is therein related." Historians have found neither hospital records nor names connected to Samson's treatment. Mann wrote that a French doctor tended to the wound on her head but that "with a penknife and needle, she extracted the ball from her thigh." Since the French doctor remained nameless and Samson allegedly treated herself for the other wound, it is impossible to verify this incident.

In Samson's later petition for back pay she stated that she was wounded in battle, but, significantly, her letters of reference did not include this information in their accounts. Instead, both commented on her service and sought to establish that Samson was in fact enlisted. The resolves of the court granting her back pay also did not comment on any wounds. If Samson was in fact not wounded during her time in the Continental army, she may have fabricated the story in subsequent requests because invalid-pension requests were granted only to soldiers wounded in battle.

It is difficult to sort out fact from fiction in the life of Deborah Samson. Documents seem to challenge the traditional portrayal of her as a woman who sacrificed her traditional female role for patriotism; economic need seems at least as important in her motivation. It is clear that economic difficulties were central in Samson's life, and her options as a single woman without family money were quite limited. Enlisting in the service provided her with a substantial sum of money up front and the promise of more to come.

Although her original discharge paper was destroyed, a replacement issued in 1786 documents that Samson did indeed receive an honorable discharge from General Henry Knox in October 1783. After returning home, according to town records in Sharon, Massachusetts, she married Benjamin Gannett and had three children. During the following years her young family struggled. Postwar inflation made living difficult for many families at this time, and Benjamin Gannett, a farmer, had little money or means. Their financial need led Samson finally to petition the government for back pay in January 1792, which she promptly received.

Five years later Herman Mann published his 1797 account drawing attention to Samson's extraordinary tale. Numerous newspaper articles had already appeared on the subject of her 1782 enlistment in the Continental army and her successful military pension request in 1792. Mann's *The Female Review* was far more sensational, describing a three-year adventure which included rescuing a girl held captive by Indians and triumphing in the Battle of Yorktown. In Mann's tale "Robert Shirtliff" fought equally hard for her virtue by fending off females struck by her heroism and inner strength, and by never allowing male comrades to put their arms around her. As mentioned earlier, when she was wounded, she removed a musket ball from her own thigh in secret, lest she be discovered by a doctor. Later in Mann's tale Samson was stricken with fever and lay dying in a Philadelphia hospital. Her doctor, fearing the worst, in checking her heartbeat thrust his hand under her shirt and to his surprise discovered what Herman Mann's readers already knew. Having been on his deathbed both literally and figuratively, the life of "Robert Shurtliff" was now over. Deborah Samson was nursed back to health, regained her strength, and received an honorable discharge.

Four years after Mann's account appeared, at the age of forty-two, Samson began a solo lecture tour, presenting a speech in uniform and demonstrating her mustering skills. Mann had written the speech, but Samson made her own arrangements and bookings in nearly a dozen towns in Massachusetts, Rhode Island, and New York. The diary she kept that year details many of her expenses and her schedule from March 1802 until her last entry in June 1803. Her income from this tour is unknown, but upon returning to Sharon she once again petitioned Congress, this time for an invalid-veteran pension. Paul Revere, who knew her personally, wrote to Congress in support of her petition, "They have few acres of poor land which they cultivate, but they are really poor." In 1818 Samson again petitioned Congress after a new pension act passed for indigent veterans who had served at least nine months. Congress granted this request, and as a condition for accepting it, Deborah signed papers attesting to her poverty. At Norfolk Circuit Court of Common Pleas, under oath, she listed her property as clothing valued at twenty dollars. Her final pension request in 1820 was rejected at a time when the government, heavily in debt, was reluctant to give out pensions.

In 1827, at the age of sixty-six, Deborah Samson's extraordinary life came to an end. Soon after, her husband, Benjamin Gannett, became the first man to receive a pension on the basis of his wife's military service. The pension was not processed, however, until after Gannett's death in 1837 and was amended the following year "for the relief of the heirs of Deborah Samson Gannett."

One ongoing dispute concerns the correct spelling of her surname. "Samson" is the spelling used in documents concerning Samson and her ancestors; her marriage was recorded with the spelling Samson. Herman Mann misspelled it in the subtitle of his book (*The Female Review: Life of Deborah Sampson* [sic], *the Female Soldier in the War of Revolution*), and by the late eighteenth century "Sampson" became the generally accepted spelling. Most published sources have picked up the spelling as "Sampson."

Although some sources claim that Samson is the only woman known to have served in the American Revolution disguised as a man, there is evidence of at least three other women who did the same. A Sally St. Clair (sometime "St. Clare"), apparently a Creole girl, was killed at the Battle of Savannah, wearing men's clothing. Anna Maria Lane fought at the Battle of Germantown, and **Ann Bailey,** also known as Samuel Gay, served briefly before her identity was discovered and she was discharged for "being a woman."

Bibliography: Archives of the Dedham, Massachusetts Historical Society and Sharon, Massachusetts, Public Library; Davis, "A 'Gallantress,' Gets Her Due," 1981; De Pauw, "Women in Combat," 1980; Foster, "In Defense of All That Is Dear and Lovely," 1995; Guba, *Deborah Samson,* 1992; Mann, *The Female Review,* 1972; Pierce, "Three American Women Pensioned for Military Service," 1975; Seeley, *American Women and the U.S. Armed Forces,* 1992; Stickley, "The Records of Deborah Sampson Gannett," 1972.

—Thomas Alan Foster

SAMSONOVA, E.P. (born?, Bialystok, Russian Poland, died ?) Military driver and nurse, Russia, First World War.

E.P. Samsonova was the daughter of a mechanic from Bialystok and a graduate of the Bestuzhev Higher Courses for Women in St. Petersburg. After the war broke out, she petitioned the minister of war for permission to serve in the active army as a military pilot. Having graduated from courses in Warsaw in automotive maintenance and operation in 1911 and military flight school in Gatchina in 1913, Samsonova was already a fully trained and accomplished driver and pilot. Her application was denied, however, on the ground of her sex (at least one woman did serve as a military aviator in the Russian Army during the First World War; see **Princess Evgeniia Mikhailovna Shakhovskaia**).

Unable to fly for the military, Samsonova entered the army as a nurse but found medical duties unsatisfying. Samsonova then set off for the Galician front and enlisted in a motorcycle company. After proving her abilities, she was allowed to join an automobile detachment and served as a driver at the front. Due to the extremely strenuous nature of the work, such as covering great distances under heavy artillery fire, Samsonova fell ill in January 1915. She was sent to Moscow to recover, and after her convalescence she hoped to return to the front in the capacity of a pilot. It is not known if she succeeded in her aspirations, as no source later than 1915 mentions her. As with other women who fought for the tsar, her achievements would not have been valued by the Bolshevik regime that took power in 1917.

Bibliography: Ardashev, Nikolai, *Velikaia Voina i zhenshchiny russkiia* (Moscow: 1915); "E.P. Samsonova," *Zhenshchiny i Voina* 1 (March 1915): 5–7.

—Laurie Stoff

SÁNCHEZ MORA, ROSARIO (born 1919, Villarejo de Salvanés, province of Madrid, Spain), also known as La Dinamitera (the Dynamiter) because she lost her hand in 1937 in an accident with explosives. Republican soldier, Spanish Civil War.

Rosario Sánchez Mora left her village for Madrid in 1935 in order to learn the trade of seamstress. In the capital she joined the Communist youth movement, Juventudes Socialistas Unificadas, and when the **Spanish Civil War** broke out in July 1936, she enlisted for front-line duty with a group of young political comrades. After the most rudimentary military instruction they were sent into the trenches near Guadalajara, where, in the first weeks of engagement, a great many of them were killed.

Subsequently Sánchez was invited to join an explosives unit operating from an old hut behind the Republican line that ran from Buitrago to Gascones. The work was extremely dangerous. Under the eye of an Asturian miner, Sánchez and her comrades made bombs and grenades with whatever was at hand. They used empty jars, old condensed-milk cans, or spent cartridge canisters. The most dangerous part of their work was closing off the container of the bomb after the percussion cap had been embedded in the dynamite. On 16 September 1937, while she was experimenting with using different wicks and containers, the dynamite with which Sánchez was working exploded, blowing off her hand. (She would later be nicknamed La Dinamitera, "the dynamiter.")

Despite horrific injury and great loss of blood, Sánchez survived. She was taken to a field hospital and then to a surgical base hospital and spent several months in convalescence in Madrid. Once recovered, she returned to her unit, where she worked first as a telephonist at military headquarters and subsequently joined the unit's postal service, sorting and delivering mail to soldiers at the front.

Her exploits were celebrated in a poem by the Republican poet Miguel Hernández that Sánchez herself read over Republican radio. With the defeat of the Republican forces by General Francisco Franco in February 1939 Sánchez was arrested and spent hard years jailed as a political prisoner until her release in March 1942.

Bibliography: Cuevas, *Cárcel de mujeres (1939–1945),* 1985; Mangini, *Memories of Resistance,* 1995.

—Judith Keene

SANDES, FLORA (born 22 January 1876, Poppleton, Yorkshire; died December 1956). Captain, Serbian army, First World War. Received Kara George Star.

Flora Sandes was, uniquely, an Englishwoman who served seven years in the Serbian army, rising from nurse during the typhus epidemic of 1915 to the rank of captain in 1919. On 12 August 1914 she left London with a British Red Cross unit for Serbia and was stationed at Kragujevatz, in a large military hospital. She worked throughout the typhus epidemic of 1915–1916 in Valjevo, even operating on patients after the hospital had lost twenty-one doctors in three weeks. After nursing with Mabel St. Clair Stobart's camp, she was attached to the Second Infantry Regiment of the Serbian army as a private on 28 November 1915 and became an active combatant. By January she had been promoted to corporal, a month later to sergeant, and in May 1916 to honorary second lieutenant by a special act of the Serbian parliament. She was wounded during a battle with the Bulgarians near Salonika and in December 1916 received the Kara George Star for NCOs and was promoted to sergeant-major. She was wounded again in July 1917, but returned to her unit the following October. She participated in the final offensive against the Austrian and Bulgarian forces and was demobilized in 1921. She was also instrumental to the Serbian forces as a fundraiser and good-will ambassador, conducting speaking tours through Australia and Britain and along the western front.

Although Flora Sandes had no formal military training, neither was she a stranger to adventure. The youngest daughter of a rector's large family, she was educated by governesses and trained as a secretary. Later on she shocked her neighbors in Thornton Heath, Surrey, by racing along country lanes in her French motorcar, climbed the Rocky Mountains, and tramped around Ireland and the pyramids in Egypt. She also received first-aid training with the Ladies' Nursing Yeomanry (see **FANY Corps**).

When war broke out in August 1914, Sandes's immediate offer of service to the War Office as a Volunteer Aid Detachment nurse was rejected. But if Britain did not want her, Serbia did. On 12 August she left London with Madame Mabel Grouitch's Red Cross nursing unit bound for Salonika, Greece. Her first journey to Serbia was fraught with difficulties: France was still mobilizing, trains were disrupted, platforms were choked with soldiers on their way to the front, and ships were often scarce. But the nurses arrived after a

387

memorable thirty-six hour voyage from Piraeus to Salonika on the deck of a Greek cattle ship in a raging thunderstorm. From there they traveled by train through the Vardar valley to Kragujevatz. A telegram was waiting when Sandes arrived, stating that her father, the Reverend Samuel Sandes, with whom she had lived until her abrupt departure, had died on 23 August.

She plunged into work at the First Reserve Hospital, where seven English nurses worked with Serbian doctors to tend more than 1,000 sick and wounded soldiers. They were casualties of the Serbs' efforts to repel the Austrian invasion across the Danube. After exhausting hours on duty, the nurses took turns sleeping on straw mattresses, sharing a single blanket, and eating, all in the same room. The hospital was so desperately short of medicine and other supplies that only the worst cases could be treated with anaesthetic.

After the first three months Sandes developed a deep commitment to the Serbian cause. When she returned to London, it was to raise funds for medical supplies, and after only six weeks, Sandes' countrywide tour yielded more than £2,000. She returned to Serbia accompanied by an American nurse, Emily Simmonds, literally sitting on packing cases containing 120 tons of cotton, gauze, and other much-needed materials. Upon their arrival at Nish, the president of Serbia's Red Cross persuaded the women to take the supplies on to Valjevo, a northern town particularly hard hit by the typhus epidemic. An American doctor they met warned that they would be dead within a month if they continued on to the "death trap of Serbia."

By this time the British nurses and doctors in Serbia had assumed political significance. Sandes visited the English consul before leaving Nish and was handed a letter from Sir Edward Grey, the British foreign secretary. Whatever assistance the nurses gave Serbia, he said, "was helping Britain and the Allies and was of inestimable benefit to the common cause." The British nurses were a highly visible sign of Allied concern.

The door was thus opened for British women to set their own course of action in Serbia. Flora Sandes became indispensable as a nurse, surgeon, and hospital administrator in Valjevo, where the death rate of typhus victims soared to 70 percent and more than 200 died each day. Although Sandes was qualified only as a nurse, she was soon performing minor surgery. The loss of medical staff to typhus was enormous. At the end of the month only one Serbian doctor, an orderly, and the nurses remained.

"Looking back," Sandes wrote in 1927, "I have just naturally drifted, by successive stages from nurse to soldier." But it was actually only fifteen days after joining the Serbian Army's 2nd Regiment's Ambulance Unit that she was asked to stay on. When the regiment pulled back to within a few miles of Monastir, regimental commander Colonel Milic required Sandes to make a decision. Unequivocally, she chose to remain with the regiment, overjoyed that "I represented England!" From the Serbs' perspective, it was entirely reasonable since there were other women in the army; enlistment was often haphazard, and Sandes's ability to shoot and ride was highly prized. At home on leave the following year she undertook a major fundraising sweep throughout England.

Whatever reservations were expressed about women in the ranks at home, however, Sandes's experience and position demanded the same respect shown to any official representative of an Allied army. She had returned home wearing the Kara George Star—the highest medal awarded to noncommissioned officers—for her bravery during the Serbian retreat into Albania. She had lived in the trenches with her comrades, shared their food, slept underneath their overcoats, and divided her last cigarettes and crusts of bread with them.

She remained fearful that any expression of weakness would be interpreted as proof of her lingering femininity. A Bulgarian bomb exploded beneath her during the Serbs' taking of Hill 1212 against the Austrian army in November 1915, smashing Sandes's right arm and wounding her back in a dozen places. As she was crying in agony from the pain, a regimental doctor warned her to "shut up and remember that she was a soldier," which Sandes claimed "did far more good than any amount of petting would have done."

An indication of her value to the Serbs as a diplomat and her commitment to their cause was reflected in coverage of Sandes's 1920 Australian tour. She was an official envoy of the Serbian army and met with the country's governor-general, Ronald Munro-Ferguson, Prime Minister Hughes, the New South Wales premier John Storey, and the defense minister Senator Pearce. She urged these Australian politicians to lend financial aid to replenish the devastating agricultural losses the Serbs had suffered during the war. Where the lines between official and ad hoc representation blurred, Sandes met with less success.

After more than seven years serving in the Serbian army Flora Sandes settled in Belgrade and found that demobilization demanded that she relinquish her hard-won honorary male status. There was no position for her in the new Yugoslavian government to continue her diplomatic work, and with peace came the end of Sandes's improvised roles. She married a fellow officer, a Russian named Yuri Yudenitch, and though they both retired to civilian life, she felt "a permanent incapacity to settle down to anything." She tried her hand at driving Belgrade's first taxicab, wrote an autobiography, acquired a speedboat license, taught English, and acted as a matron to a dancing troupe in Paris. She was called up for service again in 1941, but after the bombing of Belgrade both she and Yuri were interned by the Germans. They were released, but Yuri died soon afterwards, and Flora Sandes returned to England via South Africa. She died at Marlsford, Suffolk, in December 1956.

Bibliography: Klein, *Beyond the Home Front*, 1997; Sandes, *An English Woman-Sergeant in the Serbian Army*, 1916, and *The Autobiography of a Woman Soldier*, 1927; Wheelwright, *Amazons and Military Maids*, 1989.

—Julie Wheelwright

SCHELLINCK, MARIE-JEANNE (born 1757, Belgium; died 1840), also known as Shelling. Infantry soldier, Second Belgian Volunteers of the French revolutionary armies.

Marie-Jeanne Schellinck served for four years in campaigns with the French Armies of the North and of the Sambre-et-Meuse. As an infantry soldier serving in combat, Schellinck was wounded numerous times, including a gunshot wound in the left leg and twelve saber wounds scattered over her body from her left ear and her neck to her right arm and legs. Because of her excellent record (although her military dossier does not specify the details of her service), General Rosières recommended her continued appointment, a necessary recommendation after the French government legislated the 1793 exclusion of women from the military (see **French Revolution and Napoleonic Era, women soldiers in**). The license provided by Rosières allowed Schellinck to serve until 1795, after which she rejoined the military in disguise sometime in 1797.

According to additional records, Schellinck also served during the Napoleonic Wars in male disguise (Napoleon did not permit women to serve openly). Allegedly she was mentioned in an order of the day at Arcole in the First Italian Campaign and was recognized for her service at Austerlitz in 1805. In 1806, according to later historians, she became a sous-lieutenant significantly recognized by Napoleon I, who allegedly pinned the Legion of Honor, France's highest decoration, on her chest. It is likely that the latter story is apocryphal, although it is widely reported, since Napoleon officially conferred no military awards on women.

Schellinck was married to a Louis Joseph de Carnin. Based on her service record and testimony from military comrades and commanders, Schellinck was granted a pension of 667 livres per year for her service to France.

Bibliography: Bertaud, *La vie quotidienne*, 1985; Brice, *La femme et les armées*, n.d.; Cère, *Mme Sans-Gêne*, 1894; Dossier XR49, "Schellinck," Service historique de l'Armée, Vincennes, France.

—S.P. Conner

SECORD, LAURA INGERSOLL (born 13 September 1775, Great Barrington, Massachusetts; died 17 October 1868, Chippawa (Niagara Falls), Ontario). Canada, War of 1812.

During the War of 1812 Laura Secord accomplished an impressive and daring military mission. On 22 June 1813 she overheard two American officers discussing military plans while they were dining at her house. She immediately began an eighteen-mile trek on foot from Queenston to Beaver Dams to warn the British officer, James Fitzgibbon, that the Americans were planning to attack his outpost. As a result, two days later the Americans were ambushed by Indians at Beaver Dams, and 400 men were forced to surrender to Fitzgibbon.

Although Secord was perceived by many as a heroine, she received little official recognition. Fitzgibbon later described the event and his indebtedness to Secord: "The weather on the 22nd was very hot and Mrs. Secord whose person was slight and delicate . . . no doubt was much exhausted by the exertion she made coming to me." He added that as Secord and her family were "entire strangers" to him, her "exertions could have been made for public motive only." He therefore recommended her to the "favourable consideration" of the provincial government, but no reward was forthcoming.

In 1828 Laura Secord's husband was rewarded for her actions by a series of local appointments. By 1841 she was widowed and penniless and resorted to teaching school. Finally, at the age of eighty-five she received a small reward from the Prince of Wales. Distressed by the Canadian government's failure to recognize the contribution of Laura Secord to her nation's sovereignty in the de-

Undated portrait of Laura Ingersoll Secord. (Perry-Castañeda Library)

bate over pensions for veterans of the War of 1812, Sarah Curzon wrote a play focusing on Secord's heroic deeds (Wagner, *Women Pioneers,* 1979). In her preface to *Laura Secord, the Heroine of 1812* (1876), Curzon pointed to the injustice of showering so much attention on the male heroes of war. "To save from the sword is surely as great a deed as to save with the sword and this Laura Secord did, at an expense of nerve and muscle—fully equal to any that are recorded of the warrior."

Bibliography: Coates and Morgan, *Heroines and History,* 2001; Herrington, *Heroines of Canadian History,* 1910; McKenzie, *Laura Secord,* 1972; Prentice et al., *Canadian Women,* 1988; Wagner, *Women Pioneers,* 1979.

—Kristine Dawkins-Wright

SEMIRAMIS (fl. late ninth century BCE). Greek name of Sammuramat, queen of Assyria.

Semiramis is a figure to whom have been attributed significant military actions that may be almost completely legendary, for no direct evidence exists of her commanding forces herself. During her reign in Assyria the empire did expand through military force, but the nature of the sources makes it difficult to determine the precise role of Semiramis as head of state. In this entry "Sammuramat" refers to the historical Assyrian queen, while "Semiramis" will be used to refer to the Greek form of her name in semilegendary accounts written long after her death.

Semiramis (Assyrian Queen Sammuramat, ninth-century BC) by a mausoleum. Folio 11R of 1505 manuscript *La Vie des femmes Celebres* (Life of Famous Women), by Antoine du Four. (The Art Archive/Musée Thomas Dobrée Nantes/Dagli Orti)

Save a few short inscriptions that suggest that Sammuramat played an active role in affairs of the kingdom, there is little contemporary evidence to reconstruct the events of her life. We are dependent on several Greek historians, especially Diodorus (first century BCE), who derived his information from an earlier and now lost history of Persia and Assyria, the *Persica,* written by Ctesias of Cnidus. A Greek physician, Ctesias recounted the legends of Semiramis as he had learned them in Persia while he was employed in the court of the Persian king. Diodorus (and Ctesias), writing centuries after her death, placed Semiramis in the thirteenth century BCE, though in fact Sammuramat lived four centuries later.

The legendary Semiramis, as described by Diodorus, was an extremely beautiful woman who was married to a high-ranking officer in the Assyrian army. She caught the attention of King Ninus, founder of the Assyrian Empire, builder of Nineveh (Assyria's capital city), and conqueror of all the Mideast from eastern Persia to Egypt, when she went along with her husband on campaign in Bactria (modern Afghanistan). When the king's generals could not capture the chief citadel of Bactria, Semiramis devised a successful plan to capture it. King Ninus, informed of the plan by Semiramis's husband, summoned her to his tent. Enamored, the king soon took Semiramis from her husband, who, disgraced, committed suicide. Ninus married her, and Semiramis became his queen. Ninus died suddenly within a few years of their marriage, and Semiramis became queen-regent for her young son. According to Ctesias's history, she continued her husband's successful building programs, constructing Babylon and numerous other cities, all of which became centers of commerce along the Euphrates and Tigris Rivers. She also built numerous monuments, roads, and irrigation projects throughout the empire and tried to emulate her dead husband's military exploits. Leading the Assyrian armies westward, she conquered Libya and Ethiopia. Her eastward invasion of the Indus Valley with an army allegedly numbering some three and one-half million men was not successful, however. Conquering the region on the west bank of the Indus, she then advanced across the river. In a great battle with the Indian king Stabrobates and a subsequent retreat back across the Indus, Semiramis lost two-thirds of her army. She ruled for forty-two years before yielding the throne to her son Ninyus, who had begun to foment a palace coup against his mother. The legendary Semiramis was said to have been born of the fish-goddess Atargatis, whose chief shrine was in Ascalon, Syria. At her death Semiramis supposedly became a dove and was worshiped as a deity.

The historical Sammuramat was wife to Shamshi Adad V. Some historians believe that after his death she ruled the kingdom of Assyria as regent for their son, Adad-nirari III, in the last decade of the ninth century BCE, for there is evidence of her rule on stelae discovered in Ashur. If Sammurat was regent for her son during his minority, then the legends are likely embellishments of events occurring during her regency and the reign of her son Adad-nirari III. Sammuramat certainly, as regent, could have directed the armies of Assyria. Assyrian forces, probably under the command of Nergal-ilia, attacked the Medes in 810 BCE and were sufficiently successful to acquire Mesopotamia for the Assyrian Empire the following year. Nergal-ilia's armies took the empire to its furthest eastward conquests by fighting the Mannai in 808–807. It is in this campaign that Semiramis's legendary actions against the Bactrians and India probably had their basis.

Other legendary aspects are demonstrably untrue. Assyrian armies never reached the Indus Valley, and while Sammuramat may have dedicated new temples in Babylon, she did not found the city. As a Babylonian princess, Sammuramat may have been responsible during her reign for the widespread introduction of Babylonian religious practices into Assyria, and the resulting stories about her could have been spread by Babylonian priests. The stories surrounding the legendary Semiramis also probably represent a conflation of the deeds of Sammuramat and other politically active Assyrian queens, such as Zakutu (Naqia), the wife of King Sennacherib (680–669 BCE), who during the reign of her son, Esarhaddon, oversaw the reconstruction of Babylon, which her husband had destroyed earlier.

Bibliography: Bury, *Cambridge Ancient History*; Diodorus Siculus, *Diodorus of Sicily, 1933–1967*; Gera, *Warrior Women*, 1997; Olmstead, *History of Assyria*, 1923; Roux, *Ancient Iraq*, 1992; Schmitz, *Ancient History*, 1898.

—Paul K. Davis and Ralph F. Gallucci

SFORZA, CATERINA (born 1462, Milan, Italy; died 1509, Florence). Countess of Forlì. Conducted military operations and defended besieged fortresses in fifteenth-century Italy.

Caterina Sforza was one of the most dynamic women to emerge from turbulent Renaissance Italy. She was an illegitimate daughter of Galeazzo Maria Sforza, duke of Milan, and granddaughter of **Bianca Maria Visconti Sforza**. Raised in the duke's household, she showed a greater aptitude for sports and horseback riding than for books. At the age of ten she was betrothed to twenty-nine-year-old Girolamo Riario, a favored nephew of Pope Sixtus IV. Four years later, soon after her father's death, Caterina married Girolamo and bore him seven children (and two more to later lovers). The pope gave the young couple control of two cities in central Italy, Imola and Forlì, and they became involved in long and bloody feuds with such powerful families as the Médici of Florence.

Young, blonde, and beautiful, Caterina Sforza was a powerful presence within her small dominion. Her husband was often away fighting, and as she took up his duties, she rapidly proved herself to be strong and independent. She endured recurring bouts of fever and nearly constant pregnancies, as well as the loss of several of her children at young ages, while ruling in her husband's absence. When Pope Sixtus IV died in 1484, she acted quickly to try to ensure her family's favor with his successor. Her husband had been forbidden to enter Rome, so Caterina, though seven months pregnant, rode to Rome and seized the Castel Sant'Angelo in the name of the pope's legal successor. She seems to have accomplished this feat mainly through force of will, chasing out the occupants and bullying the garrison into obedience; Ernst Breisach wrote that they "considered her cruel and fierce but obeyed her grudgingly" (*Caterina Sforza*). The cardinals were not particularly impressed and allowed her and her husband to retain their holdings but nothing more.

During her husband's long illness in 1487 Caterina increasingly took over his responsibilities. She became personally involved in strengthening the defenses of their holdings, particularly the fortress of Ravaldino in Forlì. She seems to have enjoyed discussions of military tactics and strategy. She served as judge over a conspiracy against her family and had six people executed and quartered. In the spring of 1488 an assassination attempt against her husband succeeded, and Caterina and her children were taken captive by townspeople who hoped to reinstate the previous ruling family. However, the castellan of Ravaldino remained loyal. He demanded an audience with Caterina, which was allowed since the conspirators held her children hostage. But when Caterina was safe in the fortress, she refused to surrender it. A famous scene ensued in which the rebels threatened to kill her children. Machiavelli wrote in his *Discourses* that she went out on the ramparts, raised her skirts to reveal her private parts, and shouted down that the people were fools; didn't they realize that she could simply make more children? The eventual arrival of several thousand troops sent by Caterina's uncle, the duke of Milan, helped to quell the rebellion.

Caterina took harsh revenge. Dozens were jailed; several were hanged and publicly dismembered. Caterina secured her power as legal regent for her son Ottaviano. Now truly independent and still a young woman in her twenties, Caterina refused to remarry, but was involved, scandalously, with a series of lovers. She bore two more children and lost four mates in the next dozen years—one to illness and three to assassination. In 1495, when Caterina's unpopular lover was assassinated, she once more exacted a harsh price from the conspirators. Dozens of people suffered torture and gruesome executions. The people of Forlì turned against Caterina Sforza.

In 1492 Ottaviano's godfather, Rodrigo Borgia, became Pope Alexander VI. Within a few years the power struggles that had plagued central Italy became newly inflamed when Caterina and her uncle in Milan found themselves the targets of a new alliance between the pope and France. Caterina negotiated to gain the support of Florence, which sent her a special envoy, Niccolò Machiavelli, on his first diplomatic mission. Machiavelli failed in his task, which was to appease Caterina without promising military aid.

In late 1499 the pope declared that Caterina was a usurper in Imola and Forlì and sent his illegitimate son, Cesare Borgia, against her with a large army. The people of Imola and Forlì surrendered. However, Caterina secured herself with a few dozen supporters and about 900 soldiers within Ravaldino. She had once written her uncle, "Should I have to perish, I want to perish like a man." She is said to have walked the battlements dressed in plate armor. Borgia's artillery began firing in late December; a period of artillery exchanges followed. By mid-January 1500 Borgia's soldiers entered the fortress. Despite a determined defense and fierce fighting by Caterina herself, her soldiers were beaten and she was captured. It is commonly believed that Cesare Borgia raped her after her capture. She endured eighteen months of harsh imprisonment, but was released in 1501 and devoted the last few years of her life to her children. She died in 1509 at the age of forty-six, prematurely aged by illness and hardship.

Machiavelli used Sforza as an example in his most famous book, *The Prince*. Her fortress, he says, enabled her to retain power during the uprising after her husband's death, "yet the fortresses were later of little avail even to her, when Cesare Borgia attacked her, and her hostile people united with a foreigner." He suggests that "it would have been more secure for her, both early and late, not to have been hated by the people than to have had fortresses." Some have seen Caterina Sforza as a tyrant who ruled by terror. This is too simplistic a picture and ignores the context of her times. In *Women of the Renaissance* Margaret L. King points out that like **Joan of Arc**, the Renaissance woman who donned armor was not revered, but reviled: "She was hated because she did what men did, and triumphantly." Such was the story of Caterina Sforza.

Bibliography: Breisach, *Caterina Sforza*, 1967; Collison-Morley, *The Story of the Sforzas*, 1934; King, *Women of the Renaissance*, 1991; Machiavelli, *Discourses, The Prince*.

—Reina Pennington

SHAKHOVSKAIA, PRINCESS EVGENIIA MIKHAILOVNA (born ?; died ?, Russia). First woman to become a military pilot, Russia, First World War.

Princess Evgeniia Mikhailovna Shakhovskaia was the only early Russian female aviator to have been trained entirely abroad and to earn a foreign license. Shakhovskaia was an educated and well-traveled member of an old aristocratic Russian family who became obsessed with flying while she was in Germany in 1911. At the Wright flying school at Johannisthal, Germany, Shakhovskaia took lessons on a Wright Flyer with V.M. Abrimovich. On 16 August she became the second known Russian woman to earn her pilot's certificate, No. 247, as reported in the Western magazine *Flying* (June 1913). The other woman, Liubov Galanshchikova, reportedly went on to set an international women's altitude record. (Cottam states that two women, Lidiia Zverevskaia and Liubov Galanshchlikova, were the first to receive pilot's licenses in 1911; see *Women in War and Resistance*, 1998, xix.)

Shakhovskaia's skill at the controls of her Wright Flyer immediately earned her a position as an instructor pilot at the Flugsmachine Wright Company School at Johannisthal. Though she does not appear to have flown regularly at air shows and aviation meets, Shakhovskaia nonetheless quickly attained an international reputation. With the outbreak of the Tripolitan War between Italy and Turkey in September 1912, Shakhovskaia made the news by offering her services as an aerial scout to the Italian government. Much to her chagrin, the offer was politely turned down.

Her name continued to appear in international journals devoted to aviation, though for somewhat more orthodox reasons. On 12 November 1912 Shakhovskaia along with a woman passenger reportedly made a ten-minute flight over St. Petersburg; and in May 1913 she was involved in an accident that left her injured and killed her passenger, her former instructor Abrimovich. Neither the crash nor her earlier spurned efforts to fly as a military pilot dampened Shakhovskaia's burning desire to fly, preferably in the army. In August 1914, when the First World War erupted, Shakhovskaia wrote to the tsar himself, requesting active service as a military pilot.

Undoubtedly greeted with some amusement by the tsar, Shakhovskaia's petition to fly as a military reconnaissance pilot was granted. In November 1914 Shakhovskaia, now an ensign of engineers, was posted to active duty with the First Field Air Squadron of the Russian Northwestern Front. Officially her duties were to fly reconnaissance and artillery-direction missions, but it has been impossible to verify whether she indeed flew active missions. Still, she stands as the first woman to serve officially as a military aviator in any country.

Another woman, Nadezhda Degtereva, reportedly disguised herself as a boy and entered military air service in 1914. Like Shakhovskaia, she flew reconnaissance missions. Her disguise was discovered when she was forced to seek medical attention after being wounded while flying over enemy lines. **Sofiia Alexandrovna Dolgorukaia** later flew in 1917 after Minister of War Aleksandr Kerensky opened military service to women.

Bibliography: Cottam, *Women in War and Resistance,* 1998; Meyer, "The Impact of World War I on Russian Women's Lives," 1991; Moolman, *Women Aloft,* 1981; White, "Gossamer Wings," 1991; Smithsonian Air and Space Museum, archival materials: "LB71768" and "Robertson, Russian Women in WWI."

—Christine White

SHALIZHI (died after 1142, northeast China). Mistress Commander of Jinyuan. Leader of a self-organized militia group during the Jinb dynasty (1115–1234).

Shalizhi lived in the time of the Jinb dynasty, founded by the Jurchen (the Tungus tribes of the modern Heilongjiang Province). Her brother and husband were both military commanders. In 1122 a rebellion at Huanglong Superior Prefecture spread to where she lived. Since her husband was away on another military expedition, Shalizhi mustered around 500 inhabitants and erected camps and fences for protection. She used heavy blankets as armor and clothes as banners, and she gave armor to men and asked women to make clamorous noises. For three days she led her troop until more than 1,000 invading rebels were chased away. In 1142 she was awarded the title Mistress Commander of Jinyuan.

Bibliography: Chen Menglei, *Gujin tushu jicheng (Qin ding),* 1993; Tuotuo et al., *Jin shi,* 1975.

—Sherry J. Mou

SHAO, first name unknown (fl. fourth century, China). A cavalry soldier during the Jin dynasty (265–420).

Shao was good at military maneuvers, like her father, the regional inspector of Ji Prefecture (now southwest of Gaoyi in Hebei Province). Later the central government became very weak and China was in turmoil. During the reign of Emperor Yuan (r. 317–322) Shao's husband Liu Xia (died 326), then a rampart commander, led fighters against bandits and rebels. In one such battle, when Liu Xia was surrounded by the nomadic leader Shi Jilong, Shao led a cavalry rescue and saved her husband.

When Liu Xia died, the emperor assigned his troops to another court official. Liu Xia's brother-in-law Tian Fang and several of his chief subordinates rebelled, supporting Liu Xia's son Liu Zhao as their leader. The emperor sent Guo Mo to quell the rebellion. Shao also tried to stop her rebellious brother-in-law Tian Fang, but in vain, so she secretly burned all the weapons. Eventually Tian Fang and the other subordinates were beheaded by Guo Mo's troops, and their heads were sent to the capital for public display. Shao's son Liu Zhao inherited his father's title and rank; Shao and all other assistant commanders were moved to the capital Jiankang (now Nanjing).

Bibliography: Chen Menglei, *Gujin tushu jicheng (Qin ding)*, 1993; Fang Xuanling and Baoyuan Du, eds., *Jin shu*, 1974.

—Sherry J. Mou

SHEJIE, first name unknown (died 1303, Shuixi, southwest China). A regional leader and commander of the Yi during the Yuan dynasty (1272–1368).

During the reign of Emperor Chengzong (r. 1295–1307) the government drafted soldiers and imposed frequent and heavy taxes. Many aboriginal people were pushed to revolt by these cruel measures. In 1301 in Shuixi, Shejie led the Yi people, an ethnic group in southwestern China, in rebellion against the local administrator's demand for more military supplies. Other ethnic people nearby echoed her call, and they soon took Guizhou. The Yuan government sent troops to suppress the revolt. In the second month of 1303 Shejie and forty of her subordinates surrendered, and she was executed.

Bibliography: Shaomin, "Xin Yuan shi," 1959.

—Sherry J. Mou

SHEN YUNYING (born 1623; died 1660, Xiaoshan, Zhejiang Province, China), also known as Shen Guandi. Mobile corps commander, post commander.

As a female commander of the late Ming dynasty (1368–1644), Shen Yunying fought in Hunan Province against local bandits under Zhang Xianzhong (1605–1647), who was one of the main leaders of the peasant rebellions in late Ming times. Shen was the daughter of a post commander of Daozhou in southern Hunan. She is said to have been educated in both literary and military skills. After her father died defending the city of Daozhou, attacked in 1643 by bandits under Zhang Xianzhong, Shen exhorted the army and the people of Daozhou and succeeded in saving the city from the besieging bandits. In recognition, the emperor by special decree made her a mobile corps commander with her father's post command and gave her command over the local troops. Later, when she heard that her husband had been killed fighting bandits in Hubei Province, she resigned and returned to her native Xiaoshan. There she lived as a teacher until she died at the age of thirty-seven.

Bibliography: *Ming yiminlu*, comp. Sun Jing'an, and *Qingdai guige shiren zhenglue*, comp. Shi Shuyi, both in *Qingdai zhuanji congkan*, ed. Zhou Junfu (Taipei: 1985); Tingyu, *Ming shi*, 1974; *Yishi zhi yi*, ed. Li Yao, in *Mingdai zhuanji congkan*, ed. Zhou Junfu (Taipei: 1991).

—Doris Kehry-Kurz

SHOCHAT, MANIA WILBUSHEWICH (born 1879, Lososna, Belorussia; died 1961, Tel Aviv, Israel), also known as Manya. Radical labor leader and social activist; founding member of Bar-Giora, Hashomer, and Gedud Ha'avodah,

Jewish self-defense organizations prominent before the establishment of IDF (Israel Defense Forces) in 1948.

Mania Shochat became the guiding spirit and military leader of Hashomer (The Watchmen). Though highly involved in the organization's day-to-day activities, she was always attentive to issues of women's rights and fiercely supported egalitarianism within its ranks. Shochat and her female compatriots participated in nightly reconnaissances, rescued wounded civilians, and often smuggled firearms on their bodies.

Shochat immigrated to Palestine in 1904. Her military activities began in Paris in 1905 while she was on a fundraising mission for the first collective settlement in Palestine. An old friend approached her to assist the Jewish self-defense movement in Russia. She was to raise funds, acquire weapons and ammunition in Belgium, and transport them to Russia. Shochat raised 50,000 gold francs and smuggled arms into Russia through four European borders. On her last mission Shochat, dressed as a rabbi's wife, arrived in Odessa only to realize that her hiding place was surrounded by Russian secret police. As she was waiting with her arms shipment in the house, a pale young man knocked on the door and collapsed fainting. Shochat took him inside before realizing that he was a Russian secret agent. On discovering his true identity, she shot and killed him. Shochat hid his body in a closet. Later, when the Russian Secret Police left the scene without discovering the crime, she and her revolutionary friends placed the corpse in a crate and sent it as merchandise via train to a false address. In three days the firearms were distributed to different locations, and soon afterwards she returned to Palestine.

Shochat was arrested and imprisoned on several occasions by the Turkish rulers of Palestine. She was exiled with her husband, Israel Shochat, to Brusia, Turkey (1914–1918). When she returned, she continued her clandestine work for Hashomer. Once during Arab pogroms she disguised herself as a Red Cross nurse and infiltrated the Arab camps as a spy. On another assignment to smuggle hand grenades, her car sank into sand and was immobilized. Shochat asked for help from British soldiers who were passing by. While the soldiers were busy with the car, Shochat sat nearby shielding the two "grocery" baskets of grenades. In her memoirs Shochat described Hashomer as a tiny secret cell that succeeded because of its members' devotion, ingenuity, and the undying support of the "watchmen's" wives.

Bibliography: Ben-Zvi, *Before Golda: Manya Shochat*, 1989; Reinharz, "Toward a Model of Female Political Action," 1984; Shochat, "The Guarding of the Land," 1937, "My Path in Hashomer," 1957, and "The Collective," 1975.

—Dina Ripsman Eylon

SICHELGAITA OF SALERNO (born ca. 1036, Salerno, Italy; died 27 March 1090, Salerno). Military leader, Italy, eleventh century.

Sichelgaita was a daughter of Prince Guaimar of Salerno. Her brothers,

Guaimar and Gisulf, in turn succeeded their father as prince. In 1058 Gisulf arranged the marriage of his elder sister, Sichelgaita, as the second wife of Robert Guiscard, the Norman duke of Apulia and Calabria. Robert had arrived in southern Italy as an almost penniless younger son of a minor Norman noble, following several of his older brothers. In his earlier years he can only be described as a bandit chieftain, but as his nickname Robert the Cunning shows, he had ambition and the capability of carrying out his plans. His first marriage, to Alberada of Buonalbergo, brought him access to the 200 soldiers who formed the nucleus of his first regular army. His conquests brought him the status to make a more ambitious second marriage that in turn allowed him to broaden his activities and move against the Muslim rulers of Sicily and the Byzantine Greeks in southern Italy. Rather scandalously, Robert dissolved his first marriage to marry Sichelgaita, though his first wife was very much alive and had borne him the only one of his sons to inherit his father's warlike temperament, Bohemond of Taranto, one of the leaders of the First Crusade. Even though he was both capable and ambitious, Robert needed both of his marriages for the ties of kinship to families of higher status as well as for the troops that his wives' landed wealth could provide. In 1077 Robert drove Gisulf from Salerno, leaving Sichelgaita as de facto ruler of her native principality.

Two historians report Sichelgaita's military exploits. According to the Byzantine historian Anna Comnena, Sichelgaita in armor was a formidable sight; unfortunately, Sichelgaita's tomb was destroyed by bombs during the Second World War, so it will never be possible to determine if she was taller or stronger than other women of her time. Anna Comnena notes that Sichelgaita was accustomed to accompany her husband on campaign, and that Robert waited for her to arrive before setting out on his campaign against the Byzantine emperor. In October 1081, during the battle for possession of the city of Durazzo (Dyrrachium), some of the Norman troops broke and were in flight when Sichelgaita took up a spear, rode across their path, and drove them back. Anna Comnena also writes that Sichelgaita narrowly avoided capture during the naval battle off Corfu just before the death of her husband in May 1085, indicating that she was in the thick of the action.

William of Apulia adds that Sichelgaita was wounded by an arrow at Durazzo but managed to elude capture with the help of God. William also writes that in 1080, during an uprising of some of the Normans against her husband, Sichelgaita took command of the siege of Trani while Robert went south to take charge at Taranto. Peter of Trani later formally surrendered and asked Robert's forgiveness.

The reports of Sichelgaita's military activities cluster in the later years of her life. She and Robert had a large family, and numerous pregnancies may have limited her activities in earlier years. After Robert's death her energy was devoted to ensuring the succession of her son, Roger Borsa (Roger Moneybag) to his father's vast patrimony. The troops that Sichelgaita commanded at Trani and rallied at Durazzo may well have been her own, and her presence says as much about the limits of her husband's authority as it does about her own vigor and courage.

Bibliography: Comnena, *The Alexiad of Anna Comnena*, 1969; Guillaume de Pouille (William of Apulia), *La Geste de Robert Guiscard*, 1961; Memoli-Apicella, Dorotea, *Sichelgaita: Tra Longobardi e Normanni* (Salerno: 1997); Norwich, *The Normans in the South*, 1981; Tanner, Private-Orton, and Brooke, *Contest of Empire and Papacy*, 1926.

—Valerie Eads

SIENA, WOMEN IN SIEGE OF (1553–1555). Italy.

In January 1553, in the preparations for the defense of their city against an expected Spanish imperial attack, the women of Siena contributed to the defense effort by organizing themselves into three groups and carrying building materials to the fortifications. To this day the remains of a fort built by Baldassarre Peruzzi just outside the city walls at Porta Camollia bear the name of "Fortino delle donne," and a modern plaque (1928) commemorates "the heroic Sienese women [who] defended the freedom of their homeland during the glorious siege."

The first to mention their effort was their immediate contemporary Marco Guazzo in his *Cronica* (Venice, 1553); he was followed by Ascanio Centorio degli Ortensi in his *La seconda parte dei Commentari delle guerre e dei successi più notabili* (Venice, 1565–1569) and a variety of subsequent historians. The best-known and most accessible source for the episode, however, is the *Commentaires* of the French marshal Blaise de Monluc, leader of the Franco-Sienese forces defending the city.

Guazzo describes how, on 17 January 1553, three Sienese women, "la signora Forteguerri . . . la signora Fausta Piccolhuomini . . . la signora Livia Fausta," led three groups of women, 3,000 strong, in carrying materials to a fort that was being constructed just outside the city walls. Although Guazzo and others after him praise the women for their actions, they also basically ignore the military value of the women's contribution by focusing not on the deeds but on their wardrobe and the pageantry of the women's actions. In fact, Guazzo's narrative basically says that they marched with drums and banners and then describes what the women wore. We thus know that each group's banner bore a motto: Forteguerri's was "Pur che ilsia il vero" (As long as it be true), Piccolomini's "Pur che non lo butto" (As long as I do not throw it away), and Fausta's "Pur che l'abbia" (As long as I may have it). Forteguerri's women wore short violet dresses that left their ankles exposed, Piccolomini's group wore red dresses and carried a red banner with a white cross in it, and Fausta and her followers wore white and carried an emblem with a palm in it. Guazzo claims that they cheered, "France, France" (Siena's ally), and Monluc adds that they all sang a song in praise of France composed by the Sienese poet Laura Civoli. Guazzo concludes by saying that the contribution of these women inspired not only "gentlemen" to carry materials to the fortifications, but also the clergy of the city, who, led by the archbishop himself, undertook a similar effort twelve days later, on 29 January.

Guazzo and Monluc's description of the episode gives it the air of a "festa" and not of a valiant civic effort by the unfranchised for the survival of the homeland. The drums, banners, flags, and emblems described by Guazzo suggest a parade, while the comment that the women, dressed in short tunics, looked like "nymphs" betrays a quasi-erotic attitude on the part of the male viewer. Finally, the mottos displayed on the banners are akin to the eclectic witticisms in vogue in contemporary literary academies such as the influential Accademia degli Intronati di Siena.

The episode is also clouded by doubts regarding the identification of the women. Guazzo was not an eyewitness to the event. Monluc did see women working on the ramparts (carrying baskets of earth on their heads), but his narrative and his identification of the three leaders is based on Guazzo and on hearsay. Monluc even admits that he had not yet arrived in Siena at the time, but then says that Monsieur de Termes often retold him the story of the three women and their troops. Further doubts are cast by the fact that there is no archival record for the existence of a Livia Fausta, or even a family Fausta, in Siena at the time, while no Christian name is given for the Forteguerri woman. Tradition has subsequently identified the latter with the poet Laudomia Forteguerri.

Monluc follows this episode with the story of a nameless young Sienese working-class woman who replaced her brother on guard duty. This second episode is most probably a complete literary construct, not an actual historical event. It may have been included to complement the episode describing the leadership shown by the three noblewomen.

Regardless of the literary constructs, Monluc's admiration for the valor of the Sienese women during the siege was such that later, in Rome, he reprimanded the officers of the papal army, saying that he would prefer to defend Siena with an army of Sienese women than Rome with an army of modern Roman men. His admiration is echoed by a number of subsequent historians who narrated the fall of the Sienese Republic.

Representative Participant

Forteguerri, Laudomia (1515–1555, Siena, Italy). Defender during siege of Siena, Italy, 1553. Forteguerri is traditionally identified as one of the three women who led 3,000 other women in the defense of Siena in January 1553. Unfortunately, almost no details have been preserved regarding her exact actions. Six poems by Forteguerri have been published; five are sonnets of affection for Marguerite of Austria (1522–1586), duchess of Parma and Piacenza, while the sixth sings the beauty of another woman poet, Alda Torella Lunata. Forteguerri was the poetic and literary muse of Alessandro Piccolomini (1508–

1579), who dedicated a number of books to her. She was widely renowned for her beauty.

Bibliography: Betussi, Giuseppe, *Le imagini del tempio della Signora Giovanna Aragona* (Florence: 1556); Forteguerri, Laudomia, *Sonetti di Madonna Laudomia Forteguerri, poetessa senese del secolo XVI* (Siena: 1901); Monluc, Blaise de, *Commentaires,* ed. Paul Courteault (Paris: 1913); Guazzo, Marco, *Cronica* (Venice: 1553); Ugurgieri Azzolini, Isidoro, *Le pompe sanesi* (Pistoia: 1649).

—Konrad Eisenbichler

SMIRNOVA, ZOIA F. (born ?; died ?), also known as "Evgeni: Makarov." Infantry, nurse, Russia, First World War.

Zoia Smirnova was one of a group of twelve young women between the ages of fourteen and seventeen who left home to join the Russian army during the First World War. Concealed on a train bound for the front, Smirnova and her friends arrived at the Austrian front in July 1914. Although they had acquired uniforms from some sympathetic soldiers, their sex was quickly detected by regimental authorities. The commanders could not persuade the young zealots to return home and finally agreed to allow them to stay with the unit. Smirnova and the other young women participated in numerous battles. Some of them were wounded and even killed. Smirnova was wounded twice, and after the second time, at the end of 1915, she was awarded the St. George's Cross (see **Order of St. George**) and promoted to junior noncommissioned officer. After her convalescence Smirnova lost her original unit and was persuaded to serve for the rest of the war as a nurse.

Bibliography: Ivanova, "Prekrasneishie iz khrabrykh," 1994; "Young Girls Fighting on the Russian Front," *Current History* May 1916: 366.

—Laurie Stoff

SNELL, HANNAH (born 1723; died 8 February 1792, London, England), also known as "James Grey," "hearty Jemmy," "Molly," "the female soldier." English foot soldier, marine.

Under the guise of a male marine and later heralded as the "female soldier," Hannah Snell actively participated in several Franco-British struggles over trade and commerce in the mid-eighteenth century. Snell's surprising military career began in 1745 when she borrowed a set of men's clothes to find her way-

Hanna Snell. Illustration from a book ca. 1745. (Hulton/Archive by Getty Images)

On the Royal Navy's attitude toward women at sea in the eighteenth and nineteenth centuries:

The seaman John Nicol related the following account of [the 1798 Battle of the Nile]: "Any information we got was from the boys and women who carried the powder. The women behaved as well as the men. . . . I was much indebted to the gunner's wife, who gave her husband and me a drink of wine every now and then which lessened our fatigue much. There were some of the women wounded and one woman belonging to Leith died of her wounds . . . one woman bore a son in the heat of the action . . ."

As late as 1847, Queen Victoria directed that the Navy General Service Medal be awarded "without reservation to sex." However, when two women actually stepped forward and claimed medals for their participation in the battles of the Nile and Trafalgar, the navy pleaded an obligation to forego the two medals in order to spare itself—and the army as well—a *multitude* of similar requests. In the Committee's words, "there were many women in the fleet equally useful, and it [would] leave the Army exposed to *innumerable* applications."

—Dianne Dugaw, *Warrior Women and Popular Balladry, 1650–1850* (Cambridge: Cambridge University Press, 1989), 128–129.

ward husband. Following in his footsteps, Snell joined a foot regiment in Coventry under the alias James Grey and marched north to Carlisle. Deserting this unit soon after, Snell joined Boscowen's fleet marines headed for the East Indies. Passing as a beardless young man, Snell served as a steward and cook while at sea and fought French troops when the fleet reached the Mascarene Islands in the Indian Ocean. After moving on to southern India, Snell was shot in the groin in her first major engagement at Pondicherry. Rather than being tended by the regimental surgeon, Snell instructed a local woman to extract the bullet to preserve the secret of her gender.

After joining a man-o'-war bound for Portugal in 1750, Snell gave up her career as a marine and identity as a man when she learned that her husband had been killed. She returned to England to record her adventures in battle, which were dramatized several years later. With the royal pension she received for her wounds, Snell opened a pub called The Female Warrior in 1759 that she ran until her death.

Bibliography: *Dictionary of National Biography*; Dugaw, *Warrior Women and Popular Balladry, 1650–1850*, 1989; Holmes, Geoffrey, and Daniel Szechi, *The Age of Oligarchy: Pre-industrial Britain, 1722–1783* (Longman: 1993); Stark, *Female Tars*, 1996.

—Susanna Calkins

SOLDADERAS, also known as women warriors, *mociuaquetzque* (valiant women), *auianime* (pleasure girls), camp followers, *soldadas, capitanas, coronelas, Adelitas, Juanas, cucarachas* (cockroaches), *viejas* (old ladies), *galletas* (cookies). Central and Latin America.

The indigenous peoples of the Western Hemisphere had many stories about warrior women: the Warrior Princess (ca. CE 1035), the Toltec queen **Xochitl** (ca. CE 111), and Coyolxauhqui (Golden Bells, ca. CE 1143). Coyolxauhqui was the warrior sister of the Aztec warrior god Huitzilopochtli and vied with him for leadership of the Aztecs. Although she was defeated and mutilated by Huitzilopochtli, her death marked the ritual ascendancy of the Aztec warrior empire. Both indigenous men and women had to help in the common defense of their tribes, with women fighting either as individuals, together with men, or in separate women's groups led by women. The most common function of indigenous women was to grind and cook corn for the warriors; however, women did occasionally become involved in combat. This heritage, both legendary and historical, would be invoked by women in later centuries.

The word *soldadera* is a Spanish word and refers to the *soldada* or the pay of the soldier. The *era* ending is commonly used to refer to servants. Thus the meaning of the word *soldadera* is a female servant of the soldier's pay. The word *soldadera* was used in the book *El Cid* to refer to Spanish women camp followers. When the Spaniards

Photograph of *soldaderas* from an old pamphlet published in Mexico. (Library of Congress)

invaded the Western Hemisphere, they brought with them a military structure that did not include commissary units. During the course of their battles against indigenous peoples in the Valley of Mexico, the Spaniards came to rely on corn as their main food staple. Indigenous women corn grinders were picked for the job of providing this foodstuff for all armies. It appears that these women were not paid for their services, but rather relied on individual soldiers to hand over their wages to the *soldaderas*. While some women were conscripted to be corn grinders for armies, other women voluntarily went along with soldiers as family members. Many of the women were married or related to the men, so their presence in the armies was out of a sense of familial devotion. The word *soldadera* can best be used to identify women who traveled with soldiers in the traditional support roles of camp followers, providing logistical support necessary in premodern armies. Women also occasionally took up arms to fight in battles.

The best-known *soldadera* of the 1519 invasion of Mexico was Malinal Tenepal (also known as Doña Marina, Malinche). She was an indigenous woman who came from people who lived outside the realm of the Aztecs. Malinal was one of nineteen women given to Hernán Cortés to grind corn for his army. She had a facility with languages and already knew Aztec and Mayan dialects. Within a short time she learned Spanish and became Cortés's most important translator, advisor, and mistress. At least twelve *soldaderas* (both of European and African ancestry) were among Cortés's troops, following either husbands or brothers. Many indigenous women fought alongside their men against the Spaniards; the best known was a Tarascan woman named Erendira. Indigenous women supplied warriors with stones and arrows, prepared slings, and strung bows. The last battle between the Aztecs and the Spaniards included women dressed as male warriors upon the orders of the Aztec leader

Photograph of *soldaderas* from an old pamphlet published in Mexico. (Library of Congress)

Cuauhtemoc. Since most of his male warriors were dead, Cuauhtemoc ordered the women of Tenochtitlan to take up shields, swords, darts, and stones and fight the Spaniards.

In the process of consolidating their empire from 1521 to 1810, the Spaniards included in their military expeditions women corn grinders, cooks, foragers, guides, washerwomen, translators, and female relatives of the men. In a campaign in the 1700s against the Mayans, every fifteen-man Spanish army squad had an indigenous woman *soldadera* to make the *nixtamal* (ground corn), grind it, and make the dough into tortillas and tamales. A Spanish army officer wrote about the sorry condition of the palms of the women's hands and the joints of their fingers, which were raw and festering from the continuous grinding.

During the Mexican War of Independence against Spain (1810–1823) women of all classes participated in warfare, including Doña Leona Vicario, Antonia Nava de Catalan, and Luisa Martínez. The Mexican military continued to use women as corn grinders in all of its wars from 1821 to 1925. In most instances women amounted to 20 to 30 percent of most armies and rebel factions. While the major role of the *soldaderas* was to grind the corn, the women could, if they chose, pick up a weapon and join the men in battle and then return to being cooks and camp followers. Some women would disguise themselves as male soldiers and disappear into the ranks, while other women, with the consent of their commanding officers, would operate solely as soldiers on the line.

When Texas declared its independence from Mexico in 1836, President and General Antonio Santa Anna led troops that included *soldaderas*. Women were considered a "necessary evil" because they foraged for food, helped to find water and ground the corn, thus preventing many desertions by soldiers due to starvation. More than 1,500 *soldaderas* and children marched from Laredo to Bexar, Texas, with Santa Anna's 6,019-man army, but fewer than 300 *soldaderas* and children completed the journey because many died from starvation, thirst, and the harsh environment. *Soldadera* Panchita Alvarez, the wife of Captain Telesforo Alvarez, saved the lives of at least ninety-nine Americans who were taken captive by the Mexican army. She talked her husband and other Mexican officers out of executing the Americans even though General Santa Anna had ordered their deaths.

During the 1846–1848 Mexican-American War *soldaderas* continued to forage, grind and cook corn, and help the wounded on the battlefields. There were two women who became fused together in a composite identity as "Maria Josefa Zozaya." One *soldadera* went to the battlefield during the Battle of Monterrey and brought food and water to both Mexican and American soldiers before she was shot and killed. The other "Maria Josefa Zozaya" kept rallying the troops in Monterrey to remain firm and not desert their posts during the battle.

The 1910 Revolution was the heyday of the *soldaderas*. There were thousands of them attached to all of the major armies of the war. Many women distinguished themselves in battle, like **Petra Herrera, Petra Ruiz,** Clara Ramos, Valentina Ramirez, and **Angela Jiménez**. Women soldiers complained that they could not rise higher than the rank of lieutenant. Some the most daring women *soldadas* received honorary titles like "la Coronela" or "la Capitana," but rarely did these "battlefield" ranks hold up after the Revolution ended and all officers' ranks were reevaluated. General Francisco Villa did not like the *soldaderas* because he considered them to be a "burden" affecting rapid troop movements. In 1916, when the Villistas captured Santa Rosalia Camargo, Chihuahua, about eighty or ninety *soldaderas* and their children became his prisoners. One of the *soldaderas* shot at Villa and grazed his sombrero. Villa demanded to know who had shot at him but was unable to get the *soldaderas* to point the woman out. He then ordered the execution of all the *soldaderas*, and his soldiers complied with his command. Another officer, General Álvaro Obregón, put *soldaderas* and children in front of his troops and artillery to protect them from enemy fire.

After the 1910 Revolution women *soldadas* (soldiers) could petition for veterans' pensions based on written testimony from male officers under whom they had served. Such was not the case with women classified as *soldaderas*. Most *soldaderas* who did the "dirty work" of the camps and were corn grinders and cooks did not receive any veterans' benefits. *Soldaderas* in the Emiliano Zapata faction did join the Union de Mujeres Revolucionarias (Union of female revolutionaries) to get pensions, but not as cooks and corn grinders but rather as widows, daughters, and sisters of dead male revolutionaries. In 1941 a national committee was created to see to the needs of the *soldaderas*, not as members of the Mexican military, but rather as soldiers' wives and female relatives. The *soldaderas* have passed into history, but their legacy remains in Mexico, as literature, art, film, and music continue to portray them as "patriotic heroines" (La Adelita, La Valentina) or as whores (La Cucaracha) servicing soldiers. The film *Like Water for Chocolate* (1992) depicts a woman acting in a command role.

The 1994 revolt by the EZLN (Emiliano Zapata National Liberation Army) in Chiapas brought to the forefront Mayan women rebels. About 20 to 30 percent of the Zapatista fighters are women. Major Ana Maria was the officer in command during the capture of San Cristobal de la Casas. She joins other women leaders like Commandante Ramona and Lieutenants Amalia, Laura, Marta, and Rocio in the Zapatista army. The Mayan women rebels put together a manifesto called the "Revolutionary Women's Law." The first tenet maintains the right of women to "participate in the revolutionary struggle in a way determined by their desire and ability," and tenet nine states that women have the right to "hold military ranks in the revolutionary armed forces."

Bibliography: Alatorre, *La mujer en al Revolución Mexicana*, 1961; Gugliotta, *Women of Mexico*, 1989; Herrera-Sobek, *The Mexican Corrido*, 1990; Kentner, "The Socio-Political Role of Women in the Mexican Wars of Independence," 1974; Poniatowska, *Hasta no verte Jesús mio*, 1969; Salas, *Soldaderas*, 1990; Soto, "The Mexican Woman: A Study of her Participation in the Revolution, 1910–1940," 1977.

—Elizabeth Salas

SOSNOWSKA-KARPIK, IRENA (born 1922; died 9 March 1990, Warsaw, Poland). Deputy Wing Commander, Colonel (Ret.), Polish Air and Air Defense Forces. Former pilot-instructor, Officer Flying School in Deblin, Poland.

A career soldier, Irena Sosnowska-Karpik was a Second World War veteran who served with the Polish Armed Forces formed in the Soviet Union and became an outstanding postwar pilot-instructor in Poland. In her youth Sosnowska-Karpik completed a flying course that qualified her as a glider pilot, but she had an ambition to fly combat aircraft. Responding to an appeal made by the Union of Polish Patriots, the predecessor of the postwar Polish Communist government, on 10 November 1944 she joined the Polish Armed Forces formed in the Soviet Union.

Serving in the Polish Air and Air Defense Forces after the war as a pilot-instructor, Sosnowska-Karpik trained almost 1,000 new pilots. When she transferred to the reserves, she had approximately 4,300 flying hours to her credit, accumulated in both fixed-wing aircraft and helicopters. Decorated with the Knight's Cross of the Order of the Rebirth of Poland, Sosnowska-Karpik was also awarded the Gold and Silver Crosses of Merit as well as various air force medals and badges.

On a Croatian woman who flew in the Second World War:

Training jumps were suspended until April 1943. The largest jump made to date occurred at this time from Avia Fokker aircraft number F9 and F18 from Borongaj airfield in Zagreb. During this jump the paratroopers showed off their new uniforms (a one-piece camouflaged overall) and German-made heavy equipment containers that were individually numbered for each paratrooper. This jump was also novel because of the presence of the first woman paratrooper, Zdenka Zibrat. Although other women started the parachute course, Ms. Zibrat was the only woman to graduate with five jumps. She went on to pilot school and graduated on September 1, 1944, after which she flew in the 19th squadron based at Zagreb.

—Josip Novak and David Spencer, "Paratroopers of the Independent State of Croatia, 1942–1945," *Journal of Military Ordnance* 6.6 (1996), 11.

Bibliography: Articles in *Żołnierz Wolności:* Lukashewski, Stanislaw, "Czas służby, czas wspomnien," 13 October 1986; 1, 3; Obituary, 14 March 1990: 6, and 15 March 1990: 6.

—Kazimiera J. Cottam

SPANISH CIVIL WAR, WOMEN IN (July 1936–February 1939).

The Spanish Civil War affected women in a number of significant ways. Acute shortages of labor on the home front drew Spanish women into occupations and services that before the war had been the strict preserve of men. At the same time, the exigencies of wartime dissolved many of the restrictive conventions that had governed social interaction between the sexes. Observers who remarked on these changes in both Republican and Nationalist zones almost invariably concluded that the war had increased female liberty.

What these observers were noting perhaps could be understood more accurately as an example of what Patrice and Anne Higonnet in *Behind the Lines* have categorized as the "double helix." It describes the phenomenon whereby the increase in women's apparent freedoms in wartime always is bound within an interlocking structure of male dominance. An apparent expansion in female opportunities tends not to be of long duration and takes place within a social transformation in which male authority remains paramount. In the Spanish Civil War the most striking example of women's expanded wartime activity, though still within a "double helix" of male dominance, was the armed Spanish militiawoman. Ostensibly she shared the dangers of front-line combat as an equal with her male comrades.

Even in the Nationalist zone, where a central element of Franco's ideology was the return of Spanish women to the confines of the traditional Catholic family, the demands of war work drew women into the public sphere. The Falangist women's organization, the Sección Femenina, actively recruited women, and, as well, from mid-1937 young

Spanish Civil War recruitment poster. (Library of Congress)

women were expected to undergo a period of national service in the Auxilio Social. The latter was a state-run social service organization modeled on the Italian Fascist youth corporations. In these organizations women sewed for the soldiers at the front or themselves donned uniforms to work in military hospitals, orphanages, and soup kitchens. There was a paradox, as Frances Lannon has pointed out, between the busy public careers of the women who led these organizations and the rhetoric of female abnegation that they promoted.

In the Republican zones, to an even greater extent, women took over the munitions industry and farm work or drove buses and trains while organizations like Agrupación de Mujeres Antifascistas (AMA) rallied women to support the war effort. Perhaps the most recognizable figure on the Republican side was Dolores Ibárruri, La Pasionaria, the Communist deputy from Oviedo who was indefatigable in promoting the Republican cause within Spain and abroad. A small and tragic figure, always dressed modestly in black, La Pasionaria was an orator with formidable power. It was she who coined the slogan *no pasarán*—they shall not pass—which became the rallying cry for the Republic and its supporters.

At the beginning of the war the figure of the armed militiawoman was common in Republican Spain, where she could be seen on the street in military parades, on posters, and in newspaper photographs. Decked out in fighting gear, she usually wore a *mono,* the blue overalls worn by Spanish workers that became the de facto uniform of the militia, a leather cartridge belt, a red kerchief around her neck, and on her head a forage cap or a tin helmet. With a rifle slung on her shoulder, the *miliciana* headed off to the front to share the dangers of combat with the male comrades in her trade union or political group.

She symbolized the revolutionary change that the rising of the Spanish generals had triggered. The assessment that contemporaries made of the *miliciana* depended on how they viewed this change. In the Republican zone radical political groups, like the anarchists and the dissident Marxists of the Partido Obrero de Unificación Marxista (POUM), who argued that civil war and revolution were synonymous, tended in principle at least to favor the *miliciana.* In contrast, Republican groups and political parties like the Socialist and Communist Parties, who favored winning the war while eschewing social revolution, saw the militiawoman as part of an anarchic disorder that had to be brought under control if Franco was to be defeated.

For Franco's Nationalists, the figure of the woman in combat embodied the elements of what they found most repugnant in the Second Republic. These included women's liberation instead of deference to male authority and secular individualism over Catholic family tradition. Foreign journalists, as well, made much of these "young Amazons" but at the same time were surprised to see them acting like other soldiers. The reporters who accompanied Mary Low to the Aragon front in August 1936, for example, were taken aback to see a young militiawoman squatting to relieve herself nearby, with "her bare buttocks shining very white in the sun." In the assessment of the significance of the militiawoman by subsequent historians, Mary Nash has provided a salutary reminder that the upheaval of wartime should not be confused with real social transformation. In addition, she has pointed out that the recruitment posters of the smiling militiawomen were aimed at exhorting males rather than females to enlist.

In any event, with the centralization and professionalization of the army that began at the end of 1936, both the poster representations and the real *milicianas* within the autonomous militias became less common. The message of wartime propaganda from then on was that the business of fighting should be left to men at the front while patriotic women applied their energies to war work on the home front.

In the heyday of the militias there were militiawomen with combat units in Aragon, with Republican forces near Madrid, and on the Guadarama and Basque fronts. As well, the Rosa Luxemburg Women's Battalion fought in Majorca. Many of these women were courageous in battle, though there was no agreement over whether the presence of women at the front spurred male comrades to fight more fearlessly or encouraged reckless displays of male bravado resulting in heavy casualties.

The bravery of a number of *milicianas* under fire became part of Republican mythology, with these women cast as Republican heroines. **Lina Odena,** a Catalan and a leader of the Young Socialist League (JSU), mobilized women to fight with her on the Andalusian front. Cut off in Granada by Franco's troops in September 1936, Odena committed suicide rather than face capture. As well, there were figures like Aida de la Fuente who fought valiantly in the Asturias, or **Rosario Sánchez Mora,** of the eponymous sobriquet La Dinamitera, whose hand was blown off while she was working with an explosives unit in 1937 and whose courageous exploits were recorded in popular ballad.

What can be said with certainty about these women is that whether as individual recruits seeded into male units or as part of designated female sections attached to political battalions at the front, they were expected to wash and cook for their male comrades. In many cases *milicianas* were faced with what today would be described as sexism and harassment. It was rare that male soldiers in the Spanish Civil War treated female soldiers "simply as comrades and nothing more," as it was put by one of the militiamen in **Mika Etchebéhère**'s unit.

Etchebéhère had the notable distinction of becoming a commander of a combat unit in the POUM battalion after the death of her husband, a POUM commander. Her military position was unusual in that she insisted that *milicianas* were "not domestics" but soldiers, and that in the enterprise of winning the war men and women were equal. The fact that several militiawomen were keen to transfer into the more egalitarian environment of her unit suggests that it was not typical. Similarly, Etchebéhère has noted that it was necessary to retrain many of the men under her command before they accepted her regimen.

Given the chaotic nature of enlistment and formation of the militias in the first six months of the war, it is impossible to provide an exact estimate of the numbers of serving militiawomen. Probably there were never more than a few hundred. It is perhaps worth noting, as well, that from the descriptions of contemporaries it would seem that at least a proportion of them and those that organized women's brigades were foreigners.

These women were anti-Fascist exiles already living in Spain when the war broke out, were married to Spaniards, or, like Mika Etchebéhère, had come to Spain in order to support the Republic. Among them were Louise Gómez, the French wife of Julián Gorkin, and Olga Nin, the Russian wife of Andrés Nin, both of whom helped found the POUM Women's Secretariat. Mary Low, an Australian and a supporter of the Fourth International, had come to Barcelona with her Belgian *compañero* intending to enlist in active combat. She joined a POUM women's training regiment and later recalled the mixture of girlish shrieks and serious purpose of the female recruits as they mastered the intricacies of handling weapons. She noted, as well, that many of these women had not told their husbands or fathers that they had joined the women's reserve because their men would have forbidden it.

Once the centralization of the army began, women were discouraged from combat, and by the first months of 1937 they had almost disappeared from the front. Those who remained in POUM or anarchist militias were removed by June 1937 as their units were disarmed and dissolved. The 1995 film *Land and Freedom* by the British director Ken Loach depicts the dissolution of a militia unit on the Aragon front in which the removal of the two *milicianas* from combat to support duties presaged the disarmament of the entire unit by a battalion of the new Republican army.

The victory in February 1939 of the Nationalists brought an end to all of the political freedom and legal rights that Spanish women had enjoyed under the Second Republic. The dictatorship of General Franco imposed a repressive definition of Spanish women's roles in which female identity henceforth would be tied narrowly to the exercise of the traditional functions of devout wives and mothers. Ex-militiawomen and female activists who had embraced the potential of a new deal for women during the Second Republic were treated very harshly by the Franco state. After the civil war those who were unable to escape abroad were arrested and condemned to spend long and painful years in Franco's prisons.

Bibliography: Etchebéhère, *Ma guerre d'Espagne à moi,* 1976; Fuyola, *Mujeres antifascistas,* 1936; Keene, " 'No More than Brothers and Sister,' " 1998; Lannon, "Women and Images of Woman in the Spanish Civil War," 1991; Low, *Red Spanish Notebook,* 1937; Mangini, *Memories of Resistance,* 1995; Nash, *Defying Male Civilization,* 1995.

—Judith Keene

SPAR. The United States Coast Guard Women's Reserve. Established 23 November 1942, demobilized 30 June 1946. Served as part of the United States Coast Guard during the Second World War.

The United States Coast Guard Women's Reserve was known as SPAR from the Coast Guard motto, Semper Paratus (always ready), an acronym attributed to the SPAR director, Lieutenant Commander **Dorothy Stratton**. SPAR was one of several women's reserves established in the United States during the Second World War. Desperate for men to serve at sea, the Coast Guard realized that by filling shore jobs with women, men would be freed for sea duty. Nearly 11,000 women served as SPARs. At the height of the reserve strength of the Coast Guard, one out of every sixteen or seventeen enlisted persons was a SPAR; one out of every twelve or thirteen reserve officers was a SPAR.

SPAR was headed by a former member of the navy **WAVES,** Lieutenant Commander Dorothy Stratton. Selected as the SPAR director by WAVES director Lieutenant Commander **Mildred McAfee,** Stratton was sworn into office on 24 November 1942. The first twelve SPAR officers were volunteers from the December 1942 class of WAVES officers training at the Naval Reserve Midshipmen's School in Northampton, Massachusetts. Thirty-four enlisted members of the WAVES transferred to the Coast Guard to form the corps of enlisted women. At first the SPAR trained with the navy WAVES, but on 14 June 1943 separate SPAR training began at the Coast Guard Training Station at Palm Beach, Florida (formerly the Palm Beach Biltmore Hotel). By January 1945 the need for SPAR recruits, except for replacements and women with special skills, was filled, and training for enlisted SPARs was transferred to the Coast Guard Training Station at Manhattan Beach, Brooklyn, New York. On 28 June 1943 SPAR officers began training at the Coast Guard Academy in New London, Connecticut, making the Coast Guard the first to train women at a service academy.

Qualifications for enlistment in the SPAR were much higher than those for men joining the Coast Guard. An enlisted SPAR was required to be between the ages of twenty and thirty-six, have completed at least two years of high school or business school, be an American citizen with no dependents under eighteen, and pass a physical examination, an aptitude test, and a personal interview. Officer candidates had to be between the ages of twenty and fifty with a college degree or two years of college and two years of business or professional experience. Other requirements were the same as for an enlisted woman, except that the officer candidates were selected by a headquarters board. Black women were not accepted into the SPAR until November 1944.

SPARs served in many different occupations during the war. The largest number of SPAR officers, 37 percent, held general duty billets. These included administrative and supervisory assignments in various divisions of the Coast Guard. Twenty-three percent served as communications officers and 17 percent as pay and supply officers. A small number of SPAR officers were assigned to barracks and recruiting duty. There were a variety of ratings held by enlisted SPARs. The majority of enlisted women did clerical work, but some were assigned to other duties such as pharmacist's mates, cooks and bakers, radio technicians, link-instrument trainers, parachute riggers, and control-tower operators. The most unique job was held by the SPARs assigned to Long Range Aid to Navigation (LORAN) stations. LORAN was a highly classified system used to check the positions of ships and planes. One LORAN monitor station, Unit 21 at Chatham, Massachusetts, was believed to be the only all-female-staffed unit of its kind in the world.

SPARs served in every Coast Guard district except for the tenth (Puerto Rico). Due to legal restrictions, SPARs, along with WAVES members and **women marines,** were prohibited from assignments outside the continental United States. Wacs and nurses were the only servicewomen allowed to serve overseas. In November 1944 the law was modified and women were allowed to serve overseas in some U.S. territories. For the SPAR, this meant Alaska and Hawaii. About 200 SPARs served in Hawaii, and an additional 200 were assigned to Alaska, where they did the same type of work as back in the United States. All SPARs serving outside the continental United States were volunteers and were required to have excellent service records.

At the end of the war the SPAR was the only one of the four women's services to completely demobilize. The SPAR director, Captain Dorothy C. Stratton, resigned in January 1946 and was succeeded by Captain Helen B. Schleman. Captain Schleman served until the SPAR was demobilized in June 1946. The Coast Guard did not again recruit women until the 1970s.

On 12 August 2000 the Coast Guard cutter *SPAR* was commissioned, named in honor of the women who served in the Coast Guard during the Second World War. The *SPAR* is a Juniper "B" Class seagoing buoy tender whose home port is Kodiak, Alaska.

Bibliography: Gruhzit-Hoyt, *They Also Served*, 1995; Holm, *Women in the Military*, 1992; Litoff and Smith, *We're in This War, Too*, 1994; Lynn and Arthur, *Three Years behind the Mast*, 1946.

—Vicki L. Friedl

SPIEGEL, CHAIKE BELCHATOWSKA (born 11 November 1920, Warsaw, Poland; died 26 March 2002, Montreal, Canada). Also called Helen. Resistance fighter, Warsaw Ghetto Uprising, Poland, Second World War.

The armies of Nazi Germany overran Poland in 1939 and began the systematic deportation of Polish Jews. Chaike Belchatowska, a member of the Marxist socialist Jewish Labor Bund, took part in the efforts to urge Jews to resist deportation by all possible means. In November 1942 she escaped from the train that was taking her to the Treblinka death camp and returned to the ghetto. In January 1943 she joined the Jewish Fighting Organization (known by the Polish acronym ZOB). On 19 April 1943 ZOB and other resistance groups repulsed the Nazi attack, begun on the first night of Passover. With a handful of smuggled, outdated weapons, improvised Molotov cocktails, and little ammunition, the fighters took the Germans by surprise, causing heavy casualties. The resistance continued for three weeks. The Germans brought in flamethrowers to systematically burn down the ghetto, and on 8 May they used poison gas. It is estimated that 7,000 Jews were killed during the fighting, and 30,000 were deported to death camps. Fifty to 100 Jewish resistance fighters, including Belchatowska and her future husband, Baruch Spiegel, escaped to the woods outside of Warsaw and continued to harass the Germans until the end of the war. The Spiegels were refused an American visa and resided in Sweden and Canada after the war.

Bibliography: *New York Times,* Obituary, 7 April 2002.

—Valerie Eads

STAMIRA OF ANCONA (fl. 1172). Defender, siege of Ancona, Italy, 1172.

Stamira of Ancona represents a rare documented case of a lower-class woman participating in warfare. She was a humbly born citizen and widow, still remembered for her heroic actions in the siege of Ancona in 1172 during the Byzantine-Venetian conflict (1170–1177). Carrying arms and leading a squad of her compatriots, she boldly penetrated the imperial camp of the archbishop of Mainz and and set fire to his war engines. A modern painting commemorating her fortitude hangs in the Palazzo Comunale of Bertinoro. See also **Alruda Frangipani**.

Bibliography: Gatti, *Bertinoro: Notizie storiche,* 1968–1971; Saracini, *Notitie historiche della città d'Ancona,* 1968.

—Gloria Allaire

STANLEY, CHARLOTTE, COUNTESS OF DERBY (born December 1599, Thouars, France; died 31 March 1664, Knowsley, Lancashire, England). Born Charlotte de la Trémoille. Defender, England, English Civil War.

A staunch royalist during the English Civil War, Lady Derby, the wife of James Stanley, seventh earl of Derby, successfully defended Lathom House in Lancashire during its first siege by parliamentary forces, February to May 1644. By early 1643, with most of Lancashire supporting Parliament, Lathom House was the only significant royalist stronghold in the county. While her husband was away defending the Isle of Man, Lady Derby assumed command of Lathom House and its royalist garrison. She secretly gathered 300 men, food, and ammunition to defend against a siege. The 3,000 parliamentary troops who began the siege of Lathom House on 28 February 1644 encountered a fortress with six-foot-thick walls and towers with ordnance, surrounded by a moat and palisade. Lady Derby refused all calls for surrender and offers of safe-conduct for herself and her two daughters. She declared that the house and the people inside it would burn before surrendering. As commander in chief, she inspected the walls, oversaw distribution of food and powder, helped plan sorties, tended the wounded, and prayed regularly. Her religious faith was evident in her declaring a public thanksgiving after her soldiers captured an enemy mortar. She likewise endured all the hardships of the siege, continuing to eat dinner after a shell exploded in the dining room and refusing to change her bedroom until it had been hit several times by bullets.

Her resolute defense of Lathom House began to wear down the besiegers even before a royalist army arrived in late May to relieve the siege. Vilified by Parliamentarians as the Whore of Babylon, the woman who, after Queen **Henrietta Maria,** did most to damage England, Lady Derby herself believed that she had done her duty to husband, king, and God. Lathom House survived its first siege largely because of the sheer determination and character of Lady Derby; when it fell to Parliament in December 1645, Lady Derby was on the Isle of Man.

Bibliography: "A Brief Journall of the Siege against Lathom," 1844; *Dictionary of National Biography*; Fraser, *The Weaker Vessel*, 1984; Guizot de Witt, *The Lady of Lathom*, 1869; Higgins, "Women in the English Civil War," 1965.

—Robert W. Gee

STAUFFENBERG, MELITTA SCHILLER (born 3 January 1903, Krotoschin, West Prussia, Germany; died 8 April 1945), also known as Melitta Gräfin Schenk von Stauffenberg. Flight captain. Military test pilot, Germany, Second World War; recipient of Luftwaffe Gold Pilot's Badge and Iron Cross I and II. Member of "the plot to kill Hitler."

Melitta Schiller was born in 1903 in West Prussia and attended school there until 1918, when the area was awarded to Poland in the Treaty of Versailles. As the new Polish state did not offer upper-level German high school, Melitta completed her secondary education in Hirschberg, Silesia. As early as age sixteen, Melitta showed an interest in physics and aerodynamics. She read books on these topics voraciously and began frequenting the glider fields near Hirschberg, where war-veteran pilots taught young men flying in gliders in order to evade the restrictions of the peace treaty. Melitta so impressed the pilots there by her knowledge that she was allowed, at nineteen, to fly her first plane. Melitta later attended the Institute of Technology in Munich in order to pursue her aspirations for an aeronautical career and earned a degree in civil engineering in 1927.

Melitta's ambition to fly, however, was not met with enthusiasm, and she was forced to circumvent the rigidity of the establishment. She logged the necessary hours in the air with machines of dubious reliability and in unsafe weather conditions. Her daring efforts were criticized, and for a while she was not permitted to fly at all. Nevertheless, she acquired all existing pilot's licenses and became an "engineer pilot," testing the heaviest land and sea planes and developing instruments for the control of dive-bombing flights for the German Aviation Testing Institute in Berlin-Adlershof, a branch of the clandestine German air forces. She performed aerobatics in a Heinkel He-70 at the 1936 Berlin Olympics.

In 1936 Melitta was forced to leave her position with the Luftwaffe. After Hitler came to power, Jews were not allowed to maintain public service positions. Melitta's father informed her that her paternal grandfather had been Jewish, and although her father had converted to Lutheranism many years before, under Nazi law she was still regarded as Jewish. She applied, along with two siblings, for equal-to-Aryan status; pending the arrival of necessary documentation, she was transferred to Askania Works at Berlin-Friedenau, another secret Luftwaffe branch, and worked there as an engineer-pilot. Her knowledge in aviation was too significant, however, to be left untapped, and the military establishment placed her in another aircraft testing position in the Air War Academy at Berlin-Gatow to work on bomb sights for the Junkers 87 and 88. In 1937 she received the rank of flight captain (apparently an honorary rank).

With demonstrably superior skills as an engineer and flyer, Melitta Schiller was extraordinarily self-effacing and, in the judgment of some of her friends, much too modest about her abilities and accomplishments. She was at least as good as those with famous names, such as **Hanna Reitsch,** and she was conscious of the importance of her vanguard role in the emancipation of German women. But she preferred simply to perform her duties and did not make a public display of her accomplishments. As early as 1931 Melitta was quoted as having said that it was unimportant whether anything was published about her; her work was all a matter of course, and in a few years there would be many women aviators. But she did not fly for the sake of emancipation: "We women flyers are not suffragettes." Still, she admitted that as a woman she could less afford to make mistakes than men, and that she had to perform better and risk more. She had always hoped to use her skills, in case of war, in the service of the Red Cross, but when war came in 1939, the Air Ministry insisted that she continue her work on air force equipment and her specialty of testing dive bombers.

From 1939 on she flew as many as fifteen missions a day, primarily in the heavy and demanding Ju-88. Her workload was considered far in excess of what was medically admissible for any pilot. By the end of 1943 she had accumulated more than 2,000 dive-bombing flights, more than any other German pilot. In view of the importance of her work, the Nazi government extended her and her family equal-to-Aryan status, allowing the Schillers to avoid being sent to the death camps. Melitta was awarded the Iron Cross II and the Luftwaffe Gold Pilot's Badge with Diamonds in 1943, and in 1944 she was nominated for the Iron Cross I.

The importance of Melitta's work did not rest solely on her successes with the German air forces. In the summer of 1937 Melitta married Alexander Schenk, Count von Stauffenberg, brother to Colonel Claus Stauffenberg, the courageous leader of the German resistance. In 1944 Claus Stauffenberg decided to assassinate Hitler and asked his sister-in-law whether she could fly him to the dictator's headquarters, feign an emergency landing, wait for him to complete his mission, and then fly him back to Berlin. Stauffenberg made clear what he was planning to do, and without hesitation she agreed to help, although she had at her disposal only a slow Fieseler "Storch" that would require stops en route for fuel, so that she and Stauffenberg would likely have been arrested during a stop on their return journey. She attempted to remedy the problem of refueling and practiced frequent night flights in a Fieseler "Storch" during 17–26 June 1944. On 27 June 1944 she discussed the dilemma with her colleague and in-law, Paul von Handel. He tried to talk her out of her plan, insisting that the plane's limitation was likely to ruin Stauffenberg's mission. Melitta was frustrated; she was entirely ready to risk her own life to assist in Hitler's assassination. Although she was subsequently excused from her task, there were entries in Melitta's diary as late as 18 July 1944 that indicate that she was securing both a Ju-87 D 3 and a Storch to prepare to fly Stauffenberg to Hitler's headquarters.

The plot went forward without her help. The assassination attempt failed and the insurrection was crushed. Claus Stauffenberg was shot on the evening of 20 July 1944; his brother Berthold was hanged slowly on 10 August 1944; and Alexander and Melitta Stauffenberg were detained under the kith-and-kin arrest system. Melitta was released on 2 September 1944 because of the importance of her work and soon resumed her flight research and testing. Alexander and his brothers' widows and children remained imprisoned, mostly in concentration camps, until the end of the war. Melitta insisted on seeing her husband at least once a month, bringing him and her imprisoned in-laws food, and, in fact, carried on her military work solely on that condition. At least twice she flew to Buchenwald, and she also discovered the secret camp where the children of Claus, Berthold, and their cousin Luftwaffe Lieutenant-Colonel Caesar von Hofacker had been taken by the SS. After Claus's widow Nina gave birth to a daughter at the end of January 1945 and was moved from her prison cell to St. Joseph's Hospital at Potsdam, Melitta went to visit, in full uniform, wearing all her ribbons and medals. The head physician, who had been in the Luftwaffe, recognized her and subsequently saw to it that Nina and her child had the best available care and attention.

On 8 April 1945, while flying low along railway tracks in her unarmed Buecker 181 trainer in search of the concentration camp to which her husband had been moved, Melitta Schiller Stauffenberg was shot down from behind by an American fighter. Disciplined and tough to the last, she still managed to land her plane. She died two hours later of her wounds at the age of forty-two, less than a month before Hitler's suicide and the end of the war.

Bibliography: Archival materials at Bundesarchiv, Koblenz, Germany; Bracke, *Melitta Gräfin Stauffenberg*, 1990; Escher, "Melitta Schiller-Stauffenberg," 1972; Hoffmann, *Stauffenberg: A Family History, 1905–1944*, 1995; Rudershausen, "Taeglich fuenfzehn Sturzfluege," 5 January 1973; Schiller, "Melitta Graefin Schenk von Stauffenberg, geb. Schiller," 1988; Stauffenberg family papers.

—Peter Hoffmann and Carol Anne Hale

STRATTON, DOROTHY CONSTANCE (born 24 March 1899, Brookfield, Missouri, United States). Captain (USCG), director of the United States Coast Guard Women's Reserve, also known as SPAR, 1942–1946.

The Second World War brought such severe manpower shortages that each military service established a women's reserve. **SPAR,** the United States Coast Guard Women's Reserve, was headed by Lieutenant Commander, later Captain, Dorothy Stratton. Stratton coined the term "SPAR" from the Coast Guard motto Semper Paratus (always ready). She did not want a nickname for Coast Guard women, but in an official memorandum to the commandant of the Coast Guard wrote, "It seems to me that there is no possibility of avoiding some catch name in the press. If we do not create a name, we shall be called WARCOGS or something worse."

Stratton was born in Missouri and grew up the daughter of a Baptist minister in small towns in Missouri and Kansas. In 1920 she graduated with a B.A. from Ottawa University in Ottawa, Kansas, then worked in various educational positions, including high-school teacher, vice-principal of a junior high school, and dean of girls at a senior high school. Stratton continued her education, earning a master's degree in psychology from the University of Chicago in 1924 and a doctorate in student personnel administration from Columbia University in 1932. Her thesis, "Problems of Students in a Graduate School," was published in 1933. That same year she was appointed dean of women and associate professor of psychology at Purdue University. Stratton was an active dean, establishing the university's first residence halls for women and an employment placement center for Purdue women. In 1940 she became a full professor.

Stratton's first exposure to the military came in 1942 when she served on the selection committee of the Army 5th Corps Area, which met to select the first officer candidate class for the WAAC. Later that same year Stratton was commissioned as a lieutenant in the **WAVES,** joining because "it was a new avenue of service for women, and it seemed important that women give a good account of themselves during the war service and afterward." She was a member of the first class of WAVES at the Naval Training School at Smith College. The change from college dean to officer trainee was not an easy one to make, evidenced by Stratton's remark to a fellow trainee that she thought she had made "the worst mistake of my life." In September 1942 the newly commissioned Lieutenant Stratton was assigned as the assistant to the commanding officer at the Training Center for Radio Operators at Madison, Wisconsin. She did not serve long in this position; in November 1942 she was ordered to duty in the office of the commandant of the Coast Guard to help develop plans for a women's reserve corps. The United States Coast Guard Women's Reserve was established on 23 November 1942, and Stratton was selected as the director by the WAVES director, Lieutenant Commander **Mildred McAfee.** She was sworn in on 24 November 1942.

As SPAR director, Stratton was primarily responsible for establishing policies for the procurement, training, utilization, and maintenance of morale of SPAR. At the height of the war she commanded 1,000 officers and 10,000 enlisted women. Stratton resigned as SPAR director in January 1946, six months before the SPAR completed its demobilization. She was appointed to the Retraining and Reemployment Administration to make sure that military women were not overlooked in its mission to help veterans and war workers reintegrate into the civilian community. Stratton served as the director of personnel for the International Monetary Fund (1947–1950) and as the executive director of the Girl Scouts of America (1950–1960).

Dorothy Stratton was awarded a Legion of Merit for her service as SPAR director. In 2001 she celebrated her 102nd birthday at her home in West Lafayette, Indiana.

Bibliography: *Current Biography;* Gruhzit-Hoyt, *They Also Served,* 1995; Holm, *Women in the Military,* 1992; Lynn and Arthur, *Three Years behind the Mast,* 1946; Thomson, *The Coast Guard and The Women's Reserve in World War II,* 1992; Tilley, *A History of Women in the Coast Guard,* 1996.

—Vicki L. Friedl

STREETER, RUTH CHENEY (born 1895, Brookline, Massachusetts; died 1990, Morristown, New Jersey). Colonel, United States Marine Corps Reserve, Second World War.

Ruth Cheney Streeter was the director of the United States Marine Corps Women's Reserve during the Second World War. She received a direct commission as a major, USMCR, in January 1943. She was released from active duty on 7 December 1945 with the rank of colonel, USMCR.

Streeter entered Bryn Mawr College in 1914, but left only two years later. Born to an affluent society family in Massachusetts, she spent nearly three decades committed to raising a family and heavy involvement in community service in the state of New Jersey before starting her military service. She had also earned private and commercial pilot's licenses and flew with the Civil Air Patrol. A political ally of President Franklin Roosevelt, the forty-eight-year-old Streeter was appointed to the post of director of the Marine Corps Women's Reserve (MCWR) in January 1943. She was in office on the official creation date of MCWR on 13 February 1943. Streeter was more successful than her counterparts (**Oveta Culp Hobby, Dorothy Stratton,** and **Jacqueline Cochran**) in avoiding the application of an acronym to the women under her control. In particular, she was determined to avoid the phrase used in the First World War ("marinettes"); the women of the MCWR were simply "marines."

Throughout the war Streeter made extensive tours of the United States for recruiting purposes. The motto of the MCWR was "Free a Marine to Fight." During her tenure **women marines** performed a wide variety of vital support roles that, according to the commandant of the Marine Corps, allowed the corps to commit an additional division to amphibious operations. She advocated overseas service for military women and supported the idea that one day women would fly as marine pilots. She was released from active service on 7 December 1945. For her wartime service, Colonel Streeter was awarded the Legion of Merit Medal.

Bibliography: Meid, *Marine Corps Women's Reserve in World War II*, 1968; Soderbergh, *Women Marines: The World War II Era*, 1992; Streeter, "History of the Marine Corps Women's Reserve: A Critical Analysis of Its Development and Operation, 1943–1945," 1945, and "Oral History Transcript," n.d.; Stremlow, *Free a Marine to Fight*, 1994.

—Patrick J. O'Connor

T

TALBOT, MARY ANNE (born 2 February 1778, Lincoln's Inn Fields, London; died 4 February 1808, Shropshire), also known as John Taylor. Alleged soldier and sailor, British army and navy, French Revolutionary Wars.

Mary Anne Talbot claimed to have acted as footboy, cabin boy, drummer, powder monkey, and midshipman in the Royal Navy and in the infantry regiment of the duke of York during the late eighteenth century. Using the alias "John Taylor," she became one of Britain's most famous "amazons" of the period and joined the ranks of others such as **Hannah Snell** and **Kit Cavanaugh** who either chose or were forced to disguise themselves as men in order to join the military. If her story is true, Talbot was unique in maintaining her disguise for many years, despite hospitalization, imprisonment, and several changes of service.

Talbot was purportedly the illegitimate daughter of Lord William, first earl of Talbot. Her mother died in childbirth, and Mary Anne was raised by a wet nurse in Worthen Shropshire until she was five years old; she then attended Mrs. Tapperly's boarding school at Chester until the age of fourteen. From an older sister Talbot inherited a fortune of £30,000 with an annual income of £1,500. But her sister chose an unscrupulous guardian, a Mr. Sucker, who stole the money and placed Talbot in the care of Captain Essex Bowen of the 82nd Regiment of Foot. Bowen took Talbot to London, where, rather than placing her in school as promised, he forced her to become his unwilling sexual partner.

Then Talbot was forced to disguise herself as a boy and took the name "John Taylor" in order to sail as a passenger with Bowen aboard Captain Bishop's *Crown* from Falmouth for the Spanish colony of Santo Domingo in the Caribbean. When a gale blew up en route, "Taylor" was forced to help man the pumps and received a crash course in nautical skills.

Talbot's 1804 autobiography vividly evokes the hardships of life at sea and the difficulty of her situation, living in virtual servitude to Captain Bowen. Upon arriving in Port-au-Prince in June 1792, Captain Bowen received orders to join the duke of York's troops in France and threatened to sell Talbot into slavery unless she agreed to be enlisted as a drummer. In Flanders she says that she was "obliged to keep up a continual roll to drown the cries and confusion" on the battlefield. She was wounded at the capture of Valenciennes in northeastern France in 1793 and took advantage of Captain Bowen's death to desert the regiment and avoid detection.

On 17 September 1793, still in disguise as Taylor, she signed on with a French ship under a Captain LeSage without realizing that it was a privateer (an armed vessel with a government commission to capture enemy merchant ships) until they engaged a British ship four months later. They were captured by Lord Howe, and Talbot was taken aboard HMS *Queen Charlotte* for interrogation. She did not mention her desertion from the army, and Lord Howe accepted young "Taylor's" account, sending her to sail with Captain John Hervey on the *Brunswick* as a powder monkey (a job given to young boys during battle, hauling powder from the magazines below deck to the guns).

Captain Hervey noticed Talbot's superior manner and education and promoted "him" to principal cabin boy. Three months after Talbot came aboard, while she was serving as an assistant to the gunners, the *Brunswick* engaged a French ship on 1 June 1794. Talbot was badly wounded when grapeshot shattered her left ankle; she spent four months recuperating at the Haslar Hospital, Gosport, near Portsmouth. Retaining her male identity throughout, on recovering, "Taylor" signed on with the *Vesuvius* as a midshipman.

Vesuvius, however, was taken by two privateers off the Normandy coast, and Talbot and the crew spent eighteen months in a Dunkirk prison. After her release she signed on with an American, Captain John Field of the *Ariel*, and set sail for New York in August 1796. She returned to London on the same ship in November, where she was captured by a press gang while ashore in Wapping. She revealed her true sex to avoid impressment, saying, "The officers upbraided each other with ignorance at not discovering before, my being a woman, and readily gave me a discharge."

Talbot's retirement from the sea marked the beginning of a precarious string of occupations, which included jewelry making, acting on the London stage, and domestic service. Her poor health added to her financial troubles, and she was frequently hospitalized for treatment of her left ankle. Meanwhile, she battled the pay office of the Royal Navy for a pension (which she eventually was granted) and received presents from Queen Caroline, the duke of Norfolk, and others who heard of her military exploits. Her final employment was with Robert S. Kirby (who became the chronicler of her story) as a domestic at his house in St. Paul's Churchyard. After three years there her deteriorating health forced her to retire to a friend's home in Shropshire. She lived there for only a few weeks and died two days after her thirtieth birthday.

The preceding information is based entirely on Talbot's "autobiography" as told to Robert S. Kirby, who published a brief version in his 1803 *The Wonderful and Scientific Museum*, and expanded the tale in his 1809 *The Life and Surprising Adventures of Mary Anne Talbot*. Every later source seems to derive from the 1809 account. However, Suzanne Stark, in her book *Female Tars*, identifies a number of errors in the 1809 book that lead her to believe that Talbot's story may be pure fiction. In checking army lists, Stark found that there was no Captain Essex Bowen in the army, although a Lieutenant Essex Bowen was on navy lists of the period (but did not die until 1811). The ship in which Talbot supposedly sailed to the Caribbean with Bowen, the *Crown*, did exist, but was sailing from India to England in 1792. Stark failed to find in army lists any "John Taylor" of the right age in the right place to support Talbot's claims; she found that the *Vesuvius* was in the West Indies at the time it was allegedly captured by privateers. Although many of the regiments and ships described in the 1809 book did exist, Stark could not verify that Talbot was there, and so she discounts the entire tale.

These disputes about the truth of Talbot's life highlight the difficulties in researching the history of a low-ranking, semiliterate individual who may have lived under an assumed name. It is possible that Talbot did in fact accomplish all or most of what she claimed, and by the time she related her story to Kirby, her memory was fading; memoirs are notoriously fuzzy, and few veterans are precise on every detail of date and location. In addition, Kirby may have embellished or simply got wrong some of the information. One other piece of primary evidence may support Talbot's credibility; she was interviewed in a 1799 piece in the *Times* of London (4 November 1799) while she was in hospital, and told the reporter that she had been injured in military service.

It is thus impossible to determine, based on known sources, whether or not Talbot actually managed to serve in male disguise for four or five years. It could be pure fiction; there is little to corroborate her story. On the other hand, there could well be some truth to her claims. After all, she did not claim great heroism, but only to have done the kinds of duties performed by hundreds of teenaged boys in those years. The only sensational thing about her story is that her male disguise was so long undetected, but hundreds of other women managed that same feat in the premodern military (see Dekker and van der Pol).

Many of these women, once discharged from service, landed in a limbo world where they belonged to neither gender. A few, such as Talbot, sold their stories and even went on stage to exploit the celebrity that came with their unmasking. Talbot thus belongs to a tradition of other women who disguised themselves as men to join premodern armies and to the popular literary tradition that spread the news of their exploits. While it remains impossible to know the precise details of her individual story, those of other female sailors of the period, including Mary Read, Anne Bonnie, and Hannah Snell, suggest that her exploits are well within the bounds of credibility.

Bibliography: Dekker and van de Pol, *The Tradition of Female Transvestism in Early Modern Europe*, 1989; Gribble, *Women in War*, 1917; Stark, *Female Tars*, 1996; Wheelwright, *Amazons and Military Maids*, 1989, and "Tarts, Tars, and Swashbucklers," 1996.

—Julie Wheelwright

TAMAR, QUEEN OF GEORGIA (born ca. 1160; died 18 January 1213, r. 1184–1213), also known as Tamara, Thamar, "Mountain of God," and "King of Kartli."

Although there is no record of Queen Tamar personally engaging in battle, she did face a number of domestic and foreign military situations as the commander in chief of her armies. She issued orders for troop musters, reviewed her soldiers, received and analyzed intelligence reports, made decisions about which forces to deploy and when, and on some occasions gave battlefield exhortations to her troops prior to engagements. Under her rule the kingdom of Georgia reached the height of its power and influence in the region as well as enjoying a "golden age" in art and literature. By the time of her death her domain stretched from the Black Sea in the west to the Caspian Sea in the east, and she had effectively halted and reversed Muslim expansion into the southern part of her territories.

Tamar was the daughter of King Giorgi III of Georgia. Attempting to ensure a peaceful transition of royal power, her father had her enthroned as coruler in 1178. She became sole ruler on his death in 1184, but was initially dominated by a coalition of nobles and churchmen on the royal council who saw an opportunity to increase their own power by curbing that of the new female ruler. They insisted on a second coronation and pressured her into a marriage in 1187 with their candidate, George Bogoliubskoi, a Russian prince. Tamar's consort was popular with the more conservative elements of the Georgian aristocracy and was a capable military leader. However, he was also rumored to be drunken, violent, and prone to "unnatural acts." Tamar, with the consent of the council, divorced Bogoliubskoi in 1189 and sent him into luxurious exile in Byzantium. Her second marriage in 1190 to Ossetian prince David Soslan was more successful. Soslan proved to be an excellent military commander, and together they had two children, Giorgi in 1194 and Rusudan in 1195.

Domestically Tamar's forces put down three revolts, two involving her former husband (1191 and 1200) and a third by the lords of Samtzhe (1196). The most serious revolt was in 1190–1191 when Bogoliubskoi, supported by a conservative faction of the aristocracy largely from the western territories, was declared king and marched on the Georgian capital of Tblisi (Tiflis). Bogoliubskoi and his followers were soundly defeated by Tamar's armies. In contrast to her father's use of blinding and mutilation to deal with competitors, Tamar favored banishment over bloodshed, and Bogoliubskoi was once again sent into exile.

Control of the various social and ethnic factions that made up her kingdom was a key to Tamar's independence. Her skill at building coalitions and foresight in considering merit over political affiliation when choosing government and military leaders allowed her to gain the cooperation of the nobles who had originally sought to dominate her. Further, she actively pursued a policy of territorial expansion that kept her military forces occupied and receiving a regular supply of spoils, lands, and honors. Taking advantage of Christian religious fervor, she also assumed an aggressive posture toward the Muslim emirates to the south of Georgia and to the east in Persia. Her forces defeated a powerful Muslim coalition led by Atabag Abu-Bekr in June 1203, and she further expanded her territory in 1205–1206 with her defeat of the Seljuk sultan of Rum, Rukn-ed-Din, at the Battle of Basiani. According to the *Georgian Chronicle,* Queen Tamar marched with her troops to the site of battle and gave an impassioned speech, exhorting them to trust in God and not fear the superior numbers of the enemy. The ensuing victory over the sultan netted for Tamar the important fortified city of Kars, further strengthening her southern borders.

In 1208 she authorized a punitive raid against the sultan of Ardabil in retaliation for his earlier massacre of Christians in the city of Ani that resulted in the destruction of Ardabil and the death of the sultan. This victory was followed by an expedition into Persia that gained for the queen both abundant spoils and tribute payments. Further, taking advantage of the disorder created by the Fourth Crusade, Tamar's armies successfully detached several provinces along the southern rim of the Black Sea from Byzantium, which were placed under the control of her kinsman Alexius Comnenus as the Empire of Trebizond in 1204.

According to her biographer, years of political and military campaigning eventually took their toll on the queen's health, "for a woman's frailty could not remain unaffected in the course of continual campaigns and suffer no harm" (*Georgian Chronicle*). Tamar died at Agara on 18 January 1213 at around the age of fifty.

Bibliography: Allen, *A History of the Georgian People*, 1932; Echols and Williams, *An Annotated Index of Medieval Women*, 1992; Fraser, *The Warrior Queens*, 1989; *The Georgian Chronicle*, 1991; Lang, *The Georgians*, 1966.

—Annette Parks

TAYLOR, SUSIE KING (born 6 August 1848, Isle of Wight, Georgia, United States; died 1912), also known as Susie Baker. First South Carolina Volunteers (later known as the 33rd United States Colored Troops). Nurse, teacher, laundress, United States, American Civil War.

Susie King Taylor, a literate slave, was sent to live with relatives on the Georgia coast when war broke out. In April 1862 she fled to Union lines after Northern troops fired upon nearby Fort Pulaski. The Yankee soldiers moved the "contrabands" of war to sea islands off the South Carolina coast to assist other former slaves in operating captured cotton plantations. There, army officials asked Taylor to operate a school for former slave children.

When the army began to organize the former slaves into combat regiments, Taylor jumped at the opportunity to serve. She was fourteen at the time and was relegated to rear-echelon duty without pay. Although Taylor was originally assigned as a laundress, she rarely served in that capacity. She primarily served as a nurse and, in her spare time, taught soldiers to read and write. Besides laboring in camp hospitals, Taylor frequently traveled with the regiment as a field medic. On several occasions she moved close enough to the action to see artillery shells flying overhead.

In addition to serving the First South Carolina Volunteers, Taylor was also attached to the renowned 54th Massachusetts Infantry. Following the now famous assault upon Fort Wagner, South Carolina, in July 1863, Taylor assisted Clara Barton in treating the wounded. She worked with the respected Civil War nurse for the next eight months. After the war Taylor moved to Boston and kept in contact with her fellow veterans by organizing a local chapter of the Women's Relief Corps, an auxiliary to the postwar veterans' group, the Grand Army of the Republic. As a leader in this organization, Taylor publicly criticized the corps's Southern counterpart, the United Daughters of the

Undated portrait of Susie King Taylor. (Library of Congress)

Confederacy, for its attempt to ban the play *Uncle Tom's Cabin* at a Tennessee theater. In 1902 Taylor wrote her memoirs and became the only African American female volunteer to record her wartime experiences.

Bibliography: Taylor, *Reminiscences of My Life in Camp*, 1968.

—Robert J. Zalimas, Jr.

TELESILLA (fl. fifth century BCE). Defender of Argos against the Spartan Army in 494 BCE.

By the seventh century BCE the Spartans had subdued much of the Peloponnesus and had made alliances with most of the rest, though the city-state of Argos, Sparta's neighbor to the northeast, remained independent. Telesilla figured in a battle in which the Spartans attempted to capture Argos. They met the Argive army outside the city, drove them into a wood, and killed them all. When Telesilla learned that the Argive army had been destroyed and that the Spartans were advancing on her city, she organized the young women along with boys, old men, and slaves. She armed them with weapons from the temples, where they had been placed as in dedications, and stationed her new troops on the walls in plain view. When the Spartans broke through the city gates, the women drove them out again. Telesilla had no military training or rank. According to Plutarch, she was sickly until the Oracle commanded her to compose poetry, and her prowess as a literary figure gave her sufficient authority to be accepted as a military leader.

In accordance with the custom of burying warriors at the battle site, the women who fell in this battle were buried beside the road into the city. The surviving women were granted the privilege of putting up a dedicatory statue. Pausanias saw a relief sculpture in honor of Telesilla that showed her with poems lying forgotten at her feet and a helmet in her hand. The evidence for her is not firsthand, and some scholars doubt that she was a warrior, though her existence seems certain and her militant actions were well within the realm of probability.

The Spartans did not return to invade Argos,

The Greek word for courage (*andreia*) was derived from the word for man/men (*aner/andres*). The Greeks debated whether courage (and any other good quality) was natural or learned. If it was natural, then men would be brave because it was in their nature, and women could never be brave. If it could be taught, then women could learn to be brave. Those who thought that courage was natural to men took this as an argument for men, and not women, going into battle where courage was so obviously needed.

Some Greeks, however, recognized that women showed courage. Socrates watched as a female dancer entertained guests at a dinner party by somersaulting in and out of a circular frame set with upright sword blades, showing no fear or hesitation. He pointed out to his companions that this demonstrated that courage could be learned because this dancer was daring, in spite of being female. His friends reinforced the idea by saying that men in the army needed to learn to be brave, giving as an example a cowardly man who could not bear to look directly at a spear (Xenophon, *Symposium* 2.12).

Only rarely did Greek women fight in battle, usually of necessity when men were absent. The **Amazon** warriors were paradigms of all that was foreign to Greek culture: women engaging in combat with men and demoting men to domestic chores or fathering children. Plutarch in his collection "On the Fine Qualities of Women" gave many examples of women behaving bravely—exchanging clothing with male prisoners and allowing them to escape disguised in women's dresses while they remained behind to face the wrath of their captors; smuggling in weapons under their cloaks for their husbands; or throwing stones from the walls onto advancing armies. Only in his account of **Telesilla** do women fall in battle and receive burial as warriors.

—M. Eleanor Irwin

perhaps because victory against an army of women would bring no glory and defeat would bring further shame. Plutarch says that the Argive women arranged to make some men of neighboring cities citizens of Argos and the fathers of the next generation of Argives. In this same section of the *Moralia*, entitled "Bravery of Women," Plutarch describes how the women of Chios defended their city against an attack by Philip of Macedon.

Bibliography: Pausanias, *Description of Greece*, 1918; Plutarch, *Moralia*, 1983; *Real-Encyclopädie der classischen Altertumswissenschaft*, vol. 5A; Snyder, *The Woman and the Lyre*, 1989.

—M. Eleanor Irwin

TEUTA (fl. third century BCE), also known as Tefta. Queen of the Ardiaei during the First Illyrian War, 229 BCE.

The Illyrian queen Teuta did not fight or lead armies on the battlefield, but as head of state she determined foreign and military policy. It was Teuta who gave the Romans their first pretext to cross the Adriatic with an army as they began their conquest of the eastern Mediterranean during the interim between the First and Second Punic Wars.

Teuta succeeded her husband Agron in 231 or 230 BCE as regent for her young stepson Pinnes. The Ardiaei were at this time a powerful tribe in Illyria on the eastern coast of the Adriatic Sea (present-day Albania). Regarded by the Greeks as pirates who harassed merchant vessels, the Ardiaei were conducting a campaign of expansion southwards in the Adriatic. According to Appian, the Romans had received complaints from the Greek island of Issa about Agron's aggression and sent an embassy to investigate. It never arrived; a Roman ambassador, Coruncanius, was killed on the way by Illyrian pirates. As a result, the Romans declared war in 229. Teuta led the Illyrian defense in vain. In 228 she made an onerous peace with Rome and possibly surrendered her regency; in 219 BCE the Illyrians were defeated again by Rome, which took control of their coastal territories.

Polybius's account gives Teuta a larger military role, adding military campaigning by Teuta in 230 against Elis, Messenia, Phoenice, and Issa and again in 229, when war had become inevitable, against Corcyra and Epidamnus. In his version, Roman ambassadors investigated the complaints of Italian traders and confronted Teuta during an angry interview at Issa in 230. The interview, which is impossible by Appian's account, ended in her ordering the death of Coruncanius, which led the Romans to declare war.

In Polybius's depiction, Teuta is a potent symbol of barbarian power and danger at the fringes of the Greek and Roman world. He dwells on her greed and lack of reason, as well as her "womanly spirit." His version of events is followed and embellished by later authors, notably Florus, but there are internal reasons to doubt its reliability, and where it directly contradicts Appian, it is often now rejected.

In any event, the actions of the Ardiaei under Teuta's reign were a direct catalyst to Roman expansion. Illyria had a long history of conflict with the Macedonians, and the Roman incursions into the region were regarded as a threat by Philip V, king of Macedon, and led to a series of Macedonian Wars that ended with Roman control of the entire region. Teuta was unsuccessful in her attempt to defend her homeland against the Roman army, which places her among dozens of other tribal leaders, kings, and queens whose armies and territories would fall to Rome.

Bibliography: Appian, *Illyrike*, 7; Badian, *Studies in Greek and Roman History*, 1964; Derow, P.S., "Kleemporos," *Phoenix* 1973, 118ff; Errington, R.M., *Cambridge Ancient History*, vol. 8 (Cambridge: Cambridge University Press, 1989); Pauly et al., *Real-Encyclopädie der classischen Altertumswissenschaft*, "Teuta"; "Coruncanius" 1 and 2, 1964; Polybius, 2.2–12.

—M. Eleanor Irwin

THATCHER, MARGARET ROBERTS (born 13 October 1925, Grantham, Lincolnshire, England), also known as "the Iron Lady." Prime minister, United Kingdom of Great Britain and Northern Ireland, 1979–1990.

Margaret Thatcher was the longest-serving prime minister of the twentieth century, as well as the first female party leader and first female head of government in modern British history. Thatcher was also the first British leader to make war since the 1956 Suez incident, overseeing the Falkland Islands War with Argentina in 1982 and preparations for the Gulf War against Iraq in 1990.

Thatcher was born and raised "over the shop," the daughter of grocer Alfred Roberts, who served as alderman and later mayor of Grantham, a small

Margaret Thatcher visiting NATO, Brussels, Belgium, November 29, 1977. (NATO Photos)

town in the northeast Midlands. Thatcher's biographers make much of the fact that she seemed to idolize her father while relegating her mother, a housewife, to insignificance as a role model. From her father, Thatcher inherited a staunch belief in Victorian moral values and an indomitable confidence in herself and the righteousness of her convictions.

As a chemistry student at Oxford University during the Second World War, Thatcher involved herself in Conservative Party politics. After several unsuccessful attempts to win a seat in the House of Commons, she was nominated as the Conservative candidate for the London borough of Finchley, a "safe" seat, in 1959. A prodigious worker, Thatcher enjoyed a high profile during the 1960s. In the Conservative governments of Harold Macmillan and Edward Heath she held cabinet ministerial positions in pensions and education.

In 1974 the Conservatives lost the general election. Heath was ousted from the party leadership, and in January 1975, in a surprising turn of events, Thatcher was chosen the new Conservative Party leader, making her leader of the Opposition and shadow prime minister. The governing Labour Party's policies proved inept at addressing Britain's economic difficulties, with trade union agitation culminating in the infamous "winter of discontent" of 1978–1979. In the general election of May 1979 the Conservatives swept to power with a woman at the reins.

Thatcher's first three years were dominated by domestic policy concerns. She reduced government spending across the board, including spending on defense. The navy was trimmed to meet the Treasury's economizing demands, which had a direct effect on the opening of the Falklands crisis in 1982.

Argentina had claimed the British Falkland Islands in the South Atlantic since the early nineteenth century. However, the islands' tiny population fiercely treasured its British connection. In 1981 Argentina's government fell to a military coup; among the junta's more popular demands was the return of the Falklands. Britain seemed to signal a lack of will to resist a takeover of the islands when, as part of its 1982 defense review, it withdrew its only warship in the vicinity, HMS *Endurance,* for decommissioning. Argentina invaded and occupied the Falklands on 2 April 1982.

On 31 March the British government learned that an invasion was imminent. Thatcher, whose role as prime minister was to formulate foreign and defense policy, convened her defense and diplomatic advisors. She insisted that "if [the Falklands] are invaded, we have got to get them back." Under Thatcher's direction, on 2 April the full cabinet ordered a naval task force to the South Atlantic. Thatcher had decided to fight.

In the ensuing weeks diplomacy failed to persuade the Argentine junta to relinquish the islands. Thatcher successfully painted the Argentine move as "aggression" and went to war under Article 51 of the United Nations Charter, which sanctioned the use of force in self-defense. The *Economist* observed that Thatcher "gambled . . . on escalating the dispute from . . . the loss of a minor imperial outpost into a major confrontation between the forces of good and evil" (17 April 1982, 12).

To limit the fighting to the Falklands, Britain declared an "exclusion zone" of twelve miles from the islands' coast on 12 April. In this context Thatcher made the war's most controversial military decision. On 2 May Thatcher and her cabinet ordered a submarine to sink the Argentine battle cruiser *General Belgrano* while it was technically outside the exclusion zone. The official explanation for this action was that the ship posed a threat to the British task force preparing to invade the Falklands. The real motive seems to have been Thatcher's determination to demonstrate to the Argentines that Britain had no qualms about retaking the islands by force. Ironically, the sinking backfired in two ways: the loss of more than 380 seamen made it politically impossible for the junta to back down from the confrontation, and world opinion, which had supported Britain, now turned against it. Militarily, the sinking succeeded in persuading the Argentines to withdraw their fleet to home ports for the rest of the war; politically, it was costly, and increasing pressure was put on Britain to cease military action and negotiate.

Thatcher was unmoved. The British invasion and recapture of the Falklands commenced on 21 May. Churchill-like, she sternly declared in a 26 May speech: "Now we are present in strength on the Falkland Islands. Our purpose is to repossess them. We shall carry on until that purpose is accomplished." On 14 June the Argentines surrendered.

Thatcher also played a pivotal role in the crisis ensuing from Iraq's invasion of Kuwait in August 1990. She saw Iraq's action as "aggression" similar to Argentina's in 1982 and encouraged American president George Bush to meet force with force: "Now is not the time to go wobbly." Thatcher ordered British forces into the Persian Gulf to support the American-led coalition that later expelled Iraq from Kuwait in February 1991. By that time, however, Thatcher was no longer in charge.

The Falklands victory ensured the Conservatives' reelection in 1983 and in so doing convinced Thatcher of the correctness of her political and moral convictions. The triumph was personal; she had chosen to act decisively when the men around her counseled restraint. But one of her ministers observed that the victory "fortifies her conviction that she is right on every subject." It seemed to justify intransigence in any and all situations. Thatcher exploited the victory as a Conservative Party triumph and proceeded to fight every political battle with Falklands War intensity. By the late 1980s the British electorate and her own party were increasingly alienated by her combative style, and in a Conservative Party leadership challenge. Thatcher was forced to step down in November 1990.

Bibliography: Freedman and Gamba-Stonehouse, *Signals of War*, 1991; Howes and Stevenson, *Women and the Use of Military Force*, 1993; Thatcher, *In Defence of Freedom*, 1987, and *The Downing Street Years*, 1993; Young, *The Iron Lady*, 1989.

—Curtis F. Morgan

THÉROIGNE DE MÉRICOURT, Frenchified name of Anne-Josèphe Terwagne (born 13 August 1762, village of Marcourt, near Liège, in then Austrian Netherlands; died 8 June 1817 in La Salpêtrière prison/asylum, Paris, France), also known as "la belle Liègeoise," the "Amazon of Liberty." Militant activist, France, French Revolution.

Théroigne de Méricourt was a legendary French revolutionary activist and feminist who advocated women's legions for the defense of France in 1792. Of prosperous peasant background, she left her rural world to become a courtesan who lived in England, Italy, and France before the Revolution offered her a new moral vision of freedom.

She is reputed to have led Parisian women in the 1789 march to Versailles in the October Days astride a horse, dressed in a man's red riding coat with saber in hand. Legend (largely fabricated by the royalist press) also depicts her participating in the attacks upon the Bastille and the Tuilleries (see **French Revolution and Napoleonic Era, women soldiers in**). In reality, Théroigne de Méricourt was more a spectator than a participant in revolution; some believe that she played no role in the October Days or in the fall of the Bastille. By mythologizing Théroigne as a female war chief who defied traditional images of women as naturally sensitive, governed by emotions, and weak, conservatives portrayed the Revolution as a world turned upside down, which unleashed unbalanced women who acted contrary to their sex.

As a supporter of the Brissotin faction, Théroigne did endorse war with Austria. She was also among the first to advocate female battalions. Her theatrical call for a legion of Amazons exercising three times a week on the Champs-Élysées and her masculine attire earned her ridicule from the Jacobins. She was attacked by a mob of sans-culotte women, whipped, and publicly humiliated in 1793—an event traditionally (and probably inaccurately) believed to have precipitated her madness. Théroigne de Méricourt's uncompromising support of the Revolution, her political speeches, her habit of sometimes dressing in men's costume, and her support of women's rights led to her conservative vilification as a degenerate who combined sexual liberty with bloodthirsty politics—a threatening example of what happened when a woman violated traditional female roles.

Bibliography: Graham, "Loaves and Liberty: Women in the French Revolution," 1977; Hamel, *A Woman of the Revolution*, 1911; Roudinesco, *Théroigne de Méricourt*, 1991.

—Douglas Clark Baxter

THIRTY YEARS' WAR, WOMEN IN (1618–1648).

The series of military conflicts due partly to Christian religious controversies that took place primarily in central Europe in the first half of the seventeenth century has become known to historians as the Thirty Years' War. In these conflicts, which historians have estimated led to the deaths of up to one-fourth to one-third of the central European population, women played many essential roles. Women ruled some of the political units involved, they were active members of the huge, generally mercenary armies, providing essential support services and occasionally engaging in combat, and they staffed the "home fronts," providing labor, taxes, and other resources necessary for the war efforts.

Female rulers from the Habsburg dynasty such as the Spanish infanta María

Ana (1606–1646), who ruled as Holy Roman Empress, and her mother the Austrian archduchess Margarete, queen of Spain and Portugal (1584–1611), tied the dynasty together through their marriages and personal connections, maintaining a fairly united Habsburg front during the seventeenth-century wars. Princesses such as the Englishwoman Elizabeth Stuart, electress Palatine and queen of Bohemia (1596–1662), her sister-in-law Elizabeth of the Palatinate, electress of Brandenburg, and Stuart's predecessor Louisa-Juliana of Nassau, electress Palatine, similarly served to unite the various Protestant courts in the early years of the conflicts. In the tense years leading up to the outbreak of the war, women such as Sophia of Mecklenburg, queen of Denmark (1557–1631), **Marie de Médici,** queen-regent of France (ruled 1610–1617), and Duchess Antoinette, regent of Cleves-Jülich during the succession crisis there in 1609–1610, played important political roles.

Throughout the war, and especially in its final phase, many of the primary political units involved were ruled by women. These women include Isabella of Habsburg (1566–1633), governor-general of the Netherlands, 1621–1633. Isabella was very influential in the determination of Habsburg military policy in the Netherlands following the death of King Philip III of Spain in 1621. Another female ruler was Amalia of Solms, regent of Hesse-Kassel from 1637 to 1650. She was one of the women at the peace negotiations in Westphalia that eventually ended much of the fighting. Other rulers were Anne of Austria, queen-regent of France, 1643–1651, and Queen Christina of Sweden, who exercised personal rule in her realm from 1644 to 1654. All these female rulers were involved in organizing and directing military activities to varying degrees.

In addition to ruling political units involved in the Thirty Years' War, women also served in the large mercenary armies that fought its sieges, pitched battles, and long campaigns of attrition. Warfare was undergoing a shift in tactics, strategies, and the size of armies in the course of the sixteenth and seventeenth centuries. It is estimated that the size of the armed forces of some of the political units of western and central Europe increased by as much as ten times in the period 1500–1700. As armies grew in size to as many as 150,000 combat troops, public supply bureaucracies were insufficient.

Much of the support—particularly the feeding and the clothing of these armies—was in the hands of the women who comprised a sizable portion of each military unit. Run more by private enterprise than by state organizations, the armies often consisted of an estimated 25–40 percent or more women and children. For contemporary descriptions of these armies, see the works of the German military theorist Johann Jacobi von Wallhausen. Another famous description of one of these women who worked as army suppliers is found in the novel *The Runagate Courage,* by the German Thirty Years' War veteran Hans Jakob Grimmelshausen; this character became one of the sources for the figure of Mother Courage in Bertolt Brecht's play of the same name.

An army of 30,000 people needed more food than most early modern European cities, including approximately twenty tons of bread per day, and women played a major part in supplying this food. Due to inadequate payment systems and irregular campaigning (the armies would often simply be furloughed in the winters), female labor, including laundry services and prostitution in addition to the supply services mentioned earlier, provided essential incomes for the members of the armies. With so many women present throughout decades of chaotic conflict, inevitably many women became involved in the fighting, if only in self-defense.

Historian C.V. Wedgwood relates that on 16 November 1632 Count Albrecht von Wallenstein, military governor of Prague, known for his "ungovernable temper" and "disregard for human life," needed to bolster his army of 12,000–15,000 poorly equipped soldiers, so "he herded the camp followers out of the town, grouped them together loosely in squares, the men in front, provided them with a few standards and hoped that in the grey distance the Swedes would take them for a powerful reserve" (*The Thirty Years War*, 325, citing Foerster's *Wallenstein*). Another interesting incident was reported at Leucate in 1637, where the bishop of Albi was giving last rites to the dying. He found several women in uniform who had died in combat, and said that Castilian soldiers told him, 'They were the real men, since those who fled, including certain officers, had conducted themselves like women' " (Tallett, *War and Society*).

The sieges and field campaigns of the Thirty Years' War were tremendously expensive. They placed extraordinary demands on the financial administrations of the political units involved. It is estimated that the cost of the French armies, for example, rose from 16,000,000 livres tournois in the 1620s to more than 38,000,000 in the 1640s. Often the armies were compelled to "live off the land," and the women living in the cities and countrysides of central Europe paid a high price in confiscations, rapes, pillages, and lootings to support the mercenary armies.

In some places organized systems of compulsory male conscription seriously affected social structures. In Sweden a conscription system known as the *indelningsverk* was instituted to support the armies fighting in Germany and Poland. The loss of tens of thousands of men in these foreign wars altered Swedish society significantly. One study, of the village of Bygdea, shows the scale of these losses: of the 230 men conscripted in the 1620s and 1630s, 215 died in Germany. The total number of adult males in the parish dropped from 468 to 288. The number of households headed by women increased sevenfold.

Generations of endless warfare meant that many central European women and men knew no other ways of life than the ones associated with the military. For example, in 1648, when the war ended, many in the Swedish army at Olmütz in Moravia did not welcome the end of the fighting. Wedgwood notes that "the dazed soldiers were sunk in gloom, and in the fields about the town the camp women collected in desolate groups. 'I was born in war,' said one, 'I have no home, no country, and no friends, war is all my wealth and now whither shall I go?' " (*The Thirty Years War*, 505, citing *Chronik des Minoriten Guardians*).

Partly due to military historians' traditional emphasis on combat soldiers at the expense of discussion of other military personnel, women's roles in the Thirty Years' War have not been the subject of much extended research to date. Archival sources concerning women's roles undoubtedly exist in the pay and judicial records of early modern armies and jurisdictions. These records await future analysis by historians.

Bibliography: Anderson, *War and Society in Europe of the Old Regime*, 1988; Hacker, "Women and Military Institutions," 1981; Parker, *The Thirty Years' War*, 1987, and *The Military Revolution*, 1988; Tallett, *War and Society in Early-Modern Europe*, 1992; Wedgwood, *The Thirty Years War*, 1971.

—Joseph F. Patrouch

TOMOE GOZEN (born 1157, central Japan; died 1247? Japan). General to Minamoto (Kiso) Yoshinaka, involved in the conflict that led to the first *bakufu* government in Japan.

Tomoe Gozen is one of the best known of Japanese female warriors. She lived at the dawn of the age of samurai, when ability with a sword was nearly all that mattered and when society was undergoing a transformation that Japanese historians have called *gekokujō*, a period when rustic warriors often ruled over the court aristocracy and when life was uncertain for all. Tomoe served as a general to Minamoto (Kiso) Yoshinaka, who was in the midst of a struggle for control of Japan. She fought in many battles in Kiso Yoshinaka's quest for power, but is best known for her loyal and courageous defense of her lord in his final defeat at the Battle of Awazu in 1184. Although some skeptics doubt that Tomoe was more than a myth, there is sufficient evidence to conclude that she was a real person, and her exploits seem perfectly compatible with the tenor of her unsettled time.

Tomoe was born in 1157. Her mother was Kiso Yoshinaka's wet nurse, and Tomoe was also the younger sister of Kiso Yoshinaka's legal wife. Her father was Nakahara Kanetō, a strong supporter of Kiso Yoshinaka who put all of his daughters at Kiso Yoshinaka's disposal. Tomoe soon emerged as Kiso Yoshinaka's mistress and one of his closest confidants. Little else is known of her formative pe-

Depiction of Tomoe Gozen from a series called "Kokon him kagami" (Mirror of Beauties Past and Present), 1876. (Asian Art & Archaeology, Inc./ CORBIS)

riod, but it is likely that her education, probably conducted by her father Kanetō, included training in the martial arts and in the virtues of loyalty and courage.

What little is known about Tomoe's early career parallels Kiso Yoshinaka's fortunes in his quest for supremacy in war-torn Japan of the late twelfth century. In 1180 Kiso Yoshinaka raised an army against the Minamoto clan's rivals, the Heike clan, and swept across north central Japan on his way to the capital Kyoto, engaging the enemy in the Battles of Yokotagawa, Kurikara Ridge, and Shinohara. Tomoe's name consistently appears among the generals of Kiso Yoshinaka's army in these engagements. At the decisive Battle of Kurikara Ridge Tomoe led 1,000 cavalry in a night attack coordinated with several other companies. Her brilliant strategy of attaching torches to the tails of 500 oxen and driving them against the Heike enemy, forcing the enemy into a deep valley, was credited with defeating more than 70,000 cavalry troops in a single battle. While this number seems exaggerated and the historical fact of a "fiery oxen strategy" has been questioned by some historians, the battle did turn the tide in the Minamoto-Heike war. Historians often trace the rise of the ultimate Minamoto victor, Yoritomo, to the effects of this battle, and since Yoritomo was responsible for establishing the first shogunate in Japanese history, Japan might never have had a shogunate had it not been for the courageous acts of a military woman, Tomoe Gozen.

But Tomoe is remembered most as a loyal soldier in a hopeless cause. Kiso Yoshinaka entered Kyoto after the Heike fled in July 1183, but within months proved incapable of governing, let alone controlling his own unruly soldiers. When the emperor Goshirakawa issued an order to Kiso Yoshinaka's fellow clansman, Minamoto Yoritomo, to suppress Kiso Yoshinaka, Kiso's soldiers were faced for the first time with the prospects of fighting against fellow Minamoto forces. Most chose to run. With few soldiers left, Kiso Yoshinaka had no choice but to retreat from the capital, and on a cold day in January 1184 he left Kyoto with Tomoe as his commanding general and personal bodyguard. In retreat they encountered the legendary strongman Hatakeyama Shigetada, who was said to be able to carry his horse on his shoulders. In a mythic showdown between the Amazon and the Hercules, Tomoe and Hatakeyama locked grips, but neither was able to dismount the other. Gazing at the shreds of Tomoe's sleeve that remained in his hand, Hatakeyama is said to have wondered if his opponent was not in reality a terrible goddess of war rather than a mere mortal woman.

As Kiso Yoshinaka continued on his retreat, he was joined by the forces of Imai Kanehira, who was Tomoe's own brother. The family reunion seemed to rejuvenate the forces of Kiso Yoshinaka, and nowhere is this more evident than the changes in how Tomoe is described from this point on in the historical sources. She suddenly appears as a wild, unconstrained, yet stunningly beautiful woman clad in yellow armor, with her long black hair flowing gracefully around her tiara. Her beauty attracted another herculean enemy named

Uchida Saburō, and Uchida attempted to take Tomoe alive for his own pleasures. Tomoe responded to the challenge, and the two grappled with each other while astride their horses. When Uchida realized that he could not subdue Tomoe, he grabbed her hair and reached in desperation for his sword to slit her throat. Outraged, Tomoe struck the weapon from Uchida's hand, pinned his body against her saddle, and cut off his head with her own sword. Then, in a display of victory, she held Uchida's severed head aloft for all to see.

Tomoe's victory was but a Pyrrhic one. Massively outnumbered and with enemy arrows flying all around them, Kiso Yoshinaka's troops realized that they could not avoid doom. Tomoe begged Kiso Yoshinaka for permission to stay and die with him, her lord and lover, but he refused. To allow a woman to be present in the final battle was considered shameful, and Kiso Yoshinaka ordered Tomoe to return home. Some historians believe that Yoshinaka wanted Tomoe to report his fate to his wife (Tomoe's sister) and to hold memorial services for him. Others believe that he truly wanted to spare the life of the woman he loved. Still other historians believe that Tomoe never made it home safely.

Most historians do believe that Tomoe returned home safely, and all agree that her military career ended with the death of Kiso Yoshinaka. Some believe that she became a Buddhist nun and prayed for Kiso Yoshinaka's soul to the end of her life. There is a temple in Ōtsu city dedicated to Yoshinaka called Gichū Temple that is also known as the Temple of Tomoe, and a legend holds that the ghost of Tomoe often appears there at Yoshinaka's grave, praying for his soul. Yet the historical sources suggest that Minamoto Yoritomo, known to be cruel to his relatives, ordered Tomoe to Kamakura and forced her to serve as his mistress. There, it is believed, a man named Wada Yoshimori rescued her, and together they had a son named Asahina Yoshihide who inherited his mother's physical prowess. Tomoe Gozen has also been memorialized in the classical Japanese Noh theater with a play called *Tomoe*.

Bibliography: "Kanehira," 1970; McCullough, *The Tale of the Heike*, 1988; Tyler, "Tomoe: The Woman Warrior," 1991.

—Kevin M. Doak

TOMYRIS (fl. sixth century BCE), also known as Thamiris, Thamyris of Scythia or Amazonia. Queen of the Massagetae. Defeated the Persians ca. 530 BCE.

As queen of the Massagetae, a "great and warlike race" (*ethnos mega kai alkimon*) living east of the Caspian Sea (present-day Iran), Tomyris apparently was the first ruler to stem the rapid expansion of the Persian Empire under Cyrus the Great. Nothing is known of her background except that she assumed the throne after the death of her husband, an unnamed Massagete king. She had one son, Spargapises, who served as a military commander.

Throughout the detailed account given by Herodotus, Tomyris is in charge of her own army, and she clearly articulates all terms for Cyrus's as well.

When he encamped across a river from her territory, she gave him three choices: go away; withdraw a three days' journey and let her come over and attack; or let her withdraw a three days' journey so he could come over and attack. Cyrus decided to advance, finding it "shameful and intolerable that . . . he should give way to a woman." After Cyrus captured Spargapises by a ruse, Tomyris demanded her son's release, else "she would glut [Cyrus] with blood, even if he was insatiable." Upon learning that her son had committed suicide, she engaged Cyrus in a battle, "of all battles ever fought by barbarian men . . . the most violent." After fierce hand-to-hand combat the Massagetae finally annihilated the Persian army. Then Tomyris searched until she found Cyrus's corpse, and dropping his head into a skin filled with human blood, she said, "Though I am both living and victorious, you have undone me, taking my son by deceit; and I will glut you with blood, as I promised."

Herodotus admits that there are other accounts of Cyrus's death that he does not mention, but he claims this one as the most credible. These other accounts probably partially gave rise to variant forms of the story that have "Thamiris" or "Thamyris," "queen of Scythia" or "queen of Amazonia," carrying out similar defeats of the Persians. Tomyris's actions caught the attention of the Renaissance writers Giovanni Boccaccio and **Christine de Pisan,** who interjected new details in order to put a moral spin on the story. Christine even claims that "Thamiris" had an army of "Amazon maidens" that ambushed Cyrus's army and captured him alive, only to ritually decapitate him and his "barons" publicly.

Medieval typology made Tomyris a prefiguration of the Virgin triumphing over Satan, 1450. Painting by Andrea Del Castogno. (Perry-Castañeda Library)

Bibliography: Boccaccio, *Concerning Famous Women,* 1963; Christine de Pisan, *The City of Ladies,* 1521; Dewald, "Women and Culture in Herodotus' Histories," 1981; Herodotus, *The Histories,* 1.201–216.

—Mark W. Graham

TRIARIA (fl. first century CE; died 69?, Rome). General's wife, Roman Empire, participant in siege of Tarracina.

Triaria likely accompanied her husband, Lucius Vitellius (brother and general of the Roman emperor Aulus Vitellius) in the attack on Tarracina (modern Terracina), a city just south of Rome. This engagement was part of the ongoing civil struggle in 69 CE, the "Year of the Four Emperors." The Roman historian Tacitus suggests that she may have assisted in other battles as well.

All we know of Triaria comes from the probable year of her death. Tacitus's critical account reveals a woman "warlike beyond a female" with a boldness that could intimidate even a Roman magistrate. At the time of the attack Tarracina was held by partisans of Vitellius's rival, the future emperor Vespasian. Vitellius's invading force surprised the inhabitants in the middle of the night. Following the capture of the city, it was said that Triaria, "girded with a soldier's sword, behaved arrogantly and fiercely in the horrible massacre." It is unclear precisely what Triaria did, but she is portrayed as having a vengeful character. At the least, we can determine that this wife of a general was present at the front, and active at least in the aftermath of battle in a way that belies traditional female roles.

Triaria's military action impressed the Renaissance writers Giovanni Boccaccio and **Christine de Pisan**. Boccaccio incorporated Tacitus's descriptions into his own commentary, using Triaria as the exemplar for his moral lesson: Great is the woman who endures everything for her husband's honor. Christine, relying heavily on Boccaccio, introduced a few new elements and anachronisms as she used the story to show how such devoted love for a husband strengthens the marriage bond.

Bibliography: Boccaccio, *Concerning Famous Women,* 1963; Christine de Pisan, *The City of Ladies,* 1521; Tacitus, *Histories* 2.63–64, 3.76–77.

—Mark W. Graham

TRUNG TRAC and **TRUNG NHI** (died 43 CE, Me Linh, present-day Vinh Phu Province, Vietnam). Rebellion leaders and queens of Giao Chi (in present-day northern Vietnam), 40–43 CE.

Trung Trac and Trung Nhi led a successful rebellion in 40 CE against the Han Chinese rulers who had colonized the northern Vietnamese provinces in 111 BCE. The sisters became queens and ruled an independent state until 43 CE, when they were defeated by Chinese military forces that were sent by the Han emperor to retake the provinces.

Trung Trac and her younger sister Trung Nhi were daughters of Lac generals in the subprefecture Me Linh (Lac is the earliest name for the Vietnamese people). Trung Trac was married to Thi Sach, a Lac lord of the neighboring prefecture Chu Dien. According to many standard sources, Thi Sach was murdered by the ruthless Chinese governor, To Dinh (Su Ting in Chinese) in 40 CE. Thus the standard account relates that Trung Trac and her sister rose in rebellion to avenge the death of Thi Sach.

Historian Keith Taylor, however, argues that Thi Sach was not killed before the rebellion. Chinese sources mention Thi Sach following his wife in the rebellion. Taylor suggests that patriarchal Vietnamese historians in the thirteenth to the fifteenth centuries might have distorted the facts since it was inconceivable to them that a wife would lead rebellions and be made ruler while her husband was still alive. It was only in the thirteenth century that Vietnamese accounts of the Trung sisters were written. Much of what is known about this period is therefore based on Chinese writings. Some Vietnamese historians of the twentieth century reject the idea that Trung Trac would have been made queen over her husband. A 1965 article by Duy Hinh based on ancient Chinese material mentions Trung Trac's husband as late as 42 CE (two years after the rebellion). The writer of the article, however, states that since only Trung Trac became the ruler, Thi Sach must have died before the rebellion was successful. The assumption that Trung Trac would not have been made ruler had her husband been alive is not necessarily correct.

Whether or not Thi Sach was killed before or after the rebellion, the consensus among historians is that the uprising was fuelled by widespread resentment against Chinese domination, particularly among the Lac noble class. Once the rebellion was under way, the other districts (Cuu-Chan, Nhat-Nam, and Hop Pho) quickly joined. Soon sixty-five citadels were pacified, and the Trung sisters were made queens of Giao Chi, with the capital being Me-Linh, the sisters' birthplace.

In 41 CE the Han emperor Quan Vu (Guang Wu Di) ordered Ma Vien (Ma Yuan), a senior military general, to reconquer the Giao Chi area. Ma Vien led an army of 8,000 regular troops and 12,000 militiamen. In the spring of 42 CE the Trung sisters led their army to meet the attack of Ma Vien. Overwhelmed by the strong Chinese forces and undermined by their own undisciplined army, the Trung sisters retreated to Cam Khe (in Vinh Yen city). Ma Vien, in pursuit of the Lac army, chased the Trung sisters to Hat Mon (in Son Tay city). Here in Hat Mon (sixth day of the second lunar month, 43 CE) the sisters supposedly committed suicide by jumping into the Hat Giang River. Chinese sources, however, do not support the account of suicide. Some Chinese sources state that Ma Vien captured the sisters, while others indicate that Ma Vien had them beheaded. Taylor states that the sisters were killed in battle. In any event, they died and are regarded as martyrs.

Vietnamese still celebrate the heroism of the the Trung sisters on the sixth day of the second lunar month. Temples were built in their honor, and streets in Hanoi and Ho Chi Minh City still bear their names. The Trung sisters not only symbolize patriotism and courage, but also the important role that women have played in Vietnamese history and society. In Vinh Phu Province alone, thirty-two of the sixty-nine army generals were women. Heroines such as Le Chan (of Hai Phong), Dieu Tien (Ha Bac Province), Bao Chan, Nguyen Thai, and Nguyet Do (Hai Hung Province) and many thousands of nameless women played important roles in the rebellion. During the Second Indochina War the infamous Madame Ngo Dinh Nhu (sister-in-law of President Ngo Dinh Diem) evoked the heroism of the Trung sisters as she recounted the deed of one Phung Thi Chinh in a public speech. Apparently Phung Thi Chinh led her troops into battle against Ma Vien even while she was pregnant. She gave birth during the battle but continued fighting, stopping only long enough to tie her baby to her back. While there is no mention of Phung Thi Chinh in the standard Vietnamese historical writings, the popularity and longevity of stories about her and other heroines' deeds underscore the depth and scope of the impact that the Trung sisters continue to have on the Vietnamese consciousness.

Bibliography: Duy Hinh, "Tinh Chat Cuoc Khoi Nghia Hai Ba Trung," *Nghien Cuu Lich Su* 72.3 (1965); Ngo Si Lien et al., *Dai Viet Su Ky Toan Thu, Ngoai Ky* (compiled at the end of the seventeenth century), (Glendale, CA: Dai Nam, n.d.); Nguyen Khac Xuong, "Ve cuoc khoi nghia hai ba Trung qua tu lieu Vinh Phu," *Nghien Cuu Lich Su* 151.7–8 (1973); Taylor, *The Birth of Vietnam,* 1983; Tran Trong Kim, *Viet Nam Su Luoc,* vol. 1 (first published in Saigon in 1972; reprinted, Glendale, CA: Dai Nam, n.d.).

—Van Thanh Nguyen-Marshall

TUBMAN, HARRIET (born 1820?, Maryland; died March 1913, Auburn, New York), also known as "Moses." Second South Carolina Volunteers (later known as the 34th United States Colored Troops). Reconnaissance commander, scout, spy, nurse, United States, American Civil War.

Harriet Tubman, a former slave and abolitionist, was best known for her work as a conductor on the "Underground Railroad." During the **American Civil War** she served from the spring of 1862 to the summer of 1864 as a scout for the Union's Department of the South headquartered on the South Carolina sea islands.

A decade before the war Tubman conducted numerous clandestine raids into the Southern slave states and guided many runaway slaves to freedom. Due to this prewar experience Governor John Andrew of Massachusetts asked Tubman to assist Union military leaders in South Carolina as a scout. Shortly after her arrival she served the department as a nurse and liaison between Southern blacks and military officials. During the winter of 1862–1863 Tubman was attached to the all-black Second South Carolina Volunteers and commanded a small reconnaissance unit comprised of nine men and several riverboat pilots. The unit's mission was to slip behind enemy lines to determine Confederate troop movements and strength. Tubman's

Undated portrait of Harriet Tubman. (Library of Congress)

most famous raid occurred on 1 June 1863 along the Combahee River. There, along with the regimental commander Colonel James Montgomery, she led 150 African American soldiers up the river to clear underwater mines and destroy bridges and railroad tracks in order to disrupt Confederate supply lines. After overpowering the rebel soldiers in the area, the raiding party captured several plantations and freed more than 700 slaves. For the rest of the war she led or accompanied Northern soldiers on raids into the South Carolina interior. She finished the war as a nurse in a freedmen's hospital in Virginia.

Following the war, Tubman worked to promote rights for African American women and engaged in charity work for poor blacks. Although she served the Union army without pay, the government granted her a pension of twenty dollars a month starting in 1895. In 1982 the Smithsonian Institution recognized Tubman as the only woman in U.S. military history to lead and organize a reconnaissance mission.

Bibliography: George, *"Remember the Ladies,"* 1975; Hoefer, "Harriet Tubman: A Heroine of the Underground Goes to War," 1988; Larson, "Bonny Yank and Ginny Reb," 1990.

—Robert J. Zalimas, Jr.

TURCHIN, NADINE (born 1826, Russia; died 1904, United States). Union army. United States, American Civil War.

Nadine Turchin was born in Russia in 1826. She and her husband, John Basil Turchin, emigrated to the United States just prior to the **American Civil War**. In 1861 John Turchin was commissioned colonel of the 19th Illinois Volunteer Infantry Regiment, and Nadine Turchin accompanied her husband on campaign as a regimental nurse. As the daughter of a Russian officer, Turchin was accustomed to army life and was at ease among the men. She began to keep a diary in mid-1863, which still survives.

At the age of thirty-five, Turchin was not designated a "daughter of the regiment" like **Anna Etheridge;** that title was reserved for much younger women. Her role was not defined at first, though eventually she was listed as "regimental nurse." She served as both nurse and confidant to the men, but it appears that they trusted her as a commander as well. At least two separate reports claim that Nadine Turchin commanded her husband's regiment in a skirmish when he was too ill to lead the men himself during the spring of 1862. Several reports claim that she led the men on the battlefield, "facing the hottest fire, and fought bravely at their head." However, her diary entries do not show her on the front lines. Her husband had been court martialed in the summer of 1862 for allowing his troops to plunder and pillage, as well as for violating a regulation against military wives being present on the battlefield; Abraham Lincoln pardoned him and promoted him to brigadier general. It is likely that afterwards Nadine refrained from acting so prominently as her husband's aide, although she remained with him until he left the army in

1864. She made many comments in her diary about the quality of various troops and their training and appears to have lost respect for her husband's abilities over time. She found most of her life in camp to be "idle and useless" and was eager to be as close to the fighting as possible.

After the war the fortunes of the Turchins seem to have declined, even while the legend of Nadine's exploits grew. After John died in 1901, Nadine applied for a military pension, not in her own name, but as the widow of a soldier. An Ohio senator, a member of Turchin's regiment, testified in support of her pension application that "every man who belonged to his brigade admired her as much as they admired the General. She was with him constantly in the field, shared with him all the privations of the camp and all the dangers of battle." She died in 1904 at the age of seventy-eight.

Bibliography: Haynie, Henry, *The Nineteenth Illinois* (Chicago: 1912); Leonard, *All the Daring of the Soldier*, 1999; "Lincoln's Russian General," 1959; McElligott, "A Monotony Full of Sadness: The Diary of Nadine Turchin," 1977.

—Susannah U. Bruce

U

UNITED ARAB EMIRATES, MILITARY WOMEN IN, 1991–present.

Due to the ease with which Iraq overran Kuwait in 1990, United Arab Emirates (UAE) leader Sheik Zayed ordered the integration of women into that nation's military for the purpose of bolstering troop strength. Because of the cultural unacceptability of male officers training female recruits, the American government was requested to supply experienced American women soldiers to provide training at the new Women's Military Academy. A contingent of ten instructors subsequently began their assignment in the UAE under the command of United States Army Major Janis Karpinski. Under the overall direction of special UAE government delegate Hessa al-Khaedi, women in the UAE military continue to gain acceptance.

Bibliography: Brooks, *Nine Parts of Desire: The Hidden World of Islamic Women,* 1995.

—William Henry Foster

V

VALOIS, MARGUERITE DE (born 14 May 1553, Saint-Germain-en-Laye, France; died 27 March 1615, Paris, France), also known as Queen Margot. Queen of Navarre; queen of France during the Wars of Religion.

Unlike her Catholic mother, **Catherine de Médici,** or her Protestant mother-in-law, **Jeanne d'Albret,** both of whom greatly influenced the destiny of France, Marguerite de Valois was from her childhood a pawn between the opposing factions. Although she was in many ways a simple victim of fate, her nearly constant presence at the center of the major conflicts of her day makes her role important. Marguerite was the daughter of King Henry II of France and Catherine de Médici. Her father had been a strong leader, but her three brothers, who in turn became kings of France between 1547 and 1589 (Francis II, Charles IX, and Henry III), were weak and unstable. Her brothers always called her Margot, and it is under this name that she is remembered.

The Wars of Religion began in 1562, resulting in violent conflict between three parties: the moderate Catholics supported by the royal Valois family; the radical Catholics backed by the Guise family; and the Huguenots (French Protestants) backed by the Bourbons, who ruled in the Navarre region of France. Margot was destined from birth to serve the interests of the Crown through her marriage, and in 1572 it was decided that she would marry Henry of Navarre, the symbolic leader of the Huguenots, in an attempt to reconcile the warring factions.

Her first direct contact with the civil war took place six days after her marriage (18 August 1572). Margot recounts in her *Mémoires* that on the night of 24 August a blood-soaked man, pursued by soldiers, rushed into her bedroom begging for her help. It was the beginning of the St. Bartholomew's Day Mas-

Portrait of Marguerite de Valois by Francois Clouet, 1572. (Archivo Iconografico, S. A./Corbis)

sacre, in the middle of the palace of the Louvre. Catholic extremists began a massacre of the Huguenots that left thousands dead. By agreeing to convert to Catholicism, Margot's new husband, Henry of Navarre, escaped death, but became a prisoner at the court. Margot was able to move more freely and became involved in the political maneuverings of her husband and her brother, Henry III (who became king in 1574). For example, Margot went to Flanders on a diplomatic mission for her brother, where she was pursued by the Spanish as well as the Huguenots and barely escaped capture during her return to France (1577). In the meantime, Henry of Navarre had succeeded in escaping from the court, leaving his wife behind.

In 1578 Margot rejoined her husband. Four years later Henry and Margot were estranged and she returned to Paris. There she became involved in so many political and romantic intrigues that the following year her brother Henry III drove her from the court. She settled in Nerac and there continued her activities. In 1585 she allied herself with the ultra-Catholic Holy League and went to Agen, where she raised troops and took refuge. But as the marshal of Matignon approached, the Agenais threatened to revolt. The queen of Navarre had to flee precipitously, riding pillion behind a horseman and pursued by the lieutenants of her brother and her husband.

She took refuge at Auvergne, but in 1586, when she was blockaded without provisions or sufficient troops, she had to give herself up. On the command of her brother Henry III she was kept prisoner in the fortress of Usson, but she won over the commanders of the citadel. There Margot remained until 1605, and ensconced in her impregnable fortress she composed her *Mémoires*, all the while under the surveillance of her half nephew the count of Auvergne, bastard son of Charles IX, who was eager to take possession of Usson for himself.

With the death in 1589 of her brother Henry III, Margot's husband became the king of France as Henry IV, founder of the Bourbon dynasty that would last until the **French Revolution**. The new king needed an heir, which he had never begotten with his long-estranged wife, who in any event was now in middle age. In exchange for concessions on his part, Margot gave her consent to the annulment of their marriage (1599), which allowed Henry IV to marry **Marie de Médici**. In 1605 Margot was allowed to return to Paris, where she withdrew from political activity, and died in 1615 at the age of sixty-one.

Alexandre Dumas immortalized her in his 1845 novel *The Queen Margot,* which centers on the crucial period of the St. Bartholomew's Day Massacre and the two years that followed. Filmmakers from Desfontaines (1916) to Chéreau (1994) and, in passing, Dréville (1954) have made her famous, with the celebrated French actress Isabelle Adjani portraying Margot in Chéreau's recent film *Queen Margot*.

Bibliography: Bluche, *Dictionnaire du Grand siècle*, 1990; Castarède, Jean, *La triple vie de la Reine Margot: Amoureuse, comploteuse, écrivain* (Paris: 1992); Mariéjol, Jean-Hippolyte, *La vie de Marguerite de Valois, reine de Navarre et de France (1553–1615)* (Paris: 1928); Valois, Marguerite de, *Mémoires et lettres*, ed. François Guessard (Paris: 1842); Viennot, Éliane, *Marguerite de Valois: Histoire d'une femme, histoire d'un mythe* (Paris: 1993).

—Marie-Thérèse Lalaguë-Guilhemsans (trans. by Annette Parks)

VELAZQUEZ, LORETA JANETA (born 26 June 1842, Havana, Cuba; died ?), also known as Velasques, Velasquez, Lieutenant Harry T. Buford, Mrs. Alice Williams. Lieutenant, Confederate Army, United States, American Civil War.

Disguised as Lieutenant Harry T. Buford, complete with a glued-on beard and moustache, Loreta Janeta Velazquez recruited a group of Confederate soldiers and served as their commander during the **American Civil War**. In her memoirs Velazquez claimed that her "insatiable love for adventure; to the same overmastering desire to do difficult, dangerous, and exciting things, and to accomplish hazardous enterprises . . . induced me to assume the dress of the other sex, and to figure as a soldier on the battle-field."

In a Barroom in Memphis, Loreta Janeta Velazquez. (Library of Congress)

Velazquez claimed to have been born to a wealthy family in Cuba and raised in New Orleans by an aunt, where as a girl she thrilled to the exploits of Joan of Arc and fantasized about a military career. Nevertheless, her life seemed destined to follow a path typical for nineteenth-century women—she married young and bore three children. After the deaths of her children and her husband's decision to join the Confederate forces, however, Velazquez revived her memories of "military glory" and her desire "to win fame on the battle-field." Her attempts to enlist her husband's approval of a scheme to disguise herself as a soldier were unsuccessful, so she waited until his departure to implement her plan.

She says that she began her career in disguise as a Confederate officer, Lieutenant Harry T. Buford, in order to raise a regiment to deliver to her husband's command. But he was killed early in the war; despite her grief, Velazquez decided to continue her own military career. She claims to have fought in the First Battle of Bull Run and afterwards to have decided that she could better serve the Confederate cause as a spy. After being wounded, arrested, unmasked, imprisoned, and released, Velazquez promptly redonned her male disguise and enlisted in the Twenty-first Louisiana Regiment but soon secured a commission in the cavalry. What followed were many patrols, and Velazquez often demonstrated her military competence and courage.

Velazquez says that she married her second husband during the war, a Thomas C. DeCaulp (the only one of four husbands whom she names in her memoirs). She says that like her first husband, DeCaulp was killed in the war, but historical records show that he survived. Some historians believe that the couple had a falling-out or that DeCaulp deserted Velazquez, and in hiding this fact she introduced one of many discrepancies in her story. In any event, Velazquez writes that after being badly wounded, being unmasked again, feeling frustrated with the war, and widowed for the second time, she took on the more lucrative job of managing blockade-running operations. She also writes that at various points she performed espionage duties, sometimes in female guise as "Mrs. Alice Williams." After the war she claims to have married and been widowed a third time before marrying her fourth husband and giving birth to a son. Around 1880 Velazquez was lost to the historical record, and no information on her later life, or death, is known.

She published her memoirs, *The Woman in Battle: A Narrative of the Exploits, Adventures, and Travels of Madame Loreta Janeta Velazquez, Otherwise Known as Lieutenant Harry T. Buford, Confederate States Army*, in 1876 and was immediately labeled a fraud because of the apparent exaggeration and contradictions. Jubal Early, the former Confederate general, was among those who denounced the book (their subsequent correspondence is preserved in the Turner Family Papers, Southern Historical Collection, University of North Carolina). The sensational tone of the book makes it difficult for today's readers to accept, although it was consistent with similar memoirs of its time. However, many of the details of actual battles, weather, and daily life ring true. Most likely, her story contains both elements of truth and fiction.

Velazquez is interesting as a typical example of the several dozen women who gained fame based on a memoir or autobiography detailing their supposed exploits disguised as male soldiers. Copies of these books have been preserved, but verifying the truth of the stories is extremely challenging to the historian. In Velazquez's case, as in many others, there is no evidence to prove that she was not a soldier, and the discrepancies and exaggerations could be categorized as not untypical in the memoirs of war veterans. It is possible, or even probable, that Velazquez did serve in the army, although the true nature of her achievements cannot be determined. What is perhaps even more interesting is the likelihood that for every woman like Velazquez who lived to publish her tale and thus come to public recognition, there were many others who were killed in action or who kept their experiences forever secret, returning to traditional female roles or even maintaining their disguise long after the war had ended. See **American Civil War** and **Jenny Hodgers** for related entries.

Bibliography: Garraty et al., *American National Biography*, 1999; Hall, *Patriots in Disguise*, 1993; Hoffert, "Madame Loreta Velazquez," 1978; Leonard, *All the Daring of the Soldier*, 1999; Massey, *Bonnet Brigades*, 1966; Seeley, *American Women and the U.S. Armed Forces*, 1992; Velazquez, *The Woman in Battle*, 1972.

—Gayle Veronica Fischer

VERCHÈRES, MARIE-MADELEINE JARRET DE (born 1678, Verchères, New France; died 1747, Sainte-Anne-de-la-Pérade, New France), usually known as Madeleine (or Madelon) de Verchères. Defender, New France (present-day Quebec, Canada), eighteenth century.

In 1692, at the age of fourteen, Marie-Madeleine Jarret led the defense of her family's seigneury against Iroquois attackers. Verchères seigneury was a small estate to the southeast of Montreal, in which French settlement dated back barely twenty years. In the autumn of 1692 Iroquois warriors were pursuing a military strategy of harassing the struggling French colony of New France by conducting raids on the south shore of the St. Lawrence River. They followed the Richelieu River north and attacked recently established French settlements in the vicinity, avoiding the larger fort at Sorel.

Verchères was the eldest child of the family. Her father, a military officer, was away on duty, and her mother, who had previously defended the family fort against earlier Iroquois attackers, was absent as well when Iroquois set upon the fort. Verchères said that she narrowly escaped capture. Once back inside the fort she donned male attire in order to trick the Iroquois into thinking that the French settlers were well defended. She fired the cannon and organized a defense by her younger two brothers, an elderly man, and a

Madeline Verchères defending the Fort.

Depiction of Marie-Madeleline Jarret de Verchères from *Famous Canadian Stories Re-told for Children*, edited by Donald Graham French, illustrated by Rosalind Morely, 1923, p. 56.

frightened soldier. The duration of the Iroquois attack in some accounts was two days and nights; in others it lasted for eight days. However, it seems highly unlikely that the Iroquois remained at the fort as long as eight days, as sieges were not typical of Iroquois warfare. In fact, after the initial encounter, the Iroquois are not really mentioned in Verchères's accounts. The only firsthand descriptions of the siege were produced by Verchères herself; she signed the initial accounts of the defense of the family fort, then, in later requests for a royal pension, wrote new versions, producing some inconsistencies, such as the duration of the attack.

Verchères may have been motivated to enlarge on her story. In appealing for a pension to the wife of the minister of the marine in France, Verchères wrote, "While my sex does not permit me to have other inclinations than those it requires of me, nevertheless, allow me, madam, to tell you that I entertain sentiments which urge me on to aspire to fame quite as eagerly as many men." Her letters place little emphasis on her age, stressing her sex as more noteworthy. The *intendant* of the colony supported her request, and Verchères was granted a pension by Louis XIV in 1696. In 1722 she embellished her account further and added another story of heroism, telling how she saved her ill husband's life when a small party of natives attacked their house in another part of the colony. Her pension was further increased in the following decade.

Verchères seems to have had some recognition as a heroine among the populace of New France (which might suggest that some eyewitnesses—her brothers, for example—supported her account). Over the decades Verchères became a symbol of female heroism and nationalism in Canada, so that by the nineteenth and early twentieth centuries she was essentially a **Joan of Arc** figure, even taking on the name of the little fort she had defended (Madeleine de Verchères rather than Marie-Madeleine Jarret).

Bibliography: Coates, "Commemorating the Woman Warrior of New France," 1996; Coates and Morgan, *Heroines and History*, 2001; *Dictionary of Canadian Biography*.

—Colin Coates

VIETNAMESE REVOLUTION, WOMEN IN. Various combat and support roles, Vietnam, 1930–1972.

A central feature of Communist revolutionary strategy during the conflict in Vietnam was the concept of a "people's war," a mass struggle waged by the entire people against the French colonial regime and later against the American "imperialist invaders" and their "lackeys," the reactionary government in Saigon. In the war all Vietnamese—rural and urban, old and young, women and men—were judged primarily in terms of their prospective ability to contribute to the common endeavor of completing the struggle for the reunification of Vietnam.

The image of Vietnamese women playing an active role in defending their native soil from foreign invaders is not a recent one. The history of Vietnam is studded with the names of heroic women who fought alongside their fathers and brothers against foreign enemies. Some, like the famous **Trung** sisters, whose exploits against occupying Chinese forces in the first century CE have thrilled Vietnamese patriots for nearly two thousand years, actually commanded troops in battlefield operations against the invaders.

When the veteran revolutionary Ho Chi Minh founded the first Vietnamese Communist Party in February 1930, he and his colleagues soon concluded that Vietnamese women would be called upon to play an active role in the struggle to evict the French colonial regime, which had been established at the end of the nineteenth century. When the Party decided to create a new revolutionary army to fight against the French at the end of the Second World War, there were reportedly three women in the first thirty-four-person unit, established in December 1944.

During the ensuing conflict against the French, women played a significant role in the war effort, although usually in noncombatant positions. They were recruited for production tasks to replace men serving at the front and served on road and bridge repair teams and as members of liaison and intelligence units. They were especially useful as members of transportation units that carried vital military equipment and provisions to the troops at the front, thus earning the sobriquet of "the long-haired army."

In 1954 the Geneva Conference divided the country into two separate states, with the Communists in the north and non-Communists in the south. When scheduled national elections failed to take place, Party leaders returned to the strategy of people's war to try to overthrow the new gov-

> *One women's motivations in fighting for the Vietnamese National Liberation Front:*
>
> A woman who subsequently became an outstanding guerrilla in An Giang Province was recruited by the Communists, joined out of a spirit of adventure, and discovered that she had a real aptitude for killing and even took pleasure in it. Politics bored her, but in the seven years she remained with the Front, she absorbed a lot of ideology. She was made a Party member as a reward for the number of enemy troops she had killed, including three Americans. . . .
>
> Women fought against American and ARVN soldiers as part of male units, but Cu Chi also had an all-female fighting force, the C3 Company, which was formed in 1965. The unit was led by Tran Thi Dung, a teenager who died of an illness in 1973. All the women were skilled in firing small arms, throwing grenades, wiring and detonating mines, and assassination. Vo Thi Mo became a deputy leader of the women's platoon. . . . The young women in Mo's squad were enthusiastic about their mission. Their first real battle was against two American tanks moving down a mined and booby-trapped road. The tanks were stopped by the mines; one was put out of commission, but the other was later repaired by the enemy. . . . Although they could handle weapons, the girls were discouraged from engaging in hand-to-hand combat with the Americans because of their youth and small stature.
>
> —Sandra C. Taylor, *Vietnamese Women at War: Fighting for Ho Chi Minh and the Revolution* (Lawrence: University Press of Kansas, 1998), 57, 87–88.

ernment in South Vietnam and reunify the two zones. As before, women were expected to play a significant role in both political and military activities in support of the cause. A model to emulate was soon to appear. In January 1960 a popular uprising against the South Vietnamese regime was launched in several villages in the heart of the Mekong Delta. One of the leading figures involved in planning and carrying out the uprising was Nguyen Thi Dinh, a young woman from a local peasant family who had become a member of the revolutionary movement through the activities of male members of her family. She later took part in transporting war materials down the Ho Chi Minh Trail from North Vietnam and was named minister of defense of the Provisional Revolutionary Government, created in the late 1960s.

During the remainder of the war women played a variety of roles in the Vietnam conflict. They served as members of antiaircraft artillery units protecting Hanoi and other cities and towns in North Vietnam from American bombing raids. They were active as guerrilla fighters in South Vietnam, as couriers and transportation workers, as spies or informers, and as members of local militia units in liberated areas in the South, defending their villages against attacks by enemy troops. Statistics on female participation in military units in South Vietnam are scarce, but the percentage at lower levels was apparently quite high, and not infrequently they were found in positions of command. According to one estimate, 40 percent of all regimental commanders in resistance units in the South were women.

The nature of participation varied. In some cases women served in units alongside the men; in others all-female units were created to perform specific duties considered appropriate to their capacities. As time went on, women were increasingly viewed as a separate element in the revolutionary arsenal, presenting unique opportunities as well as potential problems. In general, it was considered disadvantageous to place women in predominantly male units. Men were sometimes resentful of their female colleagues. The love interest could present a problem, as men tended to be attracted to the younger and prettier women, sometimes leading to resentment on the part of older and frequently more experienced women in the unit. According to some sources, women were often considered inferior to men in combat, although they were particularly effective as combatants or couriers in the famous tunnel of Cu Chi, near Saigon. Other sources praise the skills of the women soldiers. Without objective measures of combat performance, the evaluation of the abilities of women soldiers is highly subjective and may reflect cultural or political bias.

Women were particularly good at certain other tasks crucial to the success of the struggle. They were often better than their male counterparts in liaison work and as informers and spies. Prostitutes were often recruited to provide information on American troop activities. Women were useful in persuading government troops to defect and were allegedly better in transporting supplies. Although men were usually stronger and thus able to carry heavier loads, women tended to possess greater stamina and were less likely to complain to their superiors. In the North women took an active part in local defense activities and were recruited to serve on antiaircraft teams, on bomb-defusing units, and as members of units directed to search out and capture downed American fliers. They also made up a high percentage of the local self-defense militia.

Women were much less active in support of the American-backed South Vietnamese government. However, there are unconfirmed reports of women combatants in the Min Top region, whose women were taller and stronger than most Vietnamese women. A half-French woman named Le Tunn Ding is said to have led a sniper movement against the Vietcong in 1962; it was claimed that her system was to use no more than one bullet per enemy, clubbing survivors to death to save ammunition. Another woman named Dho Minde reportedly could run forty-five miles without stopping and is said to have used both knife and rifle to kill Vietcong soldiers. Sally Hayton-Keeva quotes a "Vietnam veteran officer—later a CIA operative" who says that he employed female volunteers to "help flush out nests of the Viet Cong along the coastal plains." These women had all lost their families in the Tet Offensive and, he says, were filled "with a deep and almost boiling hatred" of the enemy. "As for women in combat," he says, "I would have absolutely no reservations at any time about taking them into combat with me." However, scholarly work has not yet been done to confirm the validity of these tales.

In sum, women played a prominent part in promoting the Communist cause in the Vietnam War and a much lesser role in the counterrevolution. Although the mixing of the sexes in the military units presented some problems, and women were considered more suitable for some activities than others, in general they were viewed as an essential component in the strategy of people's war and a significant factor in bringing about the reunification of the country under Communist rule.

Bibliography: Dinh, *No Other Road to Take*, 1976; Duiker, "Vietnam: War of Insurgency," 1982; Hayton-Keeva, *Valiant Women in War and Exile*, 1987; Taylor, *Vietnamese Women at War*, 1998; Tétreult, "Women and Revolution in Vietnam," 1996; Turley, "Women in the Communist Revolution in Vietnam," 1972; Turner and Phan, *Even the Women Must Fight*, 1998.

—William J. Duiker

VIKING WOMEN WARRIORS.

No reliable historical evidence exists that Viking women fought as warriors. However, around 1200 the Danish chronicler Saxo Grammaticus, in his *Gesta Danorum* (*The History of the Danes*)—a work that can only loosely be described as a "history"—tells of several women such as Stikla, who "preferr[ed] the occupations of war to those of wedlock." Saxo's account of Denmark's ancient feuds is peppered with references to sword-wielding femmes fatales such as Alfhild, who "exchanged woman's for man's attire, and, no longer the most modest of maidens, began the life of a warlike rover." He gravely relates the story of the great battle of Bravella, in which Hetha and Visna, "whose female bodies Nature had endowed with manly courage," led groups of Danes into combat. Saxo also describes a Lathgertha, who some believe was a historical figure, as "a skilled female fighter, who bore a man's temper in a girl's body, with locks flowing loose over her shoulders she would do battle in the forefront of the most valiant warriors."

All of this may be the work of vivid imagination. Viking women have been found buried with weapons, but it is not clear whether these weapons belonged to the deceased or to a male relative. Women did accompany the Vikings on their raids across Europe, but probably acted primarily in a supporting capacity, providing food, shelter, and medical care. In a male-dominated medieval society this was as close to active warfare as Viking women were likely to get, though it is possible that women were occasionally involved in defensive actions. On the other hand, historian Megan McLaughlin believes that "there is no basis to dismiss [Saxo's] references to women warriors out of hand. Historical basis has been found for many of the semi-legendary male characters." It is impossible to draw a definitive conclusion about the combat involvement of Viking women based on the available sources.

Bibliography: Haywood, ed., "Women," *Encyclopaedia of the Viking Age*, 2000; Jesch, *Women in the Viking Age*, 1991; Jones, *A History of the Vikings*, 1984; McLaughlin, "The Woman Warrior," 1990; Saxo Grammaticus, *The History of the Danes*, 1979.

—Curtis F. Morgan

VIVANDIÈRES. France and United States, Napoleonic Wars (1792–1815) and American Civil War (1861–1865).

Many women accompanied the French army during the Napoleonic Wars as independent merchants selling food, drink, and luxury items to the French soldiers. These women were known as vivandières (or sometimes as *cantinières*), and by 1800 their numbers had grown so large that Napoleon Bonaparte decreed a series of ordinances that formally recognized them as part of the French army and laid down regulations regarding membership eligibility. Under the ordinances, vivandières were to be wives of NCOs or soldiers currently on active duty. Some wore military uniforms (including pants when that was strictly illegal for civilian women) and owned and operated their own businesses (again illegal for women for much of the period). The vivandières were assigned to their husband's regiment, whose number they proudly wore inscribed on a metal disk that hung from their necks and that was also emblazoned on their wagons if they were prosperous enough to own one. In addition to her regimental disc, the most common feature of a vivandière's attire was her tonnelet, a small keg painted in revolutionary red, white, and blue and containing brandy (or other liquor) that she wore slung over her shoulder, and from which she sold spirits by the drink to soldiers.

In addition to liquor, vivandières sold sausages, cheese, pipe clay, and other items that the soldiers might need or want. They often accompanied their regiment onto the battlefield to dispense free brandy to soldiers and in emergencies carried ammunition forward to the firing line. Their numbers could be substantial; in the French armies during the Seven Years' War, for example, it is recorded that Soubise had some 12,000 sutlers, vivandières, and other noncombatants in the train of the rather modest force he took to Rossbach.

Historian Lee Kennett notes that "curiously, the hordes of these enterprising civilians were seldom the objects of complaint," and their wagons were even assigned numbers to keep them in order.

Sometimes vivandières converted their wagons into improvised ambulances to transport wounded men off the field. Perhaps typical of these women was Catherine Béguin, who joined the Fourteenth Line as a vivandière in 1800 and followed the regiment across Europe as Napoleon's Grande Armée subdued a continent. When Catherine's husband, the eagle bearer of the regiment, was wounded in battle, she carried him five miles on her back to an ambulance.

The names of most of the vivandières, like those of the enlisted men alongside whom they served, have long since been forgotten, and they are thus usually remembered by their regimental affiliation, such as the vivandière of the 57th Line who was cited for gallantry in dispatches for having twice dashed through a hail of enemy fire to distribute brandy to the men of her regiment. During the **American Civil War** women who accompanied regiments into the field and volunteered their services as laundresses, nurses, or water carriers were often referred to as vivandières after their more business-like French predecessors.

Bibliography: Blaze, *La vie militaire,* 1901; Blond, *La Grande Armée,* 1995; Elting, *Swords around a Throne,* 1988; Hall, *Patriots in Disguise,* 1993; Kennett, *The French Armies in the Seven Years' War,* 1967; Lynn, *Giant of the Grand Siècle,* 1997.

—Robert Bruce

W

WA, first name unknown (fl. sixteenth century, Tianzhou, now in Kuangsi Province, China). A commander of the southwest aboriginal people in the Ming dynasty (1368–1644).

The family of Wa's husband Chen Bangyan (died ca. 1525) had provided the aboriginal official for generations. After Chen Bangyan died, Wa and Lin, Bangyan's other wife, together raised their grandson Chen Zhi (died 1553). Later their brother-in-law Chen Bangxiang plotted to kill Chen Zhi and to take over their sole source of support, a rice paddy provided by the officials. So the two women sent Chen Zhi to report on the incident to the provincial military commander, and they had Military Inspector Lu Su appeal to the throne on Chen Zhi's behalf. Further, they sent an assassin to kill Chen Bangxiang, but Chen Bangxiang discovered the scheme and killed the assassin instead. Finally, Wa and Lu Su surrounded Chen Bangxiang's house, lured him outside at night, and had him strangled.

Wa's career as a fighter was only beginning, even though she was a grandmother. In 1555 Wa led her Tianzhou tribal soldiers to Suzhou in response to the imperial court's call against pirates. Twenty years later it is recorded that she fought under Regional Commander Yu Dayou (died 1576) and killed many pirates. The emperor awarded Wa and her two grandsons with silver coins.

Bibliography: Tingyu, *Ming shi*, 1974.

—Sherry J. Mou

WAAAF (Women's Auxiliary Australian Air Force)

WAAAF (WOMEN'S AUXILIARY AUSTRALIAN AIR FORCE). Australia, 1941–1947.

The Women's Auxiliary Australian Air Force (1941–1947) was formed by Commonwealth of Australia War Cabinet directive on 4 February 1941 in Melbourne, Victoria. On 23 March 1943 the service was legally constituted under the Air Force Act 1923–4, Permanent Air Force Regulations and Air Force (Women's Service) Regulations, as a branch of the Royal Australian Air Force (RAAF). The WAAAF pioneered the admission of women other than nurses into the **Australian Defence Forces** and contributed significantly to the country's defense. In total, 27,000 airwomen in 72 of the 120 RAAF trades worked alongside airmen under the same conditions but at two-thirds the pay. They were posted according to trade to RAAF and Allied Air Force Headquarters, to large RAAF stations, or to small specialist units throughout the country, including the operational centers and signals and intelligence units in northern Australia.

Two female machinists in the WAAAF. (Library of Congress)

After the First World War a growing percentage of Australian women had looked outside the home and family for a full-time career. Female standards of education and health had steadily risen, and the long-distance flights of the early pilots—especially Amy Johnson—had inspired a small but enthusiastic number of women to qualify for a pilot's license. After Neville Chamberlain's visit to Munich in September 1938, when war seemed increasingly imminent, voluntary organizations began training women to take an active part in the event of a national emergency. The Australian Women's Flying Club (July 1938) and the Women's Emergency Signalling Corps (July 1939) in Sydney and the Women's Air Training Corps (July 1939) in Brisbane, Melbourne, and Sydney were directly involved in the formation and development of the WAAAF.

The acute shortage of trained male wireless telegraphists in the RAAF during 1939–1940 forced a reluctant War Cabinet to approve the recruitment of 320 women: 224 ground wireless operators, 40 teleprinter operators and cipher staff, and 56 administration and domestic staff. It was essential to supplement male telegraphists with female operators if the RAAF was to meet its allotted

462

targets under the Empire Air Training Scheme and provide for home defense. The first intakes of telegraphists and teleprinter operators arrived for RAAF procedural training in March 1941 at No. 1 WAAAF Depot, Malvern, Victoria.

Despite the temporary nature of their employment, WAAAF numbers rose to 1,372 personnel in seven months, with the airwomen working in an increasing variety of trades. In October 1941 the new Labor government halted recruiting, but the Japanese attack on Pearl Harbor in December made the threat of invasion loom larger, which rapidly changed government policy. Australia declared war on Japan, and among the emergency measures hurriedly approved by the War Cabinet, the maximum use was to be made of womanpower in the services. The WAAAF was immediately to recruit an additional 500 airwomen.

Soon the bulk of RAAF signals traffic in Australia was handled by airwomen. Valda Valentine, a wireless telegraphist in Townsville, received the last messages from Singapore and Bandung and also the emergency messages from the Coral Sea Battle. A select group of special Kana-Japanese wireless telegraphy operators, part of a small RAAF unit concealed in the Queensland bush, monitored the air-to-base reports of Japanese pilots fighting in and around Papua/New Guinea. Some WAAAF members held crucial jobs as radio location (radar) operators, using newly invented technical equipment to locate and warn of German and Japanese submarine activity and the approach of enemy aircraft off Australia's coastline. They worked in intelligence and operational rooms, in the Group I male trade of meteorological assistant, and as photographers, electricians, fitters, flight riggers, armorers, instrument repairers, and flight mechanics servicing aircraft; they folded parachutes and drove oil tank trucks and aircraft-refueling tenders.

These young women proved that they had the capacity to move from civilian life into a male-dominated arena of uniforms, service discipline, and high technical standards. As the Fiftieth WAAAF Reunion demonstrated, they bonded strongly as a group, and mutual respect and comradeship developed between airmen and airwomen. Leaders naturally arose within the organization and were recognized by promotion.

The WAAAF worked calmly and efficiently under stress. Flight Officer Moira Lenore Shelton (1920–1976), a science graduate appointed as an armament officer and then as RAAF experimental officer at a highly secret RAAF Chemical Research Unit in northern Queensland, filled and checked bombs with mustard gas, supervised the work of RAAF armorers, and fully participated in the RAAF test trials.

Reports show that other WAAAF members continued to carry on with their various duties with calm efficiency during a Japanese air raid on Townsville. Flight Officer Marjorie "Nell" Palfreyman, a narrative-recording officer on duty, later wrote, "Signals WAAAF put their heads down capable and steady" when three Japanese midget submarines, evading the boom net across Sydney Harbour Heads, torpedoed a dormitory ship and just missed the USS *Chicago*.

Suburbs of Sydney and Newcastle were also shelled, and enemy submarine attacks on shipping off the eastern coast intensified.

Advances in technology during the 1940s changed the nature of warfare and also the number and the type of personnel required to prosecute it. The RAAF need for and the importance of combat-support staff had greatly increased. Developments in radar, aircraft construction, weaponry, communications, and meteorology demanded airmen and airwomen with more diverse skills and a higher standard of education. The WAAAF helped to meet that need, and its contribution during the Second World War set the stage for the reintroduction of women into the peacetime RAAF. As Prime Minister Keating stated in a speech at Parliament House during a fiftieth-anniversary commemoration of women's role in Australia's defense forces in the Second World War, "The WAAAF changed the role of [Australian] women in wartime."

Bibliography: Australian Archives, Canberra (Australian War Cabinet Papers, 1940–1943, and Australian Advisory War Council Papers, 1940–1943); Mitchell Library, State Library of NSW, Sydney (Group Officer Clare Grant Stevenson Papers); Thomson, "WAAAF Papers," Australian War Memorial Series PR 00246, and *The WAAAF in Wartime Australia*, 1991.

—Joyce A. Thomson

WAAC/QMAAC (WOMEN'S AUXILIARY ARMY CORPS/QUEEN MARY'S AUXILIARY ARMY CORPS), (February 1917 to 27 September 1921; renamed on 9 April 1918). British women's corps. Various domestic support services for the army. First World War.

The Women's Auxiliary Army Corps (WAAC) was an official British women's corps. While numerous volunteer women's organizations aided the war effort and provided the army with cooks and drivers after the summer of 1915, a great deal of manpower suitable for the front line was still tied up in administrative and support duties in France. In a logical continuation of the government's policy of substitution and dilution, the WAAC was created in February 1917; in March 1917 the first contingent was sent to France to serve at headquarters behind the lines. Service was later extended to Britain as well.

In September 1917 the WAAC assimilated the **Women's Legion**. About 9,000 women were employed in France and 29,000 at home. They often worked eighteen-hour days, seven days a week, as clerks, telephone operators, telegraphists, domestics in officers' clubs, drivers, and gardeners and in other support duties. While relatively few women served in the WAAC/QMAAC, its creation marked a milestone for women in Britain. For the first time women participated actively in the defense of their country. Mrs. Chalmers Watson, chief controller of the WAAC in 1917–1918, clashed with her deputy **Helen Gwynne-Vaughan** on the degree of militarization of women because she did not think that public opinion wanted an "amazon corps." However, the death of eight WAAC members in a air raid in April 1918 confirmed their military status to many in the army. On 9 April 1918 the queen assumed the position of commandant in chief of the WAAC, and the group was thereafter known as QMAAC (Queen Mary's Army Auxiliary Corps).

Bibliography: Bidwell, *The Women's Royal Army Corps,* 1977; Bigland, *Britain's Other Army,* 1946; Gould, "Women's Military Service in First World War Britain," 1987; Terry, *Women in Khaki,* 1988; Thomas, "Women in the Military," 1978.

—C.H.N. Hull

WAC (WOMEN'S ARMY CORPS) (1942–1978). Originated as WAAC (Women's Army Auxiliary Corps). United States, Second World War through Vietnam era.

Women gained a permanent place in the American military with the establishment of the WAC, a corps of female soldiers who performed essential wartime duty in fields from military intelligence to air-traffic control. Assigned to 225 bases worldwide, 140,000 Wacs were stationed in every theater of the war. Most held administrative and clerical jobs, though some worked in specialized military occupations as mechanics, photographers, teletype operators, parachute riggers, and cartographers. Relying on the precedent of 13,000 "yeomen (female)" in the navy during the First World War and the political leadership of Congresswoman Edith Nourse Rogers, in 1941 American women already serving as volunteers in the war effort pressed for recognition and opportunity in the military. When "manpower" shortages convinced military leaders and Congress that enlisting women was both appropriate and necessary, the Women's Army Auxiliary Corps (WAAC) was formed in May 1942. The "auxiliary" status of the corps ended on 14 September 1943 when pressure from within and administrative problems convinced the army to grant servicewomen full military status.

The conversion to regular military status helped the recruiting efforts of Colonel **Oveta Culp Hobby,** the Corps's first director, who focused on attracting the "right" type of women—those with "high moral character" and a strong educational background or work experience. Hobby and others considered the WAC a potential force of highly skilled replacement workers to handle the administrative and technical needs of a wartime army. Wacs were required to be between twenty and fifty years old and to be able to pass a fitness test and entrance exam. Although the services did not specify racial requirements and the WAC did reserve 40 spaces for African American women in its initial officer-training class of 440, the service reflected the racial prejudice of the United States during the Second World War and was not eager to include or promote women of color (see entry on **WAC, African Americans in**). Some women in Hobby's target group were dissuaded from joining the service by absurd rumors that Wacs were intended to fulfill the sexual needs of male soldiers. The rumors were so devastating to recruiting that the army investigated the slander campaign as a possible Axis plot to reduce enlistments before tracing its origins to resentful male soldiers. Some army commanders in the field were reluctant to request WAC help because of the negative publicity and their own lack of faith in women's capability, but servicewomen consistently proved their worth even in the most difficult situations. "Air Wacs" were in greatest demand, in part because of General H.H. Arnold, who was both head of the Army Air Corps and a believer in the competence of women in certain military jobs. Within the WAC itself commanders responded to rumors about the promiscuity and capability of Wacs by stressing proper behavior and comportment.

The strength of the WAC reached a peak of 100,000 women in the summer of 1945, when Wacs served around the world in jobs deemed "suitable" for women by the army. Like most men in the military, most Wacs were not directly involved in combat, though they proved their fortitude when given the opportunity. One experimental unit of sixty Wacs was integrated into the Fifth Army in North Africa, where they endured long hours and stressful conditions just twenty miles from the front lines. This special unit received praise as highly motivated soldiers who caused a minimum of disciplinary problems. Indeed, servicewomen's record for disciplinary problems and sickness was better than servicemen's under similar conditions. Pregnancy and menstrual problems were rare (initially, single Wacs who became pregnant were served with "less than honorable" discharges), and venereal disease was negligible among servicewomen (who, unlike male soldiers, were never issued prophylactics or lectured on sexually transmitted diseases).

Pregnancy rates for American women:	
Overall civilian rate	11%
Rates for women aboard ship in the U.S. Navy	7%
Overall rate for women in the army	5%
Women sent home due to pregnancy in Bosnia operation	3.5%

—Dana Priest, "Women Easily Assimilate in U.S. Armed Forces in Bosnia," *Washington Post* 3 March 1997: A01.

Although the WAC proved a vital cog in the American military machine, within days of the armistice in 1945, 98 percent of Wacs were discharged as a result of demobilization and the ensuing contraction of economic opportunity for American women. After the Second World War Wacs served continuously, though in much smaller numbers, as part of war efforts in Korea and Vietnam. In 1978 Congress abolished the WAC in favor of an integrated army. Military commanders had often found the dual chain of command regarding women to be burdensome (the army had operational command, but the WAC had administrative control). To some WAC veterans, integration was a mixed blessing, since their support network and independent traditions were subsumed into a much larger and male-dominated force. Others welcomed the opportunity to be truly integrated into the army—to simply be a "soldier" and not a "Wac." The Women's Army Corps during the Second World War was a turning point in the recognition and acceptance of American women in military uniform.

Bibliography: Litoff and Smith, *We're in This War, Too,* 1994, and *American Women in a World at War,* 1996; Meyer, *Creating G.I. Jane,* 1996; Morden, *The Women's Army Corps,* 1990; Rustad, *Women in Khaki,* 1982; Stiehm, *Arms and the Enlisted Woman,* 1988; Treadwell, *The Women's Army Corps,* 1954.

—Elizabeth Lutes Hillman

WAC, AFRICAN AMERICANS IN. Women's Army Corps, United States, Second World War and after, 1942–1978.

The quest for the "Double V" (victory over the Axis powers overseas and over racism at home) was embraced by the 6,500 African American women who joined the ranks of the **WAC** (Women's Army Corps), just as it was for the better-known case of African American men who enlisted during the Second World War. Black servicewomen overcame racial bias in recruiting, job assignments, and promotions to prove their willingness and capability to serve in the American military.

African American WACs at Fort Des Moines, Iowa, 1943. (University of North Carolina at Greensboro, Jackson Library)

At first the WAC actively recruited African American women, responding to pressure from political activists who were concerned that the appointment of a Southern aristocrat and native Texan, **Oveta Culp Hobby,** as the first director of the WAC would discourage the fair treatment and recruitment of African Americans. Hobby's first public address as WAC director took place at a Howard University sorority, part of a campaign to meet ambitious recruiting goals. The official WAC goal for recruitment of African American women was the same as the army's goal for African American men: 10.6 percent of the total force. Hobby's official statements and actions, particularly the inclusion of 39 African American women among the first officer-training class of 400, engendered early optimism about the possibilities of racial integration within the army's corps of women, unlike the whites-only female components of the other branches of service. Despite that auspicious beginning, the WAC succeeded in attracting only a small fraction of African American women into service, largely because of the racist practices that consigned most black women to menial jobs and limited their employment with regular army troops. The WAC negated its early recruiting success by canceling efforts targeted at African American women, who were also discouraged from joining by false rumors that they were to serve as consorts for African American male soldiers. About 4.3 percent of the total number of women admitted to the WAC were black, with a peak strength of just over 4,000 in December 1944.

Racial segregation was standard practice, if not WAC policy, for African American troops. Other racial minorities were treated differently; for instance, Puerto Rican Wacs were placed in a separate unit because the army was concerned about their English-language capability; Nisei women were recruited as translators; and Filipinas and Chinese American women were included in racially mixed units. Most African American Wacs were trained at Fort Des Moines in order to avoid the prejudice assumed to be more prevalent at Southern posts, although black women were also sent to Fort Oglethorpe, Georgia, Fort Devens, Massachusetts, and Daytona Beach, Florida. Strict segregation broke down at most camps because of protest from the women themselves, although War Department policy mandated "no [social] intermingling" of the races. Since white male commanders in the field were reluctant to request African American units except for domestic duties (cooking, cleaning, and laundering for soldiers were their most common tasks) and because African American officers were permitted to lead only African American units, opportunities for black servicewomen were restricted. The first two companies of black servicewomen were sent to remote Fort Huachaca, Arizona, and African American women often endured delay and disappointment in the WAC assignment process.

Still, black Wacs served in a variety of essential, nontechnical jobs at army and Army Air Corps posts throughout the United States. The only African American WAC unit stationed overseas during the war was the 6888th Central Postal Directory Battalion, commanded by Major Charity Adams (later **Charity Adams Eamley**). The 855 women of the 6888th cleared a huge backlog of soldiers' mail in Europe, and like the popular black WAC band that was reestablished after being disbanded, benefited from the political pressure exerted by groups like Mary McLeod Bethune's National Council of Negro Women. Racism could threaten African American servicewomen's safety as well as job possibilities. In one especially brutal incident uniformed black Wacs in a bus station in Kentucky were beaten with billy clubs and blackjacks for breaking Jim Crow laws and then were subjected to an army court-martial for their "violation" of the law. Adams, one of the highest-ranking African American Wacs, traveled home to South Carolina after being commissioned only to be greeted by robed Ku Klux Klansmen, who surrounded her family's home to protest her achievements.

Harriet W. West was the only African American WAC officer assigned for duty in the Personnel Division at WAC Headquarters in Washington, D.C., and by 1943 was the highest-ranking African American female officer. She evaluated allegations of racism from Wacs in the field, assigned investigators, and assessed WAC policy. Her recommendations helped the WAC leadership defuse some racial tensions, though West was aware that neither the WAC nor the American public were always comfortable with the reality of African American women in military uniform. In the spring of 1943 she was denied admission to the "Salute to Women's Services" at Constitution Hall because she was an African American, even though she was there in an official capacity representing the WAAC (the predecessor of WAC). Her most lasting contribution to military women was to chip away at the racial inequalities of the American armed forces. She retired as a lieutenant colonel in May 1952. All African American servicewomen battled racism as well as foreign enemies during the Second World War, helping to ensure a military victory and building a foundation for the civil rights movement of the postwar decades.

Undated portrait of Mary Bethune. (Library of Congress)

Bibliography: Earley, *One Woman's Army*, 1989; Johnson, *Black Women in the Armed Forces 1942–1974*, 1974; Lee, *The United States Army in World War II, Special Studies: The Employment of Negro Troops*, 1965; Moore, "Black, Female, and in Uniform," 1990, "African American Women," 1991, and *To Serve My Country*, 1996; Putney, *When the Nation Was in Need*, 1992; Treadwell, *The Women's Army Corps*, 1954.

—Elizabeth Lutes Hillman

WAFS (WOMEN'S AUXILIARY FERRYING SQUADRON), September 1942–July 1943, United States. Pilots, Second World War.

The Women's Auxiliary Ferrying Squadron (WAFS) of the Air Transport Command of the Army Air Forces (AAF), under the direction of Nancy Love, was the first auxiliary created in the United States that allowed women to fly military aircraft. It existed as a distinct group for less than a year and in August 1943 was absorbed into the **WASP** under the control of **Jacqueline Cochran**.

Nancy Harkness Love (born 1914, Houghton, Michigan; died 1976) was one of the preeminent American women pilots of the 1930s. She did not compete in high-profile air races or set world records, but she achieved many "firsts" for women pilots in her typically quiet way. She earned her private license when she was only sixteen years old. Later, as a student at Vassar College, she continued to devote her summer breaks to flying. She helped develop a network of student flying clubs. In 1933 she earned her commercial pilot's license and in 1935 was one of three women hired by the Bureau of Air Commerce to air-mark major cities in the United States. She married Robert J. Love in 1936, and together they operated a small company, Intercity Aviation, at Boston Airport. Nancy Love gained experience in ferrying aircraft by helping deliver the company's aircraft to customers. She did some flight test work and, while working with the Domestic Division early in the war, became conversant with ferry operations, especially from the logistical and administrative side. By the time she took over the WAFS in 1942, the twenty-seven-year-old Love was a commercially qualified pilot with instrument and seaplane ratings and had more than 1,200 hours of flying time.

Love was generally seen as a pilot's pilot who led by example without calling undue attention to herself, "a great leader because she was a pilot first and an administrator second." In her memoirs former WASP Marion Stegeman Hodgson described Love as "a stunning, soft-spoken, to-the-manner-born lady who was also high-spirited and adventuresome" and emanated a "woman-to-woman warmth." Vita Roth, prewar director of Women Flyers of America, saw Love as "not only one of our best pilots in the air, she is an efficient and level-headed woman on the ground."

While Jacqueline Cochran was campaigning to persuade the White House and/or AAF leadership to create a women's auxiliary, Nancy Love had been quietly working at lower command levels to persuade the Army Air Forces' Air Transport Command (ATC) to employ experienced women pilots in ferry duties. Love, whose husband was a deputy chief of staff of the ATC, believed that these women should be hired and assimilated like any other pilots. Love was interested in meeting an immediate need; only about 100 women in America had accrued the flying hours and skills necessary to qualify as a ferry pilot. Love's first proposals to admit women were rejected, but by mid-1942 production of aircraft had been dramatically increased, and a corresponding expansion of ferrying requirements was projected.

The leaders of the Ferrying Division got serious about hiring women pilots. Colonel William H. Tunner, head of the Ferrying Division, went to the air base at Wilmington, Delaware, headquarters of the 2nd Ferrying Group, to evaluate the facilities for housing and operations of the proposed women's squadron. Administrative problems delayed the plan for months. Initially it was believed that women pilots would be recruited through the Women's Auxiliary Army Corps (WAAC), in the same manner as nonflying enlisted women. However, there was no provision in the WAAC to commission flying officers or to give flight pay; congressional legislation would be required to hire women pilots as military auxiliaries. In July 1942 Colonel Baker and Nancy Love worked together to revise the proposal; this time the plan stipulated hiring women pilots as civil service employees. Love had apparently already been hired by the Second Ferrying Group at Wilmington in anticipation of starting a women pilots program. General Arnold replied that he would consider the plan only after "every possible qualified [male] pilot" had been obtained from the CAA and Civil Air Patrol. General George repeated his proposal on 3 September, and this time AAF headquarters gave the go-ahead. George's proposal specified that a director for the Women's Auxiliary Ferrying Squadron be appointed, a woman who was a qualified commercial pilot with at least 1,200 hours flying experience, and also familiar with the Air Transport Command. He appointed twenty-eight-year old Nancy Love to the position. On 5 September 1942 Love proceeded to send recruiting tele-grams to qualified women, based on the list developed from the examination of CAA records.

Love's plan was simple in concept and modest in scope. She sought to take advantage of a relatively small group of highly competent women pilots who were already qualified to fly the sort of missions required by the Ferrying Division. The ATC was already using some male civilian pilots, and the mem-bers of the WAFS were also brought in as civilians. These women were cer-tified by the same board as the men, but were paid less and had to have much higher flying qualifications.

By 17 September 1942 Love had already accepted seven women into the WAFS; by mid-December the first group of twenty-five was finalized. On av-erage, these women had 1,162 hours of flying experience. It took a few weeks for the Ferrying Division of the Air Transport Command to work out the structure of the WAFS. Initially it regarded the women as simply another group of civilian pilots, subject to the same rules and regulations as the men. In November 1942 the Ferrying Division stated for the record that "technically, there is no such activated unit as a 'Women's Auxiliary Ferrying Squadron.' " However, other agencies insisted that the women be separately organized one way or another.

Expansion of WAFS activity was already foreseen in late 1942, and in De-cember 1942 Nancy Love reported on the feasibility of creating additional WAFS units to be based near production points. In early January small cadres of WAFS, drawn from the original twenty-five members, were transferred to 5th Ferrying Group at Dallas, 3rd Ferrying Group at Romulus, Michigan, and 6th Ferrying Group at Long Beach, California. By spring 1943, the Ferrying Division wanted to increase the size of the program and decided that Nancy Love should join the Ferrying Division's headquarters staff. It took weeks before a title was chosen for Love; in June 1943 she was formally designated the "executive for WAFS."

From the creation of the WAFS as part of the Ferrying Division in September 1942 until the end of that year, women pilots ferried only primary trainers and liaison aircraft. During the first months of 1943 the range of aircraft was increasingly expanded. Women first began to ferry pursuit (fighter) aircraft in July 1943. Eventually a total of 77 different types of aircraft were ferried by American women pilots working for the Ferrying Division, including the P-47, P-51, B-17, and B-25. Some examples of the type of work done by WAFS include the following: in April 1943 Four Wilmington WAFS members, led by

Betty Gillies, ferried four slow-flying PT-26s a distance of more than 2,500 miles, from Maryland to Alberta, Canada, in just three days. The commander of the WAFS squadron at Long Beach, Barbara Erickson, received the Air Force Medal in March 1944 for an exceptionally difficult and intensive round of deliveries, in which she flew more than 8,000 miles in five days.

However, the independence of the WAFS program was under fire almost from its inception. In January 1943 ATC was instructed that it could no longer hire women pilots directly into the WAFS; all future WAFS must first complete the WFTD program (see WASP), regardless of prior experience. In March 1943 AAF headquarters directed that women graduates of the WFTD would automatically be regarded as qualified for basic ferrying duties, taking away the WAFS or ATC role in approving and selecting pilots. On 5 August 1943 the WAFS and WFTD were merged into a single organization, the Women's Airforce Service Pilots (WASP). Cochran was named Director of Women Pilots, and Nancy Love became a member of the WASP, subordinate to Cochran, with responsibility as WASP advisor to the Ferrying Division. Many saw this as a power play between Cochran and Love.

However, the conflict was not so much between Cochran and Love as between Cochran and the Ferrying Division. The Ferrying Division historian concluded in his final report that the division had an "attitude of suspicion and mistrust" toward Cochran based on its experience with her. For example, when General Arnold stopped Nancy Love and Betty Gillies from delivering a B-17 to England in 1943, most in the Ferrying Division assumed that Cochran had intervened due to her "jealousy of the Command's veteran women flyers," although there was no evidence that Cochran was responsible. Similarly, AAF headquarters noted in its final report that "almost at once" after the WASP was merged from the WAFS and WFTD, relations between Cochran's office and the Ferrying Division "were clouded by ill feeling and distrust." Hodgson noted that her feeling in mid-1943 was that "Nancy Love and Jacqueline Cochran were in conflicting and overlapping positions of authority over us. We didn't know whose child we were. Miss Cochran had gotten us as far as [the training program at] Sweetwater, but Mrs. Love was in charge of female ferry pilots, and wasn't that what we were training to be?"

Some former WAFS members adamantly make the distinction that during the war they considered themselves WAFS and not WASP, even after the merger. It was perhaps natural that Ferrying Division pilots would prefer their founder, Nancy Love, to Cochran. This led them to blame Cochran for many things. Some of the women serving with the Ferrying Division believed that they would have been able to continue serving until the end of the war, despite the defeat of the WASP militarization bill, if Cochran had not insisted on either militarization or complete dissolution. One Ferrying Division WASP member wrote in 1944, "It is too bad that the necessity of the war has not been put first in order of importance instead of the ambitions and desires of personalities." The real issue was that as long as women pilots were segregated into auxiliary organizations rather than being assimilated into the military, these organizations were vulnerable. The WAFS existed less than a year before being absorbed by the WASP, and the WASP itself was disbanded less than eighteen months after that.

Bibliography: Cochran, "Final Report on Women Pilot Program," 1945; Douglas, *United States Women in Aviation,* 1990; England, "Women Pilots of the AAF, 1941–1944," 1946; Hodgson, *Winning My Wings,* 1996; Keil, "Those Magnificent Women in Their Flying Machines," 1977; Marx, "Women Pilots in the Air Transport Command (Revised)," 1945; Pennington, "Women and Military Aviation in the Second World War," 2000; Scharr, *Sisters in the Sky,* vol.1 *The WAFS,* 1986.

—Reina Pennington

WAKEMAN, SARAH ROSETTA (born 16 January 1843, Afton, New York; died 19 June 1864, New Orleans, Louisiana), also known as Lyons Wakeman, Edwin Wakeman. Private, Union army, American Civil War.

Disguised as Private Lyons Wakeman, Sarah Rosetta Wakeman served with Company H, 153rd Regiment, New York State Volunteers, during the **American Civil War**. Wakeman was the oldest of nine children in a farming family and had worked as a domestic servant before she left her family home in 1862 at the age of nineteen. She appears to have disguised herself as a man at that time, apparently in the hope of finding better employment and to help her parents financially by securing her own future. She wrote home that she had found work on a coal barge, and when Wakeman met some soldiers from the 153rd a few months later who urged her to join the army, she did. Although Wakeman was only five feet tall, she was accepted for service.

Wakeman wrote home regularly, describing her months of service in garrison near Washington, D.C. She told her family about things like a measles epidemic and her use of tobacco as a preventative, but said little of any difficulties in maintaining her disguise. She seemed to enjoy military life and noted that she could use her gun "as well as the rest of them" in training exercises. She spoke of sinning "a good deal," by which she apparently re-

From the letters of Sarah Rosetta Wakeman, who served in disguise in the Union army:

Alexandria, VA. Fairfax Co. March the 29/63.
Dear Father, It would make your hair stand out to be where I have been. How would you like to be in the front rank and have the rear rank load and fire their guns over your shoulder? I have been there my Self.

Capitol Hill, Washington DC, December the 28/63.
Dear Father and Mother. . . . I have enjoyed my self the best since I have been gone away from home than I ever did before in my life. I have had plenty of money to spend and a good time a soldier[ing].

Grand Encore Landing, Louisiana, on the Red River, April the 14, 1864.
Dear Mother and Father, Brothers and Sisters, Our army made an advance up the river to pleasant hill about 40 miles. There we had a fight. The first day of the fight our army got whip and we had to retreat back about ten miles. . . . I was not in the first day's fight but the next day I had to face the enemy bullets with my regiment. I was under fire about four hours and laid on the field of battle all night. There was three wounded in my Co. and one killed. . . . I feel thankful to God that he spared my life and I pray to him that he will lead me safe through the field of battle and that I may return safe home.

—Lauren Cook Burgess, ed., *An Uncommon Soldier: The Civil War Letters of Sarah Rosetta Wakeman, alias Pvt. Lyons Wakeman, 153rd Regiment, New York State Volunteers, 1862–1864* (Pasadena, MD: Minerva, 1994), 25–26, 58, 77.

ferred to drinking and swearing, and noted in one letter that she had gotten into a fight with another soldier in which she got in several "good cracks." In another letter she mentioned another woman who was serving in disguise and had been discovered.

Wakeman first met the enemy on the battlefield after serving more than a year. Her unit was sent to Louisiana to participate in Major General Nathaniel P. Banks's ill-fated Red River Campaign in the spring of 1864. She survived her only apparent combat engagement on 9 April 1864 without incident. As the campaign drew to a close, Wakeman, along with many of her other comrades, developed chronic diarrhea. She reported to a regimental hospital on 3 May and transferred to Marine U.S.A. General Hospital in New Orleans; after arriving at the hospital on May 22, her condition was listed as acute. After a month of hospitalization Wakeman died on 19 June 1864, without anyone learning that she was a woman, and was buried in New Orleans beneath a tombstone reading "Lyons Wakeman, N.Y." The doctor wrote to her family that Private Wakeman had served "honestly and faithfully" and notified them that "he" left some small debts.

Sarah Rosetta Wakeman is unique in leaving behind a thorough paper trail documenting her activities. The military records confirm the enlistment, service, vaccinations, and illnesses of Private "Lyons" Wakeman. Her family kept her letters and a photo of her in uniform, together with a ring inscribed with her name and unit, stashed in a trunk, and were apparently embarrassed to speak publicly about Sarah. In 1976 the letters were rediscovered and were subsequently edited and published by Lauren Burgess in 1994 as *An Uncommon Soldier: The Civil War Letters of Sarah Rosetta Wakeman, alias Pvt. Lyons Wakeman, 153rd Regiment, New York State Volunteers, 1862–1864*. Interestingly, Wakeman signed her letters openly as "Sarah Rosetta," "Rosetta," or "R.L. Wakeman," and on occasion "Edwin R. Wakeman" (apparently after her commander's first name), but not "Lyons," although she wrote to her family to address their letters to her under that name.

Bibliography: Burgess, *An Uncommon Soldier*, 1994; Meyer, "The Soldier Left a Portrait and Her Eyewitness Account," 1995.

—Gayle Veronica Fischer

WALKER, MARY EDWARDS (born 26 November 1842; died 21 February 1919, Oswego, New York). Surgeon, Union army, American Civil War.

Mary Edwards Walker was the first woman to be commissioned as a military doctor and lieutenant in the Medical Corps. She is best known in American history as the first woman to be awarded the Congressional Medal of Honor, which was withdrawn in 1917 but restored in 1977.

Walker received her M.D. from Syracuse Medical College in 1855. After six years of practice in her home state Walker (one of only a handful of women physicians in the United States at the time) traveled to Washington in the aftermath of Fort Sumter at the outbreak of the **American Civil War,** seeking a commission as a United States Army surgeon. The daughter of reform-oriented parents, Walker was raised in an atmosphere charged with the ideas of abolitionism and sexual egalitarianism. In addition to serving her country, Walker believed that the chaos and the carnage of war might provide precisely the necessary conditions for a woman physician to achieve recognition and success and thereby widen the path for other women to enter the medical profession.

Clothed in reform dress (slacks and a knee-length dress), Walker spent most of the first three years of the war tending the sick and wounded, in hospitals and on the battlefield, in an informal, voluntary capacity, earning the respect of many of the doctors and generals (including George Thomas, Ambrose Burnside, and William T. Sherman) with whom she served, although her determination and strong character annoyed others. During this period the Union's Medical Department resisted granting her a formal position as anything but a nurse, which offer she refused on the basis of her professional status and training as a doctor.

Early in 1864, however, the untimely death of Assistant Surgeon A.J. Rosa of the 52nd Ohio Volunteers, combined with the army's desperate need for more medical personnel and the accumulated evidence of Walker's service to the army, resulted in her receiving an assignment as a noncommissioned contract surgeon, without rank, to the regiment. She remained with the 52nd Ohio until April, when, riding far from camp one night, she came upon a Confederate sentry who refused to believe her claim to be delivering letters. Suddenly Walker found herself a prisoner of the Confederacy. Both sides later accused Walker, probably inaccurately, of having been engaged in espionage activities at the time she was captured.

Her military imprisonment at Castle Thunder in Richmond lasted four months, at which time she was exchanged for a six-foot-tall "Southern officer with the rank of major." Undaunted by her experience, Walker returned to Washington and continued to press for a formal military commission as a surgeon. She never achieved that ultimate goal, but nonetheless served out the remainder of the war in unranked, noncommissioned contract-surgeon positions as the surgeon in charge, first at the Louisville Female Military Prison in Kentucky and then at an orphan asylum and refugee home in Clarksville, Tennessee.

On 5 May 1865, despite her efforts to press for a postwar commission in the peacetime army, she was dismissed. In November, as a token of appreciation, President Andrew Johnson made her the first and only woman in the history of the American military to receive the Congressional Medal of Honor, in recognition of her military service and the four months she spent as a prisoner of war. In 1917, a year before her death, Walker's medal was revoked (along with the medals of more than 900 men) when the type of service required for receiving the medal was restricted by Congress to service in combat. It was reinstated posthumously in 1977.

Bibliography: Leonard, *Yankee Women*, 1994 and *All the Daring of the Soldier*, 1999; Poynter, "Dr. Mary Walker, M.D.: Pioneer Woman Physician," 1946; Seeley, *American Women and the U.S. Armed Forces*, 1992; Snyder, *Dr. Mary Walker*, 1974; Walker, Mary E., Papers (Syracuse University Library Special Collections Department, Syracuse, New York; and Records of the War Department, Office of the Adjutant General, Record Group 94, National Archives, Washington, DC); Woodward, *The Bold Women*, 1958.

—Elizabeth D. Leonard

WARD, NANCY (born 1738?; died 1824, Chota, North Carolina), also known as Nan'Yehi, White Rose, "Ghighua." Cherokee Nation. Warrior, tribal political leader in both men and women's councils, tribal negotiator.

The Cherokees are a matrilineal society, and women leaders have played key roles in their history. Nan'yehi (later called Nancy Ward) held the singular most honorific title and role that can be bestowed upon a woman leader: "Ghighua" ("beloved woman" or "war woman"). This role is quite influential in tribal matters. After Ward's death in 1824, the Cherokees did not bestow the title again until the late 1980s.

Born around 1738 in the Overhill region of the Cherokee Nation, Nan'yehi earned the coveted title in battle with the Creeks in 1755. She married a great warrior, Kingfisher, while still in her teens. The Cherokee and Creek territories abutted each other, and war between these two tribes was constant. At a place called Taliwa another major battle occurred during which Kingfisher was killed. Women often went into battle with these tribes, and when her husband was killed, Nan'yehi picked up his weapon, rallied the Cherokees, and led them to a decisive victory over the Creeks. From that day on Nan'yehi was called "Ghighua."

She now occupied a position where she had a vote and voice in the General Council, leadership of a Women's Council, and a role as a peace negotiator. She was on one hand a fierce protector of the Cherokee Nation and on the other a voice for assimilation of some white ways. One of her special privileges was the right to save the life of any prisoner, which she exercised to save a Mrs. William Bean, who later helped the Cherokees in areas involving weaving, animal husbandry, and landownership.

Nan'yehi was a chief negotiator in 1785 and signed the Treaty of Hopewell between the United States and the Cherokees. By 1808, however, she was urging the Cherokees to sell no more land because she was now convinced that the tribe was slowly being forced off its lands. During this period she married a white trader by the name of Bryant Ward and was known from then on as Nancy Ward. The Wards ran an inn on Womankiller Creek, Tennessee. Nancy returned to her birthplace in North Carolina in 1824 and died there the same year, in her mid-eighties. She did not live, fortunately, to witness the "Trail of Tears"—the removal of the Cherokees from their native lands a decade later. Ward was buried near Benton, Tennessee, where her grave is cared for by the Daughters of the American Revolution, which has erected a pyramid of quartz stones in memorial. There is reportedly a statue of her in the Arwine Cemetery in Grainger County, Tennessee. Ward is still honored as "Ghighua," a powerful memory and spirit leader of the Cherokees.

Bibliography: De Pauw and Hunt, *Remember the Ladies,* 1976; Foreman, *Indian Women Chiefs,* 1976; Hammack, "Cherokee Phoenix," 1978; Malone, *Cherokees of the Old South,* 1956; Niethammer, *Daughters of the Earth,* 1977; O'Donnell, *Southern Indians in the American Revolution,* 1973.

—Rodney G. Thomas

WASP (WOMEN'S AIRFORCE SERVICE PILOTS). 1943–1944, United States. Pilots, Second World War.

The members of the Women's Airforce Service Pilots (WASP) were the best-known women aviators of the Second World War. They served with, but not in, the Army Air Forces (AAF). Unlike other women's auxiliary organizations in the United States, the WASP was never militarized. The WASP provides an excellent example of the way in which women who enter traditionally male occupations have been intentionally marginalized: through refusal to militarize the WASP, through reduced pay and benefits for the women compared to their male counterparts, and especially through the administrative segregation of these women aviators into separate "women's" organizations. The story of the WASP is that of a thousand patriotic and dedicated women pilots who sought to serve their country in time of war. It is also the story of personal and bureaucratic conflict and of a constant struggle over the military status of the women that was finally resolved by the refusal of Congress to militarize women pilots. It is above all a story that reveals just how resistant society is to allowing gender roles to change, except as a temporary measure. Women's roles stretched far in wartime, but once the war ended, they "snapped back" to what society deemed normal. The use of women as military pilots was hailed in 1942 and 1943 as a great contribution to the war effort; by 1944 it was seen as a direct threat to men.

From September 1942 until December 1944 American women flew as civilian auxiliary pilots, ferrying military aircraft from factories and filling various aviation support roles. These missions were performed stateside; women pilots were not permitted into theaters of war. There is no indication that anyone ever proposed that American women be permitted to fly in combat, despite the fact that the Soviet Union already had many women pilots flying in combat by the time the WASP was created. Although the WASP attained an excellent flying record, it was closed down in 1944, before the war ended, and did not receive military status until WASPs were granted veterans' rights in the 1970s.

Jacqueline Cochran, the most famous female pilot of her time, appears to have been the first person to openly propose that women pilots be admitted to military duty. In 1939 she made this suggestion to First Lady Eleanor Roosevelt; in 1941 Cochran attempted to persuade Army Air Forces (AAF) leader General "Hap" Arnold to create a women's air corps. Until the attack on Pearl Harbor American leaders were unwilling to seriously consider admitting women pilots to military service. However, the British had already begun using women pilots in their transport service, the Air Transport Auxiliary (**ATA**), in order to free male pilots for combat duties. Cochran took a group of female American volunteer pilots to England to fly with the ATA; they were the first American women pilots to make a direct contribution to the Allied war effort. Cochran's ultimate goal, however, was to establish a permanent women's air corps as part of the Army Air Forces.

Two separate organizations formed in 1942 were merged in 1943 to create the WASP. In September 1942 the **WAFS** (Women's Auxiliary Ferrying Squadron) was created in the Air Transport Command of the AAF. Members of the WAFS, under the direction of Nancy Love, were certified by the same board as the men, but were paid less and had to have much higher flying qualifications. The original WAFS was comprised of only twenty-five elite female pilots, who already had an average of 1,162 flying hours. Within days of hearing of the WAFS creation, Jacqueline Cochran implemented a much broader plan and gained command of a second organization, the WFTD (Women's Flying Training Detachment). Rather than relying on women pilots who had already attained high proficiency, as did the WAFS, the WFTD would recruit pilots with fewer flying hours (a minimum of 200 hours at the program's inception) and provide the necessary training to qualify them for military noncombat flying. This would create a continuing supply of women pilots for eventual duty with the WAFS and in other support roles. The first WFTD class began training in November 1942 in Houston, Texas. Later classes were shifted to Avenger Field in Sweetwater, Texas, where facilities were better. In May 1943 the first WFTD graduates finished training and were assigned to ATC duties with the WAFS. The four-month training program was virtually the same as that given to male aviation cadets, except that combat-related training like gunnery and formation flying was excluded. The percentage of "washouts" during training was nearly identical to that of male trainees.

The WAFS and WFTD recruited quietly, mainly through personal letters to women pilots and flying clubs. Public response was overwhelming as the word spread that women could get into military aviation; in all, more than 25,000 women applied for WASP training. The applicants even included women from Canada, England, and Brazil, although only American citizens were accepted. A total of 1,830 women were admitted, and 1,074 became operational over the duration of the program.

The WAFS and WFTD had no organizational relationship at this point, but operated independently within separate commands of the AAF. Two differing concepts were evident in the constant conflict between WAFS and WFTD. The Ferrying Division was only concerned with getting qualified pilots to serve its own purposes, while Cochran had a bigger dream of large numbers, perhaps thousands of women pilots. By November 1942 Cochran's "large numbers" concept became the official policy of the AAF. In Cochran's view, having two independent groups of women pilots was inefficient, and "the need for centralized coordination of all phases of the program became apparent." In her final report, she stressed the "experimental features" of the program that required central control over assignments and monitoring of the women's medical status. On 5 August 1943 the WAFS and WFTD were merged into a single organization, the Women's Airforce Service Pilots (WASP). Cochran was named director of women pilots, and Nancy Love became a member of the WASP, subordinate to Cochran, with responsibility as WASP advisor to the Ferrying Division.

As the number of WASP graduates increased, their duties were expanded. In general, the best-qualified women were assigned to the Ferrying Division, where the requirement to be able to fly a wide variety of aircraft demanded top skills. WASP were also assigned to a wide variety of support missions in the Air Training Command: towing targets for aerial and ground gunnery practice, serving as instructors in flight and instrument training, radio control and searchlight missions, and also test-piloting work. By July 1944 the number of women pilots in the Ferrying Division peaked at 303. Beginning in August 1944, many of these women were reassigned to other duties in Training Command, such as towing targets and flight instruction. Only the most experienced women remained with the Ferrying Division; during the last six months of 1944 an average of 140 women continued to fly with that division. In twenty-seven total months of service women pilots in the Ferrying Division had flown 12,650 ferrying missions in seventy-seven different types of aircraft, including pursuit fighters and heavy bombers. In 1944 most women pilots assigned to the Ferrying Division specialized in pursuit deliveries; by the end of the year more than 80 percent of the 140 WASP pilots in the Ferrying Division were concentrated in pursuit duties. However, only 134 WASP members in all flew pursuit aircraft, or less than 13 percent of all WASP pilots who completed training.

The second operational duty performed by WASP pilots was that of towing targets in support of antiaircraft and aerial gunnery training. A variety of aircraft were used to tow targets, including gliders, the A-24 and A-25 dive bombers, and B-17 and B-26 bombers. Aircraft would tow various kinds of targets, such as a muslin "sleeve" at the end of a long cable, that would be fired upon by ground batteries. WASP pilots stationed in tow-target squadrons performed a wide variety of functions, including simulated strafing missions, searchlight missions, tracking missions for antiaircraft gunnery crews, and radar tracking missions for radar operators.

It might have seemed that one of the most natural duties for women to perform in noncombat flying would be basic flight instruction, but male resistance seemed strongest in this area. Many believed that it would be bad for male morale to be instructed by a woman. Some WASP members did become instrument instructors. A number of women ended up in engineering test flying, especially in 1944. Most of the women assigned to this duty were stationed at locations where there were many aircraft that routinely needed repair, such as flying schools. Aircraft had to be carefully checked for safety before being cleared for cadets to fly them. Pilots in such assignments often flew other "administrative and utility" flights, such as transporting personnel; these were described by one WASP as "gofer jobs that no one else cared to do." There is no indication that Cochran, Love, or anyone else ever proposed that American women be permitted to fly in combat. The fact that this idea was apparently never even considered, at a time when the Soviet Union had three full regiments of women pilots in combat, is also revealing of American attitudes in the 1940s.

Some of the restrictions placed upon the WASPs reveal contemporary attitudes toward women flyers. The women were forbidden to fly in the same cockpit with male pilots or hitch rides in army aircraft. This meant that after delivering an aircraft, the women pilots were forced to wait for commercial transportation to return to their home bases, which increased the time required for each mission and added to the pilots' strain and fatigue. In practice, this order was sometimes disregarded. There were also standing orders that women pilots were to be grounded while they were menstruating for three days prior to and after their periods. This order was ignored, and data collected by flight surgeons eventually showed that menstruation had no effect on the women's performance; if anything, they flew slightly better on the first day of a period.

The program was still building momentum in early 1944, at which point Cochran said that plans were being considered to expand the WASP to more than 2,000 pilots and to open a second training base. Only a few months later the decision was made instead to terminate the entire program.

The military status of the WASP was always in doubt. The WAFS and WFTD were supposed to be only temporarily part of the civil service. It appears that both Love and Cochran initially thought that the women should be given military rank, just like the male pilots, but there was no provision for this within the Army Air Forces. It was suggested that the women be given rank as part of the Women's Army Corps (**WAC**), created in mid-1942 under **Oveta Culp Hobby,** but Cochran repeatedly rejected this idea because it would place the women pilots under WAC jurisdiction. In September 1943 a WASP militarization bill was introduced into Congress. At the same time, casualties among combat aviators had proven much lighter than originally estimated. Some male pilots and trainees were transferred to the ground forces. In 1944 Congress and the media became increasingly antagonistic toward the WASP. Rather than being regarded as patriotic women who were doing their best for the war effort, they were now seen as selfishly hoarding jobs that should be filled by men. The militarization bill failed, and the program was rather abruptly deactivated on 20 December 1944, before the war had ended.

Although the WAC had received full military status (including health and death benefits) in July 1943, the WASP never did during the war. The thirty-eight WASP pilots who were killed in the line of duty were buried at their own expense or, more commonly, by collections taken among their colleagues. Hearings were held only in 1977 to at last grant the WASP the status of military veterans.

Most of the small number of books about the WASPs are biographical and/or popular histories. Sally van Wagenen Keil's 1979 *Those Wonderful Women in Their Flying Machines* is the best history to date. More recently, in her book *Clipped Wings*, Molly Merryman took a theoretical approach to WASP history via feminist theory and how Americans constructed gender roles in wartime. However, the task of writing a comprehensive scholarly history of America's women pilots in the Second World War still remains to be done.

Bibliography: Cochran, "Final Report on Women Pilot Program," 1945, *The Stars at Noon*, 1954, and USAF Oral History Interviews, 1960 and 1976; Douglas, *United States Women in Aviation*, 1990; Keil, "Those Magnificent Women in Their Flying Machines," 1977; Merryman, *Clipped Wings*, 1998; Pennington, "Women and Military Aviation in the Second World War," 2000.

—Reina Pennington

WAVES (WOMEN ACCEPTED FOR VOLUNTARY EMERGENCY SERVICE). United States, Second World War (1942–1948).

WAVES was the acronym adopted to describe the women of the United States Naval Reserve. The WAVES was authorized by Public Law 689 (30 July 1942) and was created to augment the naval war effort by allowing women to serve in numerous support and technical roles. The first director was **Mildred McAfee.**

The creation of the WAVES was not unprecedented in the naval service. A Women's Naval Reserve had been created during the First World War, but that organization was much smaller and was quickly disbanded at the end of the war. Between the world wars the only women to serve in the navy were members of the Navy Nurse Corps. The principal difference between the old First World War Women's Naval Reserve and the Nurse Corps was that nurses were restricted to the medical field. Also, nurses were commissioned officers, while the WNR consisted of enlisted personnel.

The Second World War WAVES consisted of both officers and enlisted women. The WAVES and the Nurse Corps maintained separate administrative organizations throughout the war. Officers in the WAVES were initially trained at Smith and Mount Holyoke Colleges in Massachusetts; enlisted

Eleanor Roosevelt visits Smith College to review the Women Accepted for Volunteer Emergency Service (WAVES) program. (Bettmann/CORBIS)

women were trained at Oklahoma A&M, Indiana University, and the University of Wisconsin. Additional training locations were added as the ranks of the WAVES grew dramatically. The first class of 119 female officers graduated in September 1942; by the end of the war there were 8,000 officers and 76,000 enlisted women in the WAVES.

The WAVES was the first step in the integration of women into the regular establishment of the United States Navy. Unlike the Women's Auxiliary Army Corps (WAAC), the WAVES was not an auxiliary; WAVES members had military status in the navy reserve from their inception (the WAAC only achieved this in late 1943 when it became the **WAC**; the **WASP** never gained military status).

Originally, WAVES members, unlike nurses, were forbidden under public law to serve overseas. That law was amended on 27 September 1944, primarily because women were needed overseas as radio communicators. WAVES members served in dozens of locations and assignments after the change in the legal code. Unlike the WNR at the end of the first World War, the WAVES was not disbanded with the arrival of peace. Its members continued to serve, in reduced numbers, until integration into the regular establishment of the United States Navy with the Women's Armed Services Integration Act in 1948.

Bibliography: Alsmeyer, *The Way of the WAVES*, 1981, and *Old WAVES Tales*, 1982; Hancock, *Lady in the Navy*, 1972; Johnson, *Making Waves*, 1986; Weatherford, *American Women and World War II*, 1990; Willenz, *Women Veterans*, 1983.

—Patrick J. O'Connor

WILLIAMS, CATHAY (born 1844?, Independence, Missouri; died 1892–1900?), also known as William Cathay or Cathey. Private, 38th United States Infantry Regiment. Cook, United States, Indian Wars.

Cathay Williams is the first documented African American woman to serve in the United States Army following the **American Civil War**. Since women were barred from military service, she enlisted at St. Louis in November 1866 in male disguise as "William Cathay." She left no record of her life prior to enlistment; thus her reasons for volunteering under a male alias are speculative. Even her birth date cannot be confirmed and could fall between 1844 and 1850.

After Williams passed a cursory medical examination, she was assigned to the 38th United States Infantry Regiment, one of four all-black regiments under white officers organized after the war. Williams's unit traveled extensively throughout the West on long road marches, one covering 536 miles. From February 1867 to January 1868 Williams's company was stationed at various locations including Missouri, Kansas, and New Mexico. There is no record that her company fought Native American warriors. Williams spent much of her military career on sick call for various ailments; a review of her complaints suggests that she may have suffered from diabetes. Though she was treated at four different hospitals, her disguise was never uncovered by army doctors—a telling fact about medical care of the time and/or the sort of treatment given to black soldiers.

On 14 October 1868 Williams received a medical discharge from the army, following which she resumed her identity as a woman. Still sick and unable to perform manual labor (the only type of work available to a black woman in that period), Williams filed for an invalid pension in June 1891. Although she presented herself as a woman to army inspectors, the Pension Bureau rejected her claim on the grounds that her disability predated her enlistment. Shortly afterwards she died in anonymity. If she had not filed for a pension and revealed her identity, her service as "William Cathay" would have remained a secret, and anyone who had known Cathay would have regarded "him" as just another poor black soldier. What makes Williams interesting historically is her two-year stint in the United States Army in a disguise that was never discovered—raising the question of whether other women, white or black, were similarly successful.

Bibliography: Blanton, "Cathay Williams, Black Woman Soldier, 1866–1868," 1992.

—Robert J. Zalimas, Jr.

WOMAN CHIEF (born ?; died 1854). Warrior, Crow Nation.

In 1854 a Crow warrior purposefully rode into a village of hereditary Crow enemies, the Gros Ventres. It was a pilgrimage to find family, for the warrior was actually a Gros Ventres native who had been captured by the Crows at age ten. Decades of intertribal war had conditioned the response of the Gros Ventres, despite a three-year peace between the two tribes, and the warrior was killed. Although such killings were not abnormal in and of themselves, this one was: Woman Chief, one of the most revered Crow warriors that ever lived, was dead.

Woman Chief displayed a love and affinity for warriors' ways soon after her capture, eventually becoming an expert rider, shot, and hunter. She became a regular member and occasional leader of Crow raiding and war parties against other Plains tribes. On one raid against a Blackfoot village she personally captured more than seventy horses and took two scalps. Any warrior could decide to lead a raid for horses or other booty, but revenge raids were usually a corporate decision. No warrior was bound to go on any raid. Some horse raids consisted of one or two "full" warriors, with the remainder made up of those anxious to earn their title as warrior. Whenever Woman Chief declared a raid, there was never a lack of participants.

Her original name is lost to history, but the event after which she was called Woman Chief is still recalled by Crow tribal historians. An encounter with Blackfoot raiders led to a standoff. When none of the male Crow warriors with her would answer the Blackfoot challenge, she rode out alone. As the five Blackfoot attacked, she killed one with her gun, wounded two others with arrows, and chased the remaining two away. Woman Chief was thereafter accorded full rights and privileges as a Crow warrior. She even "married" four women to run her lodge. At tribal functions she could tell more "warrior stories" than most of the men.

Woman Chief's story was recorded by Edwin Thompson Denig, whom she met at Fort Union around 1842. They maintained an acquaintance until her death more than a decade later, and she gave him a scalp as a souvenir. She also met artist Rudolph Kurz in 1851, as noted in his journal. When she was killed by the Gros Ventres, Woman Chief was one of the most renowned Crow warriors. Her memory is kept alive in the Crow oral tradition.

Bibliography: Albers and Medicine, *The Hidden Half*, 1983; Denig, *Five Indian Tribes*, 1961; Ewers, "Deadlier than the Male," 1965; Kurz, *Journals of Rudolph Friederich Kurz*, 1937; Mathes, "Native American Women," 1982.

—Rodney G. Thomas

WOMEN MARINES. United States Marine Corps. 1918–present.

Women first entered the ranks of the United States Marine Corps during the First World War when the secretary of the navy authorized the enlistment of women reservists on 12 August 1918. During the war 277 women marines served in the enlisted ranks; the highest rank held was sergeant. Nicknamed "marinettes," almost all served in clerical positions in Washington, D.C., or Quantico, Virginia. Women's enlistment was considered a short-term emergency initiative, and their service was terminated at the end of the war.

During the Second World War the Marine Corps was the last of the American military services to form a women's reserve organization. This was due in large part to the resistance of the commandant of the Marine Corps, General Thomas Holcomb. General Holcomb was overruled by the ever-increasing personnel requirements of the war, as well as by the Roosevelt administration. Despite his initial hesitation, General Holcomb adamantly refused to give the new women's organization a nickname like **WAVES** or **SPAR**. He insisted that female marines be called marines and that they receive rigorous training. Women were allowed to serve as commissioned officers for the first time in the Second World War.

The official birthday of the Marine Corps Women's Reserve is 13 February 1943. Colonel **Ruth Cheney Streeter** served as the first director and principal recruiter for the organization. Officers were trained at Mount Holyoke College, Massachusetts, and enlisted personnel were trained at Hunter College, Bronx, New York. After completing Mount Holyoke or Hunter, women marines then spent six weeks of additional training at Camp Lejeune, North Carolina. Women marines were the only American military women of the Second World War to receive combat training during boot camp. Women marines served at all major stateside bases.

According to Colonel George H. Bristol, director of the Marine Corps Martial Arts Program, although the only female in the class, Sergeant Tarra R. Gundrum, motor transport operator, Headquarters Battalion, 3rd Marine Division, is one of the most capable students in the Marine Corps Martial Arts Instructor Trainer Course. April 2002. (U.S. Marine Corps)

In the first eight weeks of its existence there were 2,495 enlistees for the Women's Reserve. Within a year there were 800 officers and 14,000 enlisted women. The members of the Women's Reserve served in a variety of administrative, mechanical, and aviation-maintenance occupations. Their service was considered a huge success, yet the Marine Corps planned to disband the Women's Reserve by 1 September 1946. A major change came in August 1946 when the commandant of the Marine Corps authorized 100 women reservists to remain on active duty at Headquarters, Marine Corps, Washington, D.C.

The Marine Corps Women's Reserve was never disbanded, and in 1948 women were integrated into the corps as they were into the other services. Women marines served during the conflicts in Korea, Vietnam, the Cold War, and the Gulf War in an increasing array of military occupational specialties. In 1977 the office of the director of women marines was officially disbanded, and women were administratively integrated into the Marine Corps establishment.

Bibliography: Hewitt, *Women Marines in World War I*, 1974; Holm, *Women in the Military*, 1992; Soderbergh, *Women Marines: The World War II Era*, 1992, and *Women Marines in the Korean War Era*, 1994; Streeter, "History of the Marine Corps Women's Reserve: A Critical Analysis of Its Development and Operation, 1943–1945," 1945; Stremlow, *A History of the Women Marines*, 1986, and *Free a Marine to Fight*, 1994.

—Patrick J. O'Connor

WOMEN'S BATTALIONS OF DEATH. Organized in Russia during the summer and fall of 1917, First World War.

Women's military units in Russia were first given life in the spring of 1917 under the auspices of the Provisional Government. In an atmosphere of revived dedication to the war effort after the February Revolution, numerous women pressed the government and the Ministry of War to allow them greater participation in the activities of war, including combat. Several petitioners advanced the idea of organizing all-female military units. In late May 1917 the minister of war, Aleksandr Kerensky, gave his permission for the formation of such a unit. He instructed **Mariia Bochkareva,** a three-year veteran of the war and junior noncommissioned officer, to begin recruiting for the First Russian Women's Battalion of Death in Petrograd, with the aid of the staff of the headquarters of the Petrograd Military District. She enlisted, organized, and trained nearly 300 women during the month of June. The women were supplied with barracks, uniforms, weapons, appropriate equipment, and male military instructors. On their sleeves all members wore the special insignia of the death battalion, red and black chevrons and skull-and-crossbones emblems.

Recognizing the propaganda value and reluctant to refuse the services of any citizen, Kerensky and the Provisional Government approved the organization of further combat units composed of women volunteers in early June 1917. The formation of such units was to be overseen by the Main Directorate of the General Staff. Women volunteers were to be designated for three types of military service: combat, communications, and medical aid. In addition to the one already established by Mariia Bochkareva, two all-female infantry battalions were initially formed, one in Petrograd and one in Moscow. They were to comprise between 1,000 and 1,400 members and be allocated all necessary military subunits, including machine-gun, communications, reconnaissance, and sapper detachments. In addition, four separate communications detachments were to be organized, two in Moscow and two in Petrograd.

Throughout the summer of 1917 the women's military movement continued to grow, and a number of nongovernmentally sanctioned female units were created. Petitions from women requesting permission to join the active army continued to flow into the War Ministry. In an attempt to control these unwieldy efforts and to address popular demand, the government resolved to expand the number of women's military formations. In mid-July the Kuban Women's Shock Battalion was created from a preexisting grassroots formation of Kuban women in Ekaterinodar. Similarly, the authorities decided to create seven additional communications units, five in Kiev and two in Saratov, where women's military units had already been organized through private initiative. These developments did not, however, end the impromptu organization of private women's units. The central administration found that such efforts could not be brought under complete control. The uncertain and unmanageable nature of these independent formations made the task of formulating a consistent policy regarding the women's military movement virtually impossible. Moreover, the women's units were not given adequate attention and assistance from the military administration, which was suffering from a short-age of resources and which remained undecided about the viability of the entire experiment.

As a result of these problems, by August 1917 there was a growing incli-nation in the military establishment to discontinue the organization of women volunteers for combat purposes. Increasingly, the military authorities were moving toward a position that held that the problems caused by the women's units were greater than the advantages they might offer. They found it diffi-cult, therefore, to justify the assignment of badly needed resources to unreli-able forces. They concluded that the significance of the women's military movement had been "strongly exaggerated by the press" and by individual women and organizations who had put pressure on the government. Con-vinced that the time had already passed when the women's military forma-tions could have had a positive impact, they doubted the value of the continued existence of such units.

Of the fourteen units originally designated by the Provisional Government, only one, Bochkareva's First Russian Women's Battalion of Death, is reported to have participated in combat at the front. They fought in an attack on German positions at Smorgon, near the Vilna-Dvinsk highway. The women led the charge when their male compatriots hesitated, managing to take the first two lines of German trenches. Without reinforcements, and with a num-ber of the male soldiers reputedly engaged in drinking the stores of alcohol left by the fleeing enemy, the Battalion of Death was forced to return to its position. Its members had captured more than 200 German prisoners, though, and had undeniably demonstrated their combat ability. Regimental and di-visional commanders were highly impressed with the women's performance, but this was not enough to convince higher military authorities to sustain the movement. Moreover, male soldiers expressed hostility toward their female counterparts. While some degree of chauvinism and wounded male pride was involved, the men's animosity was primarily directed at the prowar stance of the female soldiers. The women were steadfast in their belief that the war must be continued until the Germans were driven from Russian soil, but by this time most of the men had lost all desire to continue the fighting and desperately wanted peace. When the Bolsheviks seized Petrograd on 25 Oc-tober 1917, Bochkareva's unit was still at the front, but the antagonism with which the majority of male soldiers regarded the women had grown so hostile and violent that the commander realized that she had no other alternative but to disband the battalion.

Approximately 500 members of the Moscow Women's Battalion of Death requested dispatch to the front just prior to the official disbanding of the battalion in October 1917. Without the General Staff's knowledge, they were sent to various positions along the Romanian, Southwestern, and Western Fronts, but there is no evidence that these women saw combat action.

The First Petrograd Women's Battalion also took part in fighting, but not at the front. In the weeks preceding the October Revolution the unit was in camp outside Petrograd. The women had completed their training and were awaiting orders to be sent to the front. On October 24 the male commander of the battalion received an order for the women to take up positions on the square in front of the Winter Palace and defend the Provisional Government from attack. As their goal was to fight Russia's external enemies, these female soldiers had no desire to become embroiled in the political struggle. Only a subdivision of the Second Company, consisting of 137 women, was left on the square for the purpose of assisting in the delivery of gasoline. Despite their aversion to political struggle, these women did their best to defend the palace, and it was this event that has given fame, or perhaps infamy, to the Russian woman soldier. In the face of the overwhelming difficulties, they were defeated and captured. The Soviet Military Revolutionary Committee ordered the official dissolution of the battalion on 21 November 1917. The final decree ordering any remaining women's military unit to disband was issued on 30 November.

Bibliography: Abraham, "Mariia L. Bochkareva and the Russian Amazons of 1917," 1992; Bocharnikova, "Boi v zimnem dvortse," 1962; Botchkareva, *Yashka*, 1919; Russian State Military-Historical Archives; Senin, "Zhenskie batal'ony," 1987.

—Laurie Stoff

Recruiting poster for the Women's Land Army. (Library of Congress)

WOMEN'S LAND ARMY (1917–1919 and 1939–1950). British women's corps. Agricultural work, Great Britain, First and Second World Wars.

The Women's Land Army (WLA) grew out of the desperate need for labor on British farms during the last years of the First World War. It was formed by the Women's Branch of the Ministry of Agriculture in 1917. Even with the shortages, farmers had to be convinced that women could do the work; at the WLA's peak strength, 23,000 women showed that they could. In addition to various agricultural forms of work, the WLA had a forestry and forage section.

Preparation for creating a new WLA began in May 1938, and it was officially inaugurated with government approval on 1 July 1939. It gained independence from the Ministry of Agriculture in May 1941, but at the cost of a loss of support from many in the government. The WLA put more than 70,000 women in nontraditional agricultural occupations, releasing men for other war services. It became so important to British agriculture that it was not disbanded until 1950.

Bibliography: Mant, *All Muck, No Medals,* 1994; Sackville-West, *The Women's Land Army,* 1944; Twinch, *Women on the Land,* 1990.

—C.H.N. Hull

WOMEN'S LEGION (1915–1917, November 1933–May 1936) and **EMERGENCY SERVICE** (October 1936–February 1939). British volunteer women's corps. Various support services for the army, 1915–1930s.

The first Women's Legion was created by Marchioness Edith Helen Londonderry (1879–1959), a prominent socialite with political connections. A voluntary organization, it supplied the army with about 2,000 cooks from August 1915 and about 2,000 drivers from February 1916. The success of the Women's Legion led to the creation of the **WAAC/QMAAC,** which assimilated the Women's Legion in September 1917.

The Women's Legion was reborn in late 1933 when Lady Londonderry, with the support of prominent women veterans, sought to create a private umbrella organization that would train and organize women for the three services and the Home Office. While the War Office and Royal Air Force (RAF) welcomed the proposal, the Committee of Imperial Defence did not see the need for a peacetime women's reserve, fearing the political consequences of "militarizing" women. Subsequently the Women's Legion collapsed.

Emergency Service was an officer-training organization that grew out of the remains of the Women's Legion. It trained 400 suitable women with minimal War Office assistance. Emergency Service was incorporated into the **ATS** (Auxiliary Territorial Service) when the latter was created in September 1938 as the officer-training cadre. Graduates of the Emergency Service provided a large proportion of the early officers of the ATS, and its president, Dame **Helen Gwynne-Vaughan,** became the ATS's first director.

> The following lines about military women and morality were spoken by "Tosh," a fictional British ambulance driver in the First World War, based on the author's experience:
>
> Immorality, what a chance! doesn't it make you sick? Slack as much as you can, drive your bus as cruelly as you like, crash your gears to hell, muck your engine, it's in the mechanic's hands half its time, jolt the guts out of your wounded, shirk as much as you can without actively coming up against the powers-that-be—and you won't be sent home. But one hint of immorality and back you go to England in disgrace as fast as the packet can take you. As if morality mattered two hoots when it comes to convoying wounded men. Personally, if I were choosing women to drive heavy ambulances their moral characters wouldn't worry me. It would be "are you a first-class driver?" not "Are you a first-class virgin?"
>
> —Helen Zenna Smith, *Not So Quiet . . . : Stepdaughters of War,* reprint ed. (New York: Feminist Press, 1989), 126.

Bibliography: Bidwell, *The Women's Royal Army Corps,* 1977; Gwynne-Vaughan, *Service with the Army,* 1942; Izzard, *A Heroine in Her Time,* 1969; Terry, *Women in Khaki,* 1988; Thomas, "Women in the Military," 1978.

—C.H.N. Hull

WOMEN'S MILITARY CONGRESS. 1–4 August 1917, Petrograd, Russia. First World War.

The Women's Military Congress was convened on 1 August 1917 at the Nikolaevskii Engineering School in Petrograd as a gathering of representatives from various **Women's Military Unions** and quasi-military unions and associations from across Russia. Its goal was to coordinate the activities of the disparate voluntary associations of women who sought to contribute to the war effort by offering their services in a variety of activities, including direct combat participation. Olga Nechaeva, the head of the Commission on Women's Labor Service of the Russian army, chaired the congress.

Because large numbers of women were trying to make their way to the front in an unorganized way from all parts of the country, the congress tried to determine the numbers of such women and the capacity in which they were serving. Attendees lauded the efforts of those women who had already participated in the fighting. The "little grandmother of revolution," Ekaterina Breshko-Breshkovskaia, commended the women and encouraged them to continue their activities in defense of Russia. The congress closed on 4 August 1917 after adopting a resolution to begin widespread recruitment of women for labor in the military sphere, including medical and combat service. The delegates also called on the government to grant female volunteers in the war effort the same rights as male volunteers and conscripted soldiers.

Bibliography: Stites, *The Women's Liberation Movement in Russia*, 1978; "Zhenskii Voennyi Sezd," *Rech'* 2, 3, and 6 August 1917.

—Laurie Stoff

WOMEN'S MILITARY UNIONS. Established in Russia during the period between the February and October Revolutions in 1917.

After the February Revolution Russian women hoping to aid their "newly freed" country founded a number of military and quasi-military organizations. These unions were established all over the country, in cities from Ekaterinodar to Perm, as voluntary associations of women who wanted to do more for the war effort than was possible through traditional female activities limited to the home front. To achieve this goal, these groups worked to create separate female military units that were intended for participation in combat at the front. They also established women's labor militias, ambulance detachments, and women's medical units.

The most important of these unions were the Petrograd Women's Military Union and the All-Russian Women's Union to Aid the Motherland, headquartered in Moscow. They were enlisted by the General Staff of the Russian army to assist in the process of organizing women for military activities. The Organizational Committee of the Petrograd Women's Military Union was made responsible for helping with the formation of the First Petrograd **Women's Battalion of Death,** organized in the summer of 1917. The union was headed by E.I. Malison and included prominent women such as Olga Kerenskaia (wife of the minister-president of the Provisional Government, Aleksandr Kerensky) and N.V. Brusilova (wife of the commander in chief of the Russian army, Aleksei Brusilov). In Moscow the formation of the Second Moscow Women's Battalion of Death was guided by the efforts of the All-Russian Women's Union, led by M. Rychkova and a governing board that included some of the most prominent women in the city. It was designed to unite "the women of Russia who stand for the interests of the [Provisional] government . . . independent of nationality, class, and party differences with the goal of rendering active aid to the motherland and the battle with German militarism, for freedom, honor, and existence itself."

Bibliography: Russian State Military-Historical Archives; Stites, *The Women's Liberation Movement in Russia*, 1978.

—Laurie Stoff

WRIGHT, PRUDENCE CUMINGS (born 26 November 1740, Hollis, New Hampshire; died 2 December 1824, Pepperell, Massachusetts). Commander, women's militia company. United States, Revolutionary War.

When the town of Pepperell, Massachusetts, twenty miles northwest of Concord, received the alarm in the early hours of 19 April 1775 that British regulars were on the march, local minutemen swiftly mobilized and headed out to engage the enemy, while patriot women acted to secure the area against Tory spies. The women held a town meeting in Pepperell, formed a militia company of thirty to forty women from neighboring towns, and elected Prudence Wright, a thirty-four-year-old mother of seven, as their captain. Wright named Sarah Hartwell Shattuck of Groton as her lieutenant and ordered the company to patrol the roads in and out of town. Wright posted a guard at the local bridge over the Nashua River, which any Tory messenger coming from the north would have to cross.

Wright and her guard, dressed in men's clothing and armed with muskets and makeshift weapons, apprehended Captain Leonard Whiting of Hollis, New Hampshire, a noted Loyalist who was carrying dispatches from British Canada, as he approached the bridge on horseback. They forced him to dismount, searched him, and discovered papers hidden in his boot. Under Wright's command the women held Whiting prisoner overnight in a Pepperell tavern, then marched him to Groton, where he was taken into custody and his papers forwarded to the committee of safety.

Wright and her husband David, a prominent townsman, were ardent Whigs and had even named two of their children to honor the patriot cause: Wilkes, who was six years old when his mother became a militia captain, and his brother Liberty, who had died an infant just five weeks before. Two of Wright's own brothers, Thomas and Samuel Cumings of New Hampshire, were Tory sympathizers. According to family legend, Captain Whiting had a

Loyalist companion with him on the day of his capture: Thomas Cumings, who turned back at the sight of his sister in arms at the Pepperell bridge.

Bibliography: De Pauw, "Women in Combat," 1980; Fischer, *Paul Revere's Ride*, 1994; Shattuck, *The Story of Jewett's Bridge*, 1912.

—Donna DeFabio Curtin

WULFBALD, (UNNAMED) WIDOW OF (fl. late tenth century, England). Fought to retain possession of an estate in Kent, ca. 990.

The unnamed widow of Wulfbald is the only Anglo-Saxon woman whose active participation in armed conflict is beyond reasonable doubt. When the cousin of her late husband appropriated her property, she personally led an armed party and killed the cousin and more than a dozen others. The charter from the reign of Aethelred II in which Wulfbald's widow figures (S877) illustrates the vulnerability of widows to the forcible appropriation of their marital inheritance. So far as the record enables us to judge, Wulfbald's wife had no legal claim to the land she fought for, and her victory was short-lived.

The charter relates that when Wulfbald's own father died, he had seized all the moveable property of his stepmother, then subsequently seized an estate at Brabourne held by one of his kinsmen. Notwithstanding a series of royal writs and a council resolution declaring Wulfbald's lands and life forfeit to the king, Wulfbald died unpunished and still in possession of the stolen property. Wulfbald's successful flouting of royal authority implies possession of powerful backing.

Wulfbald's own death then prompted his cousin Eadmaer to occupy the Brabourne estate. According to the charter, Wulfbald's widow went to Brabourne with her *cild* (child) and slew Eadmaer and fifteen of his companions. The number of fatalities attributed to Wulfbald's widow (even assuming that her "child" was old enough to help) suggests that Wulfbald's widow commanded a band of armed followers. Unlike Wulfbald, however, she was unable to maintain possession; by some unspecified means the king ultimately gained control of all of the lands formerly held by Wulfbald. The fate of his widow remains unknown, though her determination to fight for her family inheritance is clear.

Bibliography: Robertson, A.J., ed. and trans., *Anglo-Saxon Charters*, 2nd ed. (Cambridge: 1956), no. 63.

—Stephanie Hollis

X

XAINTRAILLES, MARIE-HENRIETTE HEINIKEN (born ?, Berlin; died 1818). Unofficial aide-de-camp and soldier, French revolutionary and Napoleonic armies, 1793–1801.

Marie-Henriette Heiniken, Prussian by birth, joined Lauthier de Xaintrailles in 1791 as his common-law wife and in 1792 followed her husband to the Sixth Battalion of Light Infantry in the Army of the Rhine. After Xaintrailles's promotion to general, Madame Xaintrailles (as she always called herself) began service with him as an unofficial aide-de-camp. Assisting wounded soldiers on the battlefield, carrying dispatches while narrowly escaping the enemy, and assisting in the capture of Prussian artillery, she built a reputation for her courage, compassion, and willingness to carry out any tasks that befell her.

After Madame Xaintrailles was expelled from military service in 1793 according to French law (see **French Revolution and Napoleonic Era, women soldiers in**), she rejoined the French military in 1795, allegedly with the knowledge of former Minister of War and member of the Directory government Lazare Carnot. She remained with the armies even after her separation from her husband in 1798 and served as an aide-de-camp to General Menou during the Egyptian Campaign. Madame Xaintrailles was seriously wounded in 1799 in a fall from horseback, requiring the removal of her left breast and underlying bone and tissue. She retired from the military in 1801, but only obtained a pension in 1810.

In an interesting letter to Napoleon I in 1804 pleading for either retirement pay or continued employment in the military, Madame Xaintrailles chronicled the deeds of her military career that merited note. What brought her the greatest consternation was her invisibility to government officials because of her sex. In a particularly strident section of the three-page petition (Service historique de l'Armée at Vincennes), Madame Xaintrailles explained, "Sire, it was not, in any manner of speaking, as a woman that I went to war; I made war as a soldier."

Napoleonic clerks and the clerks of Louis XVIII, whom Madame Xaintrailles petitioned again in 1815, frequently questioned her service record because she lacked an official military dossier. While references attested to some of her exploits, it was common for generals' wives to accompany their husbands on campaign; this tended to lessen the credibility of her requests, since it was assumed that she was just another such wife. Ultimately her settlement of 2,400 livres in compensation was confirmation of her military record. The size of this pension and its distribution from the Grand Maréchal du Palais and Ministre de la Police générale make the pension most unusual for a woman of this period.

Bibliography: Brice, *La femme et les armées*, n.d.; Dossier XR49, "Xaintrailles," Service historique de l'Armée, Vincennes, France; Hennet, Léon, "Madame Xaintrailles, chef d'escadron, aide de camp," extract from *Carnet de la Sabretache*, 1907 (Paris: n.d.).

—S.P. Conner

XI, first name unknown (fl. 696, China). Mistress of Loyalty and Integrity. Commander of a self-organized defensive troop during the Tang dynasty (618–907).

Xi's husband, Zou Baoying, was regional inspector of Ping Prefecture (now Lulong of Hebei Province), which a Qidan (Kitan Tartar) force attacked in 696–697. Zou Baoying led a counterattack in pursuit of the enemy, leaving the prefecture with little defense capability.

More Qidan came and besieged the prefecture. Xi mustered many women from the prefecture and, along with the domestic servants, formed a troop. They held out for many days, and finally the encircling Qidan retreated. Xi became well known to the officials and was given the title of Mistress of Loyalty and Integrity for her success in defending the prefecture.

Bibliography: Liu Xu, *Jiu Tang shu*, 1975; Ou-yang Xiu, *Xin Tang shu*, 1975.

—Sherry J. Mou

XIAN, first name unknown (born early sixth century; died ca. 601, Gaoliang, now Yangjiang of Guangdong Province, China). Some sources give Xian's family name as Xi. Grand Mistress of Gaoliang, Commandery Mistress of Songkang, and Mistress of Qiaoguo. Military commander of the Nanyue during the Liang (502–557), Chen (557–589), and Sui (581–618) dynasties.

Xian was influential in political and military affairs among the southern tribes in China during the second half of the sixth century. She came from a tribal chief's family in southern China and was married to a local official. She maintained peace between the tribal peoples and the central court in China for half a century.

Xian's family had ruled over 100,000 families in Nanyue (southern China) for generations. Even when she was young, she helped her parents keep peace among their subordinates and troops. Her brother Xian Ting, a regional inspector of the Liang dynasty (502–557), often used his military strength to assault neighboring prefectures. Xian reproved him and eventually placated many tribes.

At the beginning of the Datong years (535–546) Feng Rong, the regional inspector of Luozhou (now Huaxian), heard about Xian and asked to betroth her to his son Feng Bao, Grand Protector of Gaoliang. Since the Fengs were not originally from the area, their leadership was often challenged by the locals. After Feng Bao married Xian, she struck deals with her clan to settle how the people would be ruled. She also accompanied Feng Bao during sentencing and negotiation. If local chieftains broke the law, even if they were from her clan, she would not relent in meting out punishment. From then on, government and edicts became regulated, and people would not disobey the laws.

In 548 a military commander of the Liang dynasty, Hou Jing (died 552), rebelled against Emperor Wu (r. 502–549), and the central government disintegrated, leading to tribal-level conflict. When Feng Bao was invited by one regional inspector, Li Qianshi, for consultation, Xian advised Feng Bao not to go, as she believed that he intended to take Feng Bao hostage so he could take over Feng Bao's army. Instead, she volunteered to visit Li Qianshi in his place. She chose more than a thousand people to go with her and notified Li in advance that they were coming with presents. Li sent people to inspect the carriers and confirmed that they were indeed carrying gifts; pleased with the submissive gesture, he took no further precautions. As soon as Xian's party entered the barricades, they attacked, and Li ran away. Xian joined forces with the Grand Protector of Gaoyao, Chen Baxian (503–559), and defeated Li Qianshi. She returned home and suggested that her husband cooperate with Chen Baxian. Although the general area continued to have wars for several years, the Gaoliang area was peaceful, owing to Xian's political skills. Her alliance with Chen Baxian paid off very well when he finally established the Chen dynasty (557–589) in 557.

After Feng Bao died in 558, there was turmoil. Xian gathered her troops and made a coalition with other regional powers, bringing peace to the entire vicinity. She was instrumental in the Chen dynasty's unifying of the Lingnan area. She sent her son Feng Pu to lead all the chieftains to pay their respects to Chen Baxian, who was by then Emperor Wu (557–559), and in return Chen made him Grand Protector of Yangchun. Even after Chen Baxian died, Xian continued to pay loyalty to the Chen dynasty. In 569 Xian led many chieftains and sent troops to the border to quell a rebellion by the regional inspector of

Guangzhou, Ou-yang He. The Chen dynasty rewarded her for her support: she was given the title Grand Mistress of Gaoliang, a four-horse carriage, military band music, an official banner, and a staff and a team of honorary guards of the size appropriate for a regional inspector. Her son, Feng Pu, was also granted several titles.

During the reign of Zhide (583–586) Feng Pu died, and by 589 the Sui dynasty (581–618) ended the Chen dynasty. As a result, Lingnan was again in turmoil, except for a few prefectures under Xian's control. Thus the Zhuang, Li, and several other ethnic peoples worshiped her as the "Holy Mother," who protected the area and its people.

Emperor Wen (r. 581–604) sent the area commander in chief Wei Guang to pacify the area. Xu Deng, a Chen dynasty general, was resisting in Nankang, and Wei Guang dared not advance. Prince Jin (ca. 569–618) asked the last emperor, Chen Shubao (553–604), to let Xian know that the Chen dynasty had ended and that she should surrender. The letter was accompanied with a military tally and a rhinoceros horn from Funan that Xian had earlier presented to the throne. When Xian received the letter, she learned that the Chen dynasty was indeed over, so she summoned several thousand chieftains, cried for an entire day, and then sent her grandson Feng Hun to Guangzhou to welcome Wei Guang. Lingnan was peaceful again, and the Sui dynasty conferred upon Feng Hun the title of unequaled in honor and upon Xian, commandery mistress of Songkang.

In 590 a local chieftain of Fanyu (now Guangzhou) rebelled against the Sui dynasty, and many leaders of local tribes sent troops in support. Xian dispatched her grandson Feng Xuan to help Wei Guang, but he would not commit his troops to the Sui commander. Wei Guang was killed in the battles, and Xian was furious. She put Feng Xuan in the prefecture jail and sent another grandson, Feng Ang, who defeated the rebels.

Emperor Wen dispatched Pei Ju, gentleman of executive assistant, to Nanhai to coordinate military maneuvers in Lingnan. Xian put on the military regalia granted her by the imperial court, rode a tall horse, and, protected by an official brocade umbrella, led the cavalry that accompanied Pei Ju in supervising all the prefectures. All major local chieftains paid their respects and were granted titles and ranks by the Sui court. Peace again was restored to the Lingnan area.

Emperor Wen was amazed with the outcome. Xian was honored with the title mistress of Qiaoguo, with her own private secretariat, aides, and other subordinating officials. She was also given a seal and, with it, the power to dispatch troops of six prefectures in any emergency. Further, the emperor sent a decree praising her meritorious service and awarded her 5,000 pieces of brocade; the empress also sent her jewelry and a formal banquet gown. Xian put all these gifts in golden boxes and placed them in special storage, along with presents she received from the Liang and Chen courts. Every year during important festivals, she would take them out and display them in the courtyard to remind her children and grandchildren. She admonished them, stressing that it was all due to goodness of heart and loyalty that she was able to serve three dynasties and keep all these rewards, and that her posterity should continue such demeanor.

Xian died in the middle of the reign of Renshou (601–604), at the age of about eighty. After her death the court sent a thousand pieces of brocade as funeral offerings, and she received the posthumous title of Mistress Sincerity and Respect.

Bibliography: Chen Menglei, *Gujin tushu jicheng (Qin ding)*, 1993; Li Yanshou, *Bei shi*, 1974; Lin Tianwei, "Sui Qiaoguo furen shiji zhiyi ji qi xianghua yu yingxiang," *Journal of History and Philology* 43.2 (1971); Wei Zheng, *Sui shu* (Beijing: 1973); Wu Han, "Xian furen," *Chuntian ji* (Beijing: 1961).

—Sherry J. Mou

XOCHITL (ca. 1116 CE). Toltec queen.

Xochitl was seduced by the ruler Tecpancaltzin and bore his son Topiltzin, the ninth and last king of Tollan. As queen, she was said to have created a women's battalion and led it in battle until she was killed. Women's battalions were not unusual during indigenous times and can be equated to rulers sending in "reserve forces" as a last resort in a losing battle. Xochitl and her parents are considered the inventors of *pulque* (maguey wine).

Bibliography: Anton, Ferdinand, *La mujer en la America antigua* (Mexico City: 1975); Nash, "The Aztecs and the Ideology of Male Dominance," 1978; Sten, *The Mexican Codices*, 1972.

—Elizabeth Salas

Y

YAN, first name unknown (ca. 1230, Ninghua, now in Fujian Province, China), "Respectful Lady." Commander of self-organized militia groups during the Southern Song dynasty (1127–1279).

Yan built a rampart to defend her hometown from bandits and became the leader and military commander in the general area. Widowed very young, Yan decided to raise her son on her own instead of remarrying. During the reign of Shaoding (1228–1233) wandering bandits attacked Ninghua District. When the magistrate and his assistant ran away, Yan was the first to respond to an alliance with a neighboring district magistrate; she helped by sending fighters, fodder, and food. The bandits were enraged by their failure and gathered even more troops. The defenders could no longer withstand them, so Yan built a rampart by Huangniu Mountain.

Once several dozen bandits came seeking women, money, and clothes. Yan called up all her workers and said to them: "You people are clothed and fed by my family. The real meaning behind the bandits' demand for women is indeed me. For the sake of your mistress, you should try your best, and if you still can't win just kill me." She then gave her jewelry to the crowd, who gratefully expressed their determination to fight with all their might when the moment arrived.

Later, when the bandits came to attack, Yan beat the drums herself and asked her maids to beat the gongs to arouse her fighters' spirit. The bandits were again defeated. People nearby learned that they could rely on her, so they moved their families to Huangniu Mountain. Soon the refugee camp grew so big that many could not support themselves, but Yan always helped from her family provisions.

Subsequently she allied herself with the gentry of the neighboring villages, who had also built ramparts near Huangniu Mountain. Together they constructed five ramparts around the mountain so that they could flank the attackers. Furthermore, they chose some young, strong volunteers to be emergency messengers. The strategy saved the lives of tens of thousands of people in the vicinity.

When Cheng Hua, auxiliary academician of Baozhang Pavilion, sent Yan money and clothes, she gave them all away to her subordinates. Cheng Hua then rewarded the volunteers for their hard work and named the rampart after Yan's son, Wan'an. When the emperor heard about this, he conferred upon Yan the honorific title of Respectful Lady and awarded her with the hat and cape of a noblewoman. Her son was also given the title of Gentleman of Trust.

Bibliography: Chen Menglei, *Gujin tushu jicheng (Qin ding)*, 1993; Tuotuo et al., *Song shi*, 1977.

—Sherry J. Mou

YANG MIAOZHEN (died after 1231, China), also known as "Si niangzi" (the fourth lady) and "Gugu" (young aunt). Titles: Lady of Virtue; Branch Secretariat of Yidu. A leader and commander of a peasant rebel group during the Southern Song dynasty (1127–1279).

A shrewd and brave cavalry commander, Yang Miaozhen led, at one time, more than 10,000 troops against Jin, Mongol, and Song troops. During the first quarter of the thirteenth century China was in turmoil. The Jin dynasty (1115–1234) of the Jurchen in the northeast, the Mongols in the northwest, and the Song in the south were intertwined in constant warfare. Many self-defense militia groups formed, with no apparent allegiance to any one government. In the Shandong area many militias joined the Red Coat Army, one of whose most powerful leaders was Yang Miaozhen's elder brother Yang An'er (died 1215).

Yang Miaozhen was a daring fighter and very skillful at horseback riding and archery, and she was adulated as "Young Aunt" by Yang An'er's subordinates. After Yang An'er was killed in 1215 by Jin troops, Yang Miaozhen assumed leadership of the more than 10,000 fighters who remained and led them to fight around Moqi Mountain (now in Juxian, Shandong Province). Another militia group led by a Li Quan joined her group. They were impressed with each other, Yang Miaozhen soon married Li Quan, and they gave their allegiance to the Song government. Because their troops defeated the Jin in many battles, Li Quan was given the title of Grand Master of militant assistance. In 1219 he was promoted to regional inspector of Dazhou, and Yang Miaozhen was awarded the title of Lady of Virtue. For the next decade or so Li Quan received various offices, emoluments, and grain from the Song court.

In 1226 Li Quan was besieged by the Mongols for nearly a year; when rumors reported his death, another militia leader, Xia Quan, threatened the area where Yang Miaozhen remained. In early 1227, believing that Li Quan had died, Yang Miaozhen sent bribes to gain Xiao Quan's cooperation. Her message said, in part, "Now that the Li clan is extinguished, could the Xia clan exist alone? I beseech the General to consider [my proposal for cooperation] most seriously." Xia Quan agreed.

Yang Miaozhen made herself beautiful and welcomed Xiao Quan to inspect the camps, saying, "Others told me that Li Quan died. How can I, a woman, alone be on my own? I should like to serve the Defender-in-chief as my husband, and all my children, my treasure, my armory, and the granary belong to him. I beg you to accept this request without any further talk." Xia Quan was tempted, so they sat down and drank to the occasion. Afterwards, they went to bed as if nothing unusual had happened. Now that enemies had become allies, they worked together to get rid of other opponents. Later, upon return from battle, Xia Quan found that Yang Miaozhen would not let him enter Chucheng again, possibly because she had received news from her besieged husband, Li Quan.

But not long after, having been besieged well over a year and with no relief in sight, Li Quan surrendered to the Mongols. The Song court stopped sending emoluments and grain to the troops in Chuzhou, and many commanders blamed Yang Miaozhen. Hoping to regain the court's favor, they went to Yang's house and killed her brother-in-law and his wife, confusing her with Yang Miaozhen.

In the first month of 1231 Li Quan was killed by the Song, and his remaining troops followed Yang Miaozhen. The fighting continued for several months, with the Song troops gaining more ground. Yang Miaozhen devised a ruse intended to permit the honorable surrender of her forces while allowing her own escape. However, neither the Song nor the Jin courts trusted Yang Miaozhen's bandits when they asked to surrender. More bitter fighting ensued with the Song armies; suffering many losses in their retreat across the Huai River, Yang's toops lost more territory to both the Song and Jin. Eventually Yang Miaozhen led the remaining troops back to Shandong under the Mongols, and she was given the title of branch secretariat of Yidu. She employed many scholars and presided over the tribunal for the last few years of her life.

Bibliography: Rachewiltz, *In the Service of the Khan*, 1993; Shaomin, "Xin Yuan shi," 1959; Tuotuo et al., *Sung shi*, 1977.

—Sherry J. Mou

YARMŪK, WOMEN IN BATTLE OF (15–20 August 636). Arab women defenders.

Women played an important role in one of the most famous battles of the Arab-Byzantine conflict during the rise of Islam. In 636, four years after the death of Mohammed, the forces of the Byzantine emperor, Heraclius, met with and were defeated near the Yarmūk River in Syria by the Arab forces led by Khālid ibn al-Walīd. This battle was decisive for the Arabs, allowing them to secure their control over Damascus and the surrounding regions.

The sources state that the Arabs were significantly outnumbered. Early in the fighting the Byzantines made a menacing incursion into the Arabs' base camp. At this point the Arab women, who had been left in the camps to tend the wounded, played a critical role that turned the tide of the fight. Not only did they exhort the men to fight through both threats and shouts of encouragement, but they led by example, taking up arms themselves against the enemy. Among those recorded as fighting are Khawla bint Tha'laba, Umm Habība bint al'Ās, **Hind bint'Utba,** and Juwayriyya bint Abī Sufyān, who was also wounded. The Arabs rallied and defeated the Byzantine army, leading to the capture of provinces in Syria and Palestine and furthering Islamic expansion. Khawla bint Tha'laba continued her martial involvement; reportedly during the siege of Damascus she dressed herself as a man and went off to rescue her brother, who had been taken prisoner by the Byzantines.

Bibliography: Fred Donner, *The Early Islamic Conquests* (Princeton: 1981); E.J. Brill's *First Encyclopedia of Islam, 1913–1936* (Leiden: 1987); David Nicolle, *Yarmūk 636 AD* (London: 1994); al-Tabarī, *The History of al Tabarī* (New York: 1985).

—C.A. Hoffman

Z

ZAYNAB (died 1850, Zanjan), also known as Rustam-'Ali. Babi irregular fighter in the Babi urban revolt, Zanjan, Iran, 1850.

The Babis, a millenarian sect in mid-nineteenth-century Iran that later evolved into the modern Baha'i faith, were the followers of the Iranian prophet Sayyid 'Ali-Muhammad Shirazi, usually known as the Bab (1819–1850). After he announced his prophecy in 1844, his religion attracted bitter persecution by civil and religious authorities. In three places where there were significant concentrations of Babis, there was open fighting. The largest such conflict was in Zanjan, a small but strategic town in northwestern Iran. Here in 1850 a charismatic cleric known as Hujjat Zanjani led some 2,000 Babi fighters with their families in defense against an eight-month siege. The Babis, who carried out their defense with skill, energy, organization, and religious zeal, were aided by the incompetence and lack of enthusiasm of the government regular and irregular forces, eventually amounting to some 30,000 men. After eight months the Babi ranks had been reduced to fewer than a hundred fighters. When Hujjat was killed, the Babis surrendered, and most of the surviving men were executed. The women and children, after a brief informal imprisonment, were released.

Zaynab was one of two daughters of an elderly Zanjan Babi. When their father died, her sister married Hujjat and was killed by a shell near the end of the siege. Zaynab protested that the prohibition of women fighting in the holy war had been abrogated by the Bab's new revelation. Having no brother, she stated, she ought to have the right to fight on behalf of her family in the holy war (*jihad*). She was allowed to cut her hair, dress in man's clothing, and fight under the name of Rustam-'Ali. She is variously reported as having been in command of a platoon of nineteen men guarding a barricade or fighting independently where she was needed. She was killed during a sortie, having acquired a reputation among both the Babis and the besieging troops for dash and valor.

Despite rumors that the Babis had "a regiment of virgins," Zaynab was evidently atypical. The Babi women did play an important support role remarked on by most of the historians of the siege, but for the most part they did not fight. In the simultaneous siege of the Babis of Nayriz in southern Iran, women also took an active part, but again are not recorded as fighting.

Zaynab, whose story straddles folklore and history, is most important as a symbolic figure. The Bab had challenged the very legalistic Shi'ite Islam by proclaiming the abrogation of Islamic law and its replacement with a new system of religious law. Moreover, many Babis believed that they were in an interregnum in which no formal religious law applied. Since Islamic law enforced strict gender roles, the activities of individuals like Zaynab symbolized to the Babis and their Baha'i successors the liberating quality of the new revelation; to their Muslim opponents she personified the danger to the foundations of society posed by the new religion.

It is interesting that one of the Muslim clerics of Zanjan issued a ruling during the siege that Muslim women were obliged to participate in the *jihad* in Zanjan. There is no evidence that any did so.

Bibliography: 'Abd al-Ahad Zanjani, "Personal Reminiscences of the Babi Insurrection in Zanjan in 1850," 1897; Mirza Husayn Zanjani, "Tarikh-i Waqayi'-i Zanjan," Baha'i World Center MS 1632; Sipihr, *Nasikh al-Tawarikh: Dawra-yi Kamil-i Tarikh-i Qajariya* (Tehran: 1344/1965); Zarandi, *The Dawn-Breakers*, 1932.

—John Walbridge

ZENOBIA, SEPTIMIA (fl. third century), in her native Aramaic language known as Septimia Bathzabbai. Queen of Palmyra (modern Tadmor, Syria) during the period of its greatest military expansion, when she briefly ruled much of Syria, Arabia, Asia Minor, and Egypt. Defeated in battle and taken captive by the Roman emperor Aurelian in 272 CE. Date of death uncertain.

Zenobia's military successes had such an impact on the ancient world that they gave rise to many legendary tales in which she is portrayed as a great general, a fierce warrior, and a skilled hunter, with a passion for learning. The accounts also dwell, perhaps inevitably, upon her beauty and chastity. Little of this detail can be confirmed with any certainty from reliable historical sources, but her military achievements are unquestionable.

Zenobia was born in the mid-third century into one of the leading families of Palmyra, a wealthy oasis city located on the Roman side of the border with Persia. She married its greatest general, Septimius Odaenathus, and it may well have been due to him that she acquired her military experience and strategic training. After the infamous defeat and capture of the Roman emperor Valerian in 259–260 there was a power vacuum in Rome, and the eastern part of the empire was left dangerously vulnerable. Odaenathus seized the moment; he inflicted heavy losses on the retreating Persian forces and crushed the uprisings led by two local pretenders to the Roman imperial throne. As a consequence, he was entrusted by Rome with the command of all of the eastern Roman armies, and using these, plus his own Palmyrene troops and various Syrian levies, he reconquered the areas of Mesopotamia lost to the Persians and attacked deep into Persia itself. At least one chronicle notes that Zenobia accompanied him on these campaigns. The reign of Odaenathus came to an abrupt end with his murder, along with that of his eldest son and heir, the product of an earlier marriage, in 267.

The circumstances of Odaenathus's death are unclear. Some sources attribute it to a jealous cousin; others implicate Zenobia herself. What is certain is that Zenobia immediately assumed command of Odaenathus's military forces and took up the reins of civil power,

Queen Zenobia with servants (Ishtar and Tyche), funerary high relief, third century, from Palmyra, Syria. (The Art Archive/National Museum Damascus Syria/Dagli Orti)

although technically acting as regent for her own son Septimius Athenodorus or Vaballathus (Aramaic Wahballath), who was still in his minority, and that she at once set about extending Palmyra's power and influence. Odaenathus may have been content to be the loyal servant of the emperors in Rome, but Zenobia was not. She sought to exploit the lack of clear Roman authority in the East, not by leading a separatist movement but by appropriating that authority to herself, and so began a period of uneasy joint rule with the Western emperors.

Having secured the surrounding region of Syria, she appears to have won her first major victory in 268 when her Palmyrene forces destroyed a Roman army sent by the emperor Gallienus, under the command of Heraclianus, to reassert his control over the region. This strategic advantage was swiftly capitalized upon, for she then moved against the Roman province of Arabia, and in late 269 or early 270 her troops invaded and conquered Egypt. The motive for this may have been primarily economic, but she justified it by claiming descent from **Cleopatra** and the Ptolemaic rulers of Egypt, as various chronicles and an inscribed milestone bear witness. On the basis of the chronicles and a Palmyrene-led revolt following her later defeat, it appears that there was a significant section of the Egyptian population that supported her claim.

After the Egyptian campaign she extended her control north through Syria, taking the important center of Antioch, again with local support, and then overran Asia Minor as far as Ancyra (modern Ankara, Turkey). By 270 Zenobia was thus effectively ruler of the entire Eastern Roman Empire, and this situation appears to have been accepted, however reluctantly, by the new emperor in the West, Aurelian, for in 270 coins were minted with Aurelian's head on one side and that of Zenobia's son Wahballath on the other, although the all-important title Augustus (signifying absolute imperial power) was restricted to Aurelian. Even this concession was soon abandoned, for in 271 coins, legal documents, and inscriptions started to appear with Augustus placed after Wahballath's name. Even more significantly, coins were produced that bore Zenobia's portrait and the title Augusta and so acknowledged the true power broker in the East.

In 272, however, Aurelian, fresh from his military victories in Gaul and perhaps aggravated by Zenobia and Wahballath's assumption of the imperial title, turned his attention east. He marched down through Asia Minor with his army, encountering minimal resistance, until he finally reached Antioch in Syria. Here Zenobia was awaiting him to the east of the city near a town called Immae with a large army whose most significant element was the heavy cavalry for which the Palmyrenes were famed. Aurelian ordered his own cavalry to feign flight, pursued by the Palmyrenes, and when these latter were exhausted, the Romans turned and cut them down. Zenobia left a small detachment to fight a rearguard action and retreated with her army to Emesa, where they regrouped. This time the Palmyrene cavalry charge was so fierce that they appear to have destroyed much of the Roman cavalry, but in so doing they outstripped their foot soldiers and were consequently surrounded and cut down by the Roman infantry and auxiliaries. Once again Zenobia was forced to retreat, and this time she fell back upon Palmyra itself.

Palmyra was not a well-fortified city and clearly could not withstand a determined siege. In a desperate attempt to gain Persian reinforcements, Zenobia and a small escort made a run for the Persian border, but they were detected and captured. The demoralized citizens of Palmyra surrendered and were not badly treated. Another revolt later in 272, however, led to bloody suppression. So ended Zenobia's military career and the brief period of Palmyra's rule of the Eastern Roman Empire. Zenobia had resisted Roman domination more effectively than most, if only for two years; without her, Palmyra immediately faded as a power to be reckoned with in the East.

The fate of Zenobia herself is uncertain. The most famous and widely repeated story is that Zenobia was displayed to the citizens of Rome during Aurelian's triumphal march through the city, bedecked with jewels but bound with golden shackles and chains. Most sources claim that after this spectacle she married a wealthy Roman and retired to a villa in Tivoli, although others state that Zenobia died while being transported to Rome.

Bibliography: Browning, *Palmyra*, 1979; Dodgeon and Lieu, *The Roman Eastern Frontier and the Persian Wars*, 1991; Downey, "Aurelian's Victory over Zenobia at Immae, A.D. 272," 1950; Isaac, *The Limits of Empire*, 1992; Millar, *The Roman Near East, 31 BC–AD 337*, 1993; Stoneman, *Palmyra and Its Empire*, 1994.

—David G.K. Taylor

ZIMBABWE, WOMEN IN THE NATIONAL LIBERATION WAR (Chimurenga II, 1964–1980). Rhodesia/Zimbabwe.

When the decisive phase of the armed struggle for national independence in Rhodesia began in 1972, women's participation gradually increased, and by and by 1979 the Zimbabwe African National Union (ZANU) and the Zimbabwe African People's Union (ZAPU), the main nationalist political parties fighting for a democratic Zimbabwe, boasted one-third participation by women. Between 1975 and 1977 the Zimbabwe People's Army (ZIPA) or *Vashandi* (workers) movement established Wampoa College, which enforced a quota of one-third women, although there was a smaller percentage of women in its camps. It is estimated that 250,000 women were actively involved in this fight for majority rule. Women's military roles ranged from cooks to guerrilla fighters. The war ended in April 1980 when ZANU won the first democratic elections.

Directly challenging traditional roles, thousands of young women (mainly under age twenty-five) volunteered to join the armed struggle. They were trained in camps across the borders of Rhodesia, in Zambia, Botswana, Mozambique, and Tanzania, where they received political and military education. Women's participation in ZANU and ZAPU was supported by the Marxist-Leninist political philosophy of the nationalist movement. In the context of socialist transformation, women were seen as vital recruits—not just for practical reasons when male recruit numbers decreased, but because women's liberation was seen as fundamental to revolution. The actions of **Nehanda** in the first Chimurenga were invoked to encourage women to join the struggle. Most women ended up in noncombatant roles; women were initially considered incapable of being armed combatants by the leaders of ZANU and ZAPU. At the rear women filled organizational and practical roles as teachers, mechanics, drivers, cooks, and

> *Sri Lanka's rebels rely on female fighters.*
>
> Arasadithivu, Sri Lanka—
> . . . The women of the Liberation Tigers of Tamil Eelam—a rebel group waging a war for an independent homeland in this island nation—are emerging as the movement's most important weapon after thousands of men have died in battle.
> With vials of cyanide hanging from their necks, female Tigers are shooting their way into government bunkers and police stations. They are hacking to death men, women and babies. Female Tigers are wrapping their bodies with explosives and killing dozens in suicide attacks. . . .
> The Tigers' ranks were filled only with men in 1983, when the predominantly Hindu Tamil rebels started their struggle. Now, after 17 years of fighting and with more than 55,000 Sri Lankans killed, women make up a third of the fighting force, which some experts number at as many as 15,000 fighters.
>
> —Dexter Filkins, "In Sri Lanka, Dying to be Equals," *Los Angeles Times* 21 February 2000, home edition: Part A.

medical and administrative staff and also as commanders and political and military instructors. In 1973, when the first trained women emerged, they proved themselves to be capable of fighting. In the front lines women transported weapons, politicized the masses, and fought as guerrillas. A Women's Brigade was formed in ZANU and was involved in every sphere of the struggle; however, very few women were trained in the air force or artillery.

The war was mainly fought out in rural areas. Women played significant roles, maintaining the momentum of the struggle by providing food and shelter to the young male guerrillas (who trusted the women like mothers) and acting as *Chimbwidos* (lookouts, messengers, and carriers), transporting weapons and supplies. These women participated despite the threat of antiterrorist laws passed by the Ian Smith regime in Rhodesia, but the Rhodesian forces were less suspicious of women than of men.

Despite the socialist rhetoric of equality for women that was espoused during the struggle, most were involved in traditionally defined gender roles such as providing food, and in the training camps some women acted as semiwives or servants to male commanders—often not by choice. Even so, many women had high expectations of equality after independence, and were disappointed when women's emancipation did not follow national liberation.

As in many other revolutions, women in Zimbabwe made many sacrifices in the cause of independence. Much of the literature arguing for women's equality in Zimbabwe today cites women's equal participation with men in the liberation wars as evidence that they deserve equal treatment as citizens.

Bibliography: Batezat et al., "Women and Independence," 1988; Lapchick and Urdang, *The Struggle of Women in Southern Africa*, 1992; Lyons and Moore, *Written in the Revolutions*, 1995; Qunta, *Women in Southern Africa*, 1987; Staunton, *Mothers of the Revolution*, 1991; Stott, *Women and the Armed Struggle*, 1989.

—Tanya Lyons

ZRINYI, ILONA (born 1644; died 1703, Constantinople, Turkey). Defender, Austro-Turkish War.

Hungary in the seventeenth century was divided into Ottoman- and Habsburg-controlled spheres of influence, but there was no constitutional monarch, nor was constitutional law followed. The Habsburg Empire had based its claim for a constitutional presence in Hungary on the military action it engaged in when winning back parts of Hungary from the Turks.

The noble family names of Zrinyi and Rakoczi were in the forefront in pursuing unremitting opposition to both camps, as well as against other factions of the aristocracy eager to secure the Hungarian crown. Ilona Zrinyi's marriage to her first husband Ferenc Rakoczi I, the ruling prince of Transylvania (with whom she had a son, Ferenc Rakoczi II) was based on their families' common political aspirations against the Habsburgs.

The Zrinyi family had a long history of militant opposition to invaders. In 1566 Captain Miklos Zrinyi and his countess defended Szigetvar (Szigeth), a castle in West Hungary/Croatia, against Sultan Suleiman during his invasion of Austria. For weeks the Turks besieged the town and fortress; most of Zrinyi's troops were killed. The Turks broke into the castle, where the families of the soldiers waited. Countess Zrinyi

Undated portrait of Ilona Zrinyi. (Perry-Castañeda Library)

reportedly set alight the powder magazine in the fortress, committing suicide and taking hundreds (some say thousands) of the enemy along with her. Ilona Zrinyi was the great-granddaughter of Miklos Zrinyi.

When her first husband left her widowed, Ilona married Imre Thokoly, who against all odds and with unrealistic political expectations engaged in a political and military struggle to become king of Upper Hungary. He hoped to take advantage of the ongoing conflict between the two empires and to reestablish Hungarian independence. However, the Habsburg Empire used every means to put down all such activity.

Ilona Zrinyi came into prominence for organizing and conducting the defense of Thokoly's last stronghold, Munkacs Castle in northeast Hungary (Munkacsevo in Ukraine today), while her husband was occupied elsewhere. Beginning in 1686, first under General Caprara, and later under General Anton Caraffa, Habsburg military forces intermittently laid siege to the castle for nearly three years. Under Ilona Zrinyi's sole leadership the garrison resisted heavy shelling during this long siege, and both she and her son, Ferenc Rakoczi II, walked the ramparts every evening at great personal risk, in full view of the besiegers, to demonstrate their contempt and determination not to surrender.

During these politically hectic years Ilona Zrinyi at Munkacs Castle remained the sole source in Hungary offering resistance against Habsburg absolutism in order to achieve independence. Despite the provisions of the Diet of Pozsony in 1687, which recognized Habsburg claims to the Hungarian crown, Munkacs Castle did not capitulate until 1688. Ilona Zrinyi and her husband Imre Thokoly were exiled to Turkey. Ilona Zrinyi's son Ferenc Rakoczi II continued to fight for Hungarian freedom, inspired by the brave example of his mother.

Bibliography: Ember, Gyozo, *The History of Hungary* (Budapest: 1989); Farkas Emod, *Magyarorszag nagyasszonyai* (Budapest: 1911); Lelkes, Jozsef N., *A Munkacsi amazon* (Budapest: 1943).

—Antal Leisen

NUMBERED ENTRIES

46th *TAMAN'SKY* **GUARDS BOMBER AVIATION REGIMENT.** May 1942–May 1945 (disbanded 15 October 1945); founded in Engels, Soviet Union. Initially designated 588th Bomber Aviation Regiment. Flew U-2 biplanes (redesignated Po-2 in 1944), former trainers used as short-range night bombers, Red Army Air Force, Soviet Union, Second World War.

The 46th was the only one of the three women's aviation regiments created by **Marina Raskova** in 1941 that remained all-female throughout the war. It initially consisted of two squadrons; two additional squadrons were added by mid-1943, of which one functioned as a training squadron under the command of **Marina Chechneva**. The regiment was credited with having flown in excess of 24,000 combat missions on the Southern, Trans-Caucasus, North Caucasus, 4th Ukrainian, and 2nd Belorussian Fronts. Its personnel went into action in Ukraine and subsequently operated in the foothills of the Caucasus, over the Kuban' area of North Caucasus, and in the Crimea, Belorussia, and Poland, ending its campaign near Berlin. Initially subordinated to the 218th Bomber Aviation Division of the 4th Air Army, in the Crimea (4th Ukrainian Front) the regiment was temporarily attached to the 2nd *Stalingrad* Guards Bomber Aviation Division of the 8th Air Army. Back in the 4th Air Army on the 2nd Belorussian Front, it was included in the 325th Bomber Aviation Division.

In addition to bombing sorties delivered at the rate of five to eighteen per night, the regiment flew liaison, reconnaissance, and supply missions in support of Soviet ground troops. In 1943 its personnel learned, on 8 February and 9 October respectively, that their regiment had been awarded the elitist status of Guards and the honorific *Taman'sky*, in the latter case for facilitating German defeat on the Taman' Peninsula. The regiment was also awarded the

Order of Suvorov III Class (appropriate to this level) and the **Order of the Red Banner**. The unveiling of a monument dedicated to the personnel, of whom twenty-three became **Heroes of the Soviet Union,** a record number, took place on the Taman' Peninsula in October 1967.

The regiment's successes were in part due to the consistency of command provided by its sole commander Evdokiia Bershanskaia, a competent civil aviation pilot, and her harmonious relationship with Evdokiia Rachkevich, the regimental commissar (deputy commander for political affairs) and one of the very few women graduates of the "V.I. Lenin" Military Political Academy. In addition, Bershanskaia was ably assisted by her deputy Serafima Amosova, a former airline pilot, Irina Rakobol'skaia, chief of staff, and three successive chief navigators: Sofia Burzaeva, Evgenia Rudneva, and Larissa Rozanova.

Representative Participants

Aronova, Raisa Ermolaevna (born 1920, Saratov, RSFSR; died 1982, Moscow, USSR). Guards Major (Ret.), navigator, and pilot. One of several navigators in the regiment who became a pilot after improving her flying skill in the regiment's training squadron, Aronora flew 960 operational sorties and spent 1,148 hours in the air at night. She was awarded the Hero of the Soviet Union on 15 May 1946. In 1969 Aronova published what many consider the definitive memoir of the regiment, *Nochnye ved'my* (Night witches).

Gel'man, Polina Vladimirovna (born 1919, Berdichev, Ukraine). Guards Major (Ret.), navigator, and squadron communications chief. Very competent, she managed to accomplish a great deal without any fuss and got along well with all her female comrades. She flew 860 night operational missions, accumulating 1,300 flying hours, and was awarded the Hero of the Soviet Union on 15 May 1946.

Litvinova-Rozanova, Larissa Nikolaevna (born 1918 Kiev, Ukraine). Guards Captain (Ret.), chief navigator. Initially squadron navigator, Rozanova became flight commander after gaining additional flying experience in the training squadron. She replaced Evgenia Rudneva as chief navigator after the latter's death in April 1944. Credited with having flown 816 mission sorties, Rozanova was awarded the Hero of the Soviet Union on 23 February 1945.

Nosal', Evdokiia (Dusia) Ivanovna (born 1918, Burchak, Zaporozh'e Region, Ukraine; died 1943, Novorossiisk, USSR). Guards Junior Lieutenant, deputy squadron commander. At the beginning of the war her new baby was killed during the bombing of a maternity hospital, so she was determined to fly more than anyone else in the regiment. She volunteered for and was entrusted with the most difficult mission sorties. Killed on her 254th mission, she became the first in the regiment to receive the Hero of the Soviet Union posthumously on 24 May 1943.

Rudneva, Evgeniia (Zhenia) Maksimovna (born 1920, Berdiansk, Ukraine; died 1944 in the Crimea, USSR). Guards Senior Lieutenant, chief navigator. In addition to converting a number of ground support personnel to navigators, successively flying with all of the pilots, and initiating new pilots into their flying duties, Rudneva, a former astronomy student who kept an interesting diary, was the regiment's intellectual and lectured on the theory of navigation. An accurate navigator-bombardier, she was credited with destroying the headquarters of Field Marshal Baron Ewald von Kleist near Mozdok on the Trans-Caucasus Front. Shot down on her 645th mission, Rudneva was awarded the Hero of the Soviet Union posthumously on 26 October 1944.

Bibliography: Aronova, *Nochnye ved'my*, 1980; Bershanskaia et al., *46 Gvardeiskii*, n.d.; Cottam, *Women in Air War*, 1997, and *Women in War and Resistance*, 1998; Kazarinova et al., *V nebe frontovom*, 1962 and 1971 (2nd, revised edition); Noggle, *A Dance with Death*, 1994; Pennington, *Wings, Women, and War*, 2001.

—Kazimiera J. Cottam

122ND AVIATION GROUP, training unit for women's combat aviation regiments, October 1941–December 1942. Red Army Air Force, Soviet Union, Second World War.

When the Germans invaded the Soviet Union on 22 June 1941, only a few Soviet women were actively serving in military aviation. There were, however, many hundreds, possibly thousands, of trained women pilots in the civilian sector who were graduates of the **Osoaviakhim** airclubs. Many of these pilots immediately volunteered for active duty. Unlike most of the other tens of thousands of women who volunteered, the pilots had a specific technical skill to offer: the ability to fly aircraft. Nevertheless, volunteer women pilots were rejected by the Soviet military during the first weeks of the war and were told to train as nurses. Those who were already employed as airclub instructors were told that it was vital for them to remain behind and train new pilots while the male instructors went to the front.

Marina Raskova instigated the creation of all-female regiments. Using her influence as a **Hero of the Soviet Union** (awarded for her prewar exploits in aviation), she persuaded the Soviet Air Force (VVS) to permit the recruitment of women into military aviation. Order No. 0099 (8 October 1941) of the People's Commissariat of Defense directed that by 1 December three regiments would be formed and trained for combat work. Those regiments would be the **586th Fighter Aviation Regiment** (to be equipped with Yak-1 fighters), the 587th Short-Range Bomber Aviation Regiment (to receive Su-2 bombers from the reserves), and the 588th Night Bomber Regiment (which would receive U-2 biplanes). The high command of the VVS was directed to staff the regiments with women from the military and civil air fleets and from Osoav-iakhim. A training unit, later designated Aviation Group Number 122, was created for the purpose of training and equipping the three regiments.

The "tremendous flood of letters" already received by Raskova proved that there would be plenty of volunteers, but Raskova recognized her daunting task. Aviation Group Number 122 would have to train the entire personnel for three regiments: flying cadre, technicians, armorers, instrument mechanics, radio operators, and staff workers. While the call for volunteers was proceeding, Raskova gathered the core staff for the new aviation group, comprised of women who already held military rank.

Recruitment began immediately and was conducted mainly by contacting women pilots already in the military and civil air fleets and in Osoaviakhim. Potential navigators and ground crews were recruited mainly through the Komsomol (Young Communist League). Although women with some technical background were preferred, no medical or physical fitness examination was required during the initial selection process. Interviews were conducted in mid-October 1941; there were far more applicants than there were available positions. In particular, there was a great surplus of pilots, but a shortage of navigators; many women with pilot credentials had to settle for a navigator's position. Those selected for pilot placement had generally accumulated significant flying time and experience. After the initial selections were made, uniforms were issued—men's military uniforms. Women did not receive dress uniforms designed for women until 1943, and for flying, they always used standard male Soviet flying clothing and gear.

It must have been incredibly difficult to accomplish the task of forming the 122nd at that particular time. The Germans were practically on the doorstep of Moscow; everyone knew that the city was in imminent danger of occupation. Many women volunteers had come directly from digging antitank trenches to the 122nd assembly point; they knew that the situation was grave. Raskova had been urging VVS headquarters to come to a decision about transferring her new group to a training base, as it was obvious that the aviation group could not continue its work in the chaotic conditions in Moscow. On 15 October Raskova received orders to evacuate the group immediately to Engels, a city on the Volga River some 500 miles to the southeast, where a large aviation school was located, and to complete the formation and training there. On 17 October the entire contingent of Aviation Group 122 boarded a train headed east.

Upon arrival at Engels, the site of a military aviation school for pilots, the female recruits were given quarters and their hair was cut short. Then they embarked on several months of intensive study. Training consisted of as many as ten classes a day in ground school and two hours of military drill. Pilots accrued a minimum of 500 flying hours over six months, initially in open cockpit biplanes. In addition, navigators studied Morse code at night. Surprise inspections were called, sometimes in the middle of the night. All this occurred from October through May, during one of the coldest winters on record.

As each student progressed in training, Raskova and her staff determined whether she would be assigned to the fighter, dive-bomber, or night-bomber regiment. Most pilots desired the fighter assignment, but good pilots were needed in all three units. Pilots chosen for the fighter regiment had to have both outstanding flying skills and the ability to navigate. In April 1942 the 586th Fighter Aviation Regiment became the first of the units created out of the 122nd to become operational. It was assigned to the air defense forces; its duties were to protect rear targets such as cities, rail lines, and the like against enemy attack. In May 1942 the 588th Night Bomber Aviation Regiment (later the **46th Guards**) also became operational and was assigned to the Fourth Air Army on the Southern Front.

The 587th Dive Bomber Aviation Regiment (later the **125th Guards**) was slower to reach operational status because of an equipment change midway through the training program. The unit was originally slated to get the two-seat Su-2 bomber, an outdated aircraft for which the supply of spare parts was problematic. Raskova managed to get approval for new Pe-2 dive-bomber aircraft to be assigned to the 587th. This meant retraining the pilots and navigators, adding four people to each ground crew, and filling out the regimental personnel for a third flight crew position: that of radio operator/gunner. The only way Raskova could expand the regiment and still become operational by the end of 1942 was to accept men into many of the new positions. Male reservists were called up to complete the complement of personnel, and the regiment was transferred to the front in November 1942.

The 122nd Aviation Group had completed its mission; three operational regiments had been trained, equipped, and sent to active duty. The regiments entered active service at a time when days were darkest for the Soviet Air Force; it had lost strategic initiative along with massive numbers of aircraft and was outnumbered and outmatched until 1943. For the next three years the three regiments created by Raskova served in combat. Although the 122nd was an all-female organization, two of the three regiments created from it became integrated units, and none was designated as a "women's" unit.

Bibliography: Archival materials, Central Archive of the United Armed Forces of the Commonwealth of Independent States (TsAMO), Podolsk, Russia; Cottam, *In the Sky above the Front*, 1984, *Women in Air War*, 1997, and *Women in War and Resistance*, 1998; Migunova, *Prodolzheniie podviga*, 1976; Murmantseva, *Zhenshchiny v soldatskikh shineliakh*, 1971; Pennington, *Wings, Women, and War*, 2001; Raskova, *Zapiski shturmana*, 1976.

—Reina Pennington

125th "M.M. RASKOVA" *BORISOVSKY* GUARDS BOMBER AVIATION REGIMENT. January 1943–May 1945 (disbanded 28 February 1947); founded in Engels, Soviet Union. Initially designated 587th Bomber Aviation Regiment.

Flew twin-engine, medium-range Pe-2 dive bombers, Red Army Air Force, Second World War.

Sergeant Antonina Khokhova-Dubkova tells of her experiences as a tail gunner in the Pe-2 dive bomber, 125th Guards Bomber Aviation Regiment:

The second time we were shot down was on the western front, but I shot down one plane, too! I didn't know I shot it down, but the ground forces saw everything, and then we had the photographing that begins when you fire. They saw it was shot down; the bullets were tracer bullets, so our soldiers could see where they came from. One of the planes of a male regiment was burning; our plane was hit, but we weren't burning. The fuel tubes all shattered, and the fuel again was streaming out. Then Katyusha, our pilot, saw a little clearing surrounded by the forest on all sides, and she managed to land the plane safely.

The other plane that was on fire was flown by the men's crew. Probably they were conceited young boys not very well trained—they couldn't make it the last one hundred meters to that open space where we landed. They crashed in the forest and burned before our eyes. Because there was no one else around, we had to pick up their remains: one arm, one leg, all smoked and roasted. I thought I would never look at any meat after that. Well, life is life. So we collected the remains of that crew, all three of them, torn apart. No heads, all apart. We gathered them together. There was a parachute intact, so we ripped the parachute apart, covered the remains, and buried them.

—Anne Noggle, *A Dance with Death: Soviet Airwomen in World War II* (College Station: Texas A&M University Press, 1994), 115–116.

One of three women's aviation regiments created by **Marina Raskova,** the 125th was initially commanded by Raskova herself. After her tragic death in a crash on 4 January 1943, the regiment acquired a new commander, Major Valentin Markov, whose male navigator, Captain Nikolai Nikitin, was later replaced by a woman, Valentina Kravchenko. There were only two squadrons, initially commanded by **Nadezhda Fedutenko** and Evgeniia Timofeeva, former civil aviation pilots. When the latter became Markov's deputy, **Klavdiia Fomicheva** replaced her.

The 587th Bomber Aviation Regiment, as it was originally designated, was first formed as an all-female regiment. When the regiment was still in training, it had been initially assigned the outmoded Su-2 bomber, with a crew of two (pilot and navigator-bombardier). However, Raskova succeeded in upgrading the regiment to the Pe-2, a much more modern and complex aircraft, which also required a third crewmember: a radio operator/defensive gunner. There was no time to recruit and train female tail gunners before departing for the front, so at first nearly all gunners were men. There was an influx of male engineers and mechanics to deal with the need for larger numbers of specialized technical personnnel to support the Pe-2. However, a replacement squadron acquired in the spring of 1944 consisted entirely of women. Technical personnel remained partially male throughout the regiment's existence; gunners were mostly male, while nearly all the pilots and navigators were female.

The regiment went into action near Stalingrad and ended its campaign near the Baltic Sea, operating over North Caucasus, the Orel-Briansk sector, Smolensk, Belorussia, the Baltic lands, and East Prussia. It completed 1,134 missions on the Southern, Don, Western, 3rd Belorussian, and 1st Baltic Fronts. In North Caucasus the regiment was subordinated to 4th Air Army; on the 3rd Belorussian Front, to 5th Guards Air Corps of 16th Air Army; and on the 1st Baltic Front, to 4th Guards Bomber Aviation Division, 1st Guards Air Corps, of 3rd Air Army. It acquired the honorific "M.M. Raskova" on 4 May 1943 for successful operations in North Caucasus and was redesignated the 125th "M.M. Raskova" Guards Bomber Aviation Regiment on 23 September 1943. On 10 July 1944 the regiment was granted the honorific of Borisovsky for its role in the liberation of Borisov, a Belorussian town. It was also awarded the orders of Kutuzov and Suvorov III class, the level appropriate to aviation regiments. On 18 August 1945 three pilots and two navigators of the regiment became **Heroes of the Soviet Union**.

Representative Participants

Brok-Beltsova, Galina (born 1925, Moscow). Guards Lieutenant (Ret.), navigator. With pilot Antonina Bondareva-Spitsyna, Brok-Beltsova arrived in the regiment with the replacement squadron in the spring of 1944 and received her baptism of fire on 23 June 1944, the beginning of the Belorussian operation. She flew 36 combat missions during the war.

Dolina-Mel'nikova, Mariia Ivanovna (born 1920, Sharonka, Omsk Region, Siberia). Guards Major (Ret.), flight commander, deputy/acting squadron commander. During the initial months of the war she flew 200 special missions as a liaison pilot in the U-2 in the 296th Fighter Aviation Regiment (in which **Lidiia Litviak** later served) and was transferred against her will to the women's regiments. Considered one of the best pilots in her new unit, Dolina flew 72 bombing missions; she took part in the Victory Parade on Moscow's Red Square on 24 June 1945. One of her unit's five Heroes of the Soviet Union, she became postwar deputy commander of a men's aviation regiment, from which she transferred to the reserves in 1950.

Khokhlova-Dubkova, Antonina (born 1919). Senior Lieutenant (Ret.), radio operator/gunner. Khokhlova-Dubkova was the regiment's sole female gunner until the arrival of the all-female squadron in the spring of 1944. In a recent interview she described her two machine guns (out of a total of five aboard her aircraft), one of which required 60 kilograms' effort to recharge. After the war, she taught foreign languages at a military institute until 1954.

Kulkova-Maliutina, Elena (born 1917, Leningrad). Guards Lieutenant (Ret.), pilot. Kulkova-Maliutina arrived with the replacement squadron in the spring of 1944. On 24 July 1944 she was seriously wounded in the abdomen over Lithuania and, repeatedly revived by navigator Elena Iushina, managed to land safely and two months later was back in action. A participant in the Victory Parade, she subsequently flew the Tu-2 in a men's aviation regiment until her retirement in 1949.

Meriuts, Marta (born 1909). Guards Lieutenant Colonel (Ret.), Chief of Communications. Meriuts was assigned to Raskova's **122nd Aviation Group** in a nonflying role after recovering from a serious head wound and the loss of vision in one eye. In a recent interview she stated that at a postwar Kremlin reception the front commander to whom her regiment was subordinated was unaware that its aircrews consisted of women.

Smirnova, Natalia (born 1924, Moscow). Guards Sergent (Ret.), radio operator/gunner. Smirnova was a member of the replacement squadron that arrived in the spring of 1944. In a recent interview she told how, on a mission, the gunner had to stand facing the tail of the aircraft, her head sticking out of the hatchway; once an enemy shell blew open her lower hatch cover, and she was thrown upwards out of the aircraft, but managed to get back inside.

Bibliography: Cottam, *Women in Air War*, 1997, and *Women in War and Resistance*, 1998; Kazarinova et al., *V nebe frontovom*, 1962 and 1971 (2nd, revised edition); Kravchenko, *125 Gvardeiskii*, 1976; Noggle, *A Dance with Death*, 1994; Pennington, *Wings, Women, and War*, 2001.

—Kazimiera J. Cottam

586th FIGHTER AVIATION REGIMENT. 16 April 1942–May 1945. Flew Yak-series fighter aircraft, Air Defense Forces (PVO), Soviet Union, Second World War.

The 586th Fighter Aviation Regiment served from April 1942 through May 1945 as part of Fighter Aviation of the Air Defense Forces of the Soviet Union (IA/PVO). The 586th Fighter Aviation Regiment was assigned to protect fixed targets like airfields, cities, and transportation nodes from enemy attacks. It was subordinated at various times to the 144th and 101st Fighter Aviation Divisions and the 9 Fighter Aviation Corps. Flying modern Yakovlev fighters, the unit completed more than 9,000 flights, of which 4,419 were combat sorties; 38 enemy aircraft were destroyed and 42 damaged in 125 air engagements. The regiment supported the Battle of Stalingrad and performed air defense duties at Voronezh, Kursk, Kiev, Debrecen, Budapest, and Vienna. The regiment was most active during the middle period of the war, especially while it was based near Voronezh and Kursk. During the first and last months of its existence the 586th was based in areas where enemy activity was relatively light. By 1944 the Luftwaffe had increasing difficulty mustering forces to attack the fixed targets defended by PVO regiments. At least ten pilots of the 586th died during the war, or close to 30 percent of its flying personnel.

The pilots of the 586th Fighter Aviation Regiment received little recognition either in their own time or from history. In its ranks the 586th included some of the best pilots the Soviet Union had to offer. Three members of a well-known prewar women's aerobatic team, which performed before crowds of thousands at Tushino Airfield in Moscow, flew with the regiment during the war: Raisa Beliaeva, Valeriia Khomiakova, and team leader Evgeniia Prokhorova. Fighter aces **Lidiia Litviak** and Katia Budanova were first assigned to the 586th before transferring to other regiments. However, the history of

Left to right: Pilots Yamshchikova, Akimova, Solomatina, Kuznetsova, and regimental commander Aleksandr Gridnev. (Courtesy of Aleksandr Gridnev and Reina Pennington)

the 586th is the source of disagreements and disputes. Controversies focus on the circumstances surrounding the deaths of all the women just mentioned; the capabilities and reasons for dismissal of its first commander, Tamara Kazarinova; and the reasons for its failure to achieve Guards status or to receive a single **Hero of the Soviet Union** award.

The 586th began its active service at Saratov on 16 April 1942 under the command of Major Tamara Kazarinova. She commanded the regiment for only a few months, a fact that is often not evident from the published sources. She was not well liked among the pilots, and there are varying opinions regarding Kazarinova's abilities as a pilot. She was transferred to PVO headquarters following an accident in October 1942, when Valeriia Khomiakova was killed during a night sortie (see under "Representative Participants"). Kazarinova was blamed for the accident by most veterans of the 586th. Some veterans claim that Kazarinova became vengeful toward the 586th, especially toward several women who had pushed for her removal, and later worked from her headquarters position to assure that those pilots received particularly hazardous assignments and to prevent the unit receiving the Guards appellation.

On 10 September 1942 Kazarinova sent eight pilots and their ground crews to Stalingrad as replacements to aviation regiments there that had endured heavy casualties. This group arrived at Stalingrad in the worst period of the six-month battle; the Luftwaffe had attained near complete control of the air. The squadron was split into two sections and sent to two different regiments that were badly outnumbered, poorly supplied, and demoralized. Two of the women sent by the 586th became quite famous: fighter pilots Lidiia Litviak and Katia Budanova. During the Battle of Stalingrad Litviak became the first woman in the world to shoot down an enemy aircraft, but the 586th did not receive credit for this accomplishment, since she was assigned to another regiment at the time. Four of the eight pilots returned to the 586th within a few months; however, one was killed at Stalingrad, while Litviak, Budanova, and Antonina Lebedeva continued to serve in various men's regiments (all three were killed in action during the summer of 1943).

In October 1942 Soviet aircraft production had recovered sufficiently to permit the expansion of most aviation regiments to a full authorization of equipment for three squadrons. At this time the 586th received about eight male pilots to fill out its complement of personnel. Little has been written about the men who served in the 586th. They did not fly separately from the female pilots; unit records demonstrate that women and men flew side by side in the 586th. At about the same time Major Aleksandr Gridnev, former commander of the 82nd Fighter Aviation Regiment, became the second commander of the 586th. Gridnev had a checkered past: he had been arrested twice by the NKVD (the predecessor to the KGB), once in 1937 and again in 1942. Gridnev commanded the regiment until the end of the war.

From 13 February to 16 August 1943 the 586th was based at Voronezh, the site of some of the most intense combat activity the regiment experienced. During this period the 586th performed a total of 934 flights and was credited with shooting down seven Ju-88 bombers and three FW-190 fighters. In April 1943 pilots Raisa Surnachevskaia and Tamara Pamiatnykh engaged a group of forty-two enemy bombers and shot down four. The target of the German attack, a rail junction jammed with Soviet troops and fuel supplies, remained unscathed.

One of the important duties of the 586th was to provide fighter escort for various types of VIPs. While these were a relatively small percentage of flights—about 7 percent of the regiment's total combat sorties—they were considered "high-profile" missions due to the rank and prominence of the persons being escorted, including such personages as Nikita Khrushchev, political officer for the Stalingrad Front, and PVO commander General-Major Gromadin.

Representative Participants

Beliaeva, Raisa (born 25 December 1912; died 19 July 1943, Voronezh, USSR). Senior lieutenant, pilot, squadron commander. A member of a prewar women's aerobatic team; Beliaeva participated in the Battle of Stalingrad and flew as an escort pilot for Khrushchev. Gridnev remembers her as one of the best pilots he ever knew, who could beat any man in training flights and withstand g-forces better than any other pilot. On 19 July 1943 she was killed in a crash; some say that she was test-flying a fighter that had been repaired with defective parts, while others say that the crash occurred when she was returning from a combat mission.

Khomiakova, Valeriia Dmitrievna (born 3 August 1914; died 6 October 1942, Saratov, USSR). Pilot, deputy squadron commander. A member of a prewar women's aerobatic team, Khomiakova was the first woman in the world to shoot down an enemy aircraft at night. On 24 September 1942 she destroyed a Ju-88 bomber over Saratov in a nighttime engagement and on her first combat patrol. This is the first official kill credited to the 586th. Khomiakova died in a crash during a night flight on 5–6 October 1942, possibly the result of being posted to night-alert duty in a state of extreme fatigue.

Prokhorova, Evgeniia (born 1913; died 3 December 1942, Uralsk, USSR). Senior lieutenant, pilot, squadron commander. A leader of a prewar women's aerobatic team and holder of several world records in prewar competitions, Prokhorova was known as an incredibly talented pilot and "great shot" in aerial gunnery. She died on 3 December 1942 while participating in a fighter escort mission; storm conditions forced her to land in the snow, and her aircraft flipped when it landed. She was found the next day, trapped in her overturned plane, apparently frozen to death.

Bibliography: Archival materials, Central Archive of the United Armed Forces of the Commonwealth of Independent States (TsAMO), Podolsk, Russia; Cottam, *In the Sky above the Front*, 1984, *Women in Air War*, 1997, and *Women in War and Resistance*, 1998; Migunova, *Prodolzheniie podviga*, 1976; Murmantseva, *Zhenshchiny v soldatskikh shineliakh*, 1971; Pennington, "Stalin's Falcons," 2000, and *Wings, Women, and War*, 2001; Raskova, *Zapiski shturmana*, 1976.

—Reina Pennington

Timeline

Women and the military	Date of activity/event	Military history events
	~9000 BCE	Earliest material evidence of the existence of bows and arrows.
	~4000 BCE	Horses were domesticated and used by tribal cultures of the Russian/Ukrainian steppes and in eastern Europe.
	~2000 BCE	By this period the wheel, the composite bow, and the war horse were in use.
An interesting aspect of Minoan culture was the sport of bull leaping, depicted in frescoes from the Palace of Knossos. Both women and men are shown participating in the dangerous art of leaping over a bull by grabbing its horns.	~2000–1450 BCE	The Minoans on the island of Crete produced a rich, prosperous, long-lived Bronze Age culture, with wide-ranging trade but not particularly militaristic.
	1792–1750 BCE	Mesopotamia: Reign of Hammurabi, whose legal code emphasized the principle of retaliation ("an eye for an eye").
The **Amazons,** a legendary nation of women warriors, reportedly lived in the Black Sea region during the Greek Bronze Age. They fought primarily on	1600–1100 BCE	

Women and the military	Date of activity/event	Military history events
horseback, and their main weapon was the bow.		
Hatchepsut (r. ~1504 BCE–~1482 BCE) ruled Egypt as a female pharaoh for more than twenty years. She had herself depicted with the clothing, actions, and body of a male king. She maintained the territorial gains of her predecessors and left her militant successor, Tuthmosis III, a disciplined army in a high state of readiness.	1490–1482 BCE	
	~1300 BCE	Riding animals were first used in Mesopotamia.
	~1280 BCE	Iron weapons were first used by the Hittites.
According to legend, the **Amazons** came to the aid of King Priam of Troy against the Greeks, and Penthesilea, the Amazon queen, died in combat against Achilles after she had killed several Greek heroes.	~1250 BCE	The siege of Troy by the Mycenaean Greeks is believed to have occurred during this time.
	~1200 BCE	The Hebrews reentered Palestine after the Exodus (1240–1200 BCE). Organized in twelve tribes, they were involved in intermittent conflict with the local peoples, including the Philistines and the Canaanites.
	~1200 BCE	Scythians, predecessors of the Sarmatians, settled in the steppe region of Russia. By the eighth century BCE the Scythians were a "light-cavalry" culture, fighting from horseback with bows. They often served as mercenaries.
Deborah was said to have led a Hebrew (Habiru) revolt against the Canaanites, and Jael killed the Canaanite general Sisera by driving a tent peg through his temple.	~1100 BCE	The Canaanites were the Bronze Age predecessors of the Iron Age Phoenicians in the Levant. The Phoenician Period is generally dated as 1200 to 330 BCE.
Semiramis (Greek name of Sammuramat), queen of Assyria, in legend was credited with many	810–800 BCE	Assyrian forces, probably under the direct command of Nergalilia, attacked the Medes in 810

militant actions of conquest. The real Sammuramat, the basis for the legend, was an active ruler in Assyria, which added Mesopotamia to its empire in this period.

BCE and were sufficiently successful to acquire Mesopotamia for the Assyrian Empire the following year. The Assyrians were constantly at war in the ninth through seventh centuries BCE and had one of the best and most brutal armies of the era. Iron weapons, adapted from the Hittites, were in wide use.

~800 BCE	The city of Carthage was founded in North Africa by the Phoenicians.
700–500 BCE	By the eighth century BCE hoplite warfare had developed in Greece and changed little for three centuries. Heavily armed soldiers operated in tightly ranked and disciplined phalanxes. Battles were brutal head-on clashes, but generally of short duration.
600–400 BCE	

According to Herodotus, a group of **Amazons** joined with Scythians and moved beyond the Don River to the steppes of southern Russia and Kazakhstan, where they established an independent kingdom. In this society women shared equal rights with the men who fought alongside the Amazon women. Herodotus writes that the offspring of these Scythian men and Amazon women were the ancestors of the Sauromatians, who in the historic period ranged from the northern Black Sea region of the Ukraine to northwestern Uzbekistan and whose women were reported to be skilled in the arts of war and horsemanship. Sauromatian-era graves reveal that some women were buried with swords, daggers, bronze arrowheads, quivers, and whetstones for sharpening their weapons. Bowed leg bones indicate that these women spent long hours on horseback; some female remains show evidence of wounds and perhaps death inflicted in combat.

Women and the military	Date of activity/event	Military history events
Spartan women were encouraged to be physically fit and enjoyed some independence in society, but had little direct military involvement.	~600 BCE	Sparta: The Lycurgan reforms were implemented, creating a highly militarized society. All citizens owed duty to the state.
Judith, according to the Bible, killed Holofernes, one of Nebuchadnezzar's chief generals.	587 BCE	Babylonian (Chaldean) king Nebuchadnezzar II (605–562 BCE) completed the Chaldean defeat of the Assyrians and took Syria and Palestine from the Egyptians. In 587 he destroyed Jerusalem, beginning the Diaspora of the Jews.
Tomyris was queen of the Massagetae, a "great and warlike race" in present-day Iran. She was the first opponent to challenge the rapid expansion of the Persian Empire under Cyrus the Great, directing her army against his in a battle that resulted in his death.	~530 BCE	Cyrus II (the Great) of Persia (559–530 BCE) was killed by the Massagetae. Cyrus was known as one of the great conquerors of history and was famed for defeating Babylon in 539 BCE and liberating the Jews from "the Babylonian captivity."
	509 BCE	Revolt of Rome against the Etruscans and establishment of the Roman Republic.
Rome: **Cloelia** was a heroine of the early Roman Republic as an example of courage and patriotism. She was a hostage to the Etruscan king Lars Porsenna. She escaped across the Tiber River, leading a group of other young Roman women. The Romans were treaty bound to return her to the Etruscans, but Porsenna released her in recognition of her bravery.	508 BCE	Continued conflict between the new Roman Republic and the Etruscan Tarquin monarchs, including a battle at the Tiber River between the Roman Horatius Cocles and Etruscan forces under Porsenna (the legendary "Horatius at the bridge").
Greece: **Telesilla** of Argos led the defense of her city against an attack by the Spartan army.	494 BCE	Sparta dominated the Peloponnesus.
	493–264 BCE	Conquest of Italy by Rome. The legion structure of its army was developed in this period, creating a military force that was almost unstoppable by more traditional hoplite-style armies.

	490 BCE	Persian Wars: The first Persian expedition into Greece by Darius was defeated at Marathon, mainly by outnumbered Athenians.
Halicarnassus: **Artemisia I** of Halicarnassus acted as a naval commander to Xerxes of Persia and participated in the Battle of Salamis.	480 BCE	Persian Wars: The second Persian expedition into Greece was led by Xerxes. Athens and Sparta united against Persia. A Spartan force fought to the last man at the pass at Thermopylae, while the Athenians retreated to Salamis; Athens was burned. At the Battle of Salamis in September 480 BCE, the Persian fleet was defeated by the Greek fleet. A year later, the remaining Persian ground forces were forced out of Greece entirely by the combined Spartan/ Athenian army.
	460–445 BCE	The First Peloponnesian War between Athens and Sparta was a long series of skirmishes.
	431–404 BCE	Second Peloponnesian War: Sparta invaded Attica and defeated the Athenians. The toll of the wars contributed to the decline of the Greek city-states.
	359–336 BCE	Philip II of Macedon introduced many changes to military weapons and tactics, creating a flexible army that helped him unify Macedon and expand his control into Greece.
Halicarnassus: **Artemisia II** (?– 351 BCE) inherited the throne after her husband's death, prompting a revolt in Rhodes against female rule. Using clever naval strategies, she quickly suppressed the revolt.	353–352 BCE	Halicarnassus: Revolt of Rhodes.
	336 323 BCE	Reign of Alexander (the Great) of Macedon, one of the most innovative and ambitious military leaders in history. He was never defeated in battle. In just over a decade Alexander controlled most of the known world of his time, but the empire quickly broke apart after his death.

Women and the military	Date of activity/event	Military history events
Olympias (375–316 BCE), queen of Macedon, mother of Alexander the Great, was a decisive influence in Macedon from 336 to 331 BCE while Alexander was campaigning.	336–331 BCE	Alexander departed from Macedon, never to return. He invaded Persia and won sweeping victories at Granicus (334) and Issus (333), then conquered Egypt (332) before reentering Persia and ending the Persian Empire after the Battle of Gaugamela (331).
Olympias, who was hated by many Macedonians as a foreign queen, was forced out of the country in 331; she established herself in Epirus.	331 BCE	Conflicts in Macedon during Alexander's absence, partly in opposition to his assuming Persian customs during his conquest of Persia.
Cynane (357 BCE–320 BCE), half sister of Alexander and stepdaughter of **Olympias,** commanded armies during the Macedonian expansion northward into the Balkans in the fourth century BCE and played an active role in fighting.	~330–320 BCE	Macedonians expanded northward into the Balkans in the fourth century BCE.
	323 BCE	Death of Alexander the Great in Babylon.
	323–281 BCE	Wars of the Diadochi, in which the successors of Alexander fought for power and the division of his empire. In Macedon, Antipater was replaced by Perdiccas as regent for Alexander's infant son, Alexander IV.
Eurydice II (?–317 BCE), a granddaughter of Philip II and thus niece of Alexander the Great, declared her support for Cassander.	320 BCE	Macedon: Wars of the Diadochi.
Olympias led an army into Macedon against Philip III Arrhidaeus and his wife **Eurydice II** for control of Macedon. Olympias won the battle and killed Eurydice and her husband, assuming control in Macedon.	317 BCE	Macedon: The "first war between women," according to Greek historian Duris, was part of the Wars of the Diadochi.
Olympias was captured and executed by Cassander.	316 BCE	Macedon, Wars of the Diadochi: Antipater's son Cassander invaded Macedon. Six years later, he killed the heir of Alexander (Alexander IV) and the heir's mother Roxane. Conflict in Macedon continued until the estab-

		lishment of the Antigonid dynasty in 276 BCE.
	264–133 BCE	Rome's conquest of the Mediterranean was achieved through the Punic Wars and conquest in the Hellenistic kingdoms.
	264–241 BCE	First Punic War between Rome and Carthage, fought for control of Sicily.
Berenice II (273–221 BCE), Ptolemaic queen of Egypt, fought in her youth with the forces of her father Magas, king of Cyrene in modern Libya.	246–241 BCE	Third Syrian War, between Ptolemy III and Antigonus III, part of a series of wars over Palestine and Syria between the Ptolemies and Seleucids. The "Lock of Berenice (II)," wife of Ptolemy III, was a famed war trophy.
Berenice Syra (?–246 BCE), Seleucid queen of Syria, cousin of **Berenice II** and wife of Antiochus II, was involved in conflict after her husband's death.	246 BCE	
Teuta was queen of the Ardiaei of Illyria during the First Illyrian War.	229–228 BCE	First Illyrian War, in which Rome defeated the Illyrians, an aggressive pirate state that threatened Greek city-states. In the Second Illyrian War (219 BCE) Rome took control of Illyria; this led to wars between Rome and Macedon and eventual Roman domination of the Near East.
	218–201 BCE	Second Punic War between Rome and Carthage. The Carthaginian general Hannibal invaded Italy and won key battles, including the Battle of Cannae (216 BCE), one of the greatest victories in history. However, victories in the field did not translate into control of Italy, and after more than a decade Hannibal was forced to return to Carthage to meet a Roman invasion there. In 202 BCE he was beaten by the Romans at Zama, and Carthage became a Roman province.
Arsinoë III (?–204 BCE), queen of Egypt, together with her brother/husband Ptolemy IV Philopator, led the Egyptian forces in the Battle of Raphia.	217 BCE	Fourth Syrian War: At the Battle of Raphia (Palestine, 217) Ptolemy IV defeated Antiochus III of the Seleucid Empire.

Women and the military	Date of activity/event	Military history events
Chiomara, queen of Galatia, was taken prisoner by Romans during an attack. She was raped by a Roman centurion and later had him beheaded.	189 BCE	Galatia was an area in central Asia Minor that had been settled by Celts (Gauls) in the third century BCE. After the Galatians allied with Antiochus III of the Seleucids, the Romans invaded their territory in 189 BCE. The Galatian king, Ortiagon, managed to escape, but his wife, **Chiomara,** was captured along with a band of women. Galatia eventually became a Roman province in 25 BCE.
	149–146 BCE	In the Third Punic War Rome destroyed Carthage.
Cimbrian women participated in fighting against the Romans.	101 BCE	A Roman army under Marius (one of the great generals of the Republic) massacred the Cimbri people at Vercellae.
	59–49 BCE	Julius Caesar conquered Gaul.
Cleopatra VII (69–30 BCE), queen philopator and pharaoh (51–30 BCE), last Ptolemaic ruler of Egypt, became an ally of Julius Caesar, bearing a child with him and using his support to firmly establish herself on the Egyptian throne.	48–47 BCE	Julius Caesar arrived in Egypt; he reconciled a civil war between **Cleopatra VII** and her brother and coruler, Ptolemy XIII. Later he defeated Egyptian forces and killed Ptolemy at the Battle of the Nile.
Cleopatra VII followed Caesar to Rome with their son Caesarion.	46 BCE	
	43–30 BCE	Wars of the Second Triumvirate, primarily between Mark Antony and Octavian (later Augustus Caesar).
	41 BCE	Mark Antony arrived in Egypt; some say that he followed **Cleopatra VII** after meeting her in Rome.
Africa: **Candace** Amanirenas in Ethiopia ordered raids against Roman outposts in southern Egypt.	~40 BCE	
Cleopatra VII married Mark Antony, who divorced his wife Octavia (sister of Octavian, later Augustus) for her.	36 BCE	
	31 BCE, 2 September	Wars of the Second Triumvirate: Battle of Actium between the

fleets of Octavian and those of Antony and Cleopatra. Antony commanded the right wing of his fleet, while Cleopatra commanded the Egyptian naval contingent in reserve. Octavian's commander Agrippa defeated Antony's forces; Cleopatra's fleet escaped.

Egypt: **Cleopatra VII** and Mark Antony committed suicide.	30 BCE	Octavian's forces invaded Egypt. The Roman civil war ended with the deaths of Cleopatra and Mark Antony. Octavian's control was complete, and Rome was transformed from a republic into an empire.
China: **Chi Zhaoping** led a peasant revolt against Wang Mang.	21 CE	China: Wang Mang (r. 9–23) usurped power during the last years of the Former Han dynasty (206 BCE–25 CE), declaring himself emperor. He faced serious peasant revolts.
Vietnam: **Trung Trac** and Trung Nhi led a rebellion in present-day northern Vietnam against the Han Chinese rulers. Women participated in the rebellion on a large scale. One female commander, Phung Thi Chinh, allegedly delivered a child while leading troops at the front. The sisters ruled an independent state until 43, when they were defeated by Chinese military forces that were sent by the Han emperor to retake the provinces.	40–43	Vietnam: The Han dynasty faced revolts in Tonkin and other areas that were suppressed by the forces of Ma Yuan by 43.
	43	The Roman emperor Claudius invaded Britain, conquering the southern areas.
Britain: **Cartimandua,** queen of the Brigantes, a Celtic tribal state in northern Britain, formed an alliance with Rome. She was infamous for handing over Caratacus, an important tribal leader who fought the Romans, to his enemies in 51. As an ally of Rome, she maintained control of her kingdom longer than her contemporary **Boudicca,** who rebelled against the Romans.	47–70	

Women and the military	Date of activity/event	Military history events
Britain: **Boudicca** queen of the Iceni, led a military revolt against Roman domination. After early successes, including taking Londinium (London), her forces were defeated.	59–61	Romans under Suetonius Paulinus defeated the revolt of the Iceni in Britain.
Rome: **Triaria** (?–69?), married to the brother of Aulus Vitellius, accompanied her husband in campaigns and was a participant in the siege of Tarracina. She was described by Tacitus as "warlike beyond a female."	69	Rome: The "Year of the Four Emperors" followed Nero's suicide in 68. Aulus Vitellius declared himself emperor and, after killing his predecessor, became the third emperor of the year. He was defeated and succeeded by Vespasian in October 69.
Zenobia, queen of Palmyra and wife of Odaenathus, accompanied him on his Persian campaign.	262–264	Odaenathus, ruler of Palmyra (in modern Syria) and a client of Rome, invaded and conquered parts of Persia.
Zenobia became the ruler of Palmyra during the period of its greatest military expansion, when she briefly ruled much of Syria, Arabia, Asia Minor, and Egypt.	267	Odaenathus of Palmyra was murdered.
	268	Roman forces sent to pacify Palmyra were defeated by **Zenobia**'s army.
Zenobia conquered Egypt and other territories in the Near East. By 270 she had taken control of the entire Eastern Roman Empire.	268–270	
	270–273	The Roman emperor Aurelian (r. 270–275) solidified Roman control over Gaul, Britain, and Spain.
Zenobia and her general, Zobdas, were defeated in battle by Roman forces at Antioch. A Roman siege of her capital forced her to make terms with Rome. After a second revolt she was taken captive by the Roman emperor Aurelian.	272	Aurelian led an army into Palmyra and reestablished Roman control over the eastern part of the empire. He also reconquered Gaul and restored other territories to the empire.
China: After her father's death **Li Xiu** led troops to protect the people of Ningzhou against tribal incursions. She was named by	280–290	China: Emperor Wu Ti, founder of the Jin dynasty (265–420), reunited China until his death in 290. Afterwards the empire was

Emperor Wu a regional inspector of Ningzhou, placing her in charge of thirty-seven tribal divisions in the Yunnan area for more than thirty years.

		divided among his many sons. Decades of conflict and numerous rebellions and uprisings followed.
China: **Shao** (first name unknown) led a cavalry rescue and saved her husband when he was surrounded by rebels.	317–322	
China: **Lu** (first name unknown) led troops to fight and defeat a rebel who had killed her husband and three sons in 322.	322	
Mavia, queen of the Saracens, led troops into Phoenicia, Palestine, and Egypt in revolt against Rome. Her success forced the Roman emperor Valens to make terms.	373–378	Saracen revolt against Rome involving Phoenicia, Palestine, and Egypt during the reign of the emperor Valens (364–378). Valens was killed in 378, fighting a Visigoth revolt, at the Battle of Adrianople.
China: **Empress Mao,** wife of Fu Deng (ca. 334–386), fifth emperor of the Former Qin dynasty, personally led troops against a rebel chieftain.	380s	China: Former Qin dynasty (351–394).
China: In 397 Wang Xin rebelled against the Jin government. He established a women's troop and made **Kong** (first name unknown) the commander and his daughter the general.	397	China: Jin dynasty (265–420).
	~470	The stirrup was used in China, apparently by the Northern Wei dynasty (386–534). It would not be used in the West until after the seventh century.
China: **Pan** (first name unknown) hunted and fought alongside her husband, a regional inspector of Jingzhou.	500–510	China: Northern Wei dynasty (386–534).
China: **Meng** (first name unknown) commanded the defense of a prefecture during her son's absence.	504	China: Northern Wei dynasty (386–534).
China: **Xian** (first name unknown) was influential in political and military affairs among the southern tribes in China during the last half of the sixth cen-	548–601	China: Liang (502–557), Chen (557–589), and Sui (581–618) dynasties.

Women and the military	Date of activity/event	Military history events
tury. After her husband's death in 558 she was instrumental in the Chen dynasty's unification of the Lingnan area.		
Brunehaut (534–613?) and Fredegund (545–597) conducted a forty-year-long bloody feud involving warfare and assassination over succession and power in Austrasia and Neustria.	560?–613	The Frankish kingdoms of Sigibert I, Merovingian king of Austrasia (the eastern Frankish kingdom), and his brother, Chilperic I, Merovingian king of Neustria (the western Frankish kingdom), came into conflict.
Hua Mulan reportedly disguised herself as a man and fought as a soldier for twelve years.	581–600	China: The Sui dynasty (581–618) consolidated northern China (581) and then the southern area (589), reunifying China for the first time in more than 350 years.
Clotild was a nun who rebelled against her abbess Leubevére and hired an unsavory mercenary force to use against her; Leubevére defended the Abbaye Sainte-Croix.	589–590	France: Childebert II (king of Metz and Burgundy, 575–595) and Guntram (king of Orleans and Burgundy, 561–592) became involved in mediating the battle over control of the Abbaye Sainte-Croix.
Princess Pingyang commanded an army of more than 70,000 in the last years of the Sui dynasty and helped her father found the Tang dynasty (618–907).	617–623	China: Sui dynasty (581–618); Tang dynasty (618–907).
Liu (first name unknown) defended a settlement against nomadic invaders and performed other military actions.	620–680s	China: Tang dynasty (618–907).
	622	Mohammed (570–632) was forced to flee from Mecca. He preached Islam (submission to God), and those who followed Islam were called Muslims (those who submit to the will of God). After his exile his movement began to spread rapidly.
Hind bint'Utba participated in the Battle of Uhud and avenged herself on the man who had killed her father.	624	
	632	Mohammed died. He left no successor, which would lead to di-

visions within the Islamic world. Islamic Arabs embarked on a long period of military conquest.

Hind bint'Utba helped rally the Arabs at a critical moment against the forces of the Byzantine emperor Heraclius.	636	Battle of **Yarmūk** in mid-August 636, near the Yarmūk River in Syria, a decisive victory for the Arab Muslims against the Byzantines and one of the most famous battles of the Arab-Byzantine conflict during the rise of Islam.
	681–683	North Africa: Egyptian Arab Muslims invaded Morocco, but the Berbers and Byzantines from Carthage repulsed them.
Dahya bint Tatit Kāhinah was a military leader of Berber resistance during the expansion of Islam in seventh-century north Africa. After her death in 693 resistance to Islam in North Africa evaporated.	689–693	North Africa: Moslem forces under Hassān bin al-Nu'mān battled the Berber coalition under Kāhinah.
Gao (first name unknown) led the successful defense of her district against Mochuo, the khan of Tujue.	695	China: Tang dynasty (618–907) during the rule of Empress Wu (r. 683–705).
Xi (first name unknown) commanded a self-organized defensive troop against attacks by Qidan (Kitan Tartar) forces.	696–697	China: Tang dynasty (618–907) during the rule of Empress Wu (r. 683–705).
	698	North Africa: Arab Muslims secured Carthage, ending Byzantine dominance in the region.
England: **Aethelburh**, queen of Wessex, razed the fortress of Taunton in Somerset in 722.	700–725	
	712	Muslims completed the conquest of Spain.
	737–739	France: Charles Martel stopped Muslim invasions of the Frankish kingdoms.
Ren (first name unknown) formed a brigade that she led to protect Chengdu from rebels.	768	China: Tang dynasty (618–907).
	789	First recorded **Viking** raid against Britain, followed by raids against Scotland and Ireland in 794–795.

Women and the military	Date of activity/event	Military history events
Women accompanied the **Vikings** on their raids; some writers claim that some Viking women were successful warriors.	800s	Viking raids were widespread in Europe and Britain, including raids on the Netherlands (810), Paris (845), and Hamburg (851).
	877–878	England: Wessex was invaded by Danish **Vikings,** who were eventually fought off by Alfred the Great. Further invasions were repelled in the 890s.
England: **Aethelflaed** of Mercia, daughter of Alfred the Great and sister of Edward of Wessex, was military leader of Mercia (central England) during the Scandinavian invasions of England, from 911 or earlier until her death in 918. She constructed many fortifications and successfully fought off **Viking** attacks.	890s–918	England: Danish Vikings invaded in 905 and were repelled by Edward of Wessex; in 918 he killed the Danish king of East Anglia, thereby ending most of the Viking attacks against southern England.
	911	Some **Vikings** were allowed to settle in the western Frankish kingdom; they converted to Christianity, intermarried with the locals, and founded Normandy.
France: **Emma, queen of France** (?–935), wife of Ralph of Burgundy, led the defense of towns and conducted sieges against contenders for the throne.	927–933	
England: The **widow of Wulfbald** personally led an armed party against a relative who appropriated her property in Kent.	~990	
Spain: **Ermessend of Carcassonne** (980s–1050s), countess of Barcelona, fought for her son's claim to the county and later engaged in a civil war with her grandson Count Ramon Berenguer I.	1018–1057	
	1020s	Sancho III conquered and temporarily unified Christian Spain, including Barcelona, Castile, and other regions.
Spain: **Gidinild** was responsible for the capture and defense of	1026	

the town of Cervera. She then built a tower or castle there and was confirmed as its castellan by **Ermessend,** countess of Barcelona.

Latin America: Indigenous legends tell of a woman called the Warrior Princess who was militarily active in this period.

Italy: **Adelaide of Turin** (?–1091), countess of part of the March of Ivrea and of Turin in northwestern Italy, governed a vast territory. She was said to have worn armor.

France: **Mabel of Bellême** (ca. 1030s–1079) was involved in the planning and direction of military campaigns and was an ally of William of Normandy.

Italy: **Beatrice of Lorraine** (~1020–1076) was a supporter of the Roman popes who provided military protection to Popes Nicholas II, Alexander II, and Gregory VII against their enemies. A relative of Henry IV of Germany, she helped in negotiations between Henry and Pope Gregory VII.

1035		
1035–1091		
1035–1047	France: William I of Normandy consolidated control of his duchy.	
1048–1079		
1049	Henry I of France unsuccessfully attempted an invasion of the lands of William of Normandy.	
1059–1076		
1066	Norman invasion and conquest of England by William "the Conqueror" of Normandy; the Battle of Hastings was a key Norman success.	
1075–1122	The Investiture Controversy was the first great war between church and state. It developed out of civil war in the Holy Roman Empire (Germany) over the succession in which Henry IV prevailed. The key issue was the limit of papal authority over po-	

Women and the military	Date of activity/event	Military history events
litical leaders. Armed conflict was common, and armies invaded Rome in an attempt to control the papacy.		
England: **Emma FitzOsbern** (?–~1098), countess of Norfolk, was the wife of the earl of Norfolk. When her husband revolted against William the Conqueror, she was in charge of a besieged castle for three months. She and her husband were forced to flee to France. In 1096 they went on the First Crusade; they both died in Palestine around 1098.	1075–1096	England: The Anglo-Saxon nobles resisted domination by French-speaking Normans. William the Conqueror did not secure his control over the nobility until 1086.
Italy: **Matilda of Tuscany** (1046–1115) inherited the role played by her mother, **Beatrice of Lorraine**. For two decades she provided the only reliable military support for Pope Gregory VII and his successors in their conflict with Henry IV, king of Germany and Holy Roman Emperor. The large landed possessions in Lombardy and Tuscany that Matilda inherited at the age of eleven were in a strategically vital position between the combatants and controlled access to the limited roads through the Apennines. Adroitly managing numerous fortified positions, she waged a classic campaign of active defense and outlasted a competent, popular, and more powerful opponent.	1076–1097	Investiture Controversy.
Italy: **Sichelgaita of Salerno** (ca. 1036–1090), wife of Robert Guiscard, accompanied her husband on campaign and participated in fighting. Sichelgaita took command of the siege of Trani (1080) and was involved in the siege of Durazzo (1081) and a naval battle off Corfu (1085).	1077–1085	

	1081–1082	Robert Guiscard, husband of **Sichelgaita,** led his Normans against the Byzantine Empire, seizing Corfu and Durazzo.
	1081–1085, 1090–1095	Investiture Controversy: Invasions of Italy by Henry IV of Germany.
Isabel de Conches is blamed for instigating the civil war. It was said that Isabel "rode in knightly armour when the vassals took the field," but she probably did not fight.	1090	Flanders: Civil war between two brothers, the lord of Conches and William, count of Evreux.
	1095	Christian crusades were called for by Pope Urban II to take the Holy Land from Muslim control.
Women were involved in the **Crusades** in a variety of roles. Women were always present within the major crusading armies and within the Crusader States as wives, camp followers, and support personnel. Many of these women performed important logistical functions. In addition, women often assisted the soldiers. Some noblewomen had their own followings of troops, provided at their own expense. Both Christian and Muslim writers reported that some women participated in the fighting.	1096–1291	
	1096–1099	First Crusade: Christian forces captured Jerusalem and established four feudal states in the Holy Land. It was the most successful of all the **Crusades**. One result was the rise of military religious orders, such as the Templars, to protect pilgrims.
Xochitl, a Toltec queen (present-day Mexico), reputedly created a women's battalion and led it in battle until she was killed.	1116	
China: **Shalizhi** (first name unknown) (?–after 1142) was leader of a self-organized militia group.	1122	China: Northeast China, Jinb dynasty (1115–1234).

Women and the military	Date of activity/event	Military history events
China: **Liang Hongyü** (?–1135) often fought side by side with her husband, Han Shizhong (1089–1151), one of the greatest generals of the Southern Song dynasty.	1129–1135	China: Southern Song dynasty (1127–1279).
England: Empress **Matilda Augusta** of England (~1102–1167) participated in a lengthy war of succession. She was the chosen successor of her father, Henry I, but her cousin Stephen was favored by many who disliked the idea of a woman on the throne. Matilda was a militant figure who led troops and was directly involved in civil warfare against Stephen. In 1148 she was forced out of England to her husband's properties in France; from that base her son would rise to become Henry II of England in 1154.	1135–1154	England: War of succession after the death of Henry I between his daughter **Matilda** and his nephew, Stephen, count of Blois.
England: **Matilda of Boulogne,** queen of England (~1103–1152), was married to Stephen of Blois. She conducted several successful sieges against the forces of **Matilda Augusta,** and secured Stephen's release in a prisoner exchange. She was credited for her husband's success in staying on the throne.	1135–1154	England: Stephen, count of Blois and husband of Matilda of Boulogne, ruled England (1136–1154).
Eleanor of Aquitaine (1122?–1204) inherited great lands and thus power. She was directly involved in military conflict throughout her life, instigating and conducting civil wars and battles over succession. Married first to the king of France and later to the king of England, she was successively queen of those countries. In 1137 she married Louis VII, king of France.	1137	
England: **Dionisia de Grauntcourt** was said to have bested a mounted soldier, winning his horse as her trophy.	~1140	

France: **Ermengard,** viscountess of Narbonne (1120s–~1194), took an active role in protecting her inheritance, an important port in southern France. She personally led troops in battle against her feudal overlords, the counts of Toulouse.

1143–1192

Latin America: Indigenous legends describe Coyolxauhqui, the warrior sister of the Aztec warrior god Huitzilopochtli, who fought him for leadership of the Aztecs. Although she was defeated and mutilated by Huitzilopochtli, her death marked the ritual ascendancy of the Aztec warrior empire.

1143

In the Second Crusade there were reportedly two bands of women "armed as Amazons and mounted on horseback," though these were probably merely costumed noblewomen. **Eleanor of Aquitaine,** during her marriage to Louis VII, king of France, went with him on crusade to Jerusalem. She also provided troops of her own.

1147–1149   Second Crusade.

Eleanor of Aquitaine annulled her marriage to Louis VII of France and married Henry, duke of Normandy (later Henry II of England).

1152

1154   England: Henry II (r. 1154–1189) became king, resolving the twenty-year dispute over the throne. Henry II was the son of Empress **Matilda.**

Italy: **Alruda Frangipani** (?–1177), countess of Bertinoro, led an army that helped liberate Ancona from imperial siege in 1172. Her warlike spirit was widely remarked. **Stamira of Ancona** represents a rare documented case of a lower-class woman participating in warfare. She was credited with sabotaging the war engines of the besieging force.

1172   Byzantine-Venetian conflict (1170–1177), siege of Ancona.

Women and the military	Date of activity/event	Military history events
England and France: **Eleanor of Aquitaine** is believed to have initiated the rebellion of three of her sons against her husband; Henry II subsequently imprisoned her for more than sixteen years. His sons would continue to plot and revolt against him until his death in 1189, but were not punished as harshly as was Eleanor.	1172–1173	England: Great rebellion of three sons of Henry II against his rule.
France: **Ermengarde** personally led troops in battle when the nobility of Aquitaine revolted against the harsh rule of the duke of Aquitaine, King Henry II of England, the husband of **Eleanor of Aquitaine**.	1172–1173	England and France: Rebellion of Anglo-Saxons against Norman rule by Henry II in England and large areas of France.
Japan: **Tomoe Gozen** (1157–1247?) fought alongside Minamoto (Kiso) Yoshinaka, who together with Tomoe Gozen played a key role in helping his clan overturn the previous rulers.	1180–1184	Japan: Revolt of the Minamoto clan, resulting in the first shogunate of Minamoto Yoritomo (r. 1185–1199).
Tamar, queen of Georgia (ca. 1160–1213), was a militant head of state. Under her rule the kingdom of Georgia reached the height of its power and influence and stretched from the Black Sea to the Caspian Sea. Tamar's forces put down several challenges to her power.	1184–1213	
England: **Eleanor of Aquitaine** was released from imprisonment by her son Richard I. She was active in ruling the kingdom while her son was away on crusade.	1189	England: Richard I the Lionheart, son of Eleanor of Aquitaine and Henry II, succeeded to the throne upon the death of his father.
Joanna of England (1165–1199), queen of Sicily and countess of Toulouse and the daughter of **Eleanor of Aquitaine** and Henry II of England, as a young widow, accompanied her brother Richard I on the Third Crusade.	1189–1192	The Third Crusade was a response to the Islamic recapture of Jerusalem in 1187. Richard I of England participated, along with Philip II of France and Frederick I Barbarossa. Richard successfully besieged Acre and made a treaty with Saladin for Christian access to Jerusalem.

England: **Nicolaa de le Haye** (1160?–1230), the castellan and sheriff of Lincoln, defended the castle in support of John.	1191	England: Struggle in 1191 between William Longchamp, regent for Richard I, and the king's brother, John, later King John I.
England: **Eleanor of Aquitaine** actively assisted her son John to succeed his brother Richard I as king of England, overcoming armed opposition.	1199	England: Richard I died, and a struggle for succession ensued, won by his brother John (King John I, r. 1199–1216).
France: **Joanna of England,** who had married Count Raymond VII of Toulouse of 1196, was active in suppressing rebellions in his absence.	1199	
Japan: **Hōjō Masako** (1157–1225), regent after the first shogun's death, is perhaps the most important woman in Japanese military history. She was one of the principal architects of the Kamakura shogunate, a regime that dominated her country's military men and military affairs for a century and a half.	1199–1225	Japan: The Kamakura shogunate (1192–1333) was the beginning of the era of shoguns, when the samurai dominated Japan.
Tamar, queen of Georgia, took advantage of the chaos created by the Fourth Crusade to successfully annex provinces along the southern rim of the Black Sea from Byzantium.	1202–1204	Fourth Crusade: Crusaders ended up besieging the Christian city of Constantinople, capital of Byzantium.
	1209–1226	France: The Albigensian Crusade in southern France against the Cathar (Albigensian) "heresy" was organized by Pope Innocent III and led by Simon de Montfort.
Alice de Montmorency (?–ca. 1221), as the wife of Simon de Montfort, assisted in the Albigensian Crusade by raising troops and organizing supplies; she also accompanied her husband on campaign.	1210–1213	
Giralda de Laurac (?–1211) belonged to an important family of the Cathar (Albigensian) group; many Cathars took refuge in Lavaur, a heavily fortified town held by her family. When Lavaur was attacked by Simon de Mont-	1211	

Women and the military	Date of activity/event	Military history events
fort, Giralda acted as castellan and played a large role in organizing Lavaur's defense. After a lengthy siege Simon de Montfort took the town and massacred many inhabitants, including Giralda.		
	1213–1215	China: The Mongols under Genghis Khan occupied much of northern China.
China: **Yang Miaozhen,** leader and commander of a peasant rebel group, led more than 10,000 troops in Shandong Province against Jin, Mongol, and Song forces over a period of nearly two decades.	1215–1231	
Nicolaa de le Haye again successfully defended Lincoln Castle in support of King John I.	1215–1217	England: Baronial rebellion in which an attempt was made to replace John I and his heir with a French successor. Although John died in 1216, his son became Henry III (r. 1216–1272).
China: **Aluzhen** (fl. 1217) commanded a local Jurchen troop during the Jin dynasty (1115–1234).	1217	
	1218	France, Albigensian Crusade: Simon de Montfort died during the siege of Toulouse, reportedly when a female artillery crew killed him with a lucky shot.
	1219–1291	The Fifth through Eighth Crusades were all disasters and ended with the loss of all territory in the Holy Land controlled by European forces.
China: **Yan,** first name unknown, built a rampart to defend her hometown from bandits and became the leader and military commander of self-organized militia groups during the Southern Song dynasty (1127–1279).	1230	
India: **Sultan Raziya** (?–1240) was the only woman among the thirty-two sultans, or rulers, in the three-century history of the	1236–1240	India: The Delhi Sultanate (1206–1526).

Delhi Sultanate. She wore male clothing (including trousers, turban, and sword), pursued men's activities, such as hunting, and led her army in battle.

Italy: **Bianca di Rossi** (?–1253) fought alongside her husband against the forces of the notorious tyrant Ezzelino IV da Romano at the siege of Bassano in 1253.

1253

France: **Mahaut d'Artois** (ca. 1270s–1329), countess of Burgundy and Artois, defended her territories against internal and external enemies.

1285–1314

1296   Britain: Scottish-English wars began when King John of Scotland allied with France; Edward I of England invaded and annexed Scotland.

1298   Britain: Scottish revolt led by William Wallace lost the Battle of Falkirk to the forces of Edward I of England. It marked the first use of the longbow by the English in a significant battle.

China: **Shejie,** first name unknown (?–1303), commanded the Yi, an ethnic group in southwestern China, during their revolt against the Yuan dynasty (1272–1368).

1301–1303

1305   Britain: William Wallace was executed.

1306   Britain: Scottish-English wars continued, with the Scots led by Robert Bruce, who largely freed Scotland from English occupation by 1314.

Britain: **Isabel, countess of Buchan** (ca. 1287–ca. 1314), supported the accession of Robert Bruce to the Scottish throne. She was captured by the forces of Edward I of England in 1306 and imprisoned for a year in a small cage, then in other confinement.

1306

Women and the military	Date of activity/event	Military history events
Britain: **Lady Margaret Badlesmere** (ca. 1286–1333), acting as castellan in her husband's absence, refused to allow **Isabella of France**, wife of Edward II, to enter the castle of Leeds, Kent, precipitating a battle and a siege. Lady Badlesmere and her children were sent to the Tower of London for a year.	1321	Britain: Civil war between Edward II and the Lancastrians.
England: **Isabella of France** (1292–1358), wife of Edward II of England, was queen consort of England, 1308–1327 and head of government, 1327–1330. Isabella first became a participant in the conflict between her husband and his enemies during the incident at Leeds, when **Lady Margaret Badlesmere** refused her party entrance to the castle and killed several of her retainers in the ensuing fight.	1321	
England: **Isabella of France** and her young son Edward, Prince of Wales, increasingly became a focus of opposition to the tyranny of her husband.	1322–1324	England: Thomas of Lancaster, the main adversary of Edward II, was defeated and killed at Boroughbridge in 1322.
England: **Isabella of France** began to organize opposition to her husband in France in 1325 with her lover Roger Mortimer. The next year they returned to England in force and were supported by the people; Edward II died. Isabella's son was made king, but Isabella and Mortimer held de facto power.	1326–1327	England: Invasion by forces of **Isabella of France** and William II, count of Hainault. Edward II was deposed and succeeded by his teenaged son as Edward III.
	1326	First documentary evidence of guns in Europe.
	1330	Britain: The eighteen-year-old Edward III of England successfully revolted against his regent and mother, **Isabella of France**.
Marzia degli Ubaldini (?–ca. 1374) defended the castle of Cesena, Italy, against local and papal attackers. Her valiant actions	1330–1359	Italy: Continual warfare in Romagna.

won the respect of both allies and enemies and made her a legend in her own day.

Scotland: **Agnes of Dunbar, Lady Randolph** (ca. 1300–ca. 1369), led the successful defense of Dunbar Castle in 1338 against a vastly superior force of English soldiers.

1332–1341   Second Scottish War of Independence.

1337–1453   England/France: Hundred Years' War over English claims to French territory and, at times, the French throne. The war began when Edward III, son of **Isabella of France,** asserted his claim to the throne of France in 1337.

Maria of Pozzuoli, also known as the "Knight of Naples," was described by Petrarch (who saw her in 1341 and 1343) as a famous and rugged soldier.

1340s   Unidentified territorial conflict near Naples, Italy.

France: Breton Civil War. When the duke of Brittany died in 1341, the former duke's niece, **Jeanne de Penthièvre** (backed by the king of France), and his half brother, Jean de Montfort (husband of **Jeanne de Montfort** and backed by Edward III of England), both claimed the title. Two decades of bloody fighting followed. The war has sometimes been called the "War of the Two Jeannes."

Jeanne de Montfort (~1315–~1373), when her husband Jean de Montfort was imprisoned, conducted military operations and was known as a strategist. In addition to making symbolic appearances in armor and on horseback to rally the spirits of the defenders, Jeanne de Montfort took a direct and active role in military operations. Her direct role appears to have ended in 1343.

1341–1343

Jeanne de Penthièvre (1320–1384) was married to the French king's nephew Charles de Blois.

1341–1364   France: Breton Civil War. After the death of Jean de Montfort in 1345, Edward III's lieutenants

Women and the military	Date of activity/event	Military history events
Following the capture of her husband by the English in 1347, Jeanne took over the military leadership and administration of the duchy and organized the defense of her lands against the English, who besieged Nantes in 1354–1355. After her husband was killed in 1364, she was forced to make terms.		fought on behalf of Montfort's young son, later Jean IV of Brittany.
	1346	England/France: Hundred Years' War, Battle of Crécy, in which an outnumbered English force under Edward III defeated French cavalry, mainly by use of the longbow.
England: **Philippa of Hainault,** queen of England (1314–1369), was the wife of Edward III of England. Froissart's works describe a queen who took an active military role in the defense of her kingdom, including leading troops in battle against Scottish invaders at the Battle of Neville's Cross, but this view is not supported by other evidence.	1346	England versus Scotland: Battle of Neville's Cross, in which King David of Scotland was captured by forces of Edward III; Edward III himself was away in France.
	1347–1351	The Black Death (bubonic and other forms of plague) killed between one-quarter and one-half of the European population, an estimated 20–40 million people. There were periodic recurrences through 1600.
	1364	France: The Breton Civil War came to an end after the son of **Jeanne de Montfort** became duke of Brittany (Jean IV) in 1364.
France: **Julienne Du Guesclin** (ca. 1333–1405), a Benedictine nun, is said to have defended her convent, sword in hand, against an attack by an English force until the siege was lifted by her brother, Bertrand Du Guesclin, a key figure in the Hundred Years' War.	1370	France: The Hundred Years' War had resumed active conflict in the late 1360s.

France: **Jeanne de Penthièvre** allied with her former enemy, Jean IV of Brittany, to defeat efforts by the French king Charles V to annex their territories.

1373–1379

Sardinia: **Eleanora of Arborea** (1360s–1402?) was the last of the "judges" of Sardinia. She wrote an important law code and for two decades ruled Arborea, one of four administrative regions of the island kingdom of Sardinia. She succeeded to rulership after the assassination of her brother in 1383, quelled a rebellion that followed, reconquered territory held by her father, and kept Arborea in her family's hands. She is considered a national heroine for her efforts in securing the independence of Sardinia, which was in the fourteenth century essentially an Aragonese colony.

1383–1402

1389 — Balkans: The Ottoman Turks defeated an army of Serbs and other Balkan forces and gained control of the region after the Battle of Kosovo.

1402–1454 — Italy: Periodic warfare involved Milan, Venice, and Florence, as well as other states.

France: **Christine de Pisan** (ca. 1365–1430?) wrote influential military treatises during the Hundred Years' War; her book *The Book of Deeds of Arms and of Chivalry*, composed in 1408–1409, was widely studied by military leaders of her age.

1408

1415, 24 October — France, Hundred Years' War: The Battle of Agincourt was fought and won by the greatly outnumbered English forces under Henry V against the French army.

Italy: **Margherita Attendolo** was one of several militant women in the Sforza family; using force and the threat of force, she secured her brother's release from prison in Naples and held her family's fortress at Tricarico.

1415–1416

Women and the military	Date of activity/event	Military history events
Bohemia: The innovative general Jan Žižka allowed women to join his **Hussite** forces, so that some writers have incorrectly described his force as "Žižka's army of women." The activities of female soldiers seem to have been concentrated in the years 1420–1421. Women were notably active in the successful defense of Prague against Sigismund's troops and the Battle of Vitkův, both in 1420. Hungarian troops reported the capture of 156 Hussite women dressed as men, with their hair cut, and armed with swords and stones.	1419–1436	Bohemia: The Hussite Wars began after the execution of the Bohemian reformer Jan Hus for heresy in 1415. Sigismund, the Holy Roman Emperor and king of Hungary, claimed the Bohemian throne, and in 1419 conflict began. Under the leadership of Jan Žižka, Bohemians (called Hussites after the martyred Hus) achieved important victories. However, the Hussites split into factions, and Žižka died of plague in 1424. In 1436 the Hussites came to terms with Sigismund, although rebellions would recur in later decades.
Italy: The artist **Onorata Rodiana** (~1400s–1452), after killing a man who tried to rape her, disguised herself as a man and became a mercenary soldier in 1422. She was killed in battle defending her birthplace against a Venetian attack in 1452.	1422–1452	Italy: Part of the continuing warfare between Venice and other states.
France: **Joan of Arc** (~1412–1431) believed that she was an agent of God sent to defeat the English and restore the French throne. With the support of Charles VII, the dauphin (and later king), she took on a leadership and strategic role. Wearing armor and leading charges into battle, she carried (but apparently did not wield) a sword. Though Joan did not actually fight, her courage was undisputed, and she was wounded in battle. Under her direction French forces lifted the siege of Orléans in 1429 and went on to other victories. Some of Joan's plans, such as the attack on Paris in September 1429, were failures. In 1430 she was captured by French allies of the English. A church tribunal found her guilty of heresy; she was burned at the stake in 1431. In	1429–1431	France, Hundred Years' War: English forces began the siege of Orléans in 1428 but were forced to withdraw in May 1429 by French forces led by **Joan of Arc**. In June the English suffered further defeats when Joan's troops retook the Loire Valley, and in July the English lost several important cities, including Reims, to Joan. In May 1430 Joan was wounded and captured at Compiègne, north of Paris, and later executed. However, Joan's actions led to the ascendancy of France over England in this phase of the war. The French went on to retake Paris in 1436 and most of Normandy in 1449–1450; when they regained Bordeaux in 1453, the war ended.

1920 the Roman Catholic Church made her a saint.

Isabella de Lorraine (1410–1453), queen of Sicily, duchess of Anjou, Lorraine, and Bar, and countess of Provence, successfully defended against challenges to her inheritance of Lorraine and helped her husband in his unsuccessful claim to Naples and Sicily. She helped to direct the defense of Naples in 1435 against attacks by Aragon. She acted primarily on her own, as her husband was imprisoned for most of 1431–1437.	1431–1453	Italy: Alphonso V of Aragon attacked and eventually conquered Naples (1435–1442), ousting the designated heir, René of Anjou, husband of Isabella de Lorraine.
Italy: **Bona of Lombardy** was a mercenary soldier who participated in Francesco Sforza's many military campaigns to consolidate his northern Italian duchy and later served in the forces of the Venetian Republic.	1440–1470	
Italy: **Bianca Maria Visconti Sforza** (1425–1468), the consort of Francesco Sforza, often rode in armor to accompany her husband and to rally his forces in his absence.	1447–1452	Italy: Francesco Sforza gained control of Milan after a civil war (1447–1450).
Italy: **Camilla Rodolfi** fought against the forces of Francesco Sforza's siege of Vigevano in April 1449. Rodolfi led a group of armed women who held the walls when many men had been killed. Although Sforza captured the city, he reportedly liked to have Rodolfi occasionally lead the former women defenders on parade in full armor.	1449, April	Italy: Francesco Sforza besieged Vigevano.
England: **Margaret of Anjou** (1430–1482), queen of England, daughter of **Isabella de Lorraine** and René of Anjou, studied the work of **Christine de Pisan,** which may have influenced her active involvement in military affairs. When the duke of York rebelled in 1455, Margaret led Lancastrian supporters in oppos-	1455–1485	England: The Wars of the Roses over the succession to the throne began soon after the final English losses in the Hundred Years' War. The insanity of King Henry VI of the house of Lancaster and the strength of his unpopular wife **Margaret of Anjou,** led to a contest for the throne. They were opposed by Richard, the duke of

Women and the military	Date of activity/event	Military history events
ing York's claims to the throne in favor of the rightful heir, her son Edward. Both her son and her husband were killed in 1471, and she retired from the fight.		York, and later his two sons. The conflict between the Lancastrians and Yorkists continued for decades, with control of the throne changing hands several times. The direct Lancastrian line was extinguished in 1471, and York's sons ruled as Edward IV and Richard III; they were in turn supplanted by the Lancastrian Tudors in 1485.
England: **Alice Knyvet** (ca. 1420–1491) defended a castle in Norfolk that had been seized by her husband but was also claimed by King Edward IV as royal property. When Edward's forces attempted to take the castle, they were rebuffed by Alice, holding the stronghold during her husband's absence. Her husband was subsequently awarded possession of the castle.	1460–1461	England: Wars of the Roses.
Bohemia: **Johanna of Rožmitál** (?–1474), queen of Bohemia, was one in a long line of militant **Hussite** women. She commanded her own army in battle.	1460–1470s	Bohemia: Renewal of Hussite Wars (1462–1471).
Africa: **Masarico** and her followers (who became known as the Manes), using innovative weapons and tactics, subjugated and assimilated conquered peoples in the jungles of the sub-Saharan belt and the coast of central Africa. They established the Manou Empire (now western Liberia) and invaded present-day Sierra Leone.	1470–1545	
Italy: **Caterina Sforza** (1462–1509), countess of Forlì, conducted military operations and defended besieged fortresses in fifteenth-century Italy. She excelled her grandmother, **Bianca Maria Visconti Sforza,** in her involvement in military affairs.	1487–1500	

One of her most famous exploits was the seizure of Castel Sant'Angelo in Rome (1484) when she was seven months pregnant. In 1488, when her husband was assassinated during a revolt in Forlì, she defied the rebels, holding the fortress of Ravaldino until help arrived; the incident is described in Machiavelli's *Discourses*. In 1499 Pope Alexander VI sent his illegitimate son, Cesare Borgia, to seize her properties. Outnumbered and outgunned, Caterina Sforza was captured and imprisoned in 1500.

1494–1559	Italian Wars: France invaded Italy in 1494, using new and effective cannon. Spanish forces also became involved in the internecine warfare of the Italian states.

Catherine of Aragon (1485–1536), queen of England and daughter of the militant Isabella of Castile, was the first wife of Henry VIII for nearly thirty years (1509–1536). When Henry was on expedition in France in 1513, she helped organize the defeat of the Scottish at Flodden.

1509–1536	Britain: In 1513 Scotland invaded England in support of France; James IV of Scotland was killed at the bloody battle at Flodden.
1517	Germany: Martin Luther published the Ninety-five Theses, beginning the Protestant Reformation. Many European wars over religion followed.

Mexico: Many indigenous women (*soldaderas*) fought alongside their men against the Spaniards. Indigenous women supplied warriors with stones and arrows, prepared slings, and strung bows. The last battle between the Aztecs and the Spaniards included women dressed as male warriors upon the orders of the Aztec leader Cuauhtemoc. Since most of his male warriors were dead, Cuauhtemoc ordered the women of Tenochtitlan to take up shields, swords, darts, and stones and fight the Spaniards.

1519–1521	Mexico: Spaniards under Hernán Cortés conquered the Aztec Empire.

Women and the military	Date of activity/event	Military history events
Mary of Hungary (1505–1558) was ruling queen of Hungary (1521–1527), ruling queen of Bohemia (1522–1527) and regent of the Netherlands (1531–1556). She was politically active during and after the defeat of her husband by the Ottomans; that experience affected her later involvement in military affairs in the Netherlands.	1521–1527	Hungary: Suleiman I, the Ottoman ruler, invaded Hungary in 1521 and 1526 and gained control of Hungary.
Wa, first name unknown, was commander of a southwest aboriginal people in China and led her Tianzhou tribal soldiers to secure the region in support of the Ming dynasty.	1525–1576	China: Ming dynasty (1368–1644).
Mary of Hungary was named regent of the Netherlands in 1531 and was personally involved in military preparations and defensive improvements. Mary was partially responsible for the importation of Italian fortification strategies and defenses into northern Europe and was involved in the reorganization of the Dutch navy.	1540–1550s	French campaigns against the Netherlands in the 1540s and 1550s, Habsburg-Valois wars.
Scotland: **Lilliard of Ancrum** is said to have distinguished herself in battle in an English attack on her village of Maxton in 1545 and is credited with inflicting a mortal wound upon the English field commander.	1542–1550	Britain: The Scottish-English wars were renewed when England invaded Scotland in 1542; the English occupied Edinburgh in 1547 but were forced out again in 1550.
Hungary: In the continuing conflicts between the Ottomans and the Habsburgs, the castle at **Eger** came under attack by Suleiman. The women of the city played an active role in its successful defense.	1552	
Italy: The women of **Siena** actively assisted in the preparations for and conduct of the defense of their city against a Spanish siege in 1553; some 3,000 women participated in the defense.	1553–1555	Italy: Siege of Siena by Spain.

Mary I, queen of England (1516–1558), the daughter of Henry VIII and his first wife, **Catherine of Aragon,** in 1553 became England's first woman ruler since the disputed claim of **Matilda Augusta** four centuries earlier. A devout Catholic, Mary attempted to reverse her father's break with the Roman Catholic Church. Her methods were extreme and included the burning of approximately 300 Protestants, earning her the epithet "Bloody Mary." It was against her that Presbyterian author John Knox aimed his famous 1558 protest against female rule, "First Blast of the Trumpet against the Monstrous Regiment of Women."

1553–1558

1554 — England: A series of conspiracies and uprisings known as Wyatt's Rebellion began, protesting the marriage of **Mary I** of England and Philip II of Spain, but the rebels were defeated.

France: **Jeanne d'Albret** (1528–1572), queen of Navarre, became involved in the Wars of Religion on the Protestant side upon the death of her husband Antoine de Bourbon; she fought without respite to defend her kingdom and her faith and to protect the interests of her son, who would one day become Henry IV, king of France.

1555–1572

Elizabeth I (1533–1603), queen of England, was the child of Henry VIII and Anne Boleyn and the half sister of **Mary I**. Although England avoided open war during her forty-five-year reign, Elizabeth sponsored armed interventions in the French Wars of Religion and in the Netherlands and deflected the attempts of her cousin Mary, Queen of Scots, to depose her. She ruled in an age when religious wars tore apart

1558–1603

Women and the military	Date of activity/event	Military history events
and bankrupted powerful states like France and Spain, yet Elizabeth made England rich and powerful.		
France: **Catherine de Médici** (1519–1589), queen of France, widowed in 1559, controlled the destiny of France by right as the regent or by necessity as queen mother for a weak king. During the crucial time of the Wars of Religion (1562–1598) she ruled France both directly and from behind the scenes and maintained her sons' control of the throne, despite civil war, until her death.	1559–1589	France: Wars of Religion.
	1562–1598	France: Wars of Religion between the moderate Catholics (the royal family), the radical Catholics (the Guise), and the Protestant Huguenots (led by Navarre). For decades skirmishes, battles, and massacres plagued France and brought the throne itself into contest. England sometimes assisted the Huguenots. It was a series of at least eight distinct wars and part of the greater phenomenon of religious conflict in Europe.
Hungary: Captain Miklos Zrinyi and his countess defended a castle in West Hungary/Croatia against the Ottoman sultan Suleiman. After several weeks the Turks broke into the castle and killed most of the men. Countess Zrinyi reportedly set alight the powder magazine in the fortress, committing suicide and taking hundreds (some say thousands) of the enemy along with her.	1566	
France: **Margot Delaye** was a semilegendary heroine of the siege of Montélimar, one of many women who defended the town against an unsuccessful Huguenot attack.	1570	France: Wars of Religion.

Erketü Qatun (ca. 1551–1612), Mongol regent of the noble Borjigin clan and wife to four Mongol chieftains of the Borjigin clan, commanded military forces and was instrumental in keeping peace with the Ming court from the 1570s until her death.

1570s–1612 China: Ming dynasty (1368–1644).

Marguerite de Valois, also known as Queen Margot (1553–1615), queen of Navarre and queen of France during the Wars of Religion, was the daughter of the Catholic Catherine de Médici, and the daughter-in-law of Protestant Jeanne d'Albret. In 1572 she married Henry of Navarre, a marriage intended to ameliorate the religious conflicts of the country. Instead, the violence escalated, beginning with the St. Bartholomew's Day Massacre a few days after her wedding. Later estranged from her family and her husband (who became Henry IV in 1589), in 1599 she agreed to an annulment of her childless marriage, which allowed Henry to marry Marie de Médici.

1572–1599 France, Wars of Religion: The St. Bartholomew's Day Massacre (24 August, 1572) occurred soon after the marriage of Marguerite de Valois to Henry of Navarre; thousands of Protestants were killed. A new phase of violence and civil war erupted in France.

England: During a review of troops after the defeat of the Spanish Armada, Elizabeth I made a famous speech, costumed as a warrior; she is alleged to have declared, "I know I have the body but of a weak and feeble woman, but I have the heart and stomach of a king."

1588 England/Spain: The Spanish Armada sent by Philip II to attack England ended in disaster, defeated by clever British tactics and bad weather.

France: Françoise de Cezelly (~1555–1615), when her husband, the governor of Leucate, was taken prisoner and the town was besieged by members of the Catholic League, "dressed like an Amazon, with a pike in her hand," and led the defense of the town. She refused to surrender the town in exchange for her husband's life; her husband was later

1589 France: Wars of Religion.

Women and the military	Date of activity/event	Military history events
executed by the enemy. As a reward for her actions, Henry IV maintained her in the office of governor until her son was able to succeed her in 1610.		
	1589	France: Wars of Religion ended with the assassination of Henry III. Henry of Navarre became Henry IV, the first Bourbon king, and issued the Edict of Nantes, promising religious freedom for the Huguenots.
China: **Qin Liang-yü** (1574–1648), regional commander of Sichuan and a general of the late Ming dynasty (1368–1644), fought with her troops against the invading Manchus in northeastern China and against local rebellions and bandits in the southwest. She was the only woman to reach the highest post in the military command system of the Ming dynasty.	1599–1648	China: Manchu-Chinese War (1618–1659).
Latin America: **Catalina de Erauso** (1592–1642), "the Lieutenant Nun," escaped from a Spanish convent at the age of fifteen, disguised herself as a boy, and went to South America. She fought for the Spanish Crown on the Chilean frontier and was promoted to ensign. Her violent actions led to an investigation, during which she revealed her true sex. She was granted a pension by the king and papal sanction to continue dressing as a man.	1607–1627	
France: **Marie de Médici** (1573–1642), queen and queen mother of France, was the second wife of Henry IV, replacing **Marguerite de Valois**. After her husband's death she was named regent for her son Louis XIII. When her son turned sixteen seven years later, he seized power and had his mother confined. She escaped in	1610–1640s	France: Henry IV was assassinated in 1610; his wife Marie de Médici served as regent until his son Louis XIII came of age. Two more decades of conflict followed, with Marie de Médici and Louis's brother fomenting rebellion among those who disliked the influence of Cardinal Richelieu over the young king Louis.

1619, then entered into a long period of intermittent rebellion against Louis. She supported the unsuccessful efforts of her second son to take power and even in exile sought to return to France.

Women played many essential roles in the **Thirty Years' War**. Throughout the war, and especially in its final phase, many of the primary political units involved were ruled by women. Women naturally staffed the "home fronts," providing labor, taxes, and other resources necessary for the war efforts. Women were also active members of the huge, generally mercenary armies, providing essential support services; armies often consisted of an estimated 25–40 percent or more women and children. Count Albrecht von Wallenstein used women disguised as units of soldiers to try to deceive his enemies about the size of his force. Women also occasionally engaged in combat, especially during the many sieges of the war.

France: **Marie de Rohan-Montbazan, duchess of Chevreuse** (1600–1679), was, for most of her life, at war against her king and her country, allying herself with the enemies of France and drawing those around her into conspiracies against her sovereign. She instigated armed uprisings against Cardinals Richelieu and Mazarin (who remarked that "France was not calm except when she was not there").

1618–1648 Europe: The Thirty Years' War began as a religious war between Protestants and Catholics in Bohemia and Germany; it drew in forces from most of the European states, although the majority of the fighting occurred in German areas. The war ultimately was more about politics than religion; Catholic France and Catholic Spain, at war with each other, supported opposite sides in the Thirty Years' War. Millions of lives were lost—mainly civilians. Historian C.V. Wedgwood calls it an outstanding example in European history of meaningless conflict.

1618–1659 China: In the Manchu-Chinese War the Manchu took Inner Mongolia and Korea, then overthrew the Ming dynasty (1368–1644); by 1659 they controlled virtually all of China.

1625–1640s France: **Thirty Years' War;** Wars of the Fronde.

Women and the military	Date of activity/event	Military history events
France: **Madame de La Guette** (1613–~1681) defended her holdings against looters pushed into France from German lands by the **Thirty Years' War** while her husband was away fighting in that war. During the Fronde she remained loyal to the king, although her husband sided with the rebels.	1635–1653	France: **Thirty Years' War;** Wars of the Fronde.
France: **Madame de Saint-Baslemont** (1607–1660) was famous for defending her lands while her husband was away fighting in the **Thirty Years' War**. She used force to put down rebels and thieves, and others came to her for protection during unsettled times. She was known for riding with her troops, sword in hand.	1636–1643	
Canada: **Françoise de La Tour** (1602–1645) was active in the defense of her family's fort against an enemy; the conflict involved small-scale naval battles and the use of cannons.	1640s	Canada: Civil wars in Acadia.
	1642–1646	Britain: First English Civil War between the forces of Charles I (Cavaliers, generally Catholic) and Parliament (Roundheads, Protestant). In 1644 Scotland joined the war on the side of Parliament.
Britain: **Lady Brilliana Harley** (~1598–1643) and her husband were the only important Puritan gentry in Herefordshire, and their home was a center of opposition to the king and his religious policies. In her husband's absence she defended Brampton Bryan Castle against sieges by royalist forces in 1643.	1642–1643	Britain: English Civil War.
Britain: **Henrietta Maria** (1609–1669), queen consort of Charles I (king of Great Britain and Ireland, 1625–1649), helped raise	1643–1644	Britain: English Civil War.

and organize royalist troops. In 1644 she escaped to France, where she spent the remainder of her life.

China: **Shen Yunying** (1623–1660) was a female commander who fought in Hunan Province, succeeding her father as a representative of the Ming against peasant rebellions.

Britain: **Lady Mary Bankes** (?–1661) defended Corfe Castle against parliamentary forces in 1643 and 1645. By 1643 Corfe Castle was the last royalist garrison on the Dorsetshire coast. Her husband was absent during the first siege and dead before the second, leaving Lady Bankes with primary responsibility for organizing the defense of the castle. She was successful in 1643 and held out for several months in 1645–1646 until a traitor gave her enemies access.

Britain: **Charlotte Stanley, countess of Derby** (1599–1664), was a staunch royalist who, while her husband was away, successfully defended Lathom House in Lancashire during its first siege arly half a year in duration) by parliamentary forces. The castle later fell during a second siege in 1645 in Lady Charlotte's absence.

China: **Liu Shuying** (1621?–?), a loyalist of the Ming dynasty, led a private army in Hunan Province for two years after the fall of the Ming in 1644.

1643	China: Late Ming dynasty (1368–1644).
1643–1646	Britain: English Civil War.
1644	Britain: English Civil War.
1644–1646	China: Manchu-Chinese War.
1648–1651	Britain: Second English Civil War between Charles I and Parliament. In 1649 Charles I was beheaded. The parliamentary forces under Cromwell brutally put down rebellions and massacred thousands in Ireland, then defeated the Scottish forces decisively in 1651.

Women and the military	Date of activity/event	Military history events
France: **Anne-Geneviève Longueville** (1619–1679) was one of the leaders of the Wars of the Fronde. She was active in several important events of the war and sometimes disguised herself as a man.	1648–1653	France: Wars of the Fronde.
	1648–1649	France: War of the First Fronde, a rebellion against Cardinal Mazarin's influence over the boy-king Louis XIV.
	1650–1653	France: War of the Second Fronde, a continuation of the rebellion against Mazarin and Louis XIV.
France: **Anne Marie Louise d'Orléans, duchess of Montpensier** (1627–1693), was the granddaughter of Henry IV. During the Fronde, as part of the rebellion, she helped to secure her family's holding of Orléans. She led a contingent of troops into Paris and enabled the rebellious prince of Condé to enter Paris.	1651–1653	France: Wars of the Fronde.
Russia: **Alena Arzamasskaia** (?–1670) was a latter-day **Joan of Arc**. In 1669 she ran away from a convent, disguised herself as a man, and joined the peasant revolt led by Stenka Razin. She raised and led as many as 6,000 soldiers, taking the fortress city of Temnikov, among other actions. In 1670 she was captured by tsarist forces; she refused to name other rebel leaders, even under torture. She was condemned both for her treason against the tsar and (like Joan) for the crime of dressing like a man. Arzamasskaia was burned at the stake.	1669–1670	Russia: Revolt of Cossack Stepan ("Stenka") Razin against Tsar Alexis (son of Michael Romanov, founder of the Romanov dynasty). Razin inspired peoples along the Volga to declare their freedom from the control of the government and aristocracy; many peasants murdered their masters. Native groups joined in the revolt. The disorganized rebels were defeated by the imperial army, and in 1671 Razin was executed.
Wetamoo was a Wampanoag leader who played a military role in support of King Philip (her brother-in-law), and one of several women who held both polit-	1675–1676	North America: King Philip's War, between the colonists of New England and the Wampanoag leader King Philip and his allies, was a bloody affair, with

ical and military power. She personally led her warriors on the field and was killed in 1676.

France: Chevalier Balthazar (Geneviève Prémoy) (1660–?) disguised herself as a man and entered combat at the age of sixteen, later achieving promotion to officer. Her identity was discovered when she was wounded during the War of the Spanish Succession, but Louis XIV allowed her to continue to serve, modifying her uniform to add a skirt.

Hungary: **Ilona Zrinyi** (1644–1703) was among those Hungarians who opposed both the Ottoman Turks and the Austrian Habsburgs. While her husband was away, she organized and conducted the defense of Munkacs Castle in northeast Hungary against an intermittent three-year siege by Habsburg military forces. She was the great-granddaughter of the Zrinyis who were killed in a similar siege by Ottoman Turks in 1566.

France: **Marie Magdelaine Mouron** disguised herself as a man and fought with various French units in the War of the League of Augsburg. After she was

villages and settlements on both sides destroyed, killing many noncombatants. The war ended with the death of King Philip in 1676.

1676–1700s France: Franco-Dutch and Franco-Allied Wars (1672–1678) and War of the Spanish Succession (1701–1714).

1683–1697 Austro-Turkish War. Turkish forces, allied with Hungary, invaded Austria in 1683, and the conflict continued until Austria finally defeated the Turks in 1697, gaining control of Hungary in the process.

1686–1688 Hungary: Austro-Turkish War.

1688–1697 War of the League of Augsburg, also called the War of the Grand Alliance, between France and the League of Augsburg, led by William of Orange, king of England. France attacked Germany, the Netherlands, Italy, and Spain.

1690–1696 War of the League of Augsburg.

Women and the military	Date of activity/event	Military history events
wounded and her true sex was discovered, she simply enlisted in another unit. She was arrested as a deserter when she attempted to leave one unit, probably in the fear that she was about to be discovered.		
Marie-Madeleine Verchères (1678–1747) led the defense of her family's seigneury (to the southeast of Montreal) against Iroquois attackers.	1692	Canada: New France (present-day Quebec), conflict between Iroquois and colonists.
Kit Cavanaugh (1667–1739) disguised herself as a male soldier and fought in the Nine Years' War and the War of the Spanish Succession, maintaining her disguise for thirteen years, despite being wounded and imprisoned. Her true identity was revealed the third time she was wounded at the Battle of Ramillies in the Spanish Netherlands in 1706 and she was forced to leave the army.	1694–1706	Nine Years' War and the War of the Spanish Succession.
Brazil/India: Brazilian-born Dona Maria Ursula de Abreu e Lencastre escaped an arranged marriage by assuming a male identity as "Baltasar de Couto Cardoso," enlisting as a marine on a warship, and sailing for India. She served some fourteen years without being discovered. Her identity was finally revealed when she was seriously wounded in the course of rescuing her captain	1699–1713	
	1710–1714	War of the Spanish Succession between France and several other European states.
In the West African kingdom of **Dahomey**, women played a prominent military role. Women armed with muskets were first seen by European visitors to Dahomey in 1727.	1727	West Africa: Dahomey was founded by King Agaja in 1724 and embarked on a long series of wars with its neighbors, particularly the Oyo.

Austria: **Maria Theresa** (1717–1780) was archduchess of Austria and queen of Hungary and Bohemia (r. 1740–1780). When she gained the throne at the age of twenty-three, as there was no male heir, many disputed her right to rule. When Frederick the Great took one of her provinces on the pretext that he did not recognize her rule, she refused to make terms and immediately went to war. Her role in directing Austria's forces in the war has been much neglected, although her enemy Frederick receives a great deal of attention. Despite inheriting weak and poorly led armed forces, Maria Theresa endured against Frederick in the War of the Austrian Succession and would fight two more wars against him. At the same time that she was holding her own against Frederick in three wars and improving the status of her country, she bore sixteen children.

1740–1748

Europe: War of the Austrian Succession between Prussia and Austria and their allies. In 1740 both Frederick II (the Great) of Prussia and Maria Theresa rose to their thrones. Believing Austria to be weak, Frederick seized one of its provinces. The conflict ended in stalemate after eight years; Frederick kept Silesia.

1744–1748

India: First Carnatic War. As an extension of the War of the Austrian Succession, French and English fleets fought off the southern coast of India over the British bases of Madras and Fort St. George, as well as Pondicherry.

England/India: **Hannah Snell** (1723–1792) disguised herself as an English foot soldier and marine. She participated in the First Carnatic War and fought French troops in the Indian Ocean; she was wounded at Pondicherry.

1745–1750

India: First Carnatic War.

Ahilyabhai Holkar (1725–1795) was rani of Indore and military and political leader of the Maratha Confederacy. After her husband's death in 1754 she took his place in her father-in-law's campaigns and commanded the Maratha artillery at the decisive Battle of Panipat in 1761. After

1754–1795

India: An independent Maratha state, a loose alliance of Hindu peasant-warrior communities, was founded in 1646 and subsequently became embroiled in conflict with the Mughal (Moga Empire). It dominated an extensive region and supported its troops by controlling trade and

Women and the military	Date of activity/event	Military history events
the death of her son she successfully fought to retain control of Indore. Under her rule Indore became a prosperous and powerful state.		pilgrimage routes, plundering neighboring Mughal provinces, and efficiently administering its core territories. In the 1750s the power of the Mughal was broken and the Maratha invaded Punjab; other conflicts followed with the Afghans and Mysore.
	1754–1763	North America: The French and Indian War between British and French colonial forces erupted out of old tensions and soon merged with the Seven Years' War. George Washington served in the British forces. The British victory resulted in France's loss of Canada and land east of the Mississippi.
Nancy Ward (1738?–1824) was a Cherokee who held an influential role, acting as a tribal political leader in both men and women's councils and a tribal negotiator. She was famed for her role in a battle with the Creeks in 1755. She was a chief negotiator in 1785 and signed the Treaty of Hopewell between the United States and the Cherokees.	1755–1808	
Maria Theresa created the Grand Alliance of France, Russia, and Sweden, which fought Frederick the Great to a standstill, in the Seven Years' War.	1756–1763	The Seven Years' War between Prussia and Austria and their allies spread to involve many colonial areas around the world. Like its predecessor, the War of the Austrian Succession, the conflict was instigated by an attack by Frederick the Great on Austrian territory. Frederick did not defeat his enemies; he was saved by the death in 1762 of the Empress Elizabeth of Russia, who hated Frederick. Her son Peter, who adored Prussia, was assassinated and succeeded by **Catherine II** the Great, who withdrew from the war, busy with her own troubles at home. The lengthy conflict was inconclusive and ended with a return to the status quo.

Seigneuress Anne-Marie Dru-cour (?–1762) was wife of the French governor of Ile Royale (Acadia). During the British siege of Louisbourg in 1758 Madame Drucour fired artillery rounds each day throughout the five-week battle and provided aid to the wounded. The badly outnumbered French were eventually forced to surrender; Drucour and her husband survived.

1758

North America: French and Indian War.

Russia: **Catherine II** (the Great) (1729–1796) came to the throne mainly through the support of Guards military units, deposing her husband. She ruled Russia for more than thirty years, during which period Russia became a major power through great territorial expansion attained mostly by war.

1762–1796

1763

India: At the end of the Seven Years' War Britain became the primary Western influence in the region.

Russia: The forces of **Catherine II** achieved great victories over the Ottoman Empire. Her triumph was marred by domestic troubles: a massive plague epidemic in 1770–1771 and the frightening Pugachev Revolt in 1773–1774, which she brutally suppressed. However, Russia's international prestige increased as a result of Catherine's expansionist endeavors.

1768–1776

The Russo-Turkish War began when Russian forces attacked in the Balkans and Caucasus. The Russians acquired territory in the Crimea and Black Sea access. However, while most of the army was occupied fighting against Turkey, a massive revolt began in 1773, led by the Cossack Emelian Pugachev, who proclaimed himself tsar. By late 1774 the revolt was broken, and Pugachev was publicly executed in a horrific manner

Russia: **Tat'iana Markina** was a twenty-year-old Don Cossack who, during the reign of **Catherine II,** disguised herself as a man and enlisted as a soldier in an infantry regiment. She was promoted to the rank of captain. After her identity was discovered, the empress forced her to leave military service, but provided her a pension.

1770s–1790s?

Women and the military	Date of activity/event	Military history events
	1773–1774	Russia: A revolt by Cossack and other groups, led by Emelian Pugachev, was defeated by the forces of **Catherine II**.
North America: **Anne Hennis Trotter Bailey** (1742–1825), after her first husband was killed during Lord Dunmore's War in 1774, joined the militia in opposition to the British and fought in the **American Revolutionary War.** She dressed in men's clothing, carried a rifle, and served as a scout on missions between remote western areas and eastern Virginia forts. Bailey took part in campaigns against the Shawnee, who reputedly gave her the nickname of "Mad Anne." After the war she continued serving as a scout and messenger between Fort Lee and frontier posts such as Point Pleasant. In 1791 Bailey was credited with preventing an Indian attack on Fort Lee and with saving lives by delivering ammunition to the fort.	1774	North America: Lord Dunmore's War was a conflict in Virginia and Kentucky between colonists and a Shawnee coalition; the natives were defeated.
India: The exploits of **Begum Samru** (1753?–1836) are closely associated with those of the European mercenaries who joined the struggles over the remains of the Mughal Empire in northern India at the end of the eighteenth century. When her husband, an Austrian mercenary died in 1778, she took command of the army, consisting of five battalions of regular infantry, forty cannon, and some 400 cavalry, with about 300 European and Eurasian officers and gunners. She fought for the imperial forces of Shah Alam in the 1780s. She survived a revolt and an attempt to replace her in the 1790s. In 1803 she faced no less an opponent than the future duke of Wellington in the Second British-Maratha War	1775–1825	India: Maratha rebellions.

(see under 1803–1805). Amazingly, she maintained purdah (the seclusion of women) throughout her career, never appearing before her troops unveiled and conferring with her officers from behind a screen. She was one of the most successful mercenary commanders of late-eighteenth-century northern India.

North America: **"Molly Pitcher"** was a composite mythical figure of the Revolutionary War. Women who brought water in "pitchers" to cool artillery pieces during battle sometimes took over the weapons in emergency situations.

1775–1783

North America: The American Revolutionary War of the colonists against the British dragged on for nearly a decade.

North America: **Prudence Wright** (1740–1824) lived in a town near Concord, Massachusetts. When the local minutemen mobilized in response to the threat to Concord, the women acted to secure the area against Tory spies by forming a militia company, captained by Prudence Wright. Dressed in men's clothing and armed with muskets and makeshift weapons, Wright and her guard apprehended a Loyalist who was carrying British dispatches.

1775, 19 April

North America, American Revolutionary War: British attacks on Lexington and Concord were repulsed by militias.

Canada: **Mary Brant** (1736–1796) was the sister of the Mohawk chief Joseph Brant and a British ally. She was the leading matron of the important Six Nations Tribe and provided important information to the Loyalist and British armies; she is credited with playing a pivotal role in the capture of Fort Stanwix and the British victory at the Battle of Long Island.

1776

North America, American Revolutionary War: At the Battle of Long Island (August), Washington's forces were defeated by the British under General William Howe.

North America: **Margaret Cochran Corbin** (1751–1800) accompanied her husband John (apparently enlisting under her own name) and served in the artillery at the Battle of Fort Wash-

1776

North America, American Revolutionary War: Washington was pursued by the British. The Battle of Fort Washington (November) was a defeat for the Americans.

Women and the military	Date of activity/event	Military history events
ington in November 1776. When her husband was killed, Corbin took over his position at the gun; she was wounded and disabled for life. She was assigned to the Corps of Invalids that was posted to garrison duty at West Point (1779–1783), and was given a pension. She died in 1800; in 1926 her body was reinterred at West Point and marked by a monument.		
North America: **Ann Bailey** disguised herself as a man to enlist in the Continental army during the Revolutionary War (1777). She was promoted to the rank of corporal but served only a few weeks before she was discovered and arrested.	1777	North America, American Revolutionary War.
North America: **Anna Maria Lane** (?–1810) fought in disguise in her husband's unit in the American Revolution. She participated in several battles and was severely wounded at the Battle of Germantown, for which she later received a pension.	1777	North America, American Revolutionary War: The revolutionaries were defeated at the Battle of Germantown (4 October) and afterwards took refuge in Valley Forge.
North America: **Lydia Barrington Darragh** (1729–1789) lived in Philadelphia during the British occupation (1777–1778), directly opposite the headquarters of General William Howe. British officers sometimes met in her house, and when she learned of a planned surprise attack on General George Washington in December 1777, she was able to warn him so he could successfully defend himself.	1777	North America, American Revolutionary War.
North America: **Nancy Hart** (ca. 1735–1830) lived in Georgia. While her husband was with the militia, she captured several Loyalists at her home, killing two of them. She was also said to have acted occasionally as a scout or spy.	1777	North America, American Revolutionary War.

North America: **Mary Ludwig Hays McCauley** (~1754–1832) accompanied her husband into service in the Continental army during the Revolutionary War. When he was wounded at the Battle of Monmouth, she took his place and fired on the enemy. She was probably one of the sources of the legend of **"Molly Pitcher."**	1778	North America, American Revolutionary War: After the British evacuation of Philadelphia, British forces under Sir Henry Clinton and Washington's army fought at the Battle of Monmouth (28 June).
Austria: **Maria Theresa** and her son and coruler Joseph II were involved in another war against Frederick the Great of Prussia.	1778–1779	Europe: War of the Bavarian Succession between Frederick II (the Great) of Prussia and Austria.
	1779–1782	India: First British-Maratha War.
North America: Sally St. Clair, apparently a Creole girl, was found among the dead of the Continental army at Savannah, wearing men's clothing. Little else is known about her.	1779	North America, American Revolutionary War: In the southern theater the British took Savannah (December 1778), and the Continental army unsuccessfully attempted to take it back (September–October 1779).
North America: **Rebecca Brewton Motte** (1758–1815) helped the Continental army burn her own home, which the British had fortified as "Fort Motte," in 1781.	1780–1781	North America, American Revolutionary War: In the southern theater the British took Charleston (spring 1780) and the Continental army was badly defeated at the Battle of Camden (August 1780).
North America: **Deborah Samson** (1760–1827) disguised herself as a man and served for more than a year in the Continental army. There is some dispute over her experiences in the war and whether or not she was wounded.	1782–1783	North America, American Revolutionary War.
Russia: **Catherine II** visited her newly acquired territories in the Crimea in 1787 during the silver anniversary of her reign. She reviewed the army and the new southern fleet in a highly publicized tour. Grigory Potemkin staged spectacular receptions, including an "Amazon" detachment in one instance.	1783	Russia annexed the Crimean khanate, gaining access to the Black Sea.

Women and the military	Date of activity/event	Military history events
Russia: The Swedish–Russian War led to a fear of potential Swedish attacks on St. Petersburg; **Catherine II** stated her readiness to personally fight the Swedes in the streets.	1788–1790	The Swedish-Russian War over Russia's occupation of Finland ended with defeat for Russia.
France: During the upheavals of the **French Revolution** (1789–1799) gender roles were debated, and many women had opportunities to expand beyond traditional female identities. Some women expected to receive full citizenship along with the men. Pauline Léon organized street demonstrations as early as 1789 and in 1791 took a petition signed by 300 women to the National Assembly, asking that women be allowed to form militias, to train, and to march to the front should war be declared.	1789–1791	The French Revolution began in the summer of 1789.
France: **Théroigne de Méricourt** (1762–1817) was a legendary French revolutionary activist; she reputedly led Parisian women in the 1789 march to Versailles in the October Days.	1789–1792	France: French Revolution.
France: **Marie Charpentier** (1751–?) was noted for bravery in the 1789 attack on the Bastille. In 1792 she was commissioned in the national police force and served with distinction until 1793.	1789–1793	France: French Revolution
France: Many women were among the "volunteers of 1792," serving openly among the thousands of French who volunteered to fight the First Coalition, which they believed threatened the Revolution. Women who joined in this group served an average of twelve to eighteen months in most branches of the army and navy, including the infantry, heavy artillery, and rifle and grenadier units.	1792–1798	Europe: War of the First Coalition. Austria and Prussia formed an alliance and began to mobilize against the French, resulting in a French declaration of war (April 1792). During this period Louis XVI was executed in 1793, and opposing armies fought in the Low Countries, France, and Italy and along the Rhine River.

France: When war with Austria broke out, **Théroigne de Méri-court** publicly advocated the formation of women's legions for the defense of France, but she was rebuffed by the Jacobins.	1792	
France: **Sophie Julien** disguised herself as a man to follow her father into service with an artillery regiment. She was forced out of the service in 1793.	1792–1793	Europe: War of the First Coalition.
France: **Madeleine Petitjean** (1746–?) joined the military at the age of forty-six after having lost fifteen of seventeen children and having been widowed three times. For nearly a year after her third husband's death Petitjean served in the French army. During service in the Vendée in western France she was captured by the enemy and tortured. Later released, she served until September 1793, when she was seriously injured.	1792–1793	Europe: War of the First Coalition.
France: **Rose Barreau** (1773–1843) was one of the better-known women soldiers who enlisted in the French revolutionary armies during the initial year of the War of the First Coalition in 1792. She enlisted under her own name, along with her husband and her brother. She was active at Bréaton in July 1793 in combat against the Spanish. She was discharged in 1793 after fourteen months' service, but continued to follow her soldier husband in a noncombatant role until at least 1806.	1792–1793	Europe: War of the First Coalition.
France: **Marie-Barbe Parent** (1772–1829) first joined the military in male disguise and served in Belgium. She was discovered and forced to return home, but later enlisted in the Army of the Rhine and of the Moselle until she was forced out of service in 1794 for being female.	1792–1794	Europe: War of the First Coalition.

Timeline

Women and the military	Date of activity/event	Military history events
France: **Anne Quatsault** (1775–?) disguised herself as a man and enlisted in a French artillery transport unit, serving from 1791 to 1794. She served in the Vendée and in the sieges of Liège, Aix-la-Chapelle, Namur, Maastricht, and Dunkirk and was injured at Hondschoote.	1792–1794	Europe: War of the First Coalition. Allied armies besieged the French at Mainz and Dunkirk (1793), but the French responded after hasty mobilizations with a victory at Hondschoote, near Dunkirk (1793), and other locations. The French succeeded in driving their enemies from most of France by late 1793.
Britain: Disguised as a man, **Mary Anne Talbot** (1778–1808) claimed to have acted as footboy, cabin boy, drummer, powder monkey, and midshipman in the Royal Navy and in the infantry regiment of the duke of York during the War of the First Coalition. The truth of her story, told in an 1804 biography, has been much debated.	1792–1796	Europe: War of the First Coalition.
France: **Marie Duchemin** (1772–1859) served for seven years in seven campaigns. During various campaigns in Corsica and Italy, she was twice wounded in the leg and injured in both arms. She continued serving until 1799, when she was discharged and granted aid based on the severity of her injuries.	1792–1799	Europe: War of the First Coalition. In 1794 the British occupied Corsica. In 1796 Napoleon became commander of French forces in Italy.
Marie-Jeanne Schellinck (1757–1840) served with the 2nd Belgian Volunteers of the French revolutionary armies for four years in campaigns with the French Armies of the North and of the Sambre-et-Meuse. As an infantry soldier serving in combat, Schellinck was wounded numerous times, including a gunshot wound in the left leg and twelve saber wounds. During the Napoleonic Wars she apparently put on a male disguise in order to continue serving. She appears to have participated in the battle of Austerlitz.	1792–1805	Europe: War of the First Coalition.

France: **Regula Engle** (1761–1853) followed her common-law husband into the service of France. During two decades of service, primarily on campaign with Napoleon Bonaparte, Engle bore twenty-one children, of whom ten died. Although she was not a soldier, she reportedly followed her husband onto the battlefield rather than remaining in the army train. She allegedly participated in the Egyptian Campaign, the Battle of Marengo, and the Battle of Waterloo (in which she was widowed).

1792–1815

Europe: French Revolutionary and Napoleonic Wars.

France: When the Jacobins came to dominate French politics in 1793, there was a distinct political shift against military roles for women. Legislation designated women who traveled with the armies as either "useful" or "useless." A limit of four per battalion was established and all excess women were supposed to be sent home. However, evidence shows that women soldiers serving on the front distant from Paris remained reasonably unaffected by the new directives. Many commanders chose to retain their female soldiers until the end of the wars.

1793

France: The Jacobins (the party of Maximilien Robespierre and the Committee of Public Safety) came to power and enacted a retrenchment in enlistment rules for women consistent with their reactionary position against equal rights and citizenship for women.

France: **Rose Bouillon** (1764–?) served for six months in 1793 in the Army of the Moselle, accompanying her husband and leaving behind her children. Despite her husband's death, she waited for the completion of the campaign before applying for a discharge.

1793

Europe: War of the First Coalition.

France: **Reine Chapuy** (1776–?) spent nearly a year in the cavalry before being forced from service by the edict of 1793.

1793

Europe: War of the First Coalition.

Women and the military	Date of activity/event	Military history events
In the southwest and west of France a number of women took part in the War of the Vendée. Among the best-known women of the French counterrevolution were **Renée Bordereau** and **Marie-Louise Victorine de la Rochejaquelein,** whose combat is well documented. Other notable women who participated include Jeanne Robin, Madame Bulkeley, Madame Regrenil, Madame de Fief, and the chevalier "Adam."	1793–1800	France: The War of the Vendée, a counterrevolutionary civil war, erupted from anti-Catholic measures taken by the revolutionary government and the execution of the king in January 1793. This revolt was a major catalyst in the creation of the Reign of Terror, and many executions occurred in the Vendée.
France: The **Marquise de la Rochejaquelein** (1772–1857) was the wife of a counterrevolutionary general in the War of the Vendée who accompanied him on campaign. Her popular memoir is one of the best firsthand accounts of the conflict and tells of many women who fought.	1793–1795	France: War of the Vendée.
France: **Marie-Henriette Heiniken Xaintrailles** (?–1818) in 1792 followed her husband in the army of the Rhine. He was promoted to general, and Madame Xaintrailles served as an unofficial aide-de-camp. She was expelled from military service in 1793, as were many women, but rejoined in 1795 and remained with the army even after separating from her husband in 1798. She served as an aide-de-camp to General Menou during the Egyptian Campaign. She was seriously injured in 1799 and retired from the military in 1801.	1793–1801	Europe: Wars of the First and Second Coalition.
France: **Renée Bordereau** (1766–1822), dressed in men's clothes and riding a horse, took part in all the battles of the War of the Vendée. She was described as the "girl who fights like a lion." She returned to military service in 1815 at the age of nearly fifty to fight against Napoleon.	1793–1815	France: War of the Vendée.

France: **Thérèse Figueur** (1774–1861) served as a dragoon in male disguise. She reportedly met Napoleon Bonaparte at Toulon and served in the Army of the Pyrenees. She served in the Army of Italy (1795–1799) where she was wounded four times, had horses shot out from under her twice, and was made a prisoner of war. Her captors discovered her true sex and returned her to France in 1800, where she once again disguised herself and reenlisted, fighting until she was captured in Spain (1812–1815). Her distinguished service was attested by five Napoleonic generals.	1793–1815	French Revolutionary and Napoleonic Wars.
Tyrol: **Katharina Lanz** (1771–1854) became famous for her spirited defense of her village against French forces in 1797.	1797	Napoleonic Wars (Tyrol).
	1798–1802	Europe: War of the Second Coalition (Britain, Austria, Russia, Turkey, Naples, Portugal). During this period France conducted offensives in the Low Countries, Germany, Italy, Switzerland, and Egypt. Some famous engagements included the Battles of the Nile (1798) and Marengo (1800). France considered and abandoned a plan to invade England.
United States: **Woman Chief** (?–1854), a Crow warrior, was a regular member and occasional leader of Crow raiding and war parties against other Plains tribes.	1800–1840?	United States: Intertribal conflicts were endemic among the native Americans.
Begum Samru led her troops against British forces commanded by Arthur Wellesley (the future duke of Wellington) at Assaye in 1803. Her forces suffered defeat along with the rest of the Marathas, and she was forced to give up her remaining troops after the British drove the Marathas from Delhi. She later became a staunch ally of the East India	1803–1805	India: Second British-Maratha War. Major-General Arthur Wellesley (later the duke of Wellington) campaigned in India and inflicted a decisive defeat on the Marathas at Assaye (1803) and other battles.

579

Women and the military	Date of activity/event	Military history events
Company, which allowed her to retain control of her army. Begum Samru led her troops in battle for the last time in 1825 at the siege of the Jat city of Bharatpur.		
France: Napoleon's domestic policies were notably antifeminist. Women were restricted to the control of their husbands, and the Code Napoléon denied them any significant employment opportunities (including the military), consigned women to second-class citizenship, severely restricted divorce rights, limited guardianship of their children, restricted ownership of property, and required dependence on a male in circumstances of litigation. These laws greatly limited women's ability to play military roles, although many women who had entered service in the revolutionary period continued to fight, and others managed to find their way into combat even during the Napoleonic period.	1804	France: Napoleon was crowned emperor.
Marie-Jeanne Schellinck appears to have participated in the Battle of Austerlitz in the French forces.	1805–1807	Europe: Wars of the Third and Fourth Coalition, in which France was opposed by Britain, Austria, Russia, and Sweden. Some famous engagements included the Battles of Ulm and Austerlitz, resulting in Austria's surrender, and the naval battle at Trafalgar, a British victory (all 1805). Napoleon attacked Prussia in 1806, inflicting a humiliating defeat at Jena/Auerstedt, occupying Berlin, and proceeding into Poland. Fighting against Russia in 1807 ended with the Tilsit treaties, in which France gained control of most of the German states and Poland.

Virginie Ghesquière (?–1855) served in disguise in the Napoleonic armies in the cavalry. She reportedly participated in the battle at Wagram (1809) against the Austrians and in the Peninsular War in Spain.

1806–1812

Russia: Aleksandra Tikhomirova reportedly served for fifteen years in the Russian cavalry in the late eighteenth and early nineteenth centuries. She is said to have taken the place of her dead brother, a Guards officer whom she closely resembled. She gained the command of a company and was killed in 1807, whereupon her identity was discovered. She may have been fighting in the War of the Third Coalition, in which in 1807 Russian forces fought major battles against Napoleon at Eylau and Friedland.

1807

Russia: **Nadezhda Durova** (1783–1866) fought in male disguise as an officer in the Russian cavalry. She participated in combat in 1807 and 1812–1814 in the wars against Napoleon. When her identity was discovered, she appealed to Tsar Alexander I, who permitted Durova to continue to serve. She was the only woman to win the St. George Cross (**Order of St. George**) before the First World War. She was later dubbed "the Cavalry Maiden."

1807–1814 — Russia: War of the Third and Fourth Coalition, 1812 French invasion of Russia.

1807–1814 — Europe: The Peninsular War began when France occupied Portugal and Spain. Britain sent forces against France, led by Arthur Wellesley (later the duke of Wellington), who had returned from India. The extended fighting was called "the Spanish ulcer" by the French.

Spain: **Agustina Aragón** (1788–1857) helped defend her city dur-

1808–1809 — Spain: The Peninsular War, siege of Zaragoza.

Women and the military	Date of activity/event	Military history events

ing the French siege of Zaragoza in northern Spain. She replaced a fallen artilleryman and was credited with making critical shots that prevented a French entry. She was subsequently given officer rank in the Spanish artillery and thereafter served with her unit in Seville in 1809 and participated in the defense of Tortosa in Catalonia. She was famous in her own day and became an icon of Spanish resistance to Napoleon. Many other Spanish women were active in defending and fighting for their homes during the Peninsular War against the French.

Spain: **Manuela Malasaña** (?–1808) was killed during the *dos de Mayo* in Madrid in 1808, the mass uprising against the French that began on 2 May and continued throughout the year. She was said to have been assisting an artillery unit, but apparently was a bystander. Many other women took an active part in the uprising and dozens were killed, but it was Malasaña who was made into a martyr in popular memory.	1808	Spain: The Peninsular War, *dos de Mayo* in Madrid, a revolt against the imposition of Joseph Bonaparte (brother of Napoleon) as the French king of Spain. The rebellion was crushed but became symbolic of Spanish resistance.
Russia: **Nadezhda Durova** became the first woman to receive the **Order of St. George**. Awarded for bravery in combat, the four-level Order of St. George (alternatively referred to as the St. George Cross) was created exclusively for officers in 1769 by Empress **Catherine II**.	1808	
Virginie Ghesquière was among the women in Napoleon's armies who participated in the Battle of Wagram.	1809	Europe: In the War of the Fifth Coalition Britain and Austria fought France at Aspern and Wagram.
Mexico: During the Mexican War of Independence against Spain women of all classes participated in warfare (see *soldaderas*).	1810–1823	Mexico: A war of independence against Spain began as a peasant revolt, often led by Catholic priests. The rebellion was fought

mainly as an extended guerrilla war in rural areas. Mexico became independent in 1821, but the new emperor Augustín I was deposed in 1823. A republic was declared in 1824.

Mexico: **Gertrudis Bocanegra** (1765–1818) established a spy network of women tracing the movements of Spanish forces. After her husband and son were killed, she joined the forces of her son-in-law. She raised a battalion of armed women and led them until she was arrested. She was executed in 1818.

1810–1818

Mexico: War of Independence against Spain.

Latin America: **Juana Azurduy de Padilla** (1781–1862) led a group of anti-Royalist guerrillas in the east central region of Upper Peru. She and her husband kept a vital transportation corridor for independence forces secure for several years. In her first major battle at Pintatora in 1815 she left the battlefield to give birth, then returned to capture the standard of the Spanish troops and rally the patriot forces.

1811–1816

Latin America: An independence movement in Upper Peru (Bolivia) was part of widespread revolt against Spanish rule in Latin America.

1812

Russia: Napoleon invaded with more than half a million troops. The Russians were forced to retreat, and after bloody battles like Borodino, Napoleon took Moscow in September. However, the French forces were unprepared to winter in Russia. Their withdrawal began in October; they were decimated by Russian attacks, disease, and weather. Only ten percent survived to escape Russia.

United States: **Lucy Brewer** (1793?–?) reputedly served in disguise for three years as a marine sharpshooter on board the USS *Constitution* during the War of 1812. Although her military activities are disputed, she is often characterized as the "first girl marine."

1812–1814

North America: War of 1812, in which the United States declared war on Britain. Characterized by fighting along the Canadian border and a British blockade of the American coast, the war eventually ended with a return to the prewar status quo.

Women and the military	Date of activity/event	Military history events
Canada: **Laura Secord** (1775–1868) gave vital information about American plans to the British.	1813	War of 1812
	1813–1815	Europe: During the War of the Sixth Coalition Russia, Prussia, Britain, Austria, Sweden, Spain, and Portugal united against Napoleon. Their newly reformed armies inflicted defeat on Napoleon at Leipzig, and in 1814 Paris was captured. Napoleon was exiled.
At the age of fifty-four, **Regula Engle** was said to have participated in the French forces at Waterloo. Mary Dixon reportedly fought in the British army for sixteen years and was in the Battle of Waterloo. **Renée Bordereau,** who had fought in the counter-revolutionary French forces in the Vendée, returned to military service in 1815 at the age of nearly fifty to fight against Napoleon.	1815	Battle of Waterloo: Napoleon returned to confront the British and Prussians once more at Waterloo in Belgium, when he suffered his final defeat.
Latin America: **Juana Azurduy de Padilla,** who had previously fought against the Spanish in Peru, fought on in Argentina after the death of her husband. Her greatest military success occurred in 1816 during the Battle of Jumbati, when she led outnumbered and poorly armed Indian troops in a victory against the Spanish. Her bravery on the field was recognized by the independent government of Buenos Aires. She continued to fight against the Spanish until the independence of Upper Peru in 1825.	1816–1825	Argentina declared its independence from Spain in 1816 and, along with Chile, achieved military success against the Spanish.
Dahomey: Following his coup in 1818, King Gezo maintained the traditional Dahomean female bodyguard as a military center and added to his military strength an army of women.	1818	

Greece: **Laskarina Bouboulina** (1771–1825) used her family wealth to provide ships and ground troops for the cause of Greek independence, all used under her command against Turkish naval and land forces. When the war began in 1821, Bouboulina was fifty years old. Manto Mavrogenous was another Greek woman who used her wealth to outfit and command two ships; she also organized troops and fought in male attire against the Turks. Many other Greek women were active in the conflict.

1821–1832 — Greek War of Independence against the Ottomans. Greece declared its independence in 1822; fighting continued for another decade. In 1824 the British poet Lord Byron was killed fighting for Greece.

Brazil: **Maria Quitéria de Jesus** (1792–1853) enlisted in 1822 in an infantry unit organized to expel the Portuguese army from the provincial capital of Salvador. She was discharged and promoted (for pension purposes) in 1823.

1822–1823 — Brazil gained its independence in 1822, despite Portuguese opposition.

France: **Marie Duchemin** became the first woman admitted to Les Invalides, where she was granted the honorary rank of second lieutenant for her service during the revolutionary wars.

1822

India: **Begum Samru** led her troops in battle for the last time in 1825 at the siege of the Jat city of Bharatpur, fighting on the side of the British.

1825–1826 — India: British forces successfully besieged Bharatpur (Bhurtpore), which they had failed to take in 1805.

Poland: **Emilia Plater** (1806–1831) was a captain in the Polish infantry during the rebellion against Russia. Plater fought in a number of skirmishes and battles against Russian forces in Lithuania during the first half of 1831. Other Polish women also participated in the unsuccessful insurrection.

1830–1831 — Poland: The Polish Revolution, an unsuccessful rebellion against Russian rule.

Guatemala: **Petrona García Morales de Carrera** (1817–1857) accompanied her husband into battle. A French observer com-

1837 — Guatemalan Revolution.

Women and the military	Date of activity/event	Military history events
mented that she matched her husband in courage and daring, able to handle pistol or lance effectively. She was apparently a rather brutal character with a penchant for mutilation. Her husband later became chief of state of Guatemala.		
Dahomey: By the 1840s the women's army was better equipped, disciplined, and trained than that of the men. Women made up nearly one-half of the armed forces of the West African kingdom of Dahomey in the nineteenth century. Several European observers noted the exceptional military bearing of the women soldiers.	1840s	
United States: **Eliza Allen** (1826–?) served in disguise in the Mexican War, participating in the Battles of Monterrey and Cerro Gordo. She was among the American soldiers who occupied Mexico City. Sarah Borginis reportedly achieved the rank of brevet colonel under General Zachary Taylor at the attack on Fort Brown.	1846–1848	The Mexican-American War ranged from Texas to California. At the Battle of Monterrey in Mexico (September 1846) General Zachary Taylor defeated a Mexican army. General Winfield Scott inflicted another defeat on the Mexicans under Santa Anna at Cerro Gordo in 1847, then moved on to Mexico City. The United States gained massive territory in the West and Southwest as a result of this war.
	1848	Europe: A wave of liberal/nationalistic revolutions against monarchical rule in the Italian states, German states, Austria, and France all failed; collectively they are known as the revolutions of 1848.
Hungary: **Maria Lebstuck** (1830–1892) disguised herself as a man and served in the Death's Head legion of General Giron, then in the Hussars. She married a fellow officer and was pregnant when she was captured in 1849 during the surrender of the defeated Hungarian troops.	1848–1849	Hungary: Revolution of 1848 against the Austrians.

Iran: **Zaynab** "Rustam-'Ali" (?–1850) was allowed to dress as a man and represent her family during the Babi revolt. She was active in the fighting, in which she was one of the many Babi killed.

1850

Iran: The Babi were a religious sect persecuted by the Iranian government. Open fighting occurred in places such as Zanjan, where government forces besieged the Babi, who controlled the city for eight months.

~1850

The rifled musket was introduced, more than doubling the effective range and increasing the accuracy of the weapon.

France: After the Napoleonic era ended, in which the civilian and military medal of the Legion of Honor was created, thirty-six years passed before the first woman soldier of the armies of the **French Revolution** and Napoleonic period received the coveted award. **Marie Duchemin**, soldier and prisoner of war, received her cross of the Legion of Honor from Napoleon III during the Second Empire of France.

1851

West Africa: The women soldiers of **Dahomey** numbered 5,000 to 6,000 prior to a disastrous 1851 attack on the Yoruba city of Abeokuta (Nigeria), when they lost 1,000 to 2,000. In the early 1860s an epidemic of smallpox and a second fruitless attack on Abeokuta thinned their ranks to around 3,000.

1851–1860s

1853–1856

The Crimean War between Russia and Turkey (backed by Britain and France) resulted in a humiliating defeat for Russia.

India: **Laxshmi Bhai** (1827?–1858), rani of Jhansi, was a leading figure in the Indian Mutiny. As a widowed queen and regent after 1853, she was free from the traditional seclusion of high-caste women, and she was an active ruler in Jhansi. A horsewoman and a good shot, the rani dressed in jodhpurs and wore a short sword and two pistols in her belt.

1857–1858

India: The Sepoy Mutiny (also called the Indian-British War) was a widespread rebellion against the British. Inflamed by religious issues, Indians massacred the British in many locations; the British responded in kind and eventually put down the rebellion.

Women and the military	Date of activity/event	Military history events
She raised and trained an all-female regiment from among her servants. The British refused to recognize her as ruler of Jhansi, declaring the region annexed, and besieged her territory in 1858. She refused to surrender, though her forces were greatly outmatched. The Rani was personally in the thick of the fighting. When she was killed in June 1858, the regimental history of the British Eighth Hussars noted that "in her death the rebels lost their bravest and best military leader." Hazrat Mahal, the queen of Awadh during the Indian Mutiny, while not as actively involved in fighting as Laxshmi Bhai, nevertheless led and commanded armies.		
United States: Women served in a wide variety of roles in the **American Civil War,** from support, supply, and nursing to espionage and combat. Women accompanied troops into combat; "daughters of the regiment" often carried the colors. Women who participated in fighting most often did so in male disguise. The best-documented cases of women who served in male disguise were nearly all in the Union army; women were also present in the Confederate army, but less documentation has survived. Estimates of the number of women who actually fought in the Civil War vary from 400 to 1,000.	1861–1865	The **American Civil War** began when a series of Southern states seceded from the Union and established the Confederate States of America (February 1861). The first shots were fired at Fort Sumter, South Carolina. A long and bloody conflict followed with more than a million casualties and more than 600,000 dead.
United States (Confederacy): During the **American Civil War** a group of women who named themselves the "**Nancy Harts**" after the Revolutionary War heroine formed a Confederate militia company in La Grange, Georgia.	1861–1865	**American Civil War.**

United States (Union): **Anna Ella Carroll** (1815–1894) was the niece of General Winfield Scott and an ardent Union supporter. There is little evidence to support Carroll's claims that she was the author of the Tennessee River strategy (a plan to invade the Confederacy in the west by going up the Tennessee River instead of down the Mississippi River). However, she made an important contribution to the Union as a political publicist.

1861   American Civil War.

United States (Union): **Kady Brownell** (1842–1915), a South African immigrant, accompanied her husband in the 1st Rhode Island "Mechanics Rifles" and was designated the "daughter of the regiment." She participated in the First Battle of Bull Run and campaigns in Virginia and North Carolina. She and her husband were both wounded at the Battle of New Bern and left the military in 1863.

1861–1863   American Civil War: The First Battle of Bull Run (Manassas) in Virginia was the first major battle of the war; it was a Confederate victory in which "Stonewall" Jackson earned his moniker.

United States (Union): Canadian-born **Sarah Edmonds** (1841–1898) disguised herself as "Franklin Thompson" and served as a (male) nurse, participating at Bull Run (First and Second), the Peninsula Campaign, and the Battle of Fredericksburg. She deserted in 1863, allegedly due to an illness that would have meant her discovery, and wrote a famous autobiography in 1864.

1861–1863   American Civil War: The Union experienced several bloody defeats at the Second Battle of Bull Run (Manassas) in August 1862 and Fredericksburg in December 1862.

United States (Union): Russian-born **Nadine Turchin** (1826–1904) accompanied her husband, a colonel (later brigadier general) of the 19th Illinois Volunteer Infantry Regiment. He was court-martialed for violating regulations against wives being on the battlefield. Reportedly Nadine took over for him when he was ill. When she later applied for a

1861–1864   American Civil War.

Women and the military	Date of activity/event	Military history events
pension, an Ohio senator who was a veteran of the regiment testified that "every man who belonged to his brigade admired her as much as they admired the General."		
United States (Union): **Anna Etheridge** (1844–1913) received the Kearny Cross for bravery under fire. She accompanied her husband in the 2nd Michigan Volunteers in 1861 as the "daughter of the regiment." Her husband soon deserted, but she remained for the duration of the war. Etheridge served with the Army of the Potomac in twenty-eight engagements, including the Battles of Fredericksburg, Chancellorsville, Gettysburg, the Wilderness, and Petersburg. She is noted for rallying the regiment at Chancellorsville, riding along the line to encourage the men to stay and fight. She was credited with rallying the retreating Michigan Volunteers to turn and hold their position at Spotsylvania.	1861–1865	**American Civil War:** At the battle of Chancellorsville (1–3 May 1863) Robert E. Lee inflicted another bloody defeat on the Army of the Potomac. Casualties ran high on both sides; Confederate general Stonewall Jackson was accidentally killed by his own men.
United States (Confederacy): Cuban-born **Loreta Janeta Velazquez** (1842–?) disguised herself as Lieutenant Harry T. Buford and served in various Confederate units. She claimed to have fought in the First Battle of Bull Run and then to have served as a spy and later as a cavalry scout. Her story, told in an 1876 memoir, has been the subject of much debate.	1861–1865	**American Civil War**.
United States (Union): **Mary Edwards Walker** (1842–1919) was the first woman to be commissioned as a military doctor and lieutenant in the Medical Corps. She was widely known for her semiscandalous "reform dress"	1861–1865	**American Civil War**.

(slacks and a knee-length dress), which she deemed practical wear for a physician. In 1864 she was captured and spent four months as a POW in Richmond. President Andrew Johnson made her the first and only woman in the history of the American military to receive the Congressional Medal of Honor. The medal was revoked in 1917 (a year before her death) and reinstated posthumously in 1977.

United States (Union): **Dorothea Lynde Dix** (1802–1887) was appointed in 1861 as superintendent of female nurses the highest nursing post of the war and the only major federal appointment won by a woman. She organized and recruited a corps of 6,000 nurses to serve with the Union army.

United States (Union): At least four women fought in the battle of Antietam; two were wounded and one died. Clara Barton reported treating a soldier whose real name was Mary Galloway; **Sarah Emma Edmonds** said that she cared for a female soldier in disguise who died of her wounds.

United States (Union): **Harriet Tubman** (1820?–1913), a former slave and abolitionist, served from 1862 to 1864 as a scout for the Union in South Carolina. Her prewar clandestine work on the "Underground Railroad" equipped her well for military service. She commanded a small reconnaissance unit whose mission was to slip behind enemy lines to determine Confederate troop movements and strength. She also led raiding parties. Tubman served without rank and without pay.

1861–1866   **American Civil War**.

1862   **American Civil War:** An important battle was fought at Antietam Creek near Sharpsburg, Maryland (17 September). There was no clear victor, but casualties ran high on both sides, with nearly 5,000 killed. The battle has been called "America's bloodiest day."

1862–1864   **American Civil War**.

Women and the military	Date of activity/event	Military history events
United States (Union): **Sarah Rosetta Wakeman** (1843–1864) served with the 153rd Regiment, New York State Volunteers, disguised as Private Lyons Wakeman. Her unit only experienced combat in 1864 during the Red River Campaign. Wakeman subsequently died in New Orleans of disease, where she was buried under her pseudonym. Her story only became known in 1976 when her numerous letters to her family were rediscovered and later published.	1862–1864	**American Civil War.**
United States (Union): **Jennie Hodgers** (1844–1915) has the longest documented length of service by a female soldier in the Civil War. Just over five feet tall, Hodgers was assigned primarily to foraging and skirmishing duty. She took part in forty battles and was never wounded; "Albert Cashier" is listed on the Vicksburg battlefield monument to Illinois soldiers. What is remarkable about Hodgers's life is that unlike most women soldiers who fought in disguise, she retained her male identity for fifty years after the war.	1862–1865	**American Civil War.**
United States (Union): **Susie King Taylor** (1848–1912), at the age of 14, joined the First South Carolina Volunteers (later known as the 33rd United States Colored Troops) as an unpaid nurse. Following the now famous assault upon Fort Wagner, South Carolina, by the 54th Massachusetts Infantry in 1863, Taylor assisted Clara Barton in treating the wounded. She continued working with Barton for several months. Many years later she wrote her memoirs—the only African American woman to record her wartime experiences.	1862–1865	**American Civil War.**

Mexico: **Ignacia Reachy** (1816?–1866) started a women's battalion to defend against the French, fought in the Battle of Acultzingo in 1862, was captured by the French, spent a year in prison, escaped to fight again, and then commanded the Lancers of Jallsco until she was killed in battle in 1866.

1862–1866   Mexico: French intervention.

Paraguayan women were actively involved in the War of the Triple Alliance. Hundreds of women and children fought and died.

1864–1870   Latin America: War of the Triple Alliance (Paraguayan War). Paraguay invaded Brazil and declared war on Argentina, sparking an alliance of Argentina, Brazil, and Uruguay, which counterattacked into Paraguay in 1866 and dominated the country; guerrilla fighting continued until 1870.

Brazil: **Jovita Alves Feitosa** disguised herself as a boy and enlisted to fight for Brazil in the War of the Triple Alliance. Her identity was soon discovered, and after a brief period of fame she was forced to leave the army.

1865

United States: **Lozen** (1840?–1889) was a Chiricahua Apache warrior and holy woman, sister of Victorio, noted for her active role in Apache fighting against the United States Army. After her brother's death she rode with Geronimo's band until their surrender in 1886—among the last native groups to be subdued.

1866–1890   United States: Indian Wars.

United States: **Cathay Williams,** an African American woman, enlisted in the 38th United States Infantry Regiment in 1866 in male disguise as "William Cathay." Her unit traveled throughout the West and was stationed in Missouri, Kansas, and New Mexico. The regiment appears not to have been involved in combat. Williams was discharged in 1868 on medical grounds without ever being discovered in two years' service.

1866–1868

Women and the military	Date of activity/event	Military history events
United States: **Ehyophsta** (ca. 1826–1915), a Cheyenne woman, sought combat at the age of forty after the death of her husband. She participated in a battle with an army scouting party in Colorado in 1868 and later fought Shoshoni in Montana. She was admitted to the Crazy Dog Soldier Warrior Society in recognition of her coups against enemy warriors.	1868	United States: Indian Wars.
France: **Louise Michel** (1830–1905) organized women's first-aid units and attempted to acquire weapons for women to use in fighting against the Prussians.	1870–1871	Franco-Prussian War. Although Napoleon III surrendered his army in September 1870, Paris refused to accept defeat. The Prussians besieged Paris from September 1870 to January 1871. During the siege the Parisian National Guard defended the city operating independently of the military.
France: **Louise Michel** was among the instigators of the **Paris Commune**. When the barricades began to go up, women were heavily involved. Blanche Lefebvre was among the women killed fighting behind a barricade.	1871	The Paris Commune began on 18 March 1871 when the French government tried to send in troops to take the Parisian National Guard's cannon. The citizens of Paris elected a council that proclaimed Paris autonomous and announced its intent to re-create France as a confederation of communes. A socialist economic system was devised. When attacks began by the French army, many districts organized groups of barricade fighters. Government troops entered the city on 21 May, followed by seven days of bitter street fighting in which many thousands were killed or arrested.
United States: **The Other Magpie** was a Crow woman who was among the scouts working for General George Crook in 1876. At Rosebud she counted coup on a Lakota warrior and took his scalp.	1876	United States: Indian Wars. On the morning of 17 June 1876 Brigadier General George Crook's 1,300 soldiers and scouts met 1,500 Lakota and Cheyenne warriors on the Rosebud River. The battle involved more troops and

Native Americans (on both sides), had fewer casualties, and was of eventual greater historical significance than any other battle in all of the Indian campaigns. Crook's Indian allies were instrumental in preventing his troops from being overrun, permitting them to make a retreat.

Turkey: Nana Hatun participated in the fighting in the Ottoman-Russian War. A memorial was erected in remembrance of her courage and patriotism in Erzurum in eastern Turkey. Turkish women have served voluntarily in several wars as combatants.	1877–1878	Ottoman-Russian War.
Africa: Charwe (1862?–1898), a medium of militant spirit **Nehanda,** instigated rebellion against colonial rule in 1893–1896. Nehanda was captured in December 1897 and executed in April 1898. Her unrepentant behavior preceding her hanging became legendary, making her a symbol of nationalist resistance.	1893–1896	In a Southern Rhodesian anticolonial struggle known locally as Chimurenga I, tribes without firearms rebelled unsuccessfully against the British.
Dahomey: In the 1890s the women warriors were in the front ranks of the troops that defended Dahomey from an invading French colonial army. Decimated by the superior firepower of the French, the army of Dahomey (male and female soldiers alike) was disbanded when the kingdom fell to the French in 1894.	1894	West Africa: Dahomey fell to the French, becoming a protectorate.
United States: A Beebe Beam was said to have served in male disguise during the Spanish-American War.	1898	The Spanish-American War erupted when an American ship was destroyed at Havana. An American blockade and assault in Cuba followed, including Theodore Roosevelt's famous charge at San Juan Ridge. The war ended with Spanish withdrawal from Cuba and American possession of Puerto Rico, Guam, and the Philippines.
United States: The Army Nurse Corps was established. Its members had no military rank or ben-	1901	

Women and the military	Date of activity/event	Military history events
efits and received less pay than military men performing the same duties.		
Israel: **Mania Shochat** (1879–1961) was an important leader of Hashomer. Before the First World War she worked for the Jewish self-defense movement in Russia, raising funds and smuggling weapons and ammunition into Russia. An immigrant to Palestine, she was arrested and imprisoned on several occasions by the Turks.	1905–1920s?	Israel: Jewish self-defense movement Hashomer.
United Kingdom: The **FANY Corps** (First Aid Nursing Yeomanry Corps) was founded for women to provide volunteer military support services, including nursing, driving, and espionage.	1907	
United States: The Navy Nurse Corps was established as an auxiliary.	1908	
Mexico: During the 1910 Revolution thousands of *soldaderas* were attached to all of the major armies of the war. A distinction was made between *soldadas* (women who fought) and *soldaderas* (women who provided support services). *Soldadas* were often given "battlefield" ranks ("la Capitana"). After the Revolution ended, these ranks were rarely recognized, but *soldadas* could apply for pensions, unlike the *soldaderas*.	1910–1920	Mexican Revolution. When the dictator Porfirio Díaz lost an election, a decade-long civil war ensued, with casualties of up to a million.
Mexico: **Petra Herrera** first fought in male disguise in order to establish her reputation as a soldier and commander, then resumed her true identity. She reportedly commanded both men and a women's army of 300–400 female soldiers. She continued to serve the government after the revolution in activities that resulted in her murder in 1917.	1910–1917	Mexican Revolution.

Mexico: **Maria de la Luz Espinosa Barrera** fought for Zapata, at first disguised as a male soldier. Zapata acknowledged her bravery and promoted her to lieutenant colonel. She later qualified for a veteran's pension.	1910–1920	Mexican Revolution. After Porfirio Díaz was defeated in 1911, the revolutionaries became factionalized. The government changed hands several times. Key leaders were Emiliano Zapata (assassinated in 1919) and Francisco (Pancho) Villa. The civil war ended in 1920 when General Obregón became president.
Mexico: **Petra Ruiz** fought in male disguise for the Carranza faction and achieved the rank of lieutenant.	1910–1920	Mexican Revolution. Venustiano Carranza was one of the contenders for power; he took control of Mexico City in 1914. Villa and Zapata opposed him.
Mexico: **Angela Jiménez** (1886–?) served as a *soldadera* and at times in male disguise in the forces of Villa and Zapata. She later moved to California and became a civil rights activist.	1911–1920	Mexican Revolution.
	1914–1918	The First World War, sparked by the assassination of the Austrian archduke in the Balkans, quickly escalated to involve all the major powers of Europe. The first attacks were by Austria against Serbia and Germany against Belgium and France. Offensives everywhere bogged down by the end of the year and deteriorated into trench warfare, especially on the western front.
Russia: **Ekaterina Alekseeva** (1895–?), in male disguise, was among the first volunteers. She served for several months until her identity was discovered when she was wounded.	1914	First World War, eastern front: The Russian army attacked in East Prussia and Austrian areas in Poland in support of its French and Serbian friends, but was soundly defeated. Although massive, the Russian forces were severely impaired by poor leadership and even worse training and equipment. The Russians were essentially on the defensive after 1914.
Russia: Twenty-nine-year-old **Anna Krasil'nikova** put on male disguise and traveled to the front in central Poland in the early weeks of the war, where she	1914	First World War, eastern front.

Women and the military	Date of activity/event	Military history events
joined an infantry unit. She reportedly participated in nineteen battles before being wounded in November 1914, at which time her true sex was discovered. She was awarded the **Order of St. George**.		
Russia: **Kira Aleksandrovna Bashkirova** disguised herself as a man and served in cavalry reconnaissance in the early months of the war. In December 1914 she received the **Order of St. George** for bravery. Her identity was discovered soon afterwards and she was dismissed, but she was able to reenlist with another unit. She fought until she was wounded and her identity was once more discovered.	1914–1915	First World War, eastern front: In 1915 there were large-scale offensives against the Russians early in the year.
Russia: **Princess Evgeniia Shakhovskaia** earned her pilot's license before the war and served as a military reconnaissance pilot. She was apparently the first woman in the world to serve officially as a military aviator.	1914	First World War, eastern front.
Russia: Nadezhda Degtereva reportedly disguised herself as a boy and entered military air service in 1914 as a reconnaissance pilot. She served for an unknown period until she was wounded and her disguise was discovered.	1914	
Russia: **Mariia Leont'evna Bochkareva** (1889–?) petitioned the tsar in 1914 and was permitted to enlist under her own name. She served with some distinction, was wounded several times, and was decorated. Politically conservative, Bochkareva left the regular army in 1917, disgusted by the demoralized atmosphere fostered by constant defeat, poor conditions, and socialist agitation in the ranks.	1914–1917	First World War, eastern front.

Russia: **E.P. Samsonova,** a qualified pilot, was denied permission to fly in the military. She volunteered as an army nurse and then became a driver. Illness forced her out of the service in 1915.	1914–1915	First World War, eastern front.
Russia: **Zoia Smirnova** was one of twelve teenaged girls who made their way to the Austrian front in July 1914 and attempted to disguise themselves as young men. Their disguise was not effective, but they were permitted to remain at the front. Smirnova was wounded twice and in late 1915 was awarded the **Order of St. George** and promoted to junior noncommissioned officer. After recovering from her wounds, however, she was persuaded to serve for the rest of the war as a nurse.	1914–1917	First World War, eastern front.
United Kingdom: **Flora Sandes** (1876–1956) was an English-woman who served seven years in the Serbian army, rising from nurse during the typhus epidemic of 1915 to the rank of captain in 1919. She switched from nursing to infantry duty in late 1915, was wounded in 1916 and 1917, was decorated for bravery, and was promoted. After the war she acted as a fundraiser for Serbia's war relief.	1914–1921	First World War, Serbian army.
	1915	First World War: Poison gas was first used by Germany on the eastern front (January) and later in France (Second Battle of Ypres). It failed to be a decisive weapon.
	1915	First World War: The Battle of the Atlantic began in February with widespread German submarine attacks on Allied shipping. The sinking of the British *Lusitania*, in which Americans were killed, eroded American isolationism.

Women and the military	Date of activity/event	Military history events
Russia: **Princess Kati Dadeshkeliani,** a member of the Georgian aristocracy, disguised herself as a young male officer and served as an aide-de-camp to a family friend and as a cavalry courier, drawing on her skills in horsemanship.	1915–1917	First World War, eastern front.
	1915–1916	First World War, western front: The Gallipoli Campaign was a disastrous attack by Allied forces (British and Australian) against Turkish territory.
United Kingdom: The **Women's Legion,** a volunteer women's corps, provided various support services for the army from 1915 until the 1930s. In 1915 it began sending cooks to the army; in 1916 it also sent female drivers. It was assimilated by **WAAC/ QMAAC** in September 1917 and was revived in 1933.	1915–1917	First World War, western front.
	1915	First World War: Italy entered the war in support of the Allies and embarked on bloody and inconclusive fighting against Austria.
	1916	First World War, western front: Two massive assaults intended to break the stalemate both failed. The Germans attempted to rout the French at Verdun (February–December), a vicious battle of attrition involving gas warfare and costing a million casualties. At the Battle of the Somme (July–November) the British unsuccessfully sought a breakthrough with a massive artillery bombardment, then got bogged down in attritional fighting, with more than a million total Allied and Axis casualties.
	1916	First World War, Armenian Holocaust: The Turks interned and murdered 1–1.5 million Armenians, resulting in a large-scale exodus of survivors to Russia.

Russia: **Princess Sofiia Dolgoru-kaia** was a pilot who was refused permission to serve during the early years of the war, but was allowed to serve as a reconnaissance pilot after the February Revolution of 1917.

1917   First World War, eastern front.

Russia: The **Women's Battalions of Death** were the first women's military units in Russia, organized in the spring of 1917 by the Provisional Government. **Mariia Bochkareva** became the first Russian woman to command a military unit. Her First Russian Women's Battalion of Death in Petrograd had to turn away many volunteers. Bochkareva narrowed the group to about 300 women and conducted harsh training. This unit went to the front in the summer of 1917 but, in the chaotic conditions of the time, only went into combat once. The Provisional Government approved the organization of further combat units composed of women volunteers in 1917, including two fully equipped all-female infantry battalions in Petrograd and Moscow and a dozen communications detachments. Other groups like the Kuban Women's Shock Battalion were formed on the members own initiative. Most did not become operational before the Bolshevik Revolution in October dissolved all such units of the Provisional Government. Bochkareva disbanded her unit, still at the front. Another unit in Petrograd was pulled into the fighting at the Winter Palace during the revolution to defend the Provisional Government.

1917   First World War, eastern front: Widespread mutinies developed in the Russian army, leading to the abdication of Tsar Nicholas II and the establishment of a politically liberal Provisional Government in the February Revolution. The Provisional Government attempted to honor Russia's commitment to the Allies to keep a second front open in the war, with disastrous consequences. Russia's final offensive occurred in July 1917.

Russia: **Women's Military Unions** cropped up after the February Revolution. These unions were established in large numbers as voluntary associations of

1917   First World War, eastern front.

Women and the military	Date of activity/event	Military history events
women who wanted to expand women's roles in the war effort. They worked to create separate female military units intended for combat. They also established women's labor militias, ambulance detachments, and women's medical units.		
	1917, April	First World War: The United States issued a declaration of war on Germany in early April, and American naval vessels entered the Battle of the Atlantic.
United Kingdom: The **Women's Land Army** was formed by the Women's Branch of the Ministry of Agriculture in 1917 to provide farmworkers; some 23,000 women participated.	1917–1919	First World War.
United Kingdom: The Women's Auxiliary Army Corps (**WAAC**) assimilated the Women's Legion in 1917 and in 1918 was renamed Queen Mary's Auxiliary Army Corps (QMAAC) when the queen assumed leadership of the group. This organization supplemented the cooks and drivers of the Women's Legion with administrative and clerical support.	1917–1921	First World War, western front.
United Kingdom: **Dame Helen Gwynne-Vaughan** (1879–1967) headed the overseas section of the Women's Auxiliary Army Corps (**WAAC**) in February 1917. She fought unsuccessfully for equal military status for her group, despising the camp-follower status of the corps. Her accomplishments with the WAAC in France led to her appointment as head of the Women's Royal Air Force (WRAF) in August 1918.	1917–1919	First World War, western front.
United States: Secretary of the Navy Josephus Daniels enrolled women in the Naval Reserve as "yeomanettes"; 12,500 served by	1917	First World War.

the end of the war. Thirty black women served as yeomanettes in a segregated office in the Navy Department.

United States: **Joy Bright Hancock** (1898–1986) enlisted as a naval yeoman (F) in the Women's Naval Reserve during the First World War.

Russia: The **Women's Military Congress** held in August 1917, was a gathering of representatives from the **Women's Military Unions** and related groups across Russia. Because large numbers of women were trying to make their way to the front in an unorganized way from all parts of the country, its goal was to coordinate the activities of women who sought to contribute to the war effort. It supported the right of women to participate in both support and combat on an equal basis with men.

France: Mata Hari was executed by the French as a spy in October 1917.

United States: Women first entered the ranks of the United States Marine Corps when it began enrolling "marinettes" two months before the end of hostilities.

1917–1918	First World War.
1917, June	First World War, western front: American forces began arriving in France in June 1917.
1917, August	First World War, eastern front.
1917, October	First World War, western front.
1917, October	Russia: The Bolshevik Revolution occurred, overthrowing the short-lived Provisional Government. The Bolsheviks were committed to withdrawing from the war. Lenin agreed to a punitive peace with Germany (the Treaty of Brest-Litovsk) in March 1918.
1917, November	First World War, western front: The Battle of Cambrai (20 November–3 December) was the first massed use of tanks in combat.
1918	First World War.

Women and the military	Date of activity/event	Military history events
	1918	First World War, western front: Armistice was declared on 11 November 1918, ending the First World War.
Russia: The **Russian Civil War** involved large numbers of women on a much broader scale and more organized fashion than during the First World War. Unlike the women of 1917, these served primarily in integrated units. Most were in support roles (medical, administrative, and political), but there were also women in infantry, gunners, demolition troops, partisans, scouts, and spies. At least 70,000 women fought in the Red Army. Few appear to have been active on the side of the Whites. The **Order of the Red Banner,** awarded for bravery in combat, went to dozens of women recipients, primarily medical and political personnel.	1918–1922	Russian Civil War: After the Bolshevik Revolution various groups collectively called the Whites opposed the socialist Reds. A bitter and extended civil war was fought that ultimately involved half a dozen White armies, the armed forces of nearly a dozen national groups, and soldiers from fourteen foreign countries. Casualties were higher than those of the First World War, an estimated 13 million.
Russia: **Larisa Reisner** (1895–1926) served in the navy during the **Russian Civil War** in reconnaissance and intelligence and as a commissar.	1918–1921	
Russia: **A.P. Bogat** (1898–?) served as a commissar in the Red Army and was involved in extensive action, including capturing a prisoner bearing important documents. She also served in Budenny's Cavalry Army for two years as platoon commander and as chief of reconnaissance.	1918–1921	Russian Civil War.
Poland: A Women's Volunteer League (Ochotnicza Legia Kobiet, or **OLK**) was created in December 1918, ultimately comprising six battalions with several thousand women. The OLK grew out of women's militia groups that developed in the chaotic period at the end of the First World War.	1918–1922	Polish-Soviet War.

The most common roles were sentry duty, courier assignments, medical aid, and clerical work, but women also served in the infantry and in field artillery units as observers and gunners. Aleksandra Zagórska (1884–1965), who had previously served in the women's section of Józef Piłsudski's paramilitary group, was the creater and founder of OLK.

Russia: At least one assault company of female infantry served in combat in the Polish campaign.	1919–1920	The Polish-Soviet War began with Polish and Ukrainian attacks on Red forces during the civil war, followed by a Soviet offensive into Poland under Tukhachevsky. The offensive could not be supported, and the Soviets were driven back into Soviet territory.
Palestine: **Rachel Yanait Ben-Zvi** (1886–1979) was a military leader and organizer in Haganah for almost twenty years. In addition to administrative work for the secret self-defense of the Jews, she smuggled weapons and was active in recruiting.	1920–1940	Palestine: Jews created the Haganah, a paramilitary group designed to train Jewish settlers in self-defense. This group would provide a foundation for the Israel Defense Forces.
	1920	Germany: Ernst Röhm founded the Storm Troopers (SA), a paramilitary group that played a vital role in the rise of the Nazi Party.
United States: **Anita Phipps** (1886–1953) was director of women's relations, United States Army, 1921–1931. She wrote the first complete and workable plan for a women's army corps. The plan was rejected by the General Staff in 1926, and several years of bureaucratic infighting followed.	1921–1931	
United States: The Naval Reserve Act of 1916 was reworded so that instead of enlisting "citizens," the Navy was only authorized to enlist "male citizens." This was designed to prevent the enlistment of women directly into military service.	1925	

Women and the military	Date of activity/event	Military history events
	1927–1949	The Chinese Civil War was a lengthy conflict between the Kuomintang army, led by Chiang Kai-shek, and the Communists under Mao Zedong. Early urban-based uprisings failed, leading Mao to develop his strategy of a protracted war based in rural areas rather than cities.
Osoaviakhim was the Soviet Union's mass voluntary society dedicated to educating and training its members in civil defense and paramilitary skills. Women were primarily given training in auxiliary and support work, such as intelligence gathering and analysis, map reading, first aid and medical care, communications, and air and chemical defense techniques. Large numbers of women also participated in weapons training, especially rifle marksmanship. Aviation clubs sponsored by Osoaviakhim gave thousands of Soviet women the opportunity to learn to fly small aircraft. Thus a significant number of Soviet women attained valuable skills during the years prior to the Second World War, providing a pool of potential snipers and pilots.	1927–1948	
	1930	Vietnam: Ho Chi Minh founded the first Vietnamese Communist Party. He advocated an active role for Vietnamese women in the struggle to evict the French colonial regime.
United States: The position of army director of women's programs (held by **Anita Phipps**) was abolished by General Douglas MacArthur, chief of staff, as one that had "no military value."	1931	
Soviet Union: **Marina Raskova** became the first woman to qualify as an air force navigator.	1933	

1933

Germany: Hitler came to power, bringing Nazi domination first to Germany and then to much of Europe. In the same year, the concentration camp at Buchenwald was established.

United Kingdom: The **Women's Legion** of the First World War was reborn in late 1933, but sectors of the government did not see the need for a peacetime women's reserve and feared the political consequences of "militarizing" women, leading to the collapse of the organization in early 1936.

1933

China: **Kang Keqing** was the fourth wife of Zhu De (Chu The), one of the key leaders of the Communist forces. Kang commanded a battalion of 800 men whose leader was killed. She was one of the thousands of women and children who participated in the Long March; most served in support roles (collecting and preparing food, caring for the sick and wounded) and in functions such as propaganda and recruitment. Some women participated in fighting, and there were a few all-female units, such as a Women's Engineering Battalion.

1934–1935

Chinese Civil War: The Long March was a forced retreat by the Communist forces, covering a distance of thousands of miles and involving nearly constant fighting against forces of the Kuomintang army. Many key Communist leaders were on the Long March, including Mao Zedong, Zhou Enlai, and Zhu De.

Germany: **Hanna Reitsch** (1912–1979) is widely regarded as the first female test pilot in the Luftwaffe, but it is not clear whether she or **Melitta Schiller Stauffenberg** actually began this work first. Reitsch was the first to receive honorary "flight captain" rank in 1936.

1935

Germany: **Melitta Schiller Stauffenberg** (1903–1945), an engineer and private pilot, was involved in military-related test flying by 1935. She performed aerobatics during the 1936 Olympics, like her contemporary **Hanna**

1935

Women and the military	Date of activity/event	Military history events
Reitsch. Due to a Jewish grandfather she was forced out of Luftwaffe service in 1936, but was reinstated in 1937 (see under 1937).		
Women were widely involved in the **Spanish Civil War**. On the Nationalist side, which emphasized traditional Catholic virtues, women played traditional support roles. Among the Republicans, women served in both support roles and as armed *milicianas*. The armed militiawoman was a common sight in Republican Spain. Many non-Spanish women joined the fight.	1936–1939	**Spanish Civil War**: Fascist forces under General Francisco Franco (Nationalists) were backed by German and Italian troops. The Republican side was supported by the International Brigades of international volunteers, many Communist and anarchist, all opposed to fascism. The Soviet Union provided clandestine support to the Republicans.
Spain: **Lina Odena** (~1914–1936) was one of the first women to die in combat in the **Spanish Civil War**. An ardent Communist, she joined a militia unit at the outbreak of hostilities. When she was cut off by enemy forces, she committed suicide.	1936	**Spanish Civil War**.
Spain: **Rosario Sánchez Mora** (1919–) was known as La Dinamitera for her work in explosives on the Republican side. After losing a hand in 1937, she was forced to transfer into a support role.	1936	**Spanish Civil War**.
Spain: **Mika Etchebéhère** was an Argentinian Communist who, after her husband's death, became commander of a combat unit on the Republican side. She was considered a respected and innovative leader of both women and men and later published her memoirs of the war. She served from 1936 to 1938.	1936	**Spanish Civil War**.
United Kingdom: The Emergency Service developed out of the **Women's Legion** to train women auxiliary officers. The group was later absorbed by the **ATS** (Auxiliary Territorial Service) in 1939.	1936	

Soviet Union/Spain: Nora Pav-lovna Chegodaeva was among an unknown number of Soviet women who reportedly partici-pated in the **Spanish Civil War**. She later became the commander of the Soviet **Central Women's School for Sniper Training** in the Second World War.

| | 1937–1938 | **Spanish Civil War**. |

1937, June — Soviet Union: The purges reached their peak with the exe-cution of Civil War hero Mikhail Tukhachevsky in June 1937; the purge then escalated to involve large numbers of military per-sonnel (3 out of 5 marshals, 3 out of 4 army commanders, all mili-tary district commanders, 51 out of 57 corps commanders, 80 per-cent of colonels, and a total of 40,000–50,000 of 100,000 officers on active duty in 1937). Stalin murdered more high-ranking of-ficers (colonel and above) than would be killed by Germans in the Second World War. This purge of the military had cata-strophic effects on the morale, readiness, and leadership of the Red Army on the eve of the Sec-ond World War.

Germany: **Hanna Reitsch** began formal duties as a test pilot in Germany with quasi-military status. Reitsch put on a helicopter demonstration for Charles Lind-bergh's 1937 visit and was awarded the Military Flying Medal. Later she tested a proto-type troop-carrying glider.

1937 — Germany: Charles Lindbergh vis-ited Germany.

Germany: **Melitta Schiller Stauf-fenberg** was reinstated in military-related test flying with the rank of flight captain. The same year, she married Alexan-der Schenk, Count von Stauffen-berg, and became sister-in-law to Colonel Claus Stauffenberg, who attempted to assassinate Hitler in 1944.

1937

Women and the military	Date of activity/event	Military history events
	1937–1945	The Sino-Japanese War began when the Japanese invaded China in 1937, occupying much of the northern regions. In December Japan's brutal treatment of the residents of Nanking became known as the "Rape of Nanking." The conflict continued throughout the Second World War as the Japanese extended their control in China against bitter resistance.
United Kingdom: The name of the **FANY Corps** was officially changed to Women's Transport Service (FANY).	1937	
	1938, March	Europe: Nazi forces annexed Austria in the Anschluss (12 March 1938), beginning the expansion of German control in Europe.
United Kingdom: The **FANY Corps** was split in two. The Women's Transport Service (FANY) was assigned to the army to provide transport drivers; this was the unit that Princess Elizabeth joined in 1945. The original FANY headquarters element became known informally as the Free FANY or simply the Corps.	1938	
	1938, September	Europe: The Munich Agreement was signed in late September, in which Britain and France allowed Germany to annex portions of Czechoslovakia. Within a few months Germany extended its control to the entire country. This became an infamous example of appeasement.
United Kingdom: The **ATS** (Auxiliary Territorial Service) was created in September 1938 to administer women who trained and served operationally in other army branches, in order to release men for combat. Dame **Helen Gwynne-Vaughan** was	1938, September	

appointed Director in July 1939. Women's roles were at first fairly narrow, but expanded throughout the war. The ATS supplied female personnel to the Anti-Aircraft Command, which by 1943 employed 57,000 women. Many served in mixed batteries, but women were forbidden to actually fire the guns.

Soviet Union: The title **Hero of the Soviet Union,** introduced in 1934, was first awarded to women in October 1938, when **Marina Raskova,** Polina Osipenko, and **Valentina Grizodubova** were recognized for their pioneer nonstop transcontinental flight to the Far East in September 1938. Valentina Grizodubova (1910–1993) was an instructor pilot who set seven world records in the prewar years. She was the chief pilot of the *Rodina* mission in 1938.

1938, October	
1939, January	The **Spanish Civil War** ended in the first months of 1939 when the Nationalists took control of Barcelona and Madrid. Franco's government became the recognized government in Spain.
1939, April	United States: General George Marshall became chief of staff of the army in April 1939. He would be an advocate of military roles for women.
1939, August	The Kwangtung Army of Japan, based in Manchuria, attacked Soviet and Mongolian troops at the Khalkin River (Khalkin Gol) in May. General Georgii Zhukov led a successful counterattack, decisively defeating a force of 75,000 Japanese troops. This defeat would result in Japan's neutrality toward the Soviet Union during the Second World War.
1939–1945	The Second World War was the largest, most catastrophic war of human history.

Women and the military	Date of activity/event	Military history events
	1939, September	Second World War, eastern front: The first open hostilities of the war began with the German invasion of Poland in September 1939. Poland was crushed within a month. A Soviet invasion of eastern Poland, in accordance with the Nazi-Soviet Pact of 1939, began two weeks after the German attack. Britain and France declared war on Germany, soon joined by other Commonwealth nations. American President Franklin Roosevelt declared neutrality on September 5, but authorized arms shipments to the Allies.
Poland: Women comprised about 14 percent of the Polish Home Army, the **Armia Krajowa** (AK). Most served as liaison couriers and medics, plus two all-female specialty units, one of demolition experts, the other a unit created during the Warsaw Uprising to serve as guides in the city's sewer system.	1939–1944	Second World War, eastern front: Polish resistance movement.
Germany: When Germany went to war in 1939, **Melitta Schiller Stauffenberg** hoped to transfer to the Red Cross, but was required by the Air Ministry to continue work in her specialty of testing dive bombers. By the end of 1943 she had accumulated more dive-bombing flights in the Ju-88 than any other German pilot.	1939	Second World War, Germany, home front.
Germany: **Hanna Reitsch** applied for service as an active military pilot when war broke out in 1939, but was refused. She continued to work as a military test pilot.	1939	Second World War, Germany, home front.
	1939 September–1945	Second World War, Battle of the Atlantic: On the day that Britain declared war on Germany after its invasion of Poland, Germany began its submarine campaign

against Atlantic shipping, sinking more than 250 vessels without warning in 1939.

	1939, November–1940	The Soviet-Finnish War began in November 1939 when Soviet forces, having already occupied the three Baltic states (Estonia, Latvia, and Lithuania), proceeded into Finland. Despite numerical superiority, the Red Army met unexpectedly stiff resistance from the Finns, but prevailed by March 1940, with heavy casualties.
United Kingdom: The **Women's Land Army** became active once more. In the Second World War more than 70,000 women served in nontraditional agricultural occupations, releasing men for other war services. It became so important to British agriculture that it was not disbanded until 1950.	1939	Second World War, United Kingdom, home front.
United Kingdom: Women pilots entered the **ATA** beginning in 1940. Relegated at first to ferrying trainers, they began ferrying combat aircraft in 1941. After 1944 a few women made deliveries to the Continent. One hundred sixty-six women from a variety of countries, including the United States, making up 12 percent of the total, flew for the ATA during the war. Fifteen died.	1940	Second World War, United Kingdom, home front: The ATA (Air Transport Auxiliary), formed in 1939, was a civilian ferry service that delivered new and repaired aircraft to active British squadrons during the Second World War.
Poland: **Janina Lewandowska** (1908–1940) was a pilot and reserve officer in the Polish air force when the Second World War broke out. She appears to have been the only female officer to have been executed in the infamous Katyn Massacre of 1940.	1940, April	Second World War, eastern front: The Katyn Massacre occurred in Soviet-occupied Poland. Some 10,000 Polish prisoners (most of the officer corps) were massacred by the Red Army. For decades the Soviets claimed that the Germans were responsible, only admitting the truth in 1990.
	1940, April	Second World War, western front: German forces invaded Norway (April–June 1940).

Women and the military	Date of activity/event	Military history events
	1940, May	Second World War, western front: War began in western Europe with the German invasion of the Low Countries and France in May 1940. Belgium surrendered on May 28, and on the same day the British Expeditionary Force began its evacuation at Dunkirk. The Battle of France continued until the French surrendered on 25 June. In the same month Italy joined the war on the German side with attacks on Malta.
United Kingdom: The secret Special Operations Executive (SOE) was formed in July 1940 to support resistance movements in occupied areas. The women's support auxiliary known as the Free **FANY** provided assistance—packing parachutes, operating radios, and assisting in agent training. Seventy-three were themselves trained as agents and thirty-nine were dropped into France. Several led resistance groups that sabotaged enemy facilities. Many were captured but escaped to survive the war. Thirteen FANY agents died in Nazi concentration camps. The SOE also employed French women. Marie-Madeleine Fourcade was the only French woman known to have led a major resistance network; she was promoted by British intelligence to lead its 3,000-strong network.	1940, July	Second World War, western front.
	1940, August	Second World War, western front: The Battle of Britain was fought in August–October 1940. The Royal Air Force stood off repeated Luftwaffe attacks against its bases. The Germans then shifted to bombing raids against British cities, primarily from November 1940 through May 1941, though raids continued throughout the war.

	1940, December	Second World War: Fighting began in Africa between British and Italian forces.
Resistance Movements, French women: During the German occupation of France, French women assisted the Resistance's efforts in disproportionately high numbers. In late 1940 Charles de Gaulle authorized the creation of a women's auxiliary corps similar to the British **ATS** that eventually included 4,000 members. Unlike the British ATS/SOE, the French auxiliary under de Gaulle relegated most women to traditional nursing and support duties. French women were rarely allowed to fight, except in some Communist cells. However, women played a vital role in noncombat activities, including disseminating information and hiding weapons and personnel. A few women worked in demolitions.	1940–1945	Second World War, western front.
Australia: The **Australian Defence Forces** permitted no women but nurses until 1941. The Women's Auxiliary Australian Air Force (**WAAAF**) and Women's Royal Australian Naval Service (WRANS) were both established in 1941, followed by the Australian Women's Army Service (AWAS). Women were geographically restricted until late in the war; their main role was to free Australian men to join the combat arms.	1941	Second World War, Australia, home front.
Germany: **Hanna Reitsch** received the Iron Cross (second class) in 1941. She went on to test variants of the Messerschmitt-163 Komet "rocket plane" and was hospitalized in the winter of 1942–1943 after a bad crash.	1941	Second World War, Germany, home front.
Poland/United Kingdom: **Anna Leska-Daab** was one of three Polish women who had been	1941, February	Second World War, United Kingdom, home front.

Timeline

Women and the military	Date of activity/event	Military history events
military pilots before the war and joined the British **ATA**. She began ferrying duty in 1941 and continued until November 1945. She ferried a total of 1,295 aircraft, including 557 Supermarine Spitfires. She flew 93 types of aircraft and spent 1,241 hours in the air.		
Australia: The Women's Auxiliary Australian Air Force (**WAAAF**) pioneered the admission of women other than nurses into the Australian armed forces. Many served as telegraphists and teleprinter operators.	1941, March	Second World War, Australia, home front.
Resistance movements, Yugoslav women. There were diverse partisan groups in Yugoslavia, but most women joined Tito's Communist forces. By 1945 his group included about 100,000 women (12 percent of the total). Training was integrated, and women were theoretically equal to men. Women served most often as plain soldiers and medics, although some women worked in radio, artillery, political, and intelligence positions. Yugoslavian women suffered heavy casualties, with a higher rate for women in support roles than those in combat.	1941, April	Second World War: The Germans invaded Yugoslavia in April 1941, quickly gaining control. Resistance groups quickly emerged, especially the well-organized Communists under Josip Broz (Tito).
Australia: **Kathleen Best** (1910–1957) was in charge of an Australian hospital during the disastrous Allied attempt to prevent the German invasion of Greece and Crete.	1941, April	Second World War: Germany invaded Greece and quickly defeated British forces in the region, inflicting heavy casualties on both the Greeks and the British.
	1941, June	Soviet Union: The Great Patriotic War, the term used by the Soviet Union for its struggle against Germany during the Second World War, began with the massive German invasion of Soviet territory (Operation Barbarossa)

on 22 June 1941. By October the Germans had occupied large portions of the western Soviet Union and were threatening Moscow. The siege of Leningrad began and continued for nearly three years. The war continued until the spring of 1945. Three-quarters of all German troops fought in the East, and 80 percent of German casualties (close to 11 million) occurred on the eastern front. The Soviet Union lost more soldiers and civilians than any other country, with estimates of around 10 million dead and 18 million wounded in the military, and 20 million or more civilians. During the siege of Leningrad alone, one million Soviet citizens died (more than the combat deaths of the United States and United Kingdom combined).

Soviet Union: Irina Levchenko (1924–1973) began service in July 1941 as a medic. She was wounded at the battle for Moscow. In July 1942 she achieved an assignment to tank school and became a tank driver. Serving as a platoon commander near Smolensk, she was wounded again, but returned to duty on the 3rd Ukrainian Front, pushing into central Europe. She was wounded once more near Budapest and was later made a **Hero of the Soviet Union**. She continued military service after the war until 1958.

1941, July

Great Patriotic War.

Soviet Union: The 122nd Aviation Group was a training group authorized by Stalin on 8 October 1941 at the instigation of **Marina** Raskova, a famous navigator who had received the **Hero of the Soviet Union** in 1938. She advocated the use of women pilots in combat. The purpose of the group was to recruit and train

1941, October

Great Patriotic War: In the Battle of Moscow (November–December 1941) Soviet forces managed to prevent the Germans from taking Moscow. General Georgii Zhukov arrived and conducted a counteroffensive beginning on 6 December 1941—one of the first major successes of an Allied force against the Germans. Both sides

Women and the military	Date of activity/event	Military history events
women aircrews and ground support for three combat regiments. After recruitment in Moscow the regiment trained at Engels, where Raskova worked tirelessly to conduct a condensed training program. By April 1942 the first of the regiments became operational, followed by the other two. All three were in combat for the duration of the war.		suffered during a desperately cold winter, and there were massive casualties on both sides from weather as well as combat.
Soviet Union: On 29 November partisan Zoia Kosmodem'ianskaia was executed by the Germans and became a Soviet martyr.	1941, November	Great Patriotic War.
	1941, December	Second World War, Pacific theater: The Japanese attacked Pearl Harbor on 7 December 1941. The United States declared war on Japan on 8 December; Germany and Italy declared war on the United States three days later.
Soviet Union: **Liudmila Pavlichenko** (1916–1974) became the top-scoring female military sniper in history, with 309 kills (including 36 enemy snipers), which she accumulated in less than one year in combat. She volunteered at the outset of the war and began service as a sniper. She participated in the defense of Odessa and then Sevastopol and was wounded four times, taking her out of active service in June 1942. She later served as a sniper instructor and was awarded the **Hero of the Soviet Union**.	1941	Great Patriotic War: The Romanian allies of the Germans began the siege of the Black Sea port of Odessa in August 1941; it was captured in October. The Soviets maintained a hold on the Crimean port of Sevastopol until July 1942. Both sieges were bitterly fought. Odessa and the Crimea were retaken by the Red Army in the spring of 1944.
Soviet Union: Women composed approximately 10 percent of members of the Soviet **resistance** by 1944. Although most filled support roles or served as couriers, radio operators, and medics, they played a generally more active role than in other partisan forces, with many women partic-	1941–1944	Great Patriotic War, partisan movement.

ipating in fighting, sabotage, sniping, and assassination.

Soviet Union: **Anna Egorova** (1916–) started the war as a pilot in a communications squadron. After 1943 she flew the Il-2 "shturmovik" ground-attack aircraft in a mostly-male regiment.

1941–1945	Great Patriotic War.
1941	Palestine: The Palmach was organized by Jewish forces to act as a specialized strike force.
1941	Vietnam: The Indochina War (1941–1954) began. After the fall of France Japan occupied French Indochina. In 1941 Ho Chi Minh created the Viet Minh (Vietnamese Independence League), pledged to create a free Vietnam.
1942	Second World War, Pacific: Japanese forces continued their expansion in the Pacific. In the Battle of Singapore (February), Japan captured the city from the British. Burma was invaded, as well as Indonesia. The Japanese and American fleets fought at the Coral Sea (May) and Midway (June).
1942	Second World War, western front: British strategic bombing of Germany began, soon joined by American efforts.

Soviet Union: **Neonila Onilova** (1921–1942) was a renowned machine-gunner in the famous 25th "V.I. Chapaev" Division of the Independent Maritime Army on the Crimean Front. She began service in August 1941 as a medical NCO, but soon transferred to combat duty. She participated in the defense of Odessa and Sevastopol. She was wounded and decorated, then received a mortal wound on 28 February 1942.

1942, February — Great Patriotic War: Siege of Odessa; siege of Sevastopol.

Soviet Union: The **586th Fighter Aviation Regiment** served from April 1942 through May 1945 as part of Fighter Aviation of the Air Defense Forces of the Soviet Union. Flying Yak-series fighters,

1942, April–1945 — Great Patriotic War.

Women and the military	Date of activity/event	Military history events
the 586th was assigned to protect fixed targets like airfields, cities, and transportation nodes from enemy attacks. Though it started as an all-female unit, in October 1942 the regiment was expanded to include about one-third male pilots. The regiment supported the Battle of Stalingrad and performed air defense duties at Voronezh, Kursk, Kiev, Debrecen, Budapest, and Vienna.		
Soviet Union: The **46th Guards Night Bomber Aviation Regiment** entered operational service in May 1942. It operated in the Caucasus, the Crimea, Belorussia, Poland, and Berlin. In addition to night bombing sorties, the regiment flew liaison, reconnaissance, and supply missions—more than 24,000 combat missions in all. Commanded by Evdokiia Bershanskaia, the 46th devised innovative methods of training, maintaining, and turning around aircraft that accounted for its high sortie rates. It was the only one of the three women's aviation regiments created by **Marina Raskova** in 1941 that remained all-female throughout the war.	1942, May– 1945	Great Patriotic War.
Soviet Union: **Marina Chechneva** (1922–1984), a squadron commander in the **46th Guards Night Bomber Regiment,** entered combat in 1942 and served in the Soviet Air Force until 1948. Chechneva completed 810 combat sorties in the Po-2 biplane, mostly at night, and once flew 18 sorties in a single night. She later wrote a series of memoirs about the war.	1942, May	Great Patriotic War.
Soviet Union: In May 1942 **Valentina Grizodubova** became commander of the 101st Long-Range Aviation Regiment, the only Soviet woman to command an all-male aviation unit. She led	1942, May	Great Patriotic War.

missions personally, including flying supplies into blockaded Leningrad and evacuating partisan and other wounded troops. The regiment flew 1,850 supply missions to partisan areas. She left the regiment in June 1944 for a post in civil aviation.

United States: The Women's Army Auxiliary Corps (WAAC) was formed in May 1942 as a military auxiliary. Plans had been floating for some months; after the attack on Pearl Harbor General George Marshall told his staff, "I want a women's corps right away and I don't want any excuses." **Oveta Culp Hobby** (1905–1995) was director of the WAAC/WAC throughout the war. She saw the WAAC through its transition in September 1943 from WAAC to **WAC** (Women's Army Corps) when the organization shifted from auxiliary to full military status. It was the role of these women to "free a man to fight" by filling various noncombatant support jobs. Most served in the continental United States.	1942, May	Second World War, United States, home front.
United States: The Women Accepted for Voluntary Emergency Service (WAVES) was formed in the summer of 1942, with military status in the navy reserve from its inception. **Mildred McAfee** (1900–1994) was the first director of the WAVES. By the end of the war there were 8,000 officers and 76,000 enlisted women in the WAVES.	1942, July–1948	Second World War, United States, home front.
Soviet Union: **Natalia Kovshova** (1920–1942) and Maria Polivanova (1922–1942), a sniper team, served from October 1941 and tallied more than 300 kills before their deaths in combat in August 1942. Cut off, surrounded, and wounded, they blew themselves up with grenades, reportedly	1942, August	Great Patriotic War: Between October 1941 and the spring of 1942 Soviet forces were often in a desperate retreat, but unlike the first weeks of the invasion, it was a fighting retreat, punctuated by counterattacks. The German forces conducted a major offensive in the summer of 1942 that

Women and the military	Date of activity/event	Military history events
taking some of the enemy with them. They became the first female snipers to receive the **Hero of the Soviet Union**.		took them to Stalingrad on the Volga River.
	1942, August	Great Patriotic War: Battle of Stalingrad (August 1942–February 1943). German forces over-extended themselves in the attempt to take Stalingrad. Although they controlled most of the miles-long city, the Soviets refused to give up. The fighting quickly turned into an unprecedented urban war, fought by small squads, street to street and house to house. A Soviet counteroffensive in November 1942 succeeded in encircling the German Sixth Army and forcing its surrender in early 1943.
	1942, August	Second World War, Pacific: The Battle of Guadalcanal began, continuing until February 1943.
United States/Soviet Union: The famous sniper **Liudmila Pavlichenko,** after being invalided out of active duty, visited the United States at the invitation of Eleanor Roosevelt.	1942, August	
Soviet Union: During the Battle of Stalingrad fighter pilot **Lidiia Litviak** (1921–1943) became the first woman to down an enemy aircraft, with two kills on her third day in combat. She was one of eight female pilots sent by the **586th Fighter Aviation Regiment** to augment aviation units at Stalingrad.	1942, September	Great Patriotic War: Battle of Stalingrad.
United States: The Women's Auxiliary Ferrying Squadron (**WAFS**), under the direction of Nancy Love, was the first auxiliary created in the United States that allowed women to fly military aircraft. The WAFS recruited a relatively small group of highly competent women pilots who	1942, September–1943	Second World War, United States, home front.

were already qualified to fly the sort of missions required by the Ferrying Division of the Army Air Force. They served as civilian pilots. The WAFS existed as a distinct organization for less than a year and in August 1943 was absorbed into the **WASP** under the control of **Jacqueline Cochran**. Women who flew in the Ferrying Division often continued to consider themselves members of WAFS. In twenty-seven total months of service women pilots in the Ferrying Division flew 12,650 ferrying missions in seventy-seven different types of aircraft, including pursuit fighters and heavy bombers.

United States: **Jacqueline Cochran** (1910?–1980) was nearly as famous as Amelia Earhart in 1930s aviation. Cochran was a controversial figure whose ultimate goal was to establish a permanent women's air corps as part of the Army Air Forces (AAF). She led a group of female American volunteer pilots who flew with the British **ATA** in 1941 and early 1942. In September 1942 Cochran became director of the newly created WFTD. By August 1943, after engineering a merger between the WFTD and the **WAFS,** she was named director of women pilots with administrative control over all female pilots in the AAF.	1942, September–1944	Second World War, United States, home front.
United States: The Women's Flying Training Detachment (WFTD) was created by **Jacqueline Cochran** to recruit large numbers of female pilots and provide the necessary training to qualify them for noncombat military flying. The first WFTD class began training in November 1942 in Texas; the first class graduated in May 1943. On 5 August 1943	1942, September–1943	Second World War, United States, home front.

Women and the military	Date of activity/event	Military history events
the **WAFS** and WFTD were merged into the **WASP**.		
United States: **Joy Bright Hancock,** a First World War veteran, lobbied for the reestablishment of the Women's Naval Reserve and was commissioned as a lieutenant in October 1942. She was the highest-ranking woman at the navy's Bureau of Aeronautics, in which she had served as a civilian before the war. Hancock has been described as "the only WAVE leader with a clear idea of how the navy operated." She advocated gender-integrated specialist training at aviation schools, leading to the decision that permitted 3,000 women to serve as aviation machinist's mates. She was also instrumental in opening up overseas service to **WAVES**.	1942, October–1945	Second World War, United States, home front.
	1942, October	Second World War, Africa: In the Battle of El Alamein (23 October–4 November) British forces under Bernard Montgomery achieved a complete victory over Erwin Rommel's outnumbered army.
United States: The United States Coast Guard Women's Reserve, known as **SPAR,** was created in November 1942. Nearly 11,000 women served in shore jobs to free men for sea duty. Its director was **Dorothy Stratton** (1899–), who had been a full professor of psychology before the war. She joined the **WAVES** and was commissioned as a lieutenant in September 1942. In November she was selected as the first director of the SPAR, a post she filled until 1946.	1942, November	Second World War, United States, home front.
	1942, November	Second World War, Africa: American forces landed in Africa (Operation Torch).

Soviet Union: The **125th Guards Bomber Aviation Regiment** went into action in January 1943 and served throughout the war. Initially all-female, the regiment gained about one-third male personnel, primarily gunners and ground support. It flew the twin-engine, medium-range Pe-2 dive bomber. The regiment saw action at Stalingrad, the North Caucasus, Smolensk, Belorussia, the Baltic lands, and East Prussia. Its crews flew 1,134 combat missions.

Soviet Union: **Nadezhda Fedutenko** (1915–1978) was a dive-bomber pilot in the **125th Guards Bomber Aviation Regiment**. A squadron commander and respected pilot, she participated in the regiment's first operational mission on 28 January 1943, over Stalingrad, and led many dangerous sorties throughout the war. Her awards included the **Hero of the Soviet Union**.

Soviet Union: Pilot **Klavdiia Fomicheva** (1917–1958) flew in the **125th Guards Bomber Aviation Regiment** as a squadron commander. She was shot down twice and was once put out of action for several months, but returned to duty. Altogether Fomicheva flew fifty-five operational missions and was credited with shooting down eleven enemy aircraft in group combat. Her awards included the **Hero of the Soviet Union**.

United States: A political ally of President Franklin Roosevelt, the forty-eight-year-old **Ruth Cheney Streeter** (1895–1990) was appointed to the post of director of the Marine Corps Women's Reserve (MCWR) in January 1943 and served until December 1945.

1943, January–1947 Great Patriotic War.

1943, January–1946 Great Patriotic War.

1943, January–1949 Great Patriotic War.

1943, January–1945 Second World War, United States, home front.

Women and the military	Date of activity/event	Military history events
United States: The Marine Corps Women's Reserve was created on 13 February 1943. **Women marines** were the only American military women in the Second World War to receive combat training during boot camp. They served at all major stateside bases.	1943, February	Second World War, United States, home front.
Soviet Union: In March 1943 fighter pilot **Lidiia Litviak,** having scored several more kills, was wounded and sent to Moscow for recuperation. Her fame began to grow in the Soviet Union.	1943, March	Great Patriotic War.
Poland: **Chaike Belchatowska Spiegel** was among the many women who participated in the Warsaw Ghetto Uprising.	1943, April–May	Second World War, eastern front: The Warsaw Ghetto Uprising (19 April–8 May) was an armed insurrection by the last Jews remaining as the Germans emptied the ghetto, sending its inhabitants to death camps. The Jews knew that it would be a fight to the death. Despite the pathetic weaponry of the resisters, it took the Germans three weeks, flame-throwers, and poison gas to finally clear the ghetto. Some 7,000 Jews were killed during the fighting, and 30,000 were deported to death camps; fewer than 100 escaped.
Soviet Union: The **Central Women's School for Sniper Training** was formed on 21 May 1943 out of women's sniper-training courses in operation since 1942. Commanded by Nora Pavlovna Chegodaeva, a veteran of the **Spanish Civil War,** the school trained 1,885 snipers who were credited with 11,280 kills against enemy troops.	1943, May–1945	Great Patriotic War.
Poland/United Kingdom: The Pomocnicza Lotnicza Służba Kobiet (**PLSK**) was founded by the Polish government in exile in En-	1943, May–1945	Second World War, United Kingdom, home front: Poland and the United Kingdom, auxiliary military formation.

gland in mid-December 1942 on the model of the British Women's Auxiliary Air Force (WAAF) to serve with the Polish air force. Candidates began training in May 1943. Women of the PLSK served in a wide variety of support roles. The total strength of the PLSK was between 1,400 and 1,700, or about 10 percent of the Polish air force strength in the West.

Poland/Soviet Union: The **Emilia Plater Independent Women's Battalion** was the first cohesive, all-female Polish combat unit, founded in 1943 in response to the large number of volunteers who had been exiled to the Soviet Union in 1939–1941. The battalion was intended to fight alongside Soviet troops, but in practice was relegated to sentry and military police duties. It was commanded by men and was directly subordinated to Polish units fighting with the Red Army. The battalion typically consisted of 500–700 personnel; 70 were killed during the war. This battalion was only a small percentage of the total number of Polish women serving in the two Polish armies, with estimates ranging widely from 8,500 to 14,000. Many female officers were trained in the battalion to be company and platoon commanders and were sent on to front-line units of the Polish army to help offset the severe shortage of officers resulting from the Katyn Massacre of 1940.	1943, June–1945	Second World War, eastern front.
France: **Noor Inayat Khan** (1914–1944) was the first female radio operator sent to France by the British Special Operations Executive (SOE) (June 1943). She was arrested about three months later, reportedly never broke under interrogation, and attempted	1943, June	Second World War, western front.

Women and the military	Date of activity/event	Military history events
unsuccessfully to escape. She was executed at Dachau on 13 September 1944 along with three other women trained by the SOE. Khan was posthumously awarded the Croix de Guerre and was made the first female saint of the Sufis.		
Soviet Union: The **46th Guards Night Bomber Aviation Regiment** lost four aircraft and eight crewmembers to surprise attacks by German night fighters on 31 July 1943 over the Kuban' area, the squadron's worst disaster of the war.	1943, July	Great Patriotic War: The Kuban' region in the North Caucasus was the site of a key bridgehead to the Sea of Azov.
Soviet Union: Fighter pilot **Lidiia Litviak** made her last two kills on the day she disappeared. On 1 August 1943, during her third flight of the day, she participated in a mass engagement against an enemy formation of Ju-88 bombers escorted by Me-109s. She disappeared; she had been seriously wounded and managed to land before dying, but her body was not identified until 1979.	1943, August	Great Patriotic War: In July 1943 the Germans attacked the salient at Kursk, but the Soviets defeated their efforts. The Battle of Kursk was the largest of the Second World War and was known in particular for the greatest massed use of armor in history. The Soviets then began a series of offensives in early August, resulting in the recapture of Kharkov.
United States: On 5 August 1943 the Women's Airforce Service Pilots (**WASP**) was created from the merger of the **WAFS** and the WFTD. Some 25,000 women applied for WASP training, including women from Allied nations (only American citizens were accepted). A total of 1,830 women were admitted, and 1,074 became operational over the duration of the program. From September 1942 until December 1944 (including WAFS/WFTD) American women flew as civilian auxiliary pilots, ferrying military aircraft from factories and filling various aviation support roles. American female pilots were not permitted into theaters of war. Although they were not exposed	1943, August–1944	Second World War, United States, home front.

to combat, aviation is an inherently hazardous occupation; thirty-eight WASP pilots were killed in the line of duty. Unlike other women's auxiliary organizations in the United States, the WASP was never militarized.

Resistance movements, Italian women: The Italian Resistance operated between September 1943 and May 1945; of 200,000 partisans, at least 35,000 were women (650 died in combat or were executed). Some of the women had military rank and command positions and fought in combat, although most served as couriers and in support roles.

1943, September–1945

Second World War, western front.

Soviet Union: Elena Grigor'evna Mazanik (1918–?), a member of the Soviet resistance, infiltrated the household of Wilhelm Kube, the Reichskommissar for Belorussia. On the night of 22 September 1943 she assassinated him by placing a bomb under his bed. She escaped and was made a **Hero of the Soviet Union.**

1943, September

Great Patriotic War.

United States: The conversion of the Women's Army Auxiliary Corps (WAAC) to regular military status as the Women's Army Corps (**WAC**) in September 1943 helped the recruiting efforts of director Colonel **Oveta Culp Hobby.** The strength of the WAC reached a peak of 100,000 women in the summer of 1945, with about 4.3 percent African Americans.

1943, September

Second World War, United States, home front.

United States: **Charity Adams Earley** (1918–) was a member of the first **WAC** officer-training class. She became the commander of the only unit of African American women to serve overseas in the Second World War. She served until 1946; in the 1980s she wrote a well-known memoir.

1943, September

Second World War, western front.

Women and the military	Date of activity/event	Military history events
Soviet Union: The **Order of Glory,** created on 8 November 1943, was awarded to Red Army privates, NCOs, and junior lieutenants of aviation considered "the bravest among the brave" for skill in combat in the Second World War. Four women received the award.	1943, November	Great Patriotic War.
United States: Computer pioneer **Grace Hopper** (1906–1992) began military service in the United States Naval Reserve in December 1943. She was assigned to the Bureau of Ships Computation Project at Harvard University, where she worked on the Mark I, the first programmable computing machine made in America. It was during the summer of 1945, while working on the Mark II, that she is credited with coining the term "bug" to refer to strange computer malfunctions.	1943, December	Second World War, United States, home front.
Soviet Union: **Mariia Oktiabrskaia** (1902–1944) was a famed tank driver-mechanic. After most of her family was killed in the early part of the war, she decided that she would pay for a tank out of her own savings if the government would agree to let her drive it. After completing training, she went to the front in the fall of 1943. In January 1944 she received a head wound and later died. She was posthumously awarded the **Hero of the Soviet Union.**	1944, January	Great Patriotic War.
Germany: **Hanna Reitsch** met with Hitler in February 1944 to receive the Iron Cross (first class) and proposed her plan of creating a suicide squadron to fly rockets or "glider bombs" into key enemy facilities. The plan was rejected. She did, however, conduct test flights in an experimental piloted V-1 rocket.	1944, February	Second World War, Germany, home front.

France: Georgette "Claude" Gérard was unusual in heading a maquis (paramilitary group). After eighteen months as a regional leader responsible for some 5,000 people, she was arrested by the Germans in May 1944. Released during the liberation of France, she later attained the rank of major in the French army.

1944, May — Second World War, western front.

1944, June — Second World War, western front: The Allied invasion at Normandy on 6 June 1944 opened up a second front in Europe. The massive amphibious landing was followed by weeks of bloody fighting as the Allies slowly advanced into France, liberating Paris in late August.

Germany: **Melitta Schiller Stauffenberg** was involved in the plot of her brother-in-law Claus to assassinate Hitler. She agreed to act as his pilot and fake an emergency landing to get him into Hitler's headquarters; she planned and practiced for the mission, but he was able to travel on official orders by other transportation. She and her husband were arrested after Claus was caught, but Melitta was released to resume her work in aviation. She used her influence to help family members, including children, who remained imprisoned.

1944, July — Germany: In 1944 Claus Stauffenberg tried unsuccessfully to assassinate Hitler. Stauffenberg was caught and executed on 20 July 1944.

Soviet Union: **Anna Egorova** was shot down near Warsaw on 20 August 1944, on her 277th mission. With extensive injuries, she spent five months in POW camps until she was liberated by the Red Army in January 1945.

1944, August — Great Patriotic War: The Red Army conducted immense offensives during the summer of 1944. Belorussia was cleared and the Soviets advanced into Poland, coming near Warsaw before stalling. The Soviet 47th Army, the only major force near Warsaw, was joined by the 1st Polish Army on 20 August. Efforts to reach Warsaw in mid-September failed, and the forces withdrew. Warsaw was not liberated until January 1945.

Women and the military	Date of activity/event	Military history events
Poland: Women played a large role in the Warsaw Uprising. Female couriers were the primary means of notifying units of the date, times, places, and code words for the initiation of hostilities. Women also distributed arms and ammunition. During the uprising women couriers provided coordination between units engaged in combat, often moving under fire. Aleksandra Zagórska, creator of the **OLK** in 1918, was one of the participants. Many women captured after the suppression of the uprising were sent off as forced labor.	1944, August	Second World War, eastern front: The Warsaw Uprising occurred in August 1944, and fighting continued until October. Polish resistance fighters began open fighting against German occupation forces, believing that the Soviet Red Army would soon arrive to assist them. When the Red Army failed to appear, the uprising was ultimately defeated in early October with heavy casualties of both combatants and noncombatants.
Soviet Union: **Tat'iana Makarova** (1920–1944), a pilot, and Vera Belik (1921–1944), a navigator, served in the **46th Guards Night Bomber Aviation Regiment.** Makarova flew 628 combat sorties and Belik 813 in the Po-2 biplane, flying most of their missions as a crew. They died on 25 August 1944 when they were attacked by a German fighter near their base in Poland. Like most Po-2 crews, they carried no parachutes; the aircraft went down in flames. Both were awarded the **Hero of the Soviet Union** posthumously.	1944, August	Great Patriotic War.
	1944, October	Second World War, Pacific: The Battle of Leyte Gulf (24–25 October) was a major American naval victory over the Japanese.
Poland: **Irena Sosnowska-Karpik** (1922–1990) served with the Polish Armed Forces formed in the Soviet Union from November 1944. After the war she served in the Polish Air and Air Defence Forces as an instructor pilot.	1944, November	Second World War, eastern front.

Vietnam: Women were extensively involved in the **Vietnamese Revolution** from the early organization of the Vietnamese Communist Party. Active military and combat roles were soon defined. There were reportedly three women in the first thirty-four-person unit of the new revolutionary army established in December 1944.

1944, December — Vietnam: Ho Chi Minh and the Vietnamese Communist Party decided to create a new revolutionary army to fight the French, the People's Liberation Army, which would be commanded by Vo Nguyen Giap.

1944, December — Second World War, western front: The Battle of the Bulge began in the Ardennes in December 1944 and continued into January 1945. It was the last major counteroffensive by German forces. By early January American troops forced the Germans into a retreat.

United States: The **WASP** was disbanded. Although the WASP attained an excellent flying record, attempts to gain military status failed, and the program was rather abruptly deactivated on 20 December 1944, before the war had even ended. Complaints from male pilots that the WASP were taking their jobs were an important factor in closure of the program. It did not receive military status until WASPs were granted veterans' rights in the 1970s.

1944, December — Second World War, United States, home front.

United Kingdom: Princess Elizabeth (now Queen Elizabeth II) joined the Women's Transport Service **(FANY).**

1945 — Second World War, United Kingdom, home front.

1945, February — Second World War, Pacific: Battle of Iwo Jima (19 February–16 March), in which American amphibious forces took on some 25,000 Japanese defenders.

Poland/Soviet Union: **Emilia Gierczak** (1925–1945) first served in the **"Emilia Plater" Independent Women's Battalion** in 1943, then became a front-line platoon commander of male troops in the Polish army. She was killed in action on 17 March 1945.

1945, March — Second World War, eastern front.

Women and the military	Date of activity/event	Military history events
	1945, April	Second World War, Pacific: The Battle of Okinawa lasted from 1 April through 22 June. American forces landed without opposition, but faced some 140,000 defenders who fought to the death.
Germany: **Melitta Schiller Stauffenberg** was shot down on 8 April 1945, from behind, by an American fighter while flying in an unarmed trainer.	1945, April	Second World War, western front.
	1945, April	Second World War, eastern front: The Battle of Berlin (22 April-2 May) involved some two and a half million Red Army troops against a million German defenders (mostly people unfit for active duty).
Germany: **Hanna Reitsch** and Ritter von Greim flew into besieged Berlin (25–28 April) and were two of the last people to see Hitler alive. This episode, along with her unflinching support of the German regime, would make Reitsch infamous.	1945, April	Germany: Hitler committed suicide on 30 April.
	1945, May	Germany unconditionally surrendered on 7 May.
	1945, August	Second World War, Pacific: The United States dropped atomic bombs on the Japanese cities of Hiroshima (6 August) and Nagasaki (9 August). A cease-fire was agreed on 15 August.
	1945, September	Second World War, Pacific: The Japanese formally signed a surrender on 2 September.
Women were rapidly demobilized from the armed forces and auxiliaries of all countries when the Second World War came to a close. For example, in 1945 there were 265,000 American women in service; by 1948 only 14,000 remained. Of 340,000 American women who served during the war, fewer than 30,000 served overseas.	1945	

Israel: **Netiva Ben-Yehuda** (1928–?) enlisted in the Palmach in 1946 at age eighteen. She trained in demolition and bomb disposal and commanded a sapper unit. She fought during the **Israeli War of Independence** two years later. Ben-Yehuda related her military experiences in three autobiographical works.

1946

1946   Vietnam: Insurrection against the French escalated into open conflict between the French and the self-declared Democratic Republic of Vietnam, whose president was Ho Chi Minh. Some sources date the start of the Indochina War to 1946 rather than 1941.

Palestine: Of about 2,000 active members in the Irgun, 400 were women; they were mainly involved in anti-British agitation and courier duties, though some were involved with explosives.

1946, July   Palestine: The infamous terrorist bombing of the King David Hotel in Jerusalem by the Irgun, led by Menachem Begin, was characteristic of the tensions leading up to the **Israeli War of Independence.**

1947   The United Nations recommended a partition of Palestine into Arab and Jewish states and withdrawal of British forces in 1948.

United States: **Joy Bright Hancock** remained on active duty after the Second World War and was named director of the Women's Naval Reserve in 1947. She retired in 1953 and was a strong advocate of integrated training throughout her life.

1947

Israel: Women participated in both combat and support roles during the **Israeli War of Independence;** 114 were killed in action, 18 of whom were in the Palmach. Rachel Stahl commanded a Palmach company and led it in combat, one of five women to command a combat unit. Women soldiers fought in the Palmach's Negev and Harel Brigades. A female pilot, Yael Rom, flew combat missions with the tiny Israeli air force.

1948   Israeli War of Independence (May 1948–January 1949), sometimes called the First Arab-Israeli War. When the British withdrew in May 1948, the new Jewish state was attacked by the combined Arab forces of its neighbors, but Israel managed to survive the onslaught.

Women and the military	Date of activity/event	Military history events
United States: The Women's Armed Services Integration Act admitted women to regular and reserve forces as full military members. However, restrictions included the combat exclusion laws (banning women from flying aircraft engaged in combat missions, for example), exclusions of general rank, and a 2 percent ceiling on nonmedical women.	1948	
	1948	United States: President Harry Truman ordered the racial integration of the armed forces.
United States: The first African American women entered the Marine Corps.	1949	
Israel: When the IDF were formed, women lost all combat roles that they had previously filled. **CHEN** (Cheil Nashim, "Women's Corps") was created along the lines of the British **ATS** as a separate administrative chain for women in the armed forces. For decades Israel was the only nation that conscripted women into military service in peacetime. Women were generally restricted to noncombat roles until the 1990s.	1949	The Israel Defense Forces (IDF) were formed, incorporating all previous paramilitary groups such as the Palmach.
Australia: The Women's Royal Australian Army Corps (WRAAC) was founded, with **Kathleen Best** as its commanding officer. WRAAC officers received less pay than men. The WRAAC existed until women were permitted to join regular units of the Australian army in 1979. Other service auxiliaries were similarly reformed after going on hiatus at the end of the Second World War.	1950	
Women played an important role in the **Algerian-French War,** engaging in a wide variety of com-	1954–1962	Africa: The Algerian-French War, also called the Algerian War of Independence.

bat and combat-related activities, particularly among the guerrilla units. The role of women in the Algerian-French War has acquired an almost mythic status in Algeria.

	1954	United States: The last all-black units were abolished.
	1954	Vietnam: The French were defeated at Dien Bien Phu after a lengthy siege and begin their withdrawal from Vietnam.
Vietnam: Communist women were expected to play a significant role in both political and military activities in the **Vietnamese Revolution.** They had already been active during the Indochina War (1941–1954) and their roles would expand after the United States became militarily involved.	1954	Vietnam: The Geneva Conference ended the Indochina War and divided the country, with the Communists in the north and non-Communists in the south. Scheduled national elections were never held, and Ho Chi Minh and the Vietnamese Communist Party renewed the strategy of people's war to try to overthrow the new government in South Vietnam and reunify the two zones. The Vietnamese Civil War (1954–1975), also called the Vietnamese Revolution, began.
Israel: In the 1956 Sinai Campaign there were three women C-47 pilots who flew paratroopers into action; this was not considered combat duty.	1956	The Sinai-Suez War, also called the Second Arab-Israeli War, broke out in October 1956 with the Egyptian seizure of the Suez Canal. Britain, France, and Israel opposed the move and invaded the Sinai Peninsula, but were forced by international pressure to withdraw.
Hungary: Women fighters took up arms against the Hungarian as well as the Soviet protectors of the Stalinist regime in Hungary. They continued their resistance up to 10–11 November 1956. Many were then arrested, and some were executed.	1956, October	Hungarian Revolution: A chaotic insurrection started in Budapest on 23 October. On 4 November Soviet military forces began an armed suppression of the revolt.
Tibet: **Ani Pachen** (1933–2002) began her activities in 1958 as a guerrilla leader in the "Struggle to Free Tibet" movement. She was captured by the Chinese and	1958	Asia: The Chinese invaded Tibet in 1950, provoking the rise of a resistance movement.

Women and the military	Date of activity/event	Military history events
was imprisoned for more than two decades before her release in 1981.		
Vietnam: Thousands of women performed heavy physical labor, transporting war materials down the Ho Chi Minh Trail from North Vietnam. Women were allegedly better in transporting supplies; although men were usually stronger and thus able to carry heavier loads, women tended to possess greater stamina and were less likely to complain.	1959	Vietnam: The Ho Chi Minh Trail was opened as a major route for supplies and personnel to travel through Laos and Cambodia to South Vietnam.
Vietnam: Nguyen Thi Dinh (1920–) was a leading figure in the Ben Tre provincial committee and helped transport 1,000 rifles from the North. The Ben Tre uprisings consisted mainly of women, carefully organized and trained by Nguyen Thi Dinh, who used a wide variety of techniques against Army of the Republic of Vietnam (ARVN) forces from Saigon. Her memoirs of the technique of "mass uprising" became a handbook for later uprisings. Nguyen Thi Dinh was later named minister of defense of the Provisional Revolutionary Government created in the late 1960s.	1960, January	Vietnam: In January 1960 a popular uprising against the South Vietnamese regime was launched in several villages in the heart of the Mekong Delta. The Ben Tre uprisings ended with a withdrawal of ARVN troops.
United States: **Evelyn Patricia Foote** (1930–) began a long career in the United States Army in 1960, rising to brigadier general in 1986. Foote was a strong proponent of integrated training and of opening combat roles to women.	1960	
Africa: **Hanna Reitsch** created and ran a gliding school in Ghana for the dictator Kwame Nkrumah.	1962–1966	
Vietnam: Women served extensively on the Communist side as members of antiaircraft artillery	1965–1973	The Vietnam War, an expansion of the Vietnamese Civil War (1954–1975), began with active

units protecting Hanoi and other cities and towns in North Vietnam from American bombing raids. They were active as guerrilla fighters in South Vietnam, as couriers and transportation workers, as spies or informers, and as members of local militia units in liberated areas in the South. According to one estimate, 40 percent of all regimental commanders in resistance units in the South were women. There were many integrated units, as well as some all-female units. Women also participated to a lesser degree on the side of South Vietnam, but little information is available to date on their activities.

United States; **Jeanne Holm** (1921–) became director of Women in the Air Force (WAF) in 1965 and held the post until 1973. Holm had served in the WAAC/**WAC** during the Second World War. She later became the first female two-star general in American history (1973).

United States: Ceilings on ranks and numbers of military women were eliminated.

American military involvement in 1965, including Operation Rolling Thunder, a series of air attacks on North Vietnam.

1965

1967

1967   The Six-Day War, also called the Third Arab-Israeli War, began on 5 June with surprise Israeli attacks that decimated enemy aviation, mostly on the ground. In six days the IDF occupied the Sinai Peninsula, the Golan Heights, and the West Bank.

1968   The Vietnam War: The Tet Offensive by North Vietnamese forces was militarily defeated in early 1968. In March the My Lai Massacre of 150 civilians occurred. These events led to a tremendous loss of public support in the United States and elsewhere for American involvement in Vietnam.

Women and the military	Date of activity/event	Military history events
United States: Air Force Reserve Officer Training Corps (ROTC) was opened to women.	1969	
Israel: **Golda Meir** (1898–1978) was among those who signed Israel's independence proclamation in 1948. She served as Israel's first minister to the Soviet Union (1948–1949), was elected to the Knesset (parliament) in 1949, and served as minister of labor and social insurance and as foreign minister (1956–1966). She was prime minister (1969–1974) during the 1973 Yom Kippur War.	1969	
United States: The first American women were promoted to general rank: Anna May Hayes (Army Nurse Corps) and Elisabeth P. Hoisington (director, **WAC**).	1970	
United States: Women entered Army and Navy Reserve Officer Training Corps (ROTC) for the first time.	1970?	
Africa: Women were active in the war of liberation in **Zimbabwe**. An estimated 250,000 women were involved, with military roles ranging from cooks to guerrilla fighters. One famous female leader, **Nehanda** (Kunzaruwa) (?–1973), was conscripted by Zimbabwe African National Union (ZANU) guerrillas in 1971 as advisor and spiritual leader to young freedom fighters.	1971–1980	Africa: The Zimbabwean National Liberation War, also called the Zimbabwe-Rhodesia Civil War, had been brewing at a low level for some years before organized resistance began in 1971.
United States: **Jeanne Holm,** director of Women in the Air Force (WAF), was promoted to brigadier general, becoming the first woman general in the air force.	1971	
Canada: **Wendy Clay** (1943–) became the first female flight surgeon in the Canadian Forces (CF) in 1969, just one of many landmarks she achieved. In July 1972	1972	

she became the first woman in the CF to graduate from basic pilot training. She earned her military wings, but because women were not yet accepted into combat roles, she never flew operationally. In 1989, as brigadier general, she became one of Canada's first female general officers. She was promoted through the ranks to become the first female surgeon general (1995), the highest rank ever held by a woman in the CF.

United States: **Arlene Duerk** (1920–) became the first woman to achieve flag-officer rank in the United States Navy (1 June 1972). She was a veteran of the Navy Nurse Corps in the Second World War, when she served at stateside hospitals and on a hospital ship in the Pacific. On 1 July 1967 she was promoted to the rank of captain and was selected as Director of the Navy Nurse Corps in May 1970.

1972

Africa: **Joyce Mugari Nhongo,** nicknamed *Teurai Ropa* (Spill Blood) (1955–), joined ZANU in 1973 and filled a variety of roles over the next seven years. In 1978, when the camp she was in was attacked by Rhodesian soldiers, she was an active combatant, despite her advanced pregnancy; she gave birth two days later. She continued to fight until liberation in 1980 and thereafter served in the government.

1973–1980

Zimbabwean National War of Liberation: The Zimbabwe African National Union (ZANU) in Zambia, which was waging a guerrilla war against the Ian Smith regime of Rhodesia, stepped up its efforts in 1973.

United States: **Jeanne Holm,** director of Women in the Air Force (WAF), was promoted to major general, becoming the first female two star general in American history.

1973

1973

United States: End of the draft; formation of the all-volunteer force.

Women and the military	Date of activity/event	Military history events
Israel: During the Yom Kippur War in 1973 the surprise attacks on Israeli forces resulted in the deaths of three female soldiers at forward posts, and many other women were wounded.	1973	Yom Kippur War (also called the Fourth Arab-Israeli War): On 6 October 1973 Egyptian and Syrian forces launched a surprise attack against Israel in an attempt to regain territories lost in 1967. Israel rebounded and counterattacked, inflicting a humiliating defeat on the Soviet-backed Arab states.
United States: **Rosemary Mariner** (1953–) was in the first group of female flight trainees at the Naval Aviation Training Command in Pensacola, Florida—the first women pilots in any of the armed services since the **WASP** of the Second World War. Mariner was selected for jet pilot training in 1975, qualifying in the several jet attack aircraft. She accumulated more than 3,500 flying hours in fifteen types of aircraft during her navy career.	1974	
United States: **Mary Clarke** (1924–) began her army career in 1945. In 1975 she became the last director of the Women's Army Corps (**WAC**). During her three-year tenure many major changes occurred: women were admitted to the service academies, the first women graduated from Army ROTC programs, they were required to undergo mandatory weapons training, and women began attending OCS and basic training in integrated classes with men. By the end of her career Clarke would be the longest-serving woman in the army (thirty-six years.)	1975	
United States: The Coast Guard Academy first admitted women.	1975	
United States: **Rosemary Mariner** became the first woman in the navy to fly a tactical jet.	1975	

United States: The military service academies (army, navy, and air force) opened to women. — 1976

United States: *Crawford v. Cushman* prohibited military discharge for pregnancy or for having minor dependents. — 1976

Libya: The integration of women into the Libyan military began in 1977. Libyan leader Muammar Ghadafi stated that "bearing arms is a right and duty of every Libyan woman." Women reportedly serve as regular army officers, enlisted and air support personnel, and combat pilots. Women reportedly served in combat during Libya's ongoing conflict with Chad in the late 1970s and early 1980s. — 1977

Australia: The Women's Royal Australian Air Force (WRAAF) was integrated into the regular Air Force (RAAF). — 1977

Israel: Women became instructors in combat-related training, including tank instructors and jumpmasters. — 1977

United States: The Women's Army Corps (**WAC**) and other separate women's branches of service were disbanded; women were integrated into all services. — 1978

United States: **Mary Clarke** (1924–) became the first army woman promoted to two-star rank (1 November 1978) and the first woman to command a major army post (Fort McClellan, Alabama, 1978–1980) — 1978

United States: Brigadier General Hazel W. Johnson-Brown served as chief of the Army Nurse Corps from September 1979 until August 1983—the first African American woman to reach general officer rank in America. — 1979

Women and the military	Date of activity/event	Military history events
Australia: Women's auxiliaries were disbanded, and women were permitted to join regular units of the Australian army in 1979.	1979	
Libya: The Women's Military Academy (WMA) outside Tripoli was opened in 1979 as a counterpart to the Men's Military Academy.	1979	
United Kingdom: **Margaret Thatcher** (1925–) was the longest-serving prime minister of the twentieth century (1979–1990), as well as the first female party leader and first female head of government in modern British history. Thatcher was also the first British leader to make war since the 1956 Suez incident, overseeing the Falkland Islands War with Argentina in 1982 and preparations for the Gulf War against Iraq in 1990.	1979–1990	
United States: The Defense Officer Personnel Management Act (DOPMA) integrated promotion lists, ending separate women's promotions.	1980	
Australia: Integrated training of male and female recruits began.	1981	
United States: Computer pioneer **Grace Hopper** became the oldest person on active duty in the navy (seventy-six) when Admiral Hyman Rickover retired. Three years later she was promoted to the rank of rear admiral. In 1986, at the age of seventy-nine, Hopper was involuntarily retired from the navy, ending her forty-three year naval career. She died in 1992 and is buried at Arlington National Cemetery.	1982	
Turkey: Before 1955 women served in the Turkish military as doctors, nurses, teachers, engineers, secretaries, and interpret-	1982	

ers without any restrictions. Since 1982, however, Turkish women are only allowed to serve as officers.

United Kingdom: **Margaret Thatcher** was head of state during this conflict and was directly involved in operations. She acted decisively and effectively kept public opinion on her side.

1982

The Falklands (Malvinas) War (2 April–14 June) began with an Argentine occupation of the Falkland Islands, held by the British for 150 years. Within a month British forces retook the islands; the Argentine government soon collapsed as a result of its defeat in the war.

United States: The army closed twenty-three additional job categories to women.

1982

United States: The army implemented "direct combat probability coding" to exclude women soldiers, regardless of military operational specialty (MOS), from assignment to areas of combat. People who favored excluding women from combat pointed out that the majority of military "jobs" were open to women; statements such as "97 percent of air force jobs are available to women" were common. Figures like these usually refer to percentages of Air Force Specialty Codes (AFSCs), or MOSs, not to the actual number of positions. For example, in 1988, 90.5 percent of army MOSs were open to women, but this represented only 55 percent of actual positions; 80 percent of Marine Corps MOSs were open, comprising only 20 percent of positions.

1983

United States: The navy renamed the Mobile Logistics Support Force the Combat Logistics Force (CLF) in an apparent attempt to include more ships under the combat exclusion law and thus preclude women's service on those vessels.

1984

United States: The army reopened many of the job categories

1985

Women and the military	Date of activity/event	Military history events
closed in 1982 after a review was directed by the secretary of the army.		
Australia: The Women's Royal Australian Naval Service (WRANS) was abolished in 1985, and its members were integrated into the navy.	1985	
Australia: The Australian Defence Force Academy at Canberra was opened to women, creating the first integrated officer cadet education in the country.	1986	
United States: The navy opened positions on some Combat Logistics Force vessels to women.	1987	
Canada: **Sheila Hellstrom** was the first female general in the Canadian Forces (CF), promoted to brigadier general in January 1987. She retired in 1990 after a thirty-six-year career.	1987	
United States: The Marine Corps was ordered by the secretary of defense to open embassy security guard positions to women.	1988	
United States: The Department of Defense standardized the "risk rule," stating that women should be excluded only from those non-combat positions that are exposed to risk equal to or greater than that faced by associated combat units. This opened several thousand additional positions to women.	1988	
Canada: **Deanna Brasseur** (1954–) in 1980 became one of the first three women to earn her wings as a Canadian Forces (CF) military pilot qualified for active duty. In June 1989 Brasseur and Captain Jane Foster became the only two women in the world flying fighters in operational squadrons. Canada was the first country to allow women	1989	

to fly in a combat role since the Soviet Union in the Second World War.

Canada: **Heather Erxleben** became the Canadian Forces' (CF) first female infantry soldier in 1989.

United States: Captain Linda Bray, commander of the 988th Military Police Company, led a unit in seizing a Panamanian dog kennel. Much fuss was made in the media describing this as the "first modern instance of American woman engaging hostile troops in combat"; however, no casualties resulted, and details remain unclear.

United States: **Rosemary Mariner** was the first woman to command a naval aviation squadron. She also served as president of Women Military Aviators.

United States: In Desert Shield and Desert Storm 41,000 women deployed in noncombat positions (of 540,000 total personnel, or 7 percent). It was the largest wartime deployment of American military women in history. Eleven died during the war, five in combat action; two were taken prisoner.

United States: **Melissa Rathbun-Nealy** (1970–) on 31 January 1991 became the first American enlisted woman to be captured as a prisoner of war, and the first U.S. woman prisoner of war since the Second World War. She and another truck driver were both shot and captured and spent a month in captivity.

United States: Flight surgeon **Rhonda Cornum** (1954–) was

1989		
1989	Panama: After a failed coup against Manuel Noriega, the United States invaded Panama in December 1989.	
1990		
1990–1991	The Persian Gulf War began when Iraqi forces invaded Kuwait in August 1990. A six-month building of anti-Iraq coalition forces followed, designed to liberate Kuwait.	
1991	Persian Gulf War: Operation Desert Storm began with an extended air campaign by coalition forces against Iraq. The ground operation lasted only four days (24–28 February).	
1991, January	Persian Gulf War.	
1991, February	Persian Gulf War.	

647

Women and the military	Date of activity/event	Military history events
the only female officer to become a prisoner of war during the Persian Gulf War. She was one of three survivors when their Blackhawk helicopter was shot down on 27 February 1991; they were all captured. Cornum was severely injured and barely treated during her eight days as a POW. After the war she continued her career, including command positions in medical units. Her decorations include an Air Medal, a Distinguished Flying Cross, and the Purple Heart.		
United States: **Marie Rossi** (1959–1991) was a company commander in an aviation brigade during the Gulf War. She was one of the first U.S. helicopter pilots to fly into enemy territory, leading dozens of supply missions. She and her crew were killed in an accident on 1 March 1991, the day after the ground war ended.	1991, March	Persian Gulf War.
United Arab Emirates: As a response to the ease with which Iraq overran Kuwait in 1990, the United Arab Emirates ordered the integration of women into the military. A Women's Military Academy was created.	1991	
United States: The Senate voted on 31 July to eliminate combat exclusions for aircraft, permitting (but not requiring) the services to allow women to fly combat missions.	1991, July	
United States: The annual Tailhook Convention of naval aviators met in Las Vegas; twenty-six women attendees pursued charges of sexual harassment and assault.	1991, July	
United States: Most combat aviation was opened to women.	1993	

Mexico: A revolt by the Emiliano Zapata National Liberation Army (EZLN) in Chiapas brought to the forefront Mayan women rebels; about 20 to 30 percent of the Zapatista fighters are women.

1994

United States: Public attitudes shifted as a result of women's participation in the Gulf War and because of scandal over the harassment of women at the navy Tailhook Convention in Las Vegas. The Department of Defense rescinded the "risk rule" and opened about 260,000 combat-related jobs to women. Women continue to be prohibited from serving in any role in units whose primary mission is engaging in ground combat, and in units that work directly with those organizations during wartime. Each service was allowed to apply the new regulations as it saw fit. Nearly all air force jobs, including fighter and bomber pilots, were opened to women. All jobs in the navy except those on submarines and as special operations SEALs are now open. Sixty-two percent of jobs in the much smaller Marine Corps are open to women. For the first time the army allowed women to work at combat brigade headquarters, but women remain excluded from smaller combat battalions, companies, and platoons that would go further forward. Army women also can now fly combat helicopters, among other openings.

1994

Israel: The Defense Service Law was amended to enable servicewomen to attend flight school and to serve in the police force and paramilitary border police in combat positions.

1995

Israel: In March 1997, for the first time since their establishment, the Israel Defense Forces began

1997, March

Women and the military	Date of activity/event	Military history events
joint basic training for men and women.		
Israel: In November 1997 the Israeli Supreme Court opened the way for women to compete for slots in combat aviation.	1997, November	
The European Court, the highest legal body of the European Union, ruled that Britain did not have to let women into the Royal Marines, where all members of that elite service have to be ready for hand-to-hand combat.	1999	
The European Court ruled that women should be allowed to carry arms in the German military forces and said that laws banning women from combat violated European Union sex-equality regulations. However, access to certain special combat units could be refused. Prior to the ruling women were allowed to serve in the army only in the medical services or as musicians.	2000	
Israel: The Knesset opened all branches and services of the Israel Defense Forces to women. Those who wish to enter combat duty will be required to meet the same physical requirement as the men and sign up for similar terms of service.	2000	

Sources for this timeline, in addition to the entries in this book, include the following:

Brownstone, David, and Irene Franck. *Timelines of War: A Chronology of Warfare from 100,000 BC to the Present.* Boston: Little, Brown and Company, 1994.

Chambers, John Whiteclay, ed. *The Oxford Companion to American Military History.* Oxford and New York: Oxford University Press, 1999.

Cowley, Robert, and Geoffrey Parker, eds. *The Reader's Companion to Military History.* Boston: Houghton Mifflin, 1996.

Olsen, Kirstin. *Chronology of Women's History.* Westport, CT: Greenwood Press, 1994.

Parker, Geoffrey, ed. *The Cambridge Illustrated History of Warfare: The Triumph of the West.* Reprint ed. Cambridge: Cambridge University Press, 1999.

Spielvogel, Jackson. *Western Civilization.* Vol. 1, *To 1715.* 3rd ed. West Publishing Company, 1997.

———. *Western Civilization.* Vol. 2, *Since 1550.* 3rd ed. West Publishing Company, 1997.

Women as Prisoners of War: A Bibliographic Survey

Jan Bassett, Bobbie Oliver, and Reina Pennington

Throughout history civilian women have been far more likely to end up as prisoners of an enemy than have women who served with or in the military. These civilian women may not technically qualify as "prisoners of war," but their experiences are instructive in determining historical patterns in the treatment of female prisoners and in the response of women to capture, confinement, interrogation, harsh labor, and torture. A list of entries in this book that discuss women as prisoners is included in the frontmatter. What follows is a general discussion that includes information on many civilian women not covered in the main entries of the book. All books and articles are referenced in short form and can be found in the Bibliography.

The past two decades have seen a number of studies on the previously neglected subject of female prisoners of war. Some of these studies embrace a lengthy time frame, but most are specific to one period, for example, the Second World War. Two of the better-researched periods to date are frontier wars in countries such as the United States of America (1700s and 1800s) and Australia (1788–1920s), and the Second World War (1939–1945). The bulk of literature is from the Second World War, a fact that is reflected in this appendix.

ANCIENT AND MEDIEVAL HISTORY

The ancient sources contain a few references to women POWs in earlier historical eras. Examples include **Cloelia,** whom the Romans gave as a hostage to the Etruscan king Lars Porsenna in 508 BCE, and **Chiomara,** the queen of Galatia captured by the Romans in the 2nd century BCE, who reportedly had the Roman guard who had raped her beheaded. One of the most famous captives of Rome was **Zenobia,** the queen of Palmyra, who was reportedly brought to Rome in golden chains after her briefly successful defiance of Rome's expansion into her region. The Romans' encounter with the **Cimbrian women** is one of many cases in which conquered peoples—women and children included—were captured and enslaved by Rome. Women in Asia were equally likely to face capture and enslavement. Militant women who took to the field in defense of their territories were sometimes taken prisoner; one example is **Empress Mao** in fourth-century China. **Sultan Raziya** is an example of a female leader in thirteenth-century India who was captured in battle and then executed.

Although few women actually fought in the **Crusades** of the eleventh and twelfth centuries, there were reports of some being taken prisoner. Women who raised and led armies were at high risk of imprisonment. One famous woman prisoner was **Eleanor of Aquitaine,** imprisoned for many years by her husband Henry II for fomenting civil war in twelfth century England. **Caterina Sforza** was imprisoned by Cesare Borgia for her refusal to give up her holdings in early-sixteenth-century Italy. Civil wars could also lead to the imprisonment of women. **Margaret of Anjou,** captured during the English Wars of the Roses, was one example of a woman who ended up in the Tower of London.

During the medieval era just one example of the harsh treatment of some female civilian prisoners of war was that meted out by Edward I, king of England, to relatives of the Scottish king, Robert Bruce, and of his associates. Bruce's wife Elizabeth endured imprisonment in a succession of English castles from 1307 to 1314, and his sister Christian was confined at the Gilbertine nunnery in Lincolnshire for the same period. Their treatment was merciful, however, compared to that of **Isabel,** countess of Buchan, and Robert's other sister, Mary Bruce, who were sent, respectively, to Berwick and Roxburgh castles and imprisoned in wood and iron cages. Bruce's twelve-year-old daughter Marjorie was to be lodged in a similar cage, but Edward appears to have changed his mind and instead sent her to the priory of Watton, Yorkshire, where she remained for seven years. Others who were imprisoned in England included Marjory, wife of the earl of Menteith, who was sent to Wooton manor in Northamptonshire, and the wife of William Wysman, who was lodged at Roxburgh Castle.

Probably the most famous female prisoner of war of the medieval era was **Joan of Arc.** After a series of spectacular military victories Joan was captured at Compiègne by John of Luxembourg in May 1430 and imprisoned until her trial at Rouen in 1431, during which time she was paraded in various towns and cities by her English and Burgundian captors. Before her trial Joan was repeatedly interrogated. The charges against her were theological rather than political, and it was on the issue of heresy that she was tried and judged. Her main crime was not her military achievements; she was found guilty on theological charges and on the charge of wearing men's clothing. On 30 May 1431 Joan was executed by being burned at the stake as a heretic.

FRONTIER EXPERIENCES

Women were caught up in the colonial wars in North America and sometimes were made prisoner. For example, **Françoise de La Tour** died in captivity in mid-seventeenth-century Canada. However, it was more common for women to become prisoners in the conflict between settlers and native peoples than in the clashes between colonial powers or in the Revolutionary War.

The experiences of captured European and Indian women in the frontier wars in North America are well documented. It was the practice of many native groups to capture rather than kill prisoners, and women were often enslaved or sometimes adopted by "enemy" tribes (an example is **Woman Chief**). The experience of native women themselves as prisoners of other tribes is described in many works of native history; just one is Ruth Landes's *The Mystic Lake Sioux*.

Women settlers in frontier regions risked death and capture in the course of conflicts with native peoples. A number of American female settlers who were taken prisoner eventually were returned to their homes and wrote memoirs about their experiences. Some examples include the following:

Minnie Carrigan, *Captured by the Indians: Reminiscences of Pioneer Life in Minnesota* (1907)

Elizabeth Hanson, *God's Mercy Surmounting Man's Cruelty Exemplified in the Captivity of Elizabeth Hanson* (1728)

Sarah L. (Mrs.) Larimer, *The Capture and Escape; or, Life among the Sioux* (1870)

Josephine Meeker, *The Ute Massacre! Brave Miss Meeker's Captivity! Her Own Account of It, Also the Narratives of Her Mother and Mrs. Price* (1879)

Helen Mar Tarble, *The Story of My Capture and Escape during the Minnesota Indian Massacre of 1862* (1904)

Colonel Nancy B. Samuelson, who has extensively researched this field, concludes in her 1985 article "The Fate Worse than Death: Women Captives of the Indian Wars" that European women captured by the Indians were far more likely to be tortured, sexually abused, or killed than were Indian women captured by whites. Weak or ill captives were usually killed, and death was often preceded by torture. Many saw their children and other relatives subjected to a similar fate. In some cases captives were adopted by the tribe of their captors and were expected to marry a husband chosen for them.

Pocahontas was an early and legendary native woman prisoner, taken hostage by the British to keep her father Powhatan at bay (1613). According to Samuelson, Indian women were not generally subjected to widespread policies of brutality and were rarely tortured. Many were sold as slaves, and some eventually rejoined their own people. Samuelson seems to ignore the heavy physical labor and squalid living conditions endured by many native women who served the whites, and the cases in which native women were given to European trappers and hunters by their own tribes. Would such relationships be considered voluntary or coercive? If most such native women had no choice in their role, should they be called slaves? Can a slave be considered similar to a prisoner? By the time of the Indian Wars of the mid-nineteenth century, the United States Army rarely took prisoners. Many native women were simply massacred along with their villages, and defeated tribes were forced onto reservations.

In the Australian frontier wars, from the 1780s to the 1920s, the experience was different than in North America. Aborigines did not take prisoners, but Aboriginal women and children were frequently abducted and enslaved by settlers. Henry Reynolds has estimated that perhaps 3,000 white settlers and a minimum of 20,000 Aborigines died as a direct result of warfare. Aboriginal men, women, and children were tortured and murdered on numerous occasions, including a massacre that took place at Forrest River in Western Australia in 1926. Sources include Henry Reynolds, *Frontier: Aborigines, Settlers, and Land* (1987). Not much scholarly study has yet appeared on the situation of women in other frontier areas—Latin America or Africa, for example.

It is also instructive to examine the treatment of prisoners by women, especially in connection with any study of women's ability to inflict violence. Although women are stereotypically compassionate and nurturing, even in their attitude toward prisoners, there have been many cases in history where women have inflicted punishment, torture, and even death upon prisoners. These cases have been neglected, both in terms of contemporary documentation and historiographical evaluation. One of the better-known examples is that of **Native American women** and the cultural traditions in some tribes of torturing prisoners. But white women also had the capacity for cruelty and violence. In his article "The Vengeful Women of Marblehead: Robert Roules's Deposition of 1677," James Axtell examines an incident of extreme physical violence against male prisoners by colonial women. On 15 July 1677, a Sunday, two Indian prisoners believed to be responsible for the murder of some local fishermen were captured; a male observer states that women of the town surrounded the Indians and stoned and beat them to death until "we found them with their heads off and gone and their flesh in a manner pulled from their bones."

THE EARLY MODERN PERIOD (SEVENTEENTH–NINETEENTH CENTURIES)

The upheavals and revolutions of the early modern period involved many women, some of whom ended up as prisoners of the enemy. **Alena Arzamasskaia,** who had disguised herself to fight in the peasant revolts in Russia in the seventeenth century, was captured by tsarist forces and executed. Women in revolts against colonial powers were also taken prisoner; one example is **Begum Samru.** Women who became prisoners due to their participation in European wars of the period include **Kit Cavanaugh.** During the revolutionary wars in both America and France women risked capture. The widespread involvement of women in combat in the early period of the **French Revolution** resulted in a few women being captured on the battlefield, including **Thérèse Figueur** and **Madeleine Petitjean. Maria Lebstuck** fought in male disguise in the revolution of 1848 against the Austrian Empire; she was captured but released when it was discovered that she was pregnant.

Women also became prisoners of war during the **American Civil War,** often due to their suspected participation in espionage activities, but also when women serving in combat disguised as men were captured. Some examples include Florena Budwin, Amy Clark, and a number of unidentified women soldiers. One of the most famous female POWs of the Civil War was the physician **Mary Walker,** who was imprisoned in Richmond for four months and later freed in a prisoner exchange.

LATE NINETEENTH AND EARLY TWENTIETH CENTURIES

There are some recorded instances of women being imprisoned after taking an active part in rebellion or guerrilla warfare. **Gertrudis Bocanegra** created and ran an underground network of women during the Mexican War of Independence and was executed after her capture and torture by government troops in 1817. **Ignacia Reachy** was captured during the French intervention in Mexico in the mid-nineteenth century; she was released after a year in prison, but later died in combat. **Paraguayan women** were among the combatants and POWs in the War of the Triple Alliance (1864–1870).

Chin Ch'iu, who modeled herself on Joan of Arc, entered the struggle against the Manchu dynasty in China in 1898. She was captured and executed in 1907, having heroically refused under torture to implicate anyone else in her uprising.

During the First World War (1914–1918) there were several instances of nurses being captured and held as prisoners of war. In Russia in the fall of 1914, a Sister of Mercy, Henrietta Sorokina, was taken prisoner by the Germans but managed to save the flag of the 6th Libau Infantry Regiment. In November 1914, in recognition of her bravery, she was awarded simultaneously all four classes of the **Order of St. George,** being the first person to be awarded the first- and second-class medals. The British nurse Edith Cavell was captured by the Germans and executed by firing squad after being accused of spying. In the **Russian Civil War** that followed close on the heels of the First World War, thousands of women were active and risked capture. **Larisa Reisner** was one famous participant who was captured during espionage activity but managed to escape.

Other revolutionary conflicts, such as the one in Palestine around the state of Israel, drew in many women. **Mania Shochat** was arrested and imprisoned on several occasions by the Turkish rulers of Palestine for her clandestine work for Hashomer in the early twentieth century. Civil wars such as the **Spanish Civil War** of the 1930s involved women; some were taken prisoner, while others like **Lina Odena** committed suicide in order to avoid capture. **Rosario Sánchez Mora** provides just one example of the treatment of female combatants in this war; she was imprisoned at the war's end in 1939 and endured three years of hard conditions.

THE SECOND WORLD WAR: EUROPE

During the Second World War more women endured the experience of internment than ever before, partly because of the increased numbers of females in the armed services as well as the civilian populations involved. Civilian women in Europe experienced imprisonment, torture, and death on a massive scale before and during the Second World War. During the political purges of the 1930s in the Soviet Union many thousands of women were sent to concentration camps. Some of the best works on these experiences are Evgeniia Semenovna Ginzburg, *Journey into the Whirlwind* (1975), and Semen Samuilovich Vilenskii, John Crowfoot, and Zaiana Veselaia, *Till My Tale Is Told: Women's Memoirs of the Gulag* (1999).

The experience of women in the Holocaust has also produced literature with important ramifications for the study of women as prisoners. Among the outstanding books written on this topic are the following:

Fania Fenelon, *Playing for Time* (1997)

Brana Gurewitsch, *Mothers, Sisters, Resisters: Oral Histories of Women Who Survived the Holocaust* (1998)

Vera Laska, *Women in the Resistance and in the Holocaust: The Voices of Eyewitnesses* (1983)

Dalia Ofer and Lenore J. Weitzman, *Women in the Holocaust* (1998)

Ruth Schwertfeger, *Women of Theresienstadt: Voices from a Concentration Camp* (1989)

Jack Sutin, Rochelle Sutin, and Lawrence Sutin, *Jack and Rochelle: A Holocaust Story of Love and Resistance* (1995)

Women's increased military involvement in the Second World War also led to the risk of becoming a POW. The Soviet army, for example, had more than 800,000 women in military service. In his book *My Purpose Holds*, Jerome Caminada, a South African journalist who was interned at a camp in Slobozie, Romania, describes several Russian women paratroopers who were POWs. He managed to converse with one POW, Antonina: "In spattered Rumanian and a few words of German we talked quietly to her through the wire, and in a few quick words, or signs, as she came to our end, she described who she was." She had been dropped into Romania as one of a group of ten or twelve paratroopers; they were quickly surrounded, and Antonina fought alongside the men until captured. She suffered ten days in the "sweat box"—a Romanian torture chamber where it was impossible to either sit or stand—because she was accused of passing a note to a Russian prisoner. When the British were not given food, Antonina brought bowls of soup from the Russian prisoners. Later, two other female Russian paratroopers arrived and were put in Antonina's cell. Caminada recalls that the three "were a lively trio . . . they were soldiers first, and their relationship with their men comrades was on that basis. . . . the girls were a queer element in those surroundings, but they were dignified and self-possessed at all times."

Many Soviet women (and men) expressed their fear of being captured during the war. As one nurse recalled, "We always kept a cartridge for ourselves: we would rather die than be taken prisoner." In most published sources the fear of being captured is attributed to the expected atrocities they would suffer at the hands of the Germans. Rape was not the only—or the worst—fate that could befall a female POW. Svetlana Alexiyevich relates several poignant stories in her collection of interviews, *War's Unwomanly Face* (1988). One of the more horrific examples is of a nurse who was taken prisoner by the Germans. When she was found, "Her eyes had been put out, her breasts lopped off. She had been impaled. It was frosty and she was all very white, her hair completely grey. She was a young girl of nineteen." Partisan Liudmila Kashichkina, aged twenty-three years, was kicked, was beaten with whips until her skin was in ribbons, and was given a "Fascist manicure"—having needles simultaneously pushed under all her finger nails. She also suffered dislocated bones. After spending time in a concentration camp in Germany, Kashichkina was transferred to a camp in France in 1944. She subsequently escaped and joined the French Resistance. She was awarded the Croix de Guerre before returning to Russia. Partisans like Kashichkina were particularly at risk of being captured due to the dangerous nature of their activities. Among the most famous of the Soviet partisans were Elizaveta Chaikina and Zoia Kosmodem'ianskaia, both of whom were captured and executed by the Germans.

Tragically, the homecoming for Russian POWs, both women and men, often resulted in further imprisonment. Russian POWs who escaped, and those who were later repatriated, were nearly all imprisoned and interrogated by the NKVD as suspected collaborators. An example was **Anna Egorova,** a Shturmovik pilot and squadron commander, who bailed out of her burning Il-2 in August 1944. Her parachute only partially opened, and she suffered multiple injuries (broken ribs, two broken arms, a broken leg, and head injuries) as well as burns. She was captured and taken to a POW camp in Poland, where she was fortunate to encounter a Russian doctor who treated her injuries—she had received no treatment from the German authorities. When she was liberated by the Red Army in January 1945, she was imprisoned by the NKVD and subjected to horrible interrogations for nearly two weeks before being released.

An interesting side note is that a number of male POWs in Europe mention the fact that there were women soldiers among the Red Army liberating forces. For many of them, their first sight of women in months or years was a female soldier. For example, Flying Officer Stephen Johnson, RAF, notes in his book *A Kriegie's Log* that during the liberation of Stalag IIIA (Luckenwalde), "A small Russian column was charging down the lane between the wire enclosures, while all the prisoners ran about cheering. A very odd little column of Russians it was too. They had one tank and four trucks completely covered with branches of trees and they were all crammed with male and female Russians who bristled with Tommy guns."

Soviet treatment of POWs could be harsh. The Red Army captured few women since few women served with their enemies. However, the treatment of their own women in the gulag system, mentioned earlier, was an indication of what other female prisoners might expect. For example, Polish air force pilot **Janina Lewandowska** was apparently captured in the 1939 Soviet occupation of Poland and later executed in the infamous Katyn Massacre of 1940.

Few German women served in combat in the Second World War II, but large numbers of women's noncombatant auxiliary forces were captured at the end of the war. The only women recruited for active service at the front with the German army were members of Propaganda Company 689—volunteer Baltic Germans and Russians (mostly Ukrainians) who used loudspeakers on the front line to encourage Russian soldiers opposite them to desert. German soldiers were not happy when these women were sent to operate in the vicinity of their units. The Russians replied to these propaganda activities with direct artillery fire; more than half of the women who participated were killed. German female auxiliaries, clerical staff, and Red Cross nurses who were captured by the Red Army were not treated as prisoners of war, but as civilian internees. They were paid for any work that they performed, but those who were ill and could not work received no pay, and whoever did not fulfill her quota went more hungry than the others. The work quota for women was higher than for male POWs. Female miners were paid six to eight rubles a day, but their entire wage was spent feeding themselves. Two and a half pounds of bread cost eight rubles. One ex-POW recalled spending ten rubles on an onion. Whoever did not work during the day was allowed to purchase only half of the bread ration, part of which she was usually forced to sell in order to obtain money for the next day's bread. These German women remained in prison in Russia until November 1949. The story of these women is told in Franz Wilhelm Seidler's *Blitzmädchen* (1979).

German servicewomen who were captured by the Western Allies were treated as prisoners of war. With the exception of some crew members of the SS *Helferinnen,* most were interned only briefly in POW camps before being released. Some of the SS *Helferinnen* auxiliaries were held for up to two years pending an investigation of their wartime activities. Test pilot **Hanna Reitsch** became a prisoner of the American occupying forces due to her experience with military aircraft and association with Hitler. Reitsch spent more than a year in an internment camp. In most cases, in contrast to the experiences on the eastern front, treatment of POWs by Western Allies was humane.

In addition to regular forces, the prisoner-of-war experience was endured by women in revolutionary and resistance movements (see the entries on resistance movements for additional details). In Yugoslavia women played a critical role in the social and political revolution that took place during the Second World War. Many Yugoslavian women who resisted the Italian invasion were taken prisoner, tortured, and sent to POW camps in Italy. After Italy withdrew from the war, they were released and returned to their country, where many then continued fighting the German occupation. Women prisoners were the targets of some of the worst atrocities carried out by the Ustashe (Croatian Fascists). In *Sisters in the Resistance: How Women Fought to Free France, 1940–1945* (1995) Margaret Collins Weitz used material from a collection of first-person interviews to record the experiences of women who fought with the French Resistance. Women Resistance fighters recounted that they were treated exactly the same as male prisoners, whether they were being beaten or immersed in cold water or enduring other forms of torture. Women prisoners from all over France were interned at Compiègne outside Paris. They tried to communicate by banging Morse code on the pipes. There were a thousand women in the prison, of whom Resistance fighters were a small minority. Some were kept in solitary confinement and endured torture. One interviewee, Lise Lesèvre, recounted "nineteen days of torture" at the hands of the infamous Klaus Barbie, after which her "back was an immense wound" and she had "the outlines of a boot" on her abdomen. She was also subjected to having her head repeatedly submerged in a bathtub of water. After this experience Lesèvre was deported to Neuenbremme, an atrocious camp where inmates were forced to watch their fellow prisoners being killed.

A number of British and French women who served as SOE agents in occupied territories became prisoners of the Germans. **Noor Inayat Khan** is one example.

Only one American woman serving with the military is known to have become a POW in the European theater, and her fate was kept secret for decades. Second Lieutenant Reba Whittle had joined the Army Nurse Corps in June 1941 and then trained as a flight nurse. She was assigned to the 813th Medical Air Evacuation Squadron in England in 1944 and flew more than forty missions to pick up wounded Americans from France after the D-Day invasions. On 27 September 1944 her C-47, for unknown reasons, strayed into German air space and was shot down over Aachen. Whittle was slightly injured in the crash, along with two others, and one man died. The survivors were picked up by the Germans and incarcerated. Whittle was sent to the

POW hospital at Meiningen Stalag 9C, where she was permitted to help British prisoner doctors treat sick and wounded POWs. She was never abused but lived in isolation and never saw other women. She was repatriated in January 1945, but the army required her to sign a nondisclosure agreement keeping her POW experience secret. Whittle married Lieutenant Colonel Stanley Tobiason, to whom she had been engaged before her captivity. Despite suffering the symptoms of posttraumatic stress disorder, she was long denied disability benefits. Nevertheless, Whittle honored her nondisclosure pledge until a year before her death from breast cancer in 1981. She was buried in the National Cemetery at Presidio, California. Whittle was awarded the Air Medal and the Purple Heart in 1945, and in 1992 she was posthumously recognized as a POW.

THE SECOND WORLD WAR: THE PACIFIC

The experience of female prisoners of the Japanese in the Pacific war is also well documented. There were fifteen main internment camps for women and children in Japanese-occupied Southeast Asia, most of these being in the major islands such as Sumatra and New Britain. The situation of female and child prisoners of the Japanese forces in Asia and the Southwest Pacific was ambiguous. While General Tojo Hideki, Japan's prime minister, made it clear that POWs taken by his forces would not be protected by the Geneva Convention, women and children—including women who served as army nurses—were not regarded as being prisoners of war but rather as civilian internees.

The experience of American military nurses in the Pacific war is described in several books. The best overviews are provided by Theresa Kaminski, *Prisoners in Paradise: American Women in the Wartime South Pacific* (2000), and Elizabeth Norman, *We Band of Angels: The Untold Story of American Nurses Trapped on Bataan by the Japanese* (1999). Other interesting books include Dorothy S. Danner, *What a Way to Spend a War: Navy Nurse POWs in the Philippines* (1995), Margaret Sams and Lynn Z. Bloom, *Forbidden Family: A Wartime Memoir of the Philippines, 1941–1945* (1989), and Elizabeth Vaughan, *The Ordeal of Elizabeth Vaughan: A Wartime Diary of the Philippines* (1985).

Eighty-two American army and navy nurses were POWs in the Pacific theater; all were serving in the Philippines when Japanese forces invaded. Two army nurses at Camp Hay, about 200 miles north of Manila, in the path of the Japanese heading south, were captured on 27 December 1941. General Douglas MacArthur ordered fifty army nurses and one navy nurse to leave Manila for the Bataan Peninsula, where they established two emergency hospitals for U.S. and Filipino forces. In April 1942 the nurses were evacuated to Corregidor, where they joined another thirty-four nurses, and some were evacuated to Australia. The remaining fifty-four nurses on Corregidor were captured by the Japanese but were treated relatively humanely. They were transported to an internment camp at Santo Tomas in Manila, where they were joined by the two nurses from Camp Hay. On 3 February 1945, sixty-six army nurses were liberated at Santo Tomas.

Eleven navy nurses who were taken prisoner in January 1942 also spent some time at Santo Tomas, where they cared for 3,500 civilians until they voluntarily moved to Los Banos in May 1943. Here they established a new hospital and remained there until they were liberated on 23 February 1945 after thirty-seven months of internment. Five other navy nurses were taken prisoner when Japanese forces invaded Guam on 10 December 1941. They were sent to Zentsuji, Japan, on 10 January 1942 and were released in June 1942 as exchange prisoners.

The experience of Australian army nurses as prisoners of war is similarly the subject of both memoirs and scholarly works. Two good books to start with are Catherine Kenny, *Captives: Australian Army Nurses in Japanese Prison Camps* (1986), and Jessie Elizabeth Simons, *In Japanese Hands: Australian Nurses as POWS* (1985). Jan Bassett's *Guns and Brooches: Australian Army Nursing from the Boer War to the Gulf War* (1992) and Frances Murphy's *Desert, Bamboo, and Barbed Wire* (1983) are also useful.

Confusion and conflict characterized army decision making regarding the evacuation of members of the Australian Army Nursing Service (AANS) from Singapore Island in early 1942. Eventually six nurses sailed on the *Wah Sui* on 12 February, five days before Japanese forces captured Singapore. After many trials and tribulations they reached Australia safely. So, too, did the fifty-three nurses and seven physiotherapists who sailed the same day on the *Empire Star*, despite their vessel receiving three direct hits en route to Batavia.

Less fortunate were the remaining sixty-five AANS members on the island, who sailed that evening on the *Vyner Brooke*. On 14 February 1942 the *Vyner Brooke* was bombed and sank within half an hour of Sumatra. Twelve nurses drowned or were killed in the water. The rest struggled ashore on Banka Island, after periods in the sea ranging from eight to sixty-five hours. Japanese soldiers ordered a group of twenty-two nurses and a civilian woman into the sea and machine-gunned them. Only one of these women, Sister Vivienne Bullwinkel, survived by lying in the shallow water until after the troops had gone. Bullwinkel was unable to survive in the jungle and surrendered. She was reunited with the other surviving nurses from the *Vyner Brooke* and, with her colleagues, remained interned on Banka Island and Sumatra for the remainder of the war. They experienced dreadful living conditions, lack of food, harsh punishments, debilitating illnesses such as malaria, beriberi, and dysentery, and backbreaking work. Eight of these army nurses died while in captivity, leaving only twenty-four to be rescued on 16 September 1945.

Less well known is the fate of six other AANS members who had been sent to Rabaul in April 1941. After surrendering to Japanese troops on 23 January 1942, they were interned with a number of other women, mostly civilian nurses, for the remainder of the war. At first they were kept in Rabaul, but from July 1942, in Japan. Their living conditions were basic, they had few garments, their diet consisted mainly of rice, and their medical treatment was negligible. In winter they worked barefooted, shovelling snow from paths where their Japanese captors walked in boots. Not surprisingly, one of the six contracted tuberculosis in Japan and never completely recovered. She died prematurely in 1954. Like all of the nurses who were interned during the Second World War, she had paid a heavy price for her wartime service.

British and Dutch civilian women and children were also imprisoned in South Asia during this period. Agnes Newton Keith relates her experiences as a captive in Borneo in her book *Three Came Home,* and Sheila Bruhn's *Diary of a Girl in Changi, 1941–1945* is the account of a seventeen-year-old girl captured at the fall of Singapore; her long imprisonment provides a woman's view of the Japanese invasion and life in a Japanese prison camp. Lavinia Warner and John Sandilands, *Women beyond the Wire: A Story of Prisoners of the Japanese, 1942–1945* (1982), is also useful. In the late 1970s and early 1980s the Imperial War Museum in London embarked on an oral history project, recording the reminiscences of female POWs in Southeast Asia during the Pacific war. Using material from these interviews, in her 1987 article "Passive in War? Women Internees in the Far East, 1942–5" Margaret Brooks found that most interviewees were women who would have been younger than forty at the time of their internment. They were all British or European, mostly middle class, and were either professionals—nurses, missionaries, and teachers—or the wives of members of the military or businessmen. Hence they were part of the colonial system. Despite the relative similarity of their backgrounds, however, the condition in which the women arrived in camp varied considerably. Some had barely any possessions; others carried suitcases containing not only clothes but cosmetics, jewelry, photographs, prayer books, and other personal items that were not basic to survival.

The treatment of women prisoners by Japanese guards varied considerably. In general, women were not interrogated, but one hospital matron recalled being asked politely to sit and then being beaten around the head and face for sitting. Most female internees did not experience this type of brutality, but they did endure primitive living conditions, inadequate and poor food, illness, and the deaths of friends and relatives. In most of the camps the women organized themselves into groups. Where they lived in houses—often eight or ten to a room—they elected house captains and a camp leader, for the Japanese expected them to have a spokesperson. A democratic system was usually adopted, with leaders being selected by ballot. When they became ill, others took their place. In the latter stages of the war, when many were weak and ill, positions of authority were often rotated. Some women were regarded as being "leader types," these generally being professionals who were used to supervising staff, such as doctors, matrons, or, in one case, a mother superior, or the wives of senior colonial officials.

Daily tasks in camp included cooking, carrying food and supplies, and disposing of refuse and human waste, as well as working for the Japanese guards, sewing, gardening, and carrying water. In some camps the food supply was erratic. Ex-POWs recalled that they never knew how long each supply was meant to last. Sometimes the guards brought sacks of rice; other times meat was simply dumped on the ground, or a few dozen eggs had to be shared among 400 people. Both hygiene and privacy were virtually nonexistent. Toilets were often open latrine ditches. Bathing facilities were similarly basic and usually consisted of a bucket of water. Despite these trying conditions, many prisoners strove to keep up morale by organizing classes for their children, wearing makeup in the evenings, "dressing" for dinner, and creating special occasions. Christmas was celebrated, even when it was banned, as on one occasion at Bandung, Java.

Each death was accompanied by a small ceremony. The body, wrapped in a blanket, was taken outside the camp by the internee burial party, under escort, and a grave was dug. As the body was committed to the ground, the women removed the blanket—too precious an item to be buried. Usually someone read or recited from memory a few verses from the Bible or prayer book, the grave was decorated by leaves and flowers, and a rough cross was fashioned with a few words written in charcoal. Illness, malnutrition, exhaustion, and anxiety all contributed to the death toll. Those who survived were more likely to be women who lived from day to day and who were not consumed by anxiety for the safety of husbands or adult sons who were interned separately and of whom they had no word.

Conditions in camp were harsh and sometimes intolerable, but the highest death rate of civilian prisoners occurred among those who never entered a camp. In Sumatra in 1942 about eighty Dutch women and children were captured near Padang. Apparently none of the Japanese commanders in Sumatra wished to assume responsibility for the party, and they were marched from one area to another until, after two and a half years of this treatment, less than thirty survived. In Palembang after the war British author Nevil Shute met two of the survivors: Mrs. J. G. Geysel-Vonck and her son, who had been a six-month-old baby at the start of the march. Shute was inspired by their experience and used it as the basis of his excellent 1950 novel *A Town like Alice*, in which a party of British women and children were similarly marched around the Malay Peninsula because (in the words of his character, Captain Yoniata) "the Imperial Japanese Army do not make war on womans and childs . . . Japanese soldiers always kind to womans and childs."

Another category of women prisoners was the "comfort women" forced into prostitution by the Japanese. A number of studies have recently been published on their experiences:

Asian Women Human Rights Council, *War Crimes on Asian Women: Military Sexual Slavery by Japan during World War II: The Case of the Filipino Comfort Women* (1998)

George L. Hicks, *The Comfort Women: Japan's Brutal Regime of Enforced Prostitution in the Second World War* (1995)

Keith Howard et al., *True Stories of the Korean Comfort Women: Testimonies* (1995)

Sangmie Choi Schellstede and Soon Mi Yu, *Comfort Women Speak: Testimony by Sex Slaves of the Japanese Military (Includes New United Nations Human Rights Report)* (2000)

Margaret D. Stetz and Bonnie B.C. Oh, *Legacies of the Comfort Women of World War II* (2001)

Some women managed to escape from prison camps or evade capture. A particularly interesting story is related by Colonel Edward T. Imparato in *Rescue from Shangri-La.* In May 1945 an army transport plane left Hollandia, New Guinea, became lost in fog, and crashed into a mountain, killing nineteen of the twenty-four aboard. Ultimately only two men and a **WAC** corporal named Margaret Hastings survived the ordeal of returning to Hollandia. A similar harrowing experience is recounted by survivor Slavomir Rawicz in *The Long Walk: A Gamble for Life.* Rawicz escaped from a work camp in Siberia with seven Polish, American, and Lithuanian POWs. They were joined by Kristina Polanska, a seventeen-year-old Polish girl who had been deported to a Siberian communal farm in 1939 after the Russians invaded Poland. The group set off toward India, a journey of several thousand miles. After walking for five months with virtually no food, clothing, or equipment, Polanska died in crossing the Gobi Desert. Only four of the original eight survived to reach India.

AFTER THE SECOND WORLD WAR

Since the Second World War there have been increasing numbers of female soldiers used as irregular troops in independence struggles. Women were resistance fighters and were taken prisoner in the **Israeli War of Independence.** In Vietnam's struggle to throw off French colonial rule, female Vietcong soldiers also endured imprisonment, torture, and execution as POWs. Among noncombatants in regular forces, American and Australian army nurses served in Korea and Vietnam, where they cared for casualties who included the victims of female Vietcong soldiers. While no Australian army nurses were imprisoned by the Vietcong, some American nurses were not so fortunate. The case of Monika Schwinn, a nurse held for four years as a POW in the "Hanoi Hilton," is not well known although she published an account of her imprisonment in an autobiography entitled *We Came to Help.* Kate Webb, a combat correspondent for United Press International, also published her story after she was captured by North Vietnamese regulars in Cambodia. Long before her capture Kate Webb was unusual in that she routinely went on patrol in American and South Vietnamese units. One of Webb's fellow UPI correspondents has commented that she was "one of the finest war correspondents to cover Vietnam and her capture and subsequent release—and the way she handled herself—did a great deal to knock down myths about women facing the rigors of ground combat."

More recently American military women have served in Grenada, Panama, and the Gulf War. During the Gulf War Specialist **Melissa Rathbun-Nealy** became the first American enlisted woman to be captured as a prisoner of war; she was released after more than a month in captivity. Army medic and pilot **Rhonda Cornum** sustained serious injuries when her helicopter crashed, and she was captured by the Iraqis along with two other male survivors. Cornum's story received attention in the American press mainly when she admitted that she had been sexually assaulted.

Surprisingly, despite the long history of female POWs in numerous countries and in almost every continent, the specter of women becoming prisoners of war remains central to arguments against female combatants. In his 1996 article "Women as POWs: Forgetting the Rhonda Cornum Story," Elliot Gruner points out that sexual assault is regarded by the media (especially film media) as being central to the female POW experience, yet many female POWs did not suffer rape. The tragedy of this exaggeration of the occurrence of rape is twofold: women combatants are ill prepared for captivity, and, Gruner argues, in North American culture at least, they continue to be robbed of the "hero" status accorded to male prisoners of war. Any wisdom that they may have gained from the experience continues to be ignored. In Rhonda Cornum's case, her story "has not been used by the media or the government to make her a hero but instead to foreground the tragedy of women serving on the front lines." Sadly, this focus on the possibility of capture and rape among military women neglects the historical fact that civilian women have experienced a much greater risk and incidence of rape in wartime, especially in occupied territories.

Fortunately, the female POW experience has not been trivialized in all cultures. Some surprisingly positive aspects emerged from the POW experience. In the face of terrible adversity, the survivors of Japanese internment recalled that the supposed characteristics of women together—bitchiness and hysteria—were largely absent. One survivor said that she learned not only to depend on herself in a way that she had never done previously, but to respect other women. "I know [now] that women are dependable and women are strong, extremely strong, in a crisis."

Appendix B

Women, Medicine, and the Military: A Bibliographic Survey

Connie L. Reeves

The standard reference for the history of nursing in the last half of the nineteenth century and the first half of the twentieth century is Mary Adelaide Nutting and Lavinia L. Dock's four-volume work *A History of Nursing: From the Earliest Times to the Present Day with Special Reference to the Work of the Past Thirty Years* (New York: Putnam and Sons, 1907–1912). Distilling these four volumes into one is Isabelle M. Stewart and A. L. Austin's, *A History of Nursing, From Ancient to Modern Times: A World View* (New York: G.P. Putnam's Sons, 1962), a classic nursing history that contains some of the most valuable information on military nursing. Richard H. Shryock's *The History of Nursing: An Interpretation of the Social and Medical Factors Involved* (Philadelphia: Saunders, 1959) is one of the best accounts of how modern nursing has developed over time, although its history ends with the beginning of the twentieth century.

An early nursing text, *American Nursing: History and Interpretation* by Mary M. Roberts (New York: Macmillan Company, 1955), has a greater emphasis than usual on military nursing, both during and between wars. A classic nursing history, it picks up where Nutting and Dock left off. Although *Jensen's History and Trends of Professional Nursing*, edited by Gerald Joseph Griffin and Joanne King Griffin (St. Louis: C.V. Mosby Co., 1969), focuses on civilian nursing, it does provide important information on the relationship between the Red Cross and the military nursing corps. Another book on the nursing profession that includes some very good sections on military nursing and nursing during the wars, as well as integrating nursing history into traditional history, is Grace L. Deloughery's *History and Trends of Professional Nursing* (St. Louis: C.V. Mosby Company, 1977), evidently the successor to Griffin and Griffin.

A classic nursing text that includes information on the development of nursing because of and during wars is Josephine A. Dolan, *Nursing in Society: A Historical Perspective* (Philadelphia: W.B. Saunders Co., 1978). An extremely useful book is Bonnie Bullough, Vern L. Bullough, and Barrett Elcano's comprehensive *Nursing: A Historical Bibliography,* which includes a chapter of sources on military and wartime nursing and is current through 1978. *Nursing History: New Perspectives, New Possibilities,* by Ellen Condliffe Lagemann (New York: Teachers College, Columbia University, 1983), although primarily a discussion of civilian nursing, includes military nursing and nursing during wars as part of the developmental process of the profession. More analytical in approach than most nursing histories, it postulates why certain actions were taken rather than simply retelling them.

One of the most valuable books in the field of military nursing is Patricia M. Donahue, *Nursing, the Finest Art: An Illustrated History* (St. Louis: C.V. Mosby Co., 1985), which incorporates hundreds of photos with insightful interpretation of the entire history of civilian and military nursing. Another excellent book with respect to military nursing is Philip A. Kalisch and Beatrice J. Kalisch, *The Advance of American Nursing* (Boston: Little, Brown & Co., 1986), which, in addition to analyzing the development of the nursing profession, provides a detailed accounting of military nurses in each of this nation's major wars, from the Spanish-American War to the Second World War. Short biographies of the most significant individuals in the history of nursing are given by Vern L. Bullough, Olga Maranjian Church, and Alice P. Stein in *American Nursing: A Biographical Dictionary* (New York: Garland Publishing, 1988).

Other major nursing histories that provide information on military nursing include Victor Robinson, *White Caps: The Story of Nursing* (Philadelphia and New York: J.B. Lippincott, 1946), which includes general medical and historical developments and much interesting biographical and bibliographical information; Minnie Goodnow, *Outlines of Nursing History* (Philadelphia: W.B. Saunders, 1948), a much-used text in the United States, revised by Josephine A. Dolan as *Goodnow's History of Nursing,* 12th ed. (Philadelphia: W.B. Saunders Co., 1968); Foster Rhea Dulles, *The American Red Cross: A History* (New York: Harper and Brothers, 1950); Lucy Ridgely Seymer, *A General History of Nursing,* 4th ed. (New York: Macmillan, 1958), widely considered to be a major nursing history, written by an Englishwoman; Lena Dixon Dietz, *History and Modern Nursing* (Philadelphia: F.A. Davis, 1963), another widely used and highly respected nursing text; and Lyndia Flanagan, *One Strong Voice: The Story of the American Nurses' Association* (Kansas City: Lowell Press for the American Nurses' Association, 1976).

Although Major General Jeanne Holm's book *Women in the Military: An Unfinished Revolution* (Novato, CA.: Presidio Press, 1992) is amazingly comprehensive, it provides only scant information about military nurses. In the first few pages of *Women Veterans: America's Forgotten Heroines* (New York: Continuum, 1983), June A. Willenz provides some information about military nursing over the first two centuries of U.S. history. Matthew Naythons, *The Face of Mercy: A Photographic History of Medicine at War* (New York: Random House, 1993), and Richard A. Gabriel and Karen S. Metz, *A History of Military Medicine* (Westport, CT: Greenwood Press, 1992), also include some information about military nursing. Linda Grant De Pauw's *Seafaring Women* (Boston: Houghton Mifflin, 1982) provides some insight into early naval nursing. During the Revolutionary War women were paid to serve as nurses for the army and the navy. Of the few who are known, Mary Pricely served aboard the colonial warship *Defense,* and Mary Waters was an army nurse.

The only book to deal with military nursing as its sole subject is Anne Summers, *Angels and Citizens: British Women as Military Nurses, 1854–1914* (London and New York: Routledge and Kegan Paul, Ltd. 1988). The book traces British consciousness about women's sphere and the transition of women into the male nursing field in the military. Military nursing in the Crimean War, the Boer War, and other crises of the British Empire in the nineteenth and early twentieth centuries is discussed at length. Using many archival sources, this book's bibliography is extraordinarily extensive and provides research paths on nurses, hospitals, the army, wars, women, and work. *Angels and Citizens* is indispensable in unraveling the history of nursing in the British military.

Modern military nursing traces its origin to the Crimean War and Florence Nightingale, a nurse superintendent who took thirty-eight nurses to Scutari in 1854 to care for soldiers dying from cholera and battle wounds in the midst of filth and vermin. Her reorganization of the hospital and improved nutrition and sanitation procedures reduced the high mortality rates immediately and significantly. When the war was over, Nightingale was awarded £50,000 by the British government. She used the funds to establish the Nightingale Training School for Nurses, which soon became the international model. Nightingale's efforts helped diminish opposition to female nurses in the army and inspired Jean-Henri Dunant to found the International Red Cross.

Florence Nightingale's life and work have been written about extensively. The original classic work was Sir Edward Cook's *The Life of Florence Nightingale* (New York: Macmillan, 1942), a biography based upon her private and official papers, as well as government sources. Of particular interest in this book are her years in the Crimea and bibliographic mention of women's writings on the Crimean War. A biography both revered and maligned is Cecil Woodham-Smith, *Florence Nightingale* (New York: McGraw-Hill, 1951). Her work relied heavily upon Cook, and, in turn, other historians have relied upon Woodham-Smith's rendition.

A critical approach toward Nightingale is revealed in F.B. Smith, *Florence Nightingale: Reputation and Power* (New York: St. Martin's Press, 1982), in which Nightingale is portrayed as a power seeker and not necessarily altruistic. *Florence Nightingale and the Nursing Legacy* by Monica E. Baly (London: Croom

Helm, 1986) focuses on the early Nightingale schools and their influence, covering new ground instead of relying on Woodham-Smith and Cook. A chapter on military nursing covers British crises and wars during the period after the Crimean War and through the end of the nineteenth century.

Upon hearing about the privations suffered by soldiers in the Crimea, Mary Seacole, one of the best-known pioneer black nurses, left her home in Jamaica and traveled to London, seeking a position as one of Nightingale's nurses. Her request was denied, but Seacole traveled to the Crimea at personal expense and established a hotel and store for soldiers. In the evenings she worked in the Scutari hospital alongside Nightingale. Seacole recounted her life story in *Wonderful Adventures of Mrs. Seacole in Many Lands*.

Other nurses who went to the Crimea and wrote memoirs include Elizabeth Davis, *The Autobiography of . . . , a Crimean Nurse,* edited by Jane Williams, 2 vols. (London: 1857); Sister Mary Aloysius Doyle, *Memories of the Crimea* (London: 1897); and Sarah Anne Terrot, *Nurse Sarah Anne with Florence Nightingale at Scutari,* edited by Robert G. Richardson (London: 1977). Helena Concannon, *The Irish Sisters of Mercy in the Crimean War* (Dublin: n.p., 1950), is another source of information on nurses who served. John Shelton Curtiss wrote "Russian Sisters of Mercy in the Crimea, 1854–1855," *Slavic Review* 25 (1966): 84, reminding us that British and American nurses were not the only ones who served.

The history of black military nurses has been captured particularly well in Mary Elizabeth Carnegie's *The Path We Tread: Blacks in Nursing, 1854–1984* (Philadelphia: J.B. Lippincott, 1986). Carnegie specifically, though briefly, mentions Mary Seacole of the Crimean War; **Harriet Tubman, Susie King Taylor,** and Sojourner Truth of the **American Civil War;** and Namahyoke Sockum Curtis of the Spanish-American War—nursing pioneers who just happened to be black. The integration of black nurses into official military nursing, beginning with the Spanish-American War, is meticulously described in this well-written book. Taylor's experiences are also recounted in *Reminiscences of My Life in Camp with the 33rd United States Colored Troops Late 1st South Carolina Volunteers* (Boston: privately printed, 1902), apparently the only memoir from a Civil War black nurse. Jean M. Hoefer has provided a closer look at Tubman's war work in "Harriet Tubman: A Heroine of the Underground Goes to War," *Civil War Times Illustrated* February 1988: 37–41. Black nurses are further examined in "The Southern Side of 'Glory': Mississippi African-American Women during the Civil War," *Minerva: Quarterly Report on Women and the Military* 8.3 (1990): 28–36, by Noralee Frankel.

Although women have provided nursing care to armies for centuries, their presence on the battlefield in an official capacity first reached large numbers in the American Civil War. When the war began, the military used only male nurses, usually supplemented by soldiers who provided completely inadequate health care. Robert E. Denney's *Civil War Medicine: Care and Comfort of the Wounded* (New York: Sterling Pub., 1994) provides a good historical understanding of the difficulties and obstacles involved in providing military medical care. *Doctors in Blue: The Medical History of the Union Army in the Civil War*, by George Worthington Adams (New York: Henry Schuman, 1952), provides important background information on the historical role of military nurses.

Immediately after the Civil War Frank Moore wrote his classic *Women of the War: Their Heroism and Self-Sacrifice* (Hartford, CT: S.S. Scranton and Co., 1866) specifically to ensure that the women who served in the war were honored for their contributions. He devotes separate chapters to individual women, and of them, some are nurses, including "Mother" Bickerdyke. Engravings and first-person narratives from women make this truly authentic. Mary Elizabeth Massey, in *Bonnet Brigades: The Impact of the Civil War* (New York: Alfred A. Knopf, 1966), provides extraordinary research into the war's impact on women, including nurses, and concentrates on such famous figures as Clara Barton. Marilyn Mayer Culpeper, through extracts from women's letters, diaries, and memoirs, uses their own words to depict their attitudes toward nursing and battlefield medical conditions in her book *Trials and Triumphs: Women of the American Civil War* (East Lansing: Michigan State University Press, 1991).

Doctors and nurses often gave eyewitness accounts of the war and wrote about their experiences. Although vignettes from only a few women nurses are included in Harold Elk Straubing's book *In Hospital and Camp: The Civil War through the Eyes of Its Doctors and Nurses* (Harrisburg, PA.: Stackpole Books, 1993), it provides some good firsthand narratives. Mary A. Gardiner Holland compiled *Our Army Nurses: Interesting Sketches, Addresses, and Photographs of Nearly 100 of the Noble Women Who Served in Hospitals and on Battlefields during Our Civil War* (Boston: B. Wilkins and Co., 1895), which, though flowery, is important in the number of women it covers. In "Untrained but Undaunted: The Women Nurses of the Blue and the Gray," *Nursing Forum* 15.1 (1976), Beatrice J. Kalisch and Philip A. Kalisch provide a look at women on both sides of the war.

Most memoirs, books, and scholarly studies on Civil War nursing are based on the Union experience since virtually all Confederate medical records disappeared due to fire. One of the few books that discuss Union army nurses collectively is Marjorie Barstow Greenbie's *Lincoln's Daughters of Mercy* (New York: G.P. Putnam's Sons, 1944). Nina B. Smith, in "Men and Authority: The Union Army Nurse and the Problem of Power," *Minerva: Quarterly Report on Women and the Military* 6 (Winter 1988): 25–41, examines the negative receptions and difficulties that Union army nurses arriving at military hospitals encountered from doctors and male corpsmen. Julia C. Stimson, a noted nurse administrator, provided an early account with "Women Nurses with the Union Forces during the Civil War," *Military Surgeon* 62 (February 1928). The highly regarded historian Anne Douglas Wood wrote "The War within a War: Women Nurses in the Union Army," *Civil War History* 18 (1979): 197–222.

Another available look at Union nurses is Sylvia G. Dannett's "Lincoln's Ladies in White," *New York State Journal of Medicine* 61 (1961): 1944–1952.

Clara Barton, the best-known nursing figure in American history, served soldiers on the battlefields in the Civil War, providing them with medicines and supplies through her personal funds. After the war she helped to locate and bury thousands of dead soldiers. Still later Barton founded the American Red Cross and served as its president for many years. Percy H. Epler's authorized biography, *The Life of Clara Barton* (New York: Macmillan, 1919), incorporates her unpublished war diaries and letters, her conversations, observations by eyewitnesses, and published Red Cross history. Epler covers Barton's entire life and provides numerous chapters on her Civil War work, particularly focusing on Second Bull Run, Harper's Ferry, Antietam, the winter campaign before Fredericksburg, and the siege of Petersburg. In addition to Barton's Civil War and Red Cross contributions, Epler also discusses her assistance in Europe during the Franco-Prussian War and her contributions during the Spanish-American War in Cuba.

A new and outstanding biography of Clara Barton is Stephen B. Oates, *A Woman of Valor: Clara Barton and the Civil War* (New York: Free Press, 1994). Oates, like Epler, had access to Barton's papers and drew upon hundreds of other archival documents to create a living image of this legendary nurse. A biography that eulogizes is William E. Barton, *The Life of Clara Barton, Founder of the American Red Cross* (Boston: Houghton Mifflin, 1922). Other biographies include Blanche Colton Williams, *Clara Barton, Daughter of Destiny* (Philadelphia: J.B. Lippincott, 1941), and Corra Bacon-Foster, *Clara Barton, Humanitarian* (Washington, DC: n.p., 1918).

One of the most famous and beloved nursing figures on the battlefield was Mary Ann "Mother" Bickerdyke, a totally selfless woman constantly tending to her "boys." *Cyclone in Calico: The Story of Mary Ann Bickerdyke*, by Nina Brown Baker (Boston: Little, Brown and Co., 1952), is an early biography, while Adele Deleeuw's *Civil War Nurse: Mary Ann Bickerdyke* (New York: Julian Messner, Simon and Schuster, 1973), though a juvenile biography, is more recent. An article by Nancy B. Samuelson, "Mother Bickerdyke: She Outranked Everybody but God," *Minerva: Quarterly Report on Women and the Military* 5 (Summer 1987): 111–125, gives a wonderful description of her activities during the Civil War and a clear impression of her forceful personality.

Sophronia Bucklin, a Civil War nurse, and **Mary Edwards Walker,** a Civil War doctor and the only female recipient in history of the Congressional Medal of Honor, are the focal points in Elizabeth D. Leonard's *Yankee Women: Gender Battles in the Civil War* (New York: W.W. Norton, 1994). Although Leonard's primary purpose was to demonstrate how women's roles in society were affected after the war, her discussions illuminate the experiences of women who served in the military. After the war Bucklin penned her memoirs, *In Hospital and Camp: A Woman's Record of Thrilling Incidents among the Wounded in the Late War* (Philadelphia: J.E. Potter, 1869).

Mary Walker is further discussed in Charles McCool Snyder's delightful biography, *Dr. Mary Walker: The Little Lady in Pants* (New York: Arno Press, 1974). Snyder has amply depicted her struggle to become a physician, her medical work in the Civil War, her appointment as an assistant surgeon, and her award of the Medal of Honor. In "Civil War Doctress Mary: Only Woman to Win Congressional Medal of Honor," *Minerva: Quarterly Report on Women and the Military* 12 (Fall 1994): 24–35, Allen D. Spiegel and Andrea M. Spiegel discuss Walker's war contribution, the award of the Medal of Honor, her brief stint as a prisoner of war, and congressional efforts to rescind her medal. Helen Beal Woodward, in *The Bold Women* (Freeport, NY: Books for Librairies Press, 1958), includes a chapter titled "The Right to Wear Pants: Dr. Mary Walker."

Sarah Emma Edmonds, noted nurse and spy during the Civil War, recounted her experiences immediately after the war in her memoir, *Nurse and Spy in the Union Army.* As a nurse, she worked both in the field and in a number of different hospitals and recorded her thoughts of events at numerous famous battlefields, including Bull Run, Antietam, and Fredericksburg. Earlier Edmonds published *Unsexed; or, The Female Soldier* (Philadelphia: Philadelphia Publishing Co., 1864), a fictionalized account of her Civil War experiences, not mentioning that she had disguised herself as a male nurse with the name Franklin Thompson. Betty Fladeland, in her article, "Alias Franklin Thompson," *Michigan History* 42.3 (1958): 435–462, provides a discussion of Edmonds under her assumed identity.

Louisa May Alcott served as a nurse for a short time during the Civil War in a Union army hospital. Drawing upon letters she had written, she wrote *Hospital Sketches,* one of the earliest firsthand narratives about experiences with the wounded. The book met with instant success throughout the North and drew enormous attention to the plight of wounded soldiers. Not until four years later did Alcott publish and become famous for *Little Women.*

Walt Whitman, having attained national success with *Leaves of Grass* in 1855, was one of the more illustrious personages to have served as a war nurse. When his brother was wounded in the war, Whitman became a volunteer nurse, caring for his brother and working in Union army hospitals. Walter Lowenfels, author of *Walt Whitman's Civil War* (New York: Alfred A. Knopf, 1961), has provided the only known biography of Whitman's service during the war. Whitman did write his own short memoir entitled *Memoranda during the War* (n.p., n.d.).

A celebrated family of sisters, Georgeanna, Eliza, Abby, and Jane Woolsey, served in the Civil War as nurses and in the Sanitary Commission, an organization set up to provide transportation, medical assistance, food, clothing, and supplies to soldiers when the army's capability was lacking. Georgeanna and her sister, Eliza Woolsey Howland, were part of a select group of fifteen nurses invited by the Sanitary Commission in 1862 to serve aboard hospital ships as nurse matrons. Jane Stuart Woolsey published her memoirs shortly after the war as *Hospital Days* (New York: 1868), which received Louisa May Alcott's praise as one of the best hospital books to appear. Georgeanna, Jane, and Abby were each prominent after the war in establishing nursing schools for women. Much later, Abby Howland Woolsey wrote *A Century of Nursing* (New York: Putnam's, 1950). Anne L. Austin provides an intimate look at their contributions in *The Woolsey Sisters of New York: A Family's Involvement in the Civil War and a New Profession (1860–1900)* (Philadelphia: American Philosophical Society, 1971), an easily readable book that draws upon family letters.

Katharine Prescott Wormeley was another of the fifteen nurses selected to serve aboard a Sanitary Commission hospital ship. In the excellent study "Arranging a Doll's House: Refined Women as Union Nurses," Kristie Ross clearly and succinctly explains the frustrations and obstacles these hospital-ship matrons encountered, focusing on Wormeley's experiences as written in her letters home. A year later Wormeley seemed to have forgotten how she had protested against the constraints the Sanitary Commission and army doctors had imposed on her and other nurses. In her book *The United States Sanitary Commission* (Boston: 1863) Wormeley became that organization's greatest female supporter and admonished nurses to be obedient to doctors and remember their place. Many years later, Wormeley wrote *The Other Side of the War with the Army of the Potomac* (Boston: Ticknor, 1889), revised under the title *The Cruel Side of War* (Boston: Roberts, 1898) and considered to be one of the finest accounts of women's work during the war.

Another prominent woman who served as a nurse for the Union army was Mary Ashton Rice Livermore—teacher, reformer, suffragist, pastor's wife, and founder and editor of a magazine that later merged with *Woman's Journal*. Although she was married and middle aged, Livermore spent the entire war as an army nurse. Decades later she retold her experience in *My Story of the War: A Woman's Narrative of Four Years Personal Experience as a Nurse in the Union Army* (Hartford, CT: A.D. Worthington Co., 1889).

Despite the paucity of records and documentation, a number of books and articles have successfully reconstructed a picture of the Confederacy's medical services. *Doctors in Gray: The Confederate Medical Service* by H.H. Cunningham (Baton Rouge: Louisiana State University Press, 1958) is one such early attempt. One of the few articles located on Southern nurses is C.M. Kenneally, "Nurses and Nursing in the Confederacy," *Southern Hospital* April 1942.

An outstanding new study of inestimable value is Glenna R. Schroeder-Lein's *Confederate Hospitals on the Move: Samuel H. Stout and the Army of Tennessee* (Columbia: University of South Carolina Press, 1994). Stout, a hospital administrator, was unusual in that he maintained meticulous written records about the daily life of a hospital in battle and, furthermore, kept them safe for posterity. In addition to Stout's records, Schroeder-Lein's exceptional bibliography includes her use of innumerable memoirs, census records, and manuscripts. Biographies of doctors and nurses, accompanied by photos, include that of Kate Cummings, who served in Stout's hospital, and Fanny Beers, also a nurse matron. Immediately after the war Cummings published her own *Journal of Hospital Life in the Confederate Army of Tennessee* (Louisville: J. P. Morton, 1866).

Sally Louisa Tompkins had nursed Confederate soldiers at Bull Run and supervised a private hospital in Richmond. In 1861 the Confederacy acquired control of all private hospitals, but hers was granted an exception by President Jefferson Davis. To facilitate her ability to requisition supplies, Davis commissioned her as a captain in the Confederate army, the only female officer in the South. Tompkins refused to accept payment for her services and became well known for nursing the most critical patients. Her achievements are listed in *Women and the Military: Over 100 Notable Contributors, Historic to Contemporary* by John P. Dever and Maria C. Dever (Jefferson, NC: McFarland, 1995).

Ada W. Bacot, a Confederate army nurse, housekeeper, and assistant matron in military hospitals, detailed her daily routine and thoughts in a six-volume diary that Jean Berlin has skillfully edited into *A Confederate Nurse: The Diary of Ada W. Bacot, 1860–1863* (Columbia: University of South Carolina Press, 1994). Although Berlin footnotes whom Bacot is discussing in her diary, she does not interfere with the diary entries, but leaves them as Bacot wrote them—misspellings and all—which contributes to the charm of this book. Half a century after the war J. Fraise Richard compiled *The Florence Nightingale of the Southern Army: Experiences of Mrs. Ella K. Newsom, Confederate Nurse in the Great War, 1861–65* (New York: Broadway Publishing Co., 1914).

The role of the navy nurse can be traced back to the Civil War and onto the first hospital ship, the USS *Red Rover*, upon which women nurses served. *Privateers and Volunteers: The Men and Women of Our Reserve Naval Forces, 1766 to 1866* by Reuben Elmore Stivers (Annapolis, MD: Naval Institute Press, 1975) is a treasure trove of information on Civil War hospital ships, specifically the *Red Rover*, and includes a discussion of the nurses, their working conditions, and their military pay. An article specifically concerned with the *Red Rover* and the nurses who served upon it is "The U.S. Hospital Ship *Red Rover* (1862–1865)," *Military Surgeon* 77 (August 1935): 92.

Throughout history religious orders have often provided their nuns as nurses in wartime. In the Civil War approximately 600 Catholic sisters supported the Union and the Confederacy. Mary Denis Maher, in *To Bind Up the Wounds: Catholic Sister Nurses in the U.S. Civil War* (New York: Greenwood Press, 1989), documents their contributions. Protestant religious nursing groups also sent women to nurse soldiers during the war.

The French Red Cross was founded in 1864. La Société de secours aux blessés militaires des armées de terre et de mer (SSBM), a society of the Red Cross, was formed in 1866. SSBM became the designated military medical auxiliary and was placed under military authority in wartime. In the Franco-Prussian War Red Cross nurses cared for 340,000 wounded soldiers, with twenty women dying from war service. A short article by V.A.J. Swain, "The Franco-Prussian War of 1870–1: Voluntary Aid for the Wounded and Sick,"

British Medical Journal 3 (1970): 511–514, provides insight into the prevalent medical care. Women from other nations offered nursing care during the war, including Clara Barton.

After the Franco-Prussian War the French formed base and field hospitals throughout France. Red Cross nurses tended the wounded streaming into France from the Spanish civil war from 1873 to 1875. Two other Red Cross societies were formed in the late nineteenth century and eventually joined with SSBM. Thousands of French nurses, distributed among mobile teams, were poised to mobilize at any given moment.

Toward the end of the nineteenth century British surgeon-major G.J.H. Evatt, with interesting foresight, published *A Proposal to Form a Corps of Volunteer Female Nurses for Service in the Army Hospital in the Field, with Suggestions as to the Incorporation of the Nursing Profession* (Woolwich: n.p., 1885). His vision came to naught, however, and disappeared under the weight of history.

With the outbreak of the Spanish-American War, the United States desperately needed nurses and thousands of women volunteered. Military nursing is discussed briefly in *An Army for Empire: The United States Army in the Spanish-American War,* an analytical background of the war that includes medical conditions encountered by soldiers in Cuba.

Anita Newcomb McGee—scientist, doctor, wife, mother, author, lecturer, and clubwoman—offered to select nurses for the military under the auspices of the Daughters of the American Revolution. McGee was appointed acting assistant surgeon general, the first woman to serve in such a high official position and the only woman authorized to wear a United States Army officer's uniform. By war's end 1,600 women had served the army and navy in the United States, Puerto Rico, Cuba, Hawaii, and the Philippines and on the new hospital ship, USS *Relief,* dramatically decreasing the mortality rate. "Nursing in the Spanish American War," *Trained Nurse and Hospital Review* 63 (September 1919): 125–128, and "Heroines of '98: Female Army Nurses in the Spanish American War," *Nursing Research* 24 (November–December 1975): 411–429), by Philip Kalisch, are two articles that focus on their contributions. *War Nurses* by Shaaron Cosner (New York: Walker, 1988) provides some mention of the Spanish-American War. Clara Louise Maass, one of McGee's nurses, died in Cuba while undergoing a yellow fever experiment. She was buried with full military honors.

Following the war, McGee was instrumental in establishing the United States Army Nurse Corps in 1901 as a permanent military organization. She had expressed her views in two articles, "The Army Nurse Corps in 1899" and "The Growth of the Nursing Profession in the United States," both found in *Trained Nurse and Hospital Review* 24 (1900). "Brief Outline of the Organizing of the U.S. Army Nurse Corps," *Pacific Coast Journal of Nursing* 8 (December 1912): 561–562, is one of the few articles that discuss the origin of the new nursing corps. Edith A. Aynes, an army nurse before, during, and after the Second World War, and assistant to McGee, wrote *From Nightingale to Eagle:*

An Army Nurse's History (Englewood Cliffs, NJ: Prentice-Hall, 1973), providing an insider's view of supplying nurses for the Spanish-American War and developing a permanent nursing corps for the army. McGee also wrote a nursing manual in 1899 that was the standard for army and navy nurses until 1947 and assisted in establishing the Navy Nurse Corps in 1908. Dita H. Kinney became the first superintendent of the Army Nurse Corps, and Esther Voorhees Hasson was the first for the Navy Nurse Corps.

History of American Red Cross Nursing, edited by Lavinia L. Dock et al., is essential in understanding the Red Cross nurse's role in military nursing. Archival research at the Red Cross, Library of Congress, and Army Medical Department, spanning the Spanish-American War through the First World War, resulted in a monumental work. Appendixes listing all Red Cross base hospitals and training units organized for the army and navy, hospitals and units in foreign countries, and decorations awarded to individual nurses provide important data on First World War participation.

The Red Cross Nurse in Action, 1882–1948, by Portia B. Kernodle (New York: Harper and Brothers, 1949), superseded Dock's book and portrays the evolution of the United States Army Nurse Corps as part of the continuum of the developing nursing profession. Superlative information on wartime statistics and how nurses were trained for the military, coupled with an outstanding bibliography of primary sources, makes this book a necessity in studying military nursing.

British nurses participated in the Boer War in South Africa, and American nurses assisted the Japanese in the Russo-Japanese War. *The History of Nursing in the British Empire* (London: S.H. Bousfield & Co., 1906), by Sarah A. Tooley, is one of the few such studies about British nursing. Another of McGee's articles is "American Nurses in Japan," *Century Magazine* 60 (April 1905), about the group of Spanish-American War nurse veterans that she took with her to inspect Japanese hospitals and train Japanese nurses. Mary Phinney, Baroness von Olnhausen, maintained a diary during her nursing service. *Adventures of an Army Nurse in Two Wars* (Boston: Little, Brown and Co., 1903) is taken directly from her diary and correspondence.

French Red Cross nurses first served overseas in 1907 in Morocco, Oman, and Algeria, accompanying the wounded in convoys away from the battlefield, and again in Morocco in 1911 and 1913. During the Balkan wars women surgeons, doctors, and nurses of the French Red Cross served in Bulgaria, Montenegro, Serbia, Greece, and Turkey. In 1908 the French military had authorized Red Cross women to serve in military hospitals, and prior to the First World War, thousands of women knew their hospital assignments in case of wartime mobilization. *Vie et mort des français: Simple histoire de la grande guerre* (Paris: Hachette, 1959), by André Ducasse, Jacques Meyere, and Gabriel Perreux, provides excellent background to French military nursing history.

In 1909 Jane Arminda Delano, president of the American Nurses' Association, was appointed superintendent of the Army Nurse Corps and chairman of the National Committee on Red Cross Nursing Services. Her greatest contribution was establishing the Red Cross Nursing Service as the official reserve for the Army Nurse Corps. When the First World War began, Red Cross nurses could be immediately sent to belligerent nations. When the United States entered the war, 8,000 nurses were available for duty.

Gladys Bonner Clappison's book *Vassar's Rainbow Division: The Training Camp for Nurses at Vassar College* (Lake Mills, IA: Graphic Publishing Company, 1918), and "Vassar Training Camps for Nurses," *American Journal of Nursing* 75 (November 1975): 2000–2002, by Katherine Densford Dreeves, describe a unique effort toward the end of the war to recruit and train nurses for military service. Minnie Goodnow's *War Nursing: A Textbook for the Auxiliary Nurse* (Philadelphia and London: W.B. Saunders Co., 1917) was published just in time to provide guidance.

A total of 69,000 American nurses served in the military in the First World War. " 'Neither Fish, Flesh, nor Fowl': The World War I Army Nurse," a comprehensive article by Jo-Anne Mecca, describes their situation in the military, what it was like to be a nurse with the American Expeditionary Forces, and their assignments overseas. Carl J. Schneider and Dorothy Schneider's study *Into the Breach: American Women Overseas in World War I* (New York: Viking, 1991), although enveloping all military women, devotes some attention to nurses. *Black Americans in Defense of Our Nation* (Washington, DC: Office of the Deputy Assistant Secretary of Defense for Equal Opportunity and Safety Policy, 1985) includes information on black women nurses who served the military from the Civil War through the First World War.

Many women produced memoirs of their First World War experiences. Mary Dexter, an American nurse, published her memoir, *In the Soldier's Service: War Experiences of Mary Dexter, England, Belgium, France, 1914–1918* (Boston and New York: Houghton Mifflin, 1918), before the war was over. Dexter first served with the British Red Cross in England and was then accepted as a nurse with the Belgian Red Cross near the front. After a long illness and recuperation in England, she left nursing in 1917 to drive an ambulance in France near the front. Her unit was officially attached to the French army, and each woman received the Croix de Guerre in 1918 for her exceptional performance under battlefield conditions.

Other firsthand narratives are Julia C. Stimson's *Finding Themselves: The Letters of an American Army Chief Nurse in a British Hospital in France* (New York: Macmillan, 1918); *France in War Time, 1914–1915* (London: Methuen, 1915), by Maud R. Sutton-Pickhard, who served with the Red Cross in France and toured hospitals and charity works; *Mademoiselle Miss: Letters from an American Girl Serving with the Rank of Lieutenant in a French Army Hospital at the Front* (Boston: W.A. Butterfield, 1916); Grace E. Allison, "Some Experience in Active Service: France," *American Journal of Nursing* 19 (February 1919): 268–272, 354–359; and Aileen Cole Stewart in "Ready to Serve: A Nurse Recalls Her Experience during the First World War," *American Journal of Nursing* (September 1963): 85–87.

By war's end Delano had mobilized more than 20,000 nurses for overseas duty in the army, navy, and Red Cross. Lenah S. Higbee, second superintendent of the Navy Nurse Corps, was awarded the navy's highest decoration, the Navy Cross, and became the first woman for whom a combat ship was named.

Thousands of women from many nations besides America served during the First World War, fanning out to serve in all the belligerent countries. Lyn Macdonald, the preeminent First World War historian, has portrayed both American and British nurses in *The Roses of No Man's Land* (New York: Atheneum, 1989), an insightful look into the feelings, thoughts, and experiences of a nurse on the front lines during this trench war. Photos and oral histories enliven this glimpse of women's wartime contributions.

The most poignant and classic woman's autobiography to spring from the war was Vera Brittain's *Testament of Youth: An Autobiographical Study of the Years 1900–1925*. Brittain was a British nurse who served in several capacities during the war. In this powerful and moving book, she describes the war's impact on her generation.

An excellent source about British, German, and Russian nurses is *Female Soldiers—Combatants or NonCombatants? Historical and Contemporary Perspectives*, edited by Nancy Loring Goldman (Westport, CT: Greenwood Press, 1982). Goldman's book specifically mentions Edith Cavell, undoubtedly the most famous heroine in the First World War. While nursing soldiers in occupied Belgium in 1915, Cavell was captured by the Germans and accused of espionage. Despite enormous international outrage, the Germans executed Cavell in October for providing refuge to Allied soldiers and assisting them in their escape efforts.

The British female experience in the First World War is particularly well documented. J. Piggot wrote *Queen Alexandra's Royal Army Nursing Corps* (London: Leo Cooper, 1975) about the British Army Nursing Service that had been renamed Queen Alexandra's Imperial Military Nursing Service in 1902. Britain's Naval Nurses had been established in 1902, and Princess Mary's Royal Air Force Nursing Service was organized in 1918. Arthur Marwick's classic, *Women at War, 1914–18* (London: Fontana Paperbacks, 1977), a thorough history of British women's military organizations and civilian efforts during the war, accompanied by photos, includes many nurses and their efforts. Barbara McLaren in the outstanding *Women of the War* (London: Hodder and Stoughton, 1918) identifies the contributions of numerous women in diverse occupations. The medical services of Elsie Inglis, Mrs. St. Clair Stobart, the Heroines of Pervyse, Violetta Thurstan, Mrs. Harley, Dr. Garrett Anderson, Dr. Flora Murray, and Lady Paget are specifically noted.

Inglis, a surgeon and gynecologist, founded Scottish Women's Hospitals in

Serbia, France, Corsica, Salonika, Romania, and Russia. These all-female units of doctors, nurses, orderlies, cooks, laundresses, chauffeurs, and mechanics served under battlefield conditions and moved along the front with the army. Inglis was taken prisoner in 1915 during the Serbian retreat and became the first woman to receive the Serbian decoration of the White Eagle. In 1916 Inglis led another unit to South Russia. They were later attached to a Serbian field hospital, were forced to evacuate, and then nursed Romanian wounded. When the Serbian army was in disarray, Inglis and her hospital supported the Russian army, receiving the Russian **Order of St. George** for their work under fire. Inglis died in Serbia in November 1917. Eva Shaw McLaren edited *A History of the Scottish Women's Hospitals* (London: Hodder and Stoughton, 1919), a moving testament to these amazing women and their triumphs.

Mrs. St. Clair Stobart was in charge of an ambulance unit under the St. John Ambulance Society. She took the unit to Brussels, where she was captured by the Germans and accused of spying. She escaped, established a hospital in Antwerp and another in Cherbourg, and then left for Serbia, where she established a tent hospital and then a flying-field hospital. As a commander, Stobart was also made a major in the Serbian army, the first woman to achieve this rank. Her unit, with sixty Serbian soldiers attached, became the First Serbian-English Field Hospital. During the German and Austrian invasion, in the dead of winter, she led her unit by foot over the Montenegrin mountains to safety in Albania. Stobart told her own story in *The Flaming Sword in Serbia and Elsewhere* (London: Hodder and Stoughton, 1916).

The Heroines of Pervyse, Elsie Knocker and Mairi Chisholm, had been part of a Scottish flying ambulance corps assisting the Belgian army. The two women alone established a first-aid post on the front lines in Pervyse, a Belgian village, treating severely wounded soldiers en route to hospitals. They were awarded the Order of Leopold by King Albert in 1915, and when the Allies prohibited women at the front, Belgium requested an exception. The Heroines of Pervyse were officially attached to the Third Division of the Belgian army in the field. In 1917 both women were awarded the Military Medal of Britain and the Order of St. John of Jerusalem. In 1918 both were badly gassed. Geraldine Edith Mitton elaborated on their courage and perseverance in *The Cellar-House at Pervyse* (London: A&C Black, 1917).

Violetta Thurstan took nurses to Brussels in 1914. The Germans captured her, placed her in charge of a hospital that treated Allied prisoners, and later sent her to the Danish front. She then worked for the Russian Red Cross in Petrograd, base hospitals, and a flying ambulance column, as well as in Poland during the Russian retreat, helping to evacuate 18,000 wounded from Lodz. Thurstan was wounded while nursing soldiers in the trenches and was awarded the Russian Order of St. George. After organizing British hospital units for service in Russia, Thurstan worked in a Belgian hospital five miles from the front and was decorated by the Belgian king. She also wrote *Field Hospitals and Flying Column* (London: G.P. Putnam's Sons, 1915).

The administrator of the first Scottish Women's Hospital, Mrs. Harley, began serving in France in 1914. She established a French military hospital in 1915 and took her unit to Salonika with the French Expeditionary Force in 1915, on to Serbia, and then in retreat to Salonika. In 1916 she led a flying ambulance column to the Macedonian front in Serbia, close to the front lines. Harley was killed by exploding shells during a Bulgarian bombardment and was posthumously awarded France's highest decoration, the Croix de Guerre with palm leaves.

Dr. Garrett Anderson, a surgeon, and Dr. Flora Murray, a physician, organized a volunteer female hospital unit under the auspices of the French Red Cross and a hospital near Boulogne. When the British War Office attached the latter to its Royal Army Medical Corps, Murray became a female lieutenant-colonel in the British army. Lady Paget formed a hospital unit in Serbia in 1914, was taken prisoner in the Bulgarian invasion in 1915, and fed and clothed 70,000 Serbian refugees from her unit's supplies by 1916. She was awarded the Order of St. Sava, the first time a nonroyal woman had received this honor.

Reginald Hargreaves with *Women-at-Arms: Their Famous Exploits throughout the Ages* (London: Hutchinson and Co., 1930) and John Laffin with *Women in Battle* (New York: Abelard-Schuman, 1967) both illustrate the wartime experience of **Flora Sandes.** Sandes served as a nurse in Serbia in 1914 in a British ambulance unit. She contracted typhus, was separated from her unit while recuperating, and ended up serving in the ambulance unit for the Second Serbian Infantry Regiment. During the Serbian retreat over the mountains in 1915, wounded were abandoned and her nursing skills were useless. Sandes quickly became an infantry soldier, rising from the rank of corporal to second lieutenant by 1918. She was decorated with the Order of St. Sava and the Kara George Star.

In 1914 the French military acquired control over all French hospitals and allocated Red Cross resources as needed. The first military hospital in the world staffed completely by women was in France. More than 63,000 French women served as unpaid Red Cross nurses during the war, some at aid posts on the front lines, in mobile surgical teams, in evacuation hospitals, on trains, at railway stations, and overseas in Romania, Salonika, Serbia, Italy, Morocco, Russia, Greece, Senegal, and Annam. Almost 1,000 French women received the Croix de Guerre, and more than 300 were awarded the Croix de la Légion d'Honneur for their bravery under fire or their courageous deaths.

Comtesse de Roussy de Sales, upon mobilization, served with the Red Cross in Reims until the German advance necessitated evacuation. The Marquise d'Andigne, a Red Cross nurse and president of a war relief organization, was decorated twice for bravery under fire. Madame Olivier arrived at her post on the first day of the war, caring for soldiers on evacuation trains and eventually heading Val de Grace, the oldest Parisian military hospital. Madame Fouriaux organized a military hospital in 1914 and evacuated patients from

Reims under fire. Mademoiselle Canton-Baccara at Vauxbuin evacuated men to the rear, provided aid under fire, walked to Soissons under fire to obtain medical supplies, struggled to care for her patients and the townspeople under German control, and received the Légion d'Honneur. A French female doctor was mistakenly mobilized into the army rather than the Red Cross. By the time the error was corrected, she was at Verdun supervising an operating unit. Rather than being removed, she remained there for two years. The list of French women who died, refused to leave their posts, were wounded, became ill, stayed under German control, founded hospitals, aided refugees, removed wounded from the battlefield, and performed endless other tasks is too lengthy to mention them all.

Madame Panas and her assistants remained with their wounded patients after their hospital was shelled during the Battle of Yser until a general forced them to leave. At Ypres, Notre Dame Hospital nuns nursed patients while shells fell around them. Mademoiselle Godfroy and Mademoiselle Marniere rescued wounded soldiers under fire and evacuated children to the south in the winter of 1914. Mademoiselle Germaine Sellier, hospital director, moved her patients to cellars after their hospital was bombed, venturing out for food and supplies. Mademoiselle Daems established a hospital in her home in Wissembach, cared for German soldiers after occupation, and treated the wounded under fire. Madame Hugue and Madame Dessin organized a 400-bed hospital in Saint-Quentin under German occupation. Mademoiselle de Latour-Maubourg, Mademoiselle Jacquin, and Mademoiselle Armagnac remained behind with their patients in Maubeuge when the Germans took over the town and eventually nursed German soldiers as well.

Sister Sainte-Suxanne was killed and Sister Saint-Pierre of Saint-Jean Hospital was wounded by exploding shells. Mademoiselle Caillot-Sagot was killed by shells while nursing her men in Alsace. At a hospital in Luneville, Mademoiselle Gille refused to leave her men and was killed by shellfire. Mademoiselle Dussart refused to leave her post and received the Croix de Guerre for assistance to an army corps. Mademoiselle Caron and a nun were both awarded the Croix de Malte for aiding eighty wounded British soldiers during a German advance after the Battle of Senlis. In Compiègne Mademoiselle Cleret, Mademoiselle Barber, Madame Antoinette Pillet-Well, and Sister Triviez, and in Villers-Cotterets, Mademoiselle Bobenothi and Mademoiselle Ferdon all remained with their hospitals and were decorated for bravery under fire. Mademoiselle Eugenie Antoine single-handedly nursed wounded soldiers from the battlefield at Vailly-sur-Aisne and received the English Order of the Royal Red Cross. Sister Marie Lemoine and Madame Alice Batut were decorated by the French army for rendering aid to thousands of soldiers in hospitals under fire, as were all the nurses assigned to the field hospital in Arras. Madame Charlotte Maitre refused to leave the front lines even when wounded and was decorated twice for her work under fire in underground shelters.

Individual French nurses' stories can be found in "French Women during

World War I: Their Contributions to the National Defense," by Connie L. Reeves (master's thesis, George Washington University, 1987). In addition to nursing, Reeves provides detailed information about the many diverse activities in which French women engaged during the war. She also discusses British, German, and Russian women's wartime contributions in separate chapters. Primary sources from which French nurses' stories were taken include Louis Barthou, *L'effort de la femme française* (Paris: Bloud & Gay, 1917); Gertrude Atherton, *The Living Present* (New York: Frederick A. Stokes, 1917); R. Louise Fitch, *Madame France* (n.p., 1919); Constance E. Maud, "What Frenchwomen Are Doing," *Living Age* 298 (10 August 1918): 321–334; Michele J. Shover, "War-Time Women of France," *Bellman* 23 (1 December 1917): 42; Margerite Yates, "Frenchwomen in War Time," *Englishwoman* (November 1917): 122–130; and Louise Zeys, "Les Femmes et la Guerre," *Revue des Deux Mondes* 6 per 35 (1 September 1916): 176. Raymond Caire's *La femme militaire: Des origines à nos jours* (Paris and Limoges: Lavauzelle, 1981), primarily concentrates on the period after the Second World War II but includes a small section on women's participation from several nations in the First World War.

Léon Abensour, with his oft-quoted *Les vaillantes: Héroines, martyres, et remplaçantes* (Paris: Libraire Chapelot, 1917), relates activities of Frenchwomen in the First World War, giving numerous individual examples. One of the most important works is L. Ruault's *Cent ans de Croix-Rouge française au service de l'humanité* (Paris: Hachette, 1963), which gives significant attention to the French Red Cross's participation in the First World War and lists those nurses who died in its service. James F. McMillan's outstanding *Housewife or Harlot: The Place of Women in French Society, 1870–1940* (New York: St. Martin's Press, 1981), although primarily concerned with the cult of domesticity and the war's impact, includes some important information on French nurses, in addition to an excellent bibliography.

Russia had also established a national Red Cross, and Russian women from all levels of society worked as nurses and physicians, in canteens and on medical trains, supervising hospitals, and providing quarters for refugees. Tatiana Aleksinskaia's *With the Russian Wounded* (London: T. Fisher Unwin, 1916) and Nina Nikolaevna Selivanova's *Russia's Women* (New York: E.P. Dutton, 1923) each discuss Russia's Red Cross war effort to some degree. "Russia: Revolution and War," by Anne Eliot Griesse and Richard Stites, includes additional information.

The German military relied upon the Red Cross, the Vaterländische Frauenvereine, the Catholic Sisters, and the Lutheran nurses for medical and social services. The Vaterländische Frauenvereine, formed in 1866, was designed to provide wartime service in conjunction with the Red Cross. One million trained nurses were immediately available for duty when the war began. They worked in hospitals directly behind the front as well as in garrison. Further information can be found in Catherine E. Boyd's " 'Nationaler Frauendienst': German Middle-Class Women in Service to the Fatherland, 1914–18" (Ph.D.

dissertation, University of Georgia, 1979); Marie-Elisabeth Lüders, *Das unbekannte Heer: Frauen kämpfen für Deutschland* (Berlin: Verlag von E.S. Mittler & Sohn, 1936); Ursula von Gersdorff's *Frauen im Kriegdienst, 1914–45* (Stuttgart: Deutsche Verlags-Anstalt, 1969); Franz W. Seidler's *Frauen zu den Waffen? Marketenderinnen, Helferinnen, Soldatinnen* (Coblenz: Wehr & Wissen, 1978); Jeff M. Tuten's "Germany and the World Wars"; Sophie von Boetticher's "Mitwirkung der Frau bei der Verwundeten und Krankenpflege im Kriege," *Vierteljahrsschrift für Innere Mission* 35.2 (1915): 193–199; and G. Bianquis's "Les femmes allemandes et la guerre," *Revue des Deux Mondes* 6 per 38 (1 March 1917): 182–204.

Histories of the United States Army Nurse Corps began appearing after the First World War. Julia C. Stimson wrote "The Army Nurse Corps," *Medical Department of the United States Army in the World War*, vol. 13, pt. 2 (Washington, DC: U.S. Surgeon General's Office, U.S. Government Printing Office, 1927); "Earliest Known Connection of Nurses with Army Hospitals in the United States," *American Journal of Nursing* 25 (January 1925): 15; "The Forerunners of the American Army Nurse," *Military Surgery* 58 (February 1926): 133–141; and "History and Manual of the Army Nurse Corps," *Army Medical Bulletin* 41 (1937). Francis A. Winter published "The Army Nurse in the Past," *Military Surgery* 65 (July 1929): 133–137. Nursing sisters were not forgotten by Ellen R. Jolly, who wrote *Nuns of the Battlefield* (Providence, RI: Providence Visitor Press, 1927).

The United States Navy Nurse Corps also began taking a look at its history. Beatrice J. Bowman published "The History and Development of the Navy Nurse Corps," *American Journal of Nursing* 25 (May 1925): 356–360; "History of Nursing in the Navy," *U.S.: Navy Medical Bulletin* 26 (January 1938): 123–131; and "Public Health Nursing in the Navy," *American Journal of Nursing* 17 (May 1927): 541–542. Esther V. Hasson wrote a section on Navy nursing in Richmond Cranston Holcomb's *A Century with Norfolk (Va.) Naval Hospital, 1830–1930* (Portsmouth, VA.: Printcraft, 1930).

Although the history of American women who served in the Second World War continually expands, that portion pertaining to military nurses remains relatively unexplored. D'Ann Campbell, in *Women at War with America: Private Lives in a Patriotic Era* (Cambridge, MA.: Harvard University Press, 1984), includes military nurses in her scholarly study of American women during the Second World War. Doris Weatherford's *American Women and World War II* (New York: Facts on File, 1990) includes a section on military nurses. Olga Gruhzit-Hoyt published *They Also Served: American Women in World War II* (New York: Carol Publishing Group, 1995), which contains short vignettes from veteran nurses. An earlier study is Brenda McBryde, *Quiet Heroines: Nurses of the Second World War* (London: Chatto and Windus, Hogarth Press, 1985).

Colonel Florence Aby Blanchfield, the first woman to receive a regular army commission and instrumental in eliminating the system of relative rank for women, served as seventh superintendent of the Army Nurse Corps. She recruited, trained, and supervised the 57,000 army nurses who served in the Second World War. An excellent and comprehensive new book is *G.I. Nightingales: The Army Nurse Corps in World War II* by Barbara Brooks Tomblin (Lexington: University Press of Kentucky, 1996). Tomblin conducted numerous interviews with Second World War nurse veterans and includes an extensive bibliography at the end of this well-written and meticulously documented book. Judith A. Bellafaire provided a look at army nurse service with *The Army Nurse Corps: A Commemoration of World War II Service* (Washington, DC: Center of Military History, n.d.). Susanne Teepe Gaskins produced "G.I. Nurses at War: Gender and Professionalization in the Army Nurse Corps during World War II" (Ph.D. dissertation, University of California, Riverside, 1994). "Army Nurses in Southern France," *American Journal of Nursing* 44 (October 1944): 996, discusses women in the European theater, and Frederick Clayton's "Front-Line Surgical Nurses," *American Journal of Nursing* 44 (March 1944): 234–235, spotlights those nearest the battlefield. The new field of flight nursing has been covered by Judith Barger, who wrote "The History of Flight Nursing in the United States Army Air Forces during World War II" (Ph.D. dissertation, Catholic University, 1977).

Approximately 12,000 navy nurses served during the war, overseas, in the United States, and onboard hospital ships. *Navy Nurse,* by Page Cooper (New York: McGraw-Hill, 1946), is one of the few books that exist on navy nursing. Its primary focus is navy nurses in the Second World War, particularly those who served on hospital ships and in the Pacific, and it includes photos. *The First Navy Flight Nurse on a Pacific Battlefield: A Picture Story of a Flight to Iwo Jima,* by Lieutenant Gill DeWitt (Fredericksburg, TX: Admiral Nimitz Foundation, 1983), is an annotated photo album that portrays a day in the life of a navy flight nurse in the Pacific. Ensign Jane Kendeigh was the first woman to land on Iwo Jima during the Second World War after it had been captured from the Japanese. Barbara Tomblin first published "Beyond Paradise: The U.S. Navy Corps in the Pacific in World War II," parts 1 and 2, in *Minerva: Quarterly Report on Women and the Military* 11.1: 33–53; II.3/4: 37–55, and later incorporated it into *G.I. Nightingales.*

Nurse memoirs from the Second World War are scarce. Juanita Redmond's *I Served on Bataan* (Philadelphia and New York: J.B. Lippincott, 1943) stands out for its informative, humorous, and conversational style and because it is one of the few first-person accounts. *Thank You, Uncle Sam: Letters of a World War II Army Nurse from North Africa and Italy* (Bryn Mawr, PA: Dorrance, 1987), by Eugenia J. Kielar, is also available. *G.I. Nightingale* (New York: W.W. Norton, 1945) by Theresa Archard is another look at World War II nurses. Roberta Love Tayloe has published her memoir, *Combat Nurse: A Journal of World War II* (Santa Barbara, CA: Fithian, 1988). Robert S. LaForte and Ronald E. Marcello have compiled *Remembering Pearl Harbor: Eyewitness Accounts by U.S. Military Men and Women* (Wilmington, DE: 1991), which includes some reminiscences by female military nurses.

Eighty-two female military nurses became prisoners of war in the Pacific and one in Europe, many spending more than three years in Japanese internment camps before their release. Dorothy S. Danner has described their experiences in *What a Way to Spend a War: Navy Nurse POWs in the Philippines* (Annapolis, MD: Naval Institute Press, 1995). Philip A. Kalisch and Beatrice J. Kalisch also wrote about the nurses in the Pacific with "Nurses under Fire: The World War II Experience of Nurses on Bataan and Corregidor," *Nurses Research* 25 (1976): 409–429, while Alice R. Clarke wrote "Thirty-Seven Months as Prisoners of War," *American Journal of Nursing* 45 (May 1945): 342–345. Mary E.V. Frank provided a detailed and well-researched article in *Minerva: Quarterly Report on Women and the Military* 6.2 (1988): 82–90 entitled "Army and Navy Nurses Held as Prisoners of War during World War II." Often considered the forgotten POW, flight nurse Reba Zitella Whittle (later Tobiasen) was a German prisoner for five months following a plane crash in 1944.

Almost one-third of all women nurses were decorated for meritorious service or bravery under fire. Mary Ann Sullivan received the Legion of Merit for valor for remaining with her patients behind enemy lines at Kasserine Pass in North Africa. Ruth M. Gardiner was the first army nurse killed in the war; a hospital was named for her in Chicago. Mary Roberts, Elaine Roe, Virginia Rourke, and Ellen Ainsworth were the first women awarded the Silver Star for evacuating patients at Anzio during a bombing raid.

In the Soviet Union all nurses and nearly half of the medical corps were women, serving in field hospitals, on hospital trains, at front-line first-aid posts, and in rear hospitals. Nurses at the front often rescued wounded soldiers from the battlefield while under fire and experienced a casualty rate second only to that of the infantry. Reina Pennington, in "Offensive Women: Women in Combat in the Red Army," published in *Time to Kill: The Soldier's Experience of War in the West* (Pimlico Press, 1997), provides specific information on the heroic efforts of individual Soviet nurses in the Second World War.

Female medics usually crawled under fire to reach the wounded men and crawled back under fire with a heavy body and weapon, sometimes carrying the soldier to an aid station kilometers away. A.M. Strelkova would often venture out five or six times during one attack, and Zinaida Usnolobova-Marachenko lost both arms and legs in a rescue attempt. Maria Smirnova, with the 333rd Division, Fifth-sixth Army, is credited with bringing almost 500 wounded men out of the battlefield while under fire. Olga Omelchenko recounted a horrible experience in 1943 when she allegedly amputated a soldier's arm with her teeth when no scissors or knives were available. Tamara Umniagina served aboard a hospital evacuation barge where men in utter despair threw themselves overboard.

Many female nurses engaged in combat occasionally, or even became combat soldiers, and female soldiers were expected to serve as medics in addition to their regular duties. Zinaida Korzh, medic with the Fourth Cossack Cavalry Corps, shot Germans emerging from a disabled tank. Katiusha Mikhailova, medic in a naval infantry battalion, trained to fight as well as tend the wounded, was expected to use her grenades, antitank grenades, and machine gun. Olga Omelchenko served on a firing squad when male volunteers were lacking. Elena Kovalchuk and Sophia Kuntsevich led small attacks after unit commanders had been killed. Sergeant-Major Elena Yákovleva, pressured to join as a nurse, fled to the front to serve as a soldier.

Other histories of military nursing began to appear during the war and afterwards. Julia O. Flikke wrote *Nurses in Action: The Story of the Army Nurse Corps* (Philadelphia: J.B. Lippincott, 1943); the United States Navy Nurse Corps published *White Task Force* (Washington, DC: U.S. Government Printing Office, 1943); the United States Army Nurse Corps offered *The Army Nurse* (Washington, DC: U.S. Government Printing Office, 1944); the United States Army Medical Department published *The Tradition and Destiny of the U.S. Army Nurse Corps* (Washington, DC: U.S. Army Recruiting Publicity Bureau, 1949); and from the United States Public Health Service appeared *The U.S. Cadet Nurse Corps and Other Federal Nurse Training Programs* (Washington, DC: 1950).

Mabel K. Staupers was instrumental in integrating blacks into military nursing and included that story in her nursing history of the National Association of Colored Graduate Nurses, *No Time for Prejudice: A Story of the Integration of Negroes in Nursing in the United States* (New York: Macmillan, 1961). The chapter on military integration is very detailed and provides a valuable historical framework toward comprehending how and why black women were first not permitted and then integrated, beginning with the First World War and ending with the Second World War. In Darlene Clark Hine's superlative *Black Women in White: Racial Conflict and Cooperation in the Nursing Profession, 1890–1950* (Bloomington: Indiana University Press, 1989), " 'We Shall Not Be Left Out': World War II and the Integration of Nursing" excellently reveals Staupers's efforts. Hine includes numerous full-caption photos and an extensive bibliography. Another informative article, "Mabel K. Staupers and the Integration of Black Nurses into the Armed Forces," appears in Judith Walzer Leavitt, *Women and Health in America: Historical Readings* (Madison: University of Wisconsin Press, 1984)

Jesse J. Johnson's *Black Women in the Armed Forces, 1942–1974 (A Pictorial History)* (Hampton, VA: Hampton Institute, 1974) is invaluable. Through numerous photos and an informed text, Johnson portrays the history of black women in each of the services, highlighting many individuals as they broke new barriers. Hine also provided "The Call That Never Came: Black Women Nurses and World War II, an Historical Note," *Indiana Military History Journal* (1983): 23–27.

Genevieve de Galard-Terraude, mentioned in *Hellraisers, Heroines, and Holy Women* by Jean F. Blashfield (New York: Superlative House, 1981), was a flight nurse at Dien Bien Phu, Vietnam. Stranded when the helicopter she was on was damaged, she helped nineteen male doctors care for 1,200 wounded soldiers, the only woman and nurse present. When Dien Bien Phu fell to the Vietnamese, she remained behind with the wounded until her release nineteen days later. Blashfield also discusses Valerie André, a French neurosurgeon assigned to Indochina in 1949 who became a helicopter pilot to extract the wounded from the jungle. André flew sixty-five missions, often under fire, rescued 150 men, and parachuted twice to operate on men who could not be moved. In 1976 she was promoted to brigadier general.

A few more histories of the military nursing corps have appeared, among them E.S Popiel, "The Army Nurse Corps: Try to Remember Our Heritage," *Colorado Nurse* 67 (February 1967): 5–9, and "The Navy Nurse Corps," *Colorado Nurse* 67 (April–May 1967): 5–7. C. Raven wrote "Achievements of Women in Medicine, Past and Present—Women in Medical Corps of the Army," *Military Medicine* 125 (1960): 105–111. Philip A. Kalisch and Margaret Scobey have written "Female Nurses in American Wars: Helplessness Suspended for the Duration," *Armed Forces and Society* 9 (1983): 215–243. An unpublished, undated eleven-volume work, "The History of the Army Nurse Corps," with only one known copy, is located at the U.S. Army Center of Military History Library in Washington, D.C. Rosemary A. Byrne wrote "Women, War, and Nursing: The Army Nurse Corps, 1901–1952" (master's thesis, Arizona State University, 1986). Connie L. Reeves has published "The Military Woman's Vanguard: Nurses," in *It's Our Military, Too! Women and the U.S. Military* (Philadelphia: Temple University Press, 1996), currently the only consolidated history of American military nursing from the Revolutionary War through Vietnam. The only significant historical treatment of United States Army nurses is *Highlights in the History of the Army Nurse Corps,* edited by Elizabeth A. Shields (Washington, DC: U.S. Army Center of Military History, 1981). This work is a revision of previous similar efforts and has itself been updated by a 1997 version available over the Internet through the U.S. Army Center of Military History's Web site. Events are listed in chronological order with no added interpretation, which is its only drawback.

Sources on the Korean War, in which 540 army nurses served, are sorely lacking. Donahue, Gabriel and Metz, Holm, and Shields provide some information. "Bright Side of Korea," *Women's Home* 78 (July 1952): 22, by C. Howard; "Army Nurses in Korea," *What's New* 159 (July/August 1985): 11–18, by John Groth; G. Samuels's "Miracle in a Korean Hospital," *New York Times Magazine* 25 February 1951: 7, and "With Army Nurses Somewhere in Korea," *New York Times Magazine* 15 April 1951: 14–15; "Good Voyage Home, Flight Nurses," *Women's Day* 78 (July 1951): 21–25; and "Flight Angel, Charlotte Cooley," *Cosmopolitan* 134 (May 1953): 112–121, are some of the few articles that are available. Genevieve Smith, the only nurse to die in the war, was killed in a plane crash en route to become chief nurse in Korea.

Writings on the approximately 6,250 military nurses who served in Vietnam have been increasing in recent years. Spurgeon Neel's *Medical Support of the U.S. Army in Vietnam, 1965–1970* (Washington, DC: Department of Defense, 1991) includes a valuable chapter on nursing. Linda Alkana has written "Women Warriors, Women Healers: American Women Nurses in Vietnam," *Valley Forge Journal* 4 (December 1989): 352–361. "Angels in Vietnam: U.S. Military Nurses," *Today's Health* 45 (August 1967): 16–23, provides another glimpse of their activities.

Elizabeth Norman's *Women at War: The Story of Fifty Military Nurses Who Served in Vietnam* (Philadelphia: University of Pennsylvania Press, 1990) is an excellent compilation of women's stories and includes an extensive bibliography. Kathryn Marshall has also provided experiences of a few nurses with *In the Combat Zone: An Oral History of American Women in Vietnam, 1966–1975* (Boston: Little, Brown, 1987). Another group of oral histories, mostly of nurses, can be found in *A Piece of My Heart: The Stories of Twenty-Six American Women Who Served in Vietnam* (Novato, CA: Presidio Press, 1986), as told to Keith Walker. Al Santoli's *Everything We Had: An Oral History of the Vietnam War by Thirty-Three American Soldiers Who Fought It* (New York: Random House, 1981) includes two chapters by women nurses. *Another Kind of War Story: Army Nurses Look Back to Vietnam* (Lebanon, PA: Thompson, 1993) provides yet another retrospective.

Lynda Van Devanter, with *Home before Morning: The Story of an Army Nurse in Vietnam* (New York: Beaufort, 1983), provided the earliest first-person narrative and began raising the nation's consciousness about women Vietnam veterans. *American Daughter Gone to War: On the Front Lines with an Army Nurse in Vietnam*, by Winnie Smith (New York: William Morrow, 1992), is an insightful and interesting memoir. Bobbi Hovis, a retired navy nurse, has written the colorful *Station Hospital Saigon: A Navy Nurse in Vietnam, 1963–1964* (Annapolis, MD: Naval Institute Press, 1991). Marlene Jezierski, a flight nurse in World War II and Vietnam, discusses her experiences in "The Violence of War: A Nurse Veteran Reflects," *Journal of Emergency Medicine* 3 (June 1991): 183–185.

Dan Freedman and Jacqueline Rhoads are the editors of *Nurses in Vietnam: The Forgotten Veterans* (Austin: Texas Monthly Press, 1987), focusing on the eight women—Sharon Ann Lane, Elizabeth Ann Jones, Carol Ann Elizabeth Drazba, Annie Ruth Graham, Eleanor Grace Alexander, Hedwig Diane Orlowski, Pamela Dorothy Donovan, and Mary Therese Klinker—whose names are engraved on the Vietnam War Memorial. A Vietcong rocket attack on her hospital killed Lane; the others died in helicopter or plane crashes.

The most celebrated heroine of Desert Storm was **Rhonda Cornum,** an American flight surgeon captured by the Iraqis and held prisoner for several days. Her book, *She Went to War: The Rhonda Cornum Story* (Novato, CA: Presidio Press, 1992), is a comprehensive look at her military life. "The Most Wounded, the Most Sick, the Most Tired," *Reader's Digest* 58 (June 1951): 9–10, by H. Ely, is primarily about nurses in Desert Storm, although mention is made of the Ely's Vietnam experience.

Bibliography

'Abd al-Ahad Zanjani, Aqa. "Personal Reminiscences of the Babi Insurrection in Zanjan in 1850." *Journal of the Royal Asiatic Society* 29 (1897): 761–827.

Abraham, Richard. "Mariia L. Bochkareva and the Russian Amazons of 1917." *Women and Society in Russia and the Soviet Union*. Ed. Linda Edmondson. Cambridge: Cambridge University Press, 1992.

Addis, Elisabetta, Valeria E. Russo, and Lorenza Sebesta, eds. *Women Soldiers: Images and Realities*. New York: St. Martin's Press, 1994.

Alavi, Seema. *The Sepoys and the Company: Tradition and Transition in Northern India, 1770–1830*. New York: Oxford University Press, 1995.

Albers, Patricia, and Beatrice Medicine, eds. *The Hidden Half: Studies of Plains Indian Women*. Washington, DC: University Press of America, 1983.

Alexander, John. *Catherine the Great*. New York: Oxford University Press, 1989.

———. "Amazon Autocratrixes: Images of Female Rule in 18th Century Russia." *Gender and Sexuality in Russian Civilization*. Ed. P. Barta, Harwood, 2001.

Alexiyevich, Svetlana. *War's Unwomanly Face* [U voiny—ne zhenskoe litso . . .]. Trans. Keith Hammond and Lyudmila Lezhneva. Moscow: Progress Publishers, 1988.

Alie, Joe A.D. *A New History of Sierra Leone*. London: Macmillan, 1990.

Allaire, Gloria. "The Warrior Woman in Late Medieval Prose Epics." *Italian Culture* 12 (1994): 33–43.

Allan, Sheila. *Diary of a Girl in Changi, 1941–45*. Kenthurst, NSW: Kangaroo Press, 1994.

Allen, Peter. *The Yom Kippur War*. New York: Scribner, 1982.

Allen, W.E.D. *A History of the Georgian People*. London: Kegan Paul, Trench, Trubner and Co., 1932.

Alloisio, Mirella, and Giuliana Beltrami. *Volontarie della libertá* [Volunteers for liberty]. Milan: Mazzotta, 1981.

Almeida-Topor, Hélène d'. *Les Amazones: Une armée de femmes dans l'Afrique précoloniale*. Paris: 1984.

Alsmeyer, Marie Bennett. *The Way of the WAVES: Women in the Navy.* Conway, AR: HAMBA, 1981.

———. *Old WAVES Tales: Navy Women: Memories of World War II.* Conway, AR: HAMBA, 1982.

———. "A Preliminary Survey of Literature about World War II Women in the Navy." *Minerva: Quarterly Report on Women and the Military* 1.4 (1983): 71–76.

Amrane, Djamila. *La femme algérienne et la guerre de libération nationale (1954–62).* Actes du Colloque d'Oran, 1980.

Anderson, M.S. *War and Society in Europe of the Old Regime, 1618–1789.* New York: St. Martin's Press 1988.

Androw of Wyntoun. *Orygynale Cronykil of Scotland.* 3 vols. Edinburgh: Edmonston and Douglas, 1872–1879.

The Anglo-Saxon Chronicle. Trans. G.N. Garmonsway. Rev. ed. London: Dent, 1954.

Ani Pachen, and Adelaide Donnelley. *Sorrow Mountain: The Journey of a Tibetan Warrior Nun.* New York: 2000.

Anishchenkov, Panteleimon Stepanovich, and Vasilii Yerofeyevich Shurinov. *Tret'ia vozdushnaia: Voenno-istoricheskii ocherk o boevom puti VVS Kalininskogo fronta i 3-i vozdushnoi armii v gody Velikoi Otechestvennoi voiny.* [The Third Air Army: A military-historical essay of the campaign record of the Air Forces of the Kalinin Front and the Third Air Army during the Great Patriotic War]. Moscow: Voenizdat, 1984.

Annecchino, Raimondo. *Storia di Pozzuoli e della zona flegrea.* Pozzuoli: Comune di Pozzuoli, 1960.

Appian. *Appian's Roman History.* Trans. Horace White. 4 vols. Cambridge, MA: Harvard University Press, 1972–1979.

Aralovets, Nina Dmitrievna. *Natasha Kovshova.* Moscow: Molodaia gvardiia, 1952.

Arnold, Henry Harley. *Global Mission.* New York: Harper, 1949.

Arnulf. "Gesta archiepiscoporum Mediolanensium." *Monumenta Germaniae Historica, Scriptores.* Ed. George H. Pertz. Vol. 8. Hannover: 1848. Facsimile reprint, Stuttgart: Hiersemann, 1992. 8:18.

Aronova, Raisa E. *Nochnye ved'my* [Night witches]. 2nd ed. Moscow: Sovetskaia Rossiia, 1980.

Arrian. *History of the Successors of Alexander.*

Asian Women Human Rights Council. *War Crimes on Asian Women: Military Sexual Slavery by Japan during World War II: The Case of the Filipino Comfort Women.* Manila: Asian Women Human Rights Council, 1998.

Asimov, Isaac. *Asimov's Guide to the Bible.* New York: Avon, 1968.

Atkinson, Dorothy. "Society and Sexes in the Russian Past." *Women in Russia.* Ed. Dorothy Atkinson, Alexander Dallin, and Gail Warshofsky Lapidus. Stanford: Stanford University Press, 1977. 3–38.

Axtell, James. "The Vengeful Women of Marblehead: Robert Roules's Deposition of 1677." *William and Mary Quarterly* 31.4 (1974): 647–652.

Bachrach, Bernard S., ed. *Liber historiae Francorum.* Lawrence, KS: Coronado Press, 1973.

Badian, E. *Studies in Greek and Roman History.* New York: Barnes & Noble, 1964.

Bagley, J.J. *Margaret of Anjou, Queen of England.* London: Herbert Jenkins, 1948.

Bain, J., ed. *Calendar of Documents Relating to Scotland.* Vol. 3. Edinburgh: Scottish Record Office, 1881–1888.

Ball, Eve. *In the Days of Victorio: Recollections of a Warm Springs Apache.* Tucson: University of Arizona Press, 1970.

Bandel, Betty. "The English Chroniclers' Attitude toward Women." *Journal of the History of Ideas* 16 (1955): 113–118.

Bankes, George. *The Story of Corfe Castle and of Many Who Have Lived There.* London: J. Murray, 1853.

Barine, Arvède. *La jeunesse de la Grande Mademoiselle (1627–1652).* 4th ed. Paris: Hachette, 1905.

Barlow, Frank. *The Feudal Kingdom of England, 1042–1216.* London: Longmans, 1955.

Barmin, A. "Kavaler ordena Slavy." *Docheri Rossii.* Ed. I. Cherniaeva. Moscow: Sovetskaia Rossiia, 1975. 65–70.

Baron, Salo Wittmayer. *A Social and Religious History of the Jews.* 2nd, rev. and enl. ed. New York: Columbia University Press, 1952.

Barrow, G.W.S. *Feudal Britain: The Completion of the Medieval Kingdoms, 1066–1314.* London: Arnold, 1956.

Bashkirov, B., and N. Semenkevich. "Geroini Sovetskogo neba." *Kryl'ia Rodiny* March 1969.

Bassett, Jan. *Guns and Brooches: Australian Army nursing from the Boer War to the Gulf War.* Melbourne: Oxford University Press, 1992.

———. *As We Wave You Goodbye: Australian Women and War.* Melbourne and New York: Oxford University Press, 1998.

Bataille, Gretchen M. *Native American Women: A Biographical Dictionary.* Vol. 1. Biographical Dictionaries of Minority Women. Garland, 1993.

Batezat, E., M. Mwalo, and K. Truscott. "Women and Independence: The Heritage and the Struggle." *Zimbabwe's Prospects: Issues of Race, Class, State, and Capital in Southern Africa.* Ed. Colin Stoneman, London: Macmillan, 1988.

Batiffol, Louis. *La duchesse de Chevreuse: Une vie d'aventures et d'intrigues sous Louis XIII.* Paris: Hachette, 1913.

Baturina, K.S., ed. *Pravda stavshaia legendoi* [Truth became a legend]. Moscow: 1964.

Bay, Edna. "The Royal Women of Abomey." Ph.D. dissertation, Boston University, 1977.

———. *Wives of the Leopard: Gender, Politics, and Culture in the Kingdom of Dahomey.* Charlottesville: University Press of Virginia, 1998.

Bellefaire, Judith A. *The Women's Army Corps: A Commemoration of World War II Service.* Washington, DC: U.S. Army Center of Military History, 1993.

Bellis, Alice Ogden. *Helpmates, Harlots, and Heroes: Women's Stories in the Hebrew Bible.* Louisville: John Knox Press, 1994.

Ben-Yehuda, Netiva. *1948–Bein Hasefirot.* Jerusalem: Keter Publishing, 1981.

———. *Keshepartza Hamilchama.* Jerusalem: Maxwell-Macmillen-Keter, 1991.

———. *Mibaad La'avotot.* Jerusalem: Domino Press, 1985.

Ben-Zvi, Rachel Yanait. *Coming Home.* Tel Aviv: Massadah–P.E.C. Press, 1963.

———. *Derachai Siparti* [The paths I followed]. Jerusalem: Kiryat-Sefer, 1972.

———. *Before Golda: Manya Shochat: A Biography.* Trans. Sandra Shurin. New York: Biblio Press, 1989.

Benton, Margaret Fukazawa. "Hōjō Masako: The Dowager Shōgun." *Heroic with Grace: Legendary Women of Japan.* Ed. Chieko Irie Mulhern. Armonk, NY: M.E. Sharpe, 1991. 162–207.

Bernstein, Alison R. *American Indians and World War II.* Norman, OK: University of Oklahoma Press, 1991.

Bershanskaia, Evodokia, Irina Rakobol'skaia, Irina Sebrova, Anna Stepanova, and Raisa Iushina, eds. *46 Gvardeiskii Tamanskii zhenskii aviatsionyi polk.* [The 46th Guards Taman Women's Aviation Regiment.] N.p.: Tsentral'nyi Dom Sovetskoi Armii imeni M.v. Frunze, n.d.

Bertaud, Jean-Paul. *La vie quotidienne des soldats de la Révolution, 1789–1799.* Paris: Hachette, 1985.

Bertolini, M.G. "Beatrice di Lorena." *Dizionario biografico degli Italiani.* Vol. 7. Rome: 1960.

Bidwell, Shelford. *The Women's Royal Army Corps.* London: Leo Cooper, 1977.

Bigland, Eileen. *Britain's Other Army: The Story of the A.T.S.* London: Nicholson & Watson, 1946.

Billings, Charlene W. *Grace Hopper: Navy Admiral and Computer Pioneer.* Hillside, NJ: Enslow Publishers, 1989.

Billings, Eliza Allen. *The Female Volunteer; or, The Life and Wonderful Adventures of Miss Eliza Allen, a Young Lady of Eastport, Maine.* N.p., 1851; Reprint, microopaque, Louisville, KY: Lost Cause Press, 1965.

Bingham, Caroline. *The Crowned Lions: The Early Plantagenet Kings.* Newton Abbott: David & Charles, 1978.

Binkin, Martin. *Who Will Fight the Next War? The Changing Face of the American Military.* Washington, DC: Brookings Institution, 1993.

Binkin, Martin, and Shirley J. Bach. *Women and the Military.* Washington, DC: Brookings Institution, 1977.

Birch, Walter de Gray, ed. *Cartularium Saxonicum: A Collection of Charters Relating to Anglo-Saxon History.* 3 vols. London: Whiting, 1885–1893. Reprinted, New York: Johnson, 1964.

Blanco, Richard L., ed. *The American Revolution, 1775–1783, An Encyclopedia.* Vol. 1. New York: Garland, 1993.

Blanton, DeAnne. "Cathay Williams, Black Woman Soldier, 1866–1868." *Minerva: Quarterly Report on Women and the Military* 10.3–4 (1992): 1–21.

Blaze, Elzéar. *La vie militaire.* Paris: Garnier Frères, 1901.

Blok, Josine H. *The Early Amazons: Modern and Ancient Perspectives on a Persistent Myth.* Leiden: E.J. Brill, 1995.

Blond, Georges. *La Grande Armée.* London: Arms and Armour Press, 1995.

Bloom, Anne R. "Israel: The Longest War." *Female Soldiers—Combatants or Noncombatants? Historical and Contemporary Perspectives.* Ed. Nancy Loring Goldman. Westport, CT: Greenwood Press, 1982. 137–162.

———. "Women in the Defense Forces." *Calling the Equality Bluff: Women in Israel.* Ed. Barbara Swirski and Marilyn P. Safir. New York: Pergamon Press, 1991. 128–138.

Bloom, Anne R., and Rivka Bar-Yosef. "Israeli Women and Military Service: A Socialization Experience." *Women's Worlds.* Ed. Marilyn Safir and Barbara Swinski. New York: Praeger, 1985. 260–269.

Bluche, François, ed. *Dictionnaire du Grand siècle.* Paris: Fayard, 1990.

Boccaccio, Giovanni. *Concerning Famous Women.* Trans. Guido A. Guarino, New Brunswick, NJ: Rutgers University Press, 1963.

Bocharnikova, Mariia. "Boi v zimnem dvortse." *Novyi zhurnal* 68 (1962): 215–227.

Bochkareva, E., and S. Liubimova. *Svetlyi put': Kommunisticheskaia partiia Sovetskogo Soiuza—Borets za svobodu, ravnopravie i schast'e zhenshchiny* [Shining path: The Communist Party of the Soviet Union, fighter for the liberation, equal rights, and happiness of women]. Moscow: Politizdat, 1967.

Bogat, A.P. *Rabotnitsa i krest'ianka v Krasnoi Armii* [Women workers and peasants in the Red Army]. Moscow and Leningrad: Gosizdat, 1928.

———. *Rabotnitsa i krest'ianka na strazhe SSSR* [Women workers and peasants guard the Soviet Union]. Moscow: Moskovskii Rabochii, 1930.

———. "V ogne Grazhdanskoi Voiny." *Oktyabrem Rozhdennye.* Moscow: Politizdat, 1967.

Bone, Quentin. *Henrietta Maria, Queen of the Cavaliers.* Urbana: University of Illinois Press, 1972.

Bonnassie, P. *La Catalogne du milieu du Xe à la fin du XIe Siècle.* Vol. 1. Toulouse: Association des publications de l'Université de Toulouse–Le Mirail, 1975–1976.

Boom, Ghislaine de. *Marie de Hongrie.* Brussels: La Renaissance du Livre, 1956.

Boom, Kathleen M. "Women in the A.A.F." *The Army Air Forces in World War II.* Ed. Wesley Frank Craven and James Lea Cate. Chicago: University of Chicago Press, 1958. 7:503–540.

Bondereau, Renée. *Mémoires de Renée Bordereau, rédigées par elle-même.* Paris: 1814.

Bortolotti, Franca Pieroni. *Le donne della Resistenza antifascista e la questione femminile in Emilia, 1943–1945.* [Women of the anti-Fascist Resistance and the woman question in Emilia, 1943–1945]. Milan: Vangelista, 1978.

Botchkareva, Maria. *Yashka: My Life as Peasant, Officer and Exile.* New York: Frederick A. Stokes Company, 1919.

Bothmer, D. von. *Amazons in Greek Art.* Oxford: Clarendon Press, 1957.

Boulding, Elise. *The Underside of History: A View of Women through Time.* Boulder, CO: Westview, 1976.

Boulting, William. *Woman in Italy.* New York: Brentano's, 1910.

Bouyer, Christian. *La Grande Mademoiselle: Anne Marie Louise d'Orléans, duchesse de Montpensier.* Paris: Albin Michel, 1986.

Bowersock, Glen W. "Mavia, Queen of the Saracens." *Studien zur Antiken Sozialgeschichte* 28 (1980): 477–495.

Boxer, C.R. *Women in Iberian Expansion Overseas, 1415–1815: Some Facts, Fancies, and Personalities.* New York: Oxford University Press, 1975.

Bracke, Gerhard. *Melitta Gräfin Stauffenberg: Das Leben einer Fliegerin.* Munich: Langen Müller, 1990.

Breisach, Ernst. *Caterina Sforza: A Renaissance Virago.* Chicago: University of Chicago Press, 1967.

Brentari, Ottone. *Ecelino Da Romano Nella Mente Del Popolo E Nella Poesia.* Cittadella: Biblos, 1994.

Brice, Raoul. *La femme et les armées de la Révolution et de l'Empire.* Paris: Librairie Ambert, n.d.

"A Brief Journall of the Seige Against Lathom." *Remains Historical & Literary Connected with the Palatine Counties of Lancaster and Cheshire, vol. II.* Manchester: The Chettam Society, 1844. 159–186.

Brij Bushan, Jamila. *Sultan Raziya, Her Life and Times: A Reappraisal.* New Delhi: Manohar Publications, 1990.

British South Africa Company. *The '96 Rebellions: Reports of the Native Disturbances in Rhodesia.* London: 1898.

Brontman, Lazar Konstantinovich, and L. Khvat. *The Heroic Flight of the Rodina.* Moscow: Foreign Languages Publishing House, 1938.

Brooks, Geraldine. *Nine Parts of Desire: The Hidden World of Islamic Women.* New York: Anchor Books, 1995.

Brooks, Margaret. "Passive in War? Women Internees in the Far East, 1942–5." *Images of Women in Peace and War.* Ed. Sharon Macdonald, Pat Holden, and Shirley Ardener. London: Macmillan, 1987. 166–178.

Brown, James, and Constantina Safilios-Rothschild. "Greece: Reluctant Presence." *Female Soldiers—Combatants or Noncombatants? Historical and Contemporary Perspectives.* Ed. Nancy Lorin Goldman. Westport, CT: Greenwood Press, 1982. 165–177.

Browning, Iain. *Palmyra.* Park Ridge, NJ: Noyes Press, 1979.

Brundage, James A. "Prostitution, Miscegenation, and Sexual Purity in the First Crusade." *Crusade and Settlement: Papers Read at the First Conference of the Society for*

the Study of the Crusades and the Latin East and Presented to R.C. Smail. Ed. Peter
W. Edbury. Cardiff: Cardiff Press, 1985. 57–65.

Brust, James S. "Into the Face of History." *American Heritage* 43.7 (1992): 104–113.

———. "John H. Fouch: First Photographer at Fort Keogh." *Montana, the Magazine of
Western History* 44.2 (1994): 2–17.

Bruzzone, Anna Maria. "Women in the Italian Resistance." *Our Common History.* Ed.
Paul Thompson and Natasha Burchardt. London: Pluto Press, 1982. 273–283.

Bryant, Louise. *Six Red Months in Russia: An Observer's Account of Russia Before and
During the Proletarian Dictatorship.* New York: George H. Doran Company, 1918.

Bryant, Sir Arthur. *The Age of Chivalry.* New York: New American, 1970.

Buccella, Biffignandi, and Pietro Giorgio. *Memorie istoriche della città e contado di Vigevano.* Vigevano: 1810.

Buffalohead, Priscilla K. "Farmers, Warriors, Traders: A Fresh Look at Ojibway
Women." *Minnesota History* 48 (1983): 236–244.

Burgess, Lauren Cook, ed. *An Uncommon Soldier: The Civil War Letters of Sarah Rosetta
Wakeman, alias Pvt. Lyons Wakeman, 153rd Regiment, New York State Volunteers,
1862–1864.* Pasadena, MD: Minerva, 1994.

Burgoyne, Bruce E. "Women with Hessian Military Units." *Brigade Dispatch* 26.3 (1996): 2–
10; "Women with the Hessian Auxiliaries during the American Revolutionary War,
Part 1." *Brigade Dispatch* 26.1 (1996): 2–8; "Women with the Hessian Auxiliaries during the American Revolutionary War, Part 2." *Brigade Dispatch* 26.2 (1996): 19–23.

Burton, Richard. *A Mission to Gelele, King of Dahome.* London: 1864.

Burway, Mukund Wamanrao, and Ramakrishna Ganesh Burway. *Life of Subhedar Malhar Rao Holkar, Founder of the Indore State, 1693–1766 A.D.* Indore: Holkar State
Printing Press, 1930.

Bury, J.B. *The Cambridge Ancient History.* Vol. 3. Cambridge: Cambridge University
Press.

Butler, Kenneth D. "Woman of Power behind the Kamakura Bakufu: Hōjō Masako."
Great Historical Figures of Japan. Ed. Murakami Hyoe and Thomas J. Harper.
Tokyo: Japan Culture Institute, 1978. 79–90.

Butler, Pierce. *Women of Mediaeval France.* Vol. 5. Philadelphia: Barrie, 1907.

Caminada, Jerome. *My Purpose Holds.* London: Jonathan Cape, 1952.

Campbell, D'Ann. *Women at War with America: Private Lives in a Patriotic Era.* Cambridge, MA: Harvard University Press, 1984.

———. "Servicewomen of World War II." *Armed Forces and Society* 16.2 (1990): 251–
270.

———. "Women in Combat: The World War II Experience in the United States, Great
Britain, Germany, and the Soviet Union." *Journal of Military History* 57.2 (1993):
301–323.

Cantù, Cesare. *Ezelino da Romano: Storia d'un Ghibellino.* Torino: 1852.

Car, Edward. *Kobiety w szeregach Polskich Sil Zbrojnych na zachodzie, 1940–1948* (Women
in the ranks of the Polish Armed Forces in the West 1940–1948). Warsaw: Ad-
iutor, 1995.

Carrera, Rafael. *Memorias del General Carrera, 1837 a 1840.* Ed. Francis Polo Sifontes.
2nd ed. Guatemala: Instituto de Antropología e Historia, 1979.

Carrigan, Minnie Buce. *Captured by the Indians: Reminiscences of Pioneer Life in Minnesota.*
Forest City, SD: n.p., 1907.

Carta Raspi, Raimondo. *Storia della Sardegna.* Milan: Mursia, 1987.

Castellani, Maria. *Italian Women, Past and Present* (Translation of *Donne italiane di ieri e
di oggi*). Rome: Novissima, 1939.

Catherine II. *Memoirs of Catherine the Great* Trans. Katharine Anthony. New York:
Knopf, 1927.

Cazals, Rémy, and Daniel Fabre. *Les Audois: Dictionnaire biographique.* Carcassonne: Amis des Archives de l'Aude, 1990.

Cère, Emile. "Mme Sans-Gêne." *Revue hebdomadaire* 74 (1893): 414.

———. *Mme Sans-Gêne et les femmes soldats, 1792–1815.* Paris: Plon, 1894.

Chand, Lalla Gokul. *The History of Zeb-ul-Nissa, the Begum Samru of Sardhana.* Translated from the Persian of Lalla Gokul Chand; edited and annotated by Nicholas Shreeve. Crossbush: Bookwright, 1994.

Chartrand, René. "Notes Concerning Women in the 18th Century French Army." *Brigade Dispatch* 25.3 (1995): 2–4.

Chechneva, Marina. *Boevye podrugi moi: knigi vtoraia* [My Fighting Women Friends]. Moscow: DOSAAF, 1968.

———. *'Lastochki' nad frontom* ['Swallows' Over the Front]. Moscow: DOSAAF, 1984.

———. *Nebo ostaetsia nashim* [The Sky Remains Ours]. Moscow: Voenizdat, 1976.

———. *Samolety ukhodiat v noch'* [Aircraft Go Out Into the Night]. Moscow: Voenizdat, 1961.

Chen Menglei, ed. *Gujin tushu jicheng (Qin ding).* [Synthesis of books and illustrations of ancient and modern times]. Reprint of 1934 ed. Shanghai: Shanghai wenyi chubanshe, 1993.

Cherniaeva, I., ed. *Docheri Rossii [Daughter of Russia].* Moscow: Sovetskaia Rossiia, 1975.

Cheesman, E.C. *Brief Glory (the Story of A.T.A.).* London: Petty and Sons, 1946.

Chibnall, Marjorie. *The World of Orderic Vitalis.* Oxford: Clarendon Press, 1984.

———. *The Empress Matilda: Queen Consort, Queen Mother, and Lady of the English.* Oxford: Blackwell, 1991.

Child, Francis James, ed. *The English and Scottish Popular Ballads.* 5 vols. New York: Folklore Press, 1956.

Chirkov, P.M. "Zhenshchiny v Krasnoi Armii v gody Grazhdanskoi Voiny i Imperialisticheskoi Interventsii (1918–1920)." [Women in the Red Army in the years of the Civil War and imperialist intervention, 1918–1920.] *Istoriia SSSR* 6 (1975): 103–114.

Christine de Pisan. *The City of Ladies.* London: 1521.

———. *The Book of Deeds of Arms and of Chivalry.* Trans. Sumner Williard, ed. Charity Cannon Williard. University Park: Pennsylvania State University Press, 1999.

The Chronicle of Lanercost, 1272–1346. Trans. Sir Herbert Maxwell. Glasgow: James Maclehose and Sons, 1913.

Clausius, Gerhard P. "The Little Soldier of the 95th: Albert D.J. Cashier." *Journal of the Illinois State Historical Society* 51.4 (1958): 380–387.

Clement, Clara Erskine. *Women in the Fine Arts.* Reprint of 1904 Cambridge ed. New York: Hacker Art Books, 1974.

Clinton, Catherine, and Nina Silber, eds. *Divided Houses: Gender and the Civil War.* New York: Oxford University Press, 1992.

Coates, Colin M. "Commemorating the Woman Warrior of New France: Madeleine de Verchères, 1696–1930." *Gender and History in Canada.* Ed. Joy Parr and Mark Rosenfeld. Toronto: Copp Clark, 1996. 120–136.

———, and Cecilia Louise Morgan. *Heroines and History: Representations of Madeleine de Verchères and Laura Secord.* Toronto: University of Toronto Press, 2001.

Cochran, Jacqueline. "Final Report on Women Pilot Program." HQ Army Air Forces. Air Force Historical Research Agency, Maxwell AFB, Alabama, AFHRA 220.0721-2, 1 June 1945.

———. *The Stars at Noon.* Boston: Little, Brown, 1954.

———. USAF Oral History Interview with Kenneth Leish, May 1960. Air Force Historical Research Agency, Maxwell AFB, Alabama, USAF Oral History Interview K146.34-30.

————. USAF Oral History Interview with Capt. Robert S. Bartanowicz and Maj. John "Fred" Shiner, 11–12 March 1976, USAF Academy, CO. Air Force Historical Research Agency, Maxwell AFB, Alabama, USAF Oral History Interview K239.0512-940.

Cochran, Jacqueline, and Maryann Bucknum Brinley. *Jackie Cochran: The Autobiography of the Greatest Woman Pilot in Aviation History*. New York: Bantam, 1987.

Cockayn, G.E. *The Complete Peerage*. Rev. ed. Vol. I. London: St. Catherine's Press, 1910–1959.

Cognasso, Francesco. *Storia di Torino*. Milan: Martello, 1959.

Cohen, Daniel. "The Female Marine in an Era of Good Feelings: Cross Dressing and the 'Genius' of Nathaniel Coverly, Jr." *Proceedings of the American Antiquarian Society* 103 (1993): 359–394.

Cohen, Daniel, ed. *The Female Marine and Related Works: Narratives of Cross-Dressing and Urban Vice in America's Early Republic*. Amherst: University of Massachusetts Press, 1997.

Cole, Adelaide M. "Anne Bailey: Woman of Courage." *Daughters of the American Revolution Magazine* 114 (1980): 322–325.

Collison-Morley, L. *The Story of the Sforzas*. New York: Dutton, 1934.

Comnena, Anna. *The Alexiad of Anna Comnena*. Trans. E.R.A. Sewter. New York: Penguin, 1969.

Contamine, Philippe. *War in the Middle Ages*. Trans. Michael Jones. London: Blackwell, 1984.

Cooke, Miriam. *Women and the War Story*. Berkeley: University of California Press, 1996.

Cooley, John K. *Baal, Christ, and Mohammed: Religion and Revolution in North Africa*. New York: Holt, Rinehart and Winston, 1965.

Cornum, Rhonda. *She Went to War: The Rhonda Cornum Story*. Novato, CA: Presidio Press, 1992.

Coryell, Janet. "Anna Ella Carroll and the Historians." *Civil War History* 35 (1989): 120–137.

————. *Neither Heroine nor Fool: Anna Ella Carroll of Maryland*. Kent, OH: Kent State University Press, 1990.

Cotera, Martha. *Diosa y hembra*. Austin, TX: Information Systems Development, 1976.

Cottam, Kazimiera J. "Veterans of Polish Women's Combat Battalion Hold a Reunion." *Minerva: Quarterly Report on Women and the Military* 4 (1986): 1–7.

————. "Soviet Women Soldiers in World War II: Three Biographical Sketches." *Minerva: Quarterly Report on Women and the Military* 18.3–4 (2001).

————, ed. *In the Sky above the Front: A Collection of Memoirs of Soviet Air Women Participants in the Great Patriotic War*. Manhattan, KS: Sunflower University Press, 1984.

————. *Women in Air War: The Eastern Front of World War II*. Rev. ed. Nepean, Ontario: New Military Publishing, 1997.

————. *Women in War and Resistance: Selected Biographies of Soviet Women Soldiers*. Nepean, Ontario: New Military Publishing, 1998.

Coughlin, Kathryn M. "Women, War and the Veil: Muslim Women in Resistance and Combat." *A Soldier and a Woman: Sexual Integration in the Military*. Ed. Gerald J. DeGroot and Corinna Peniston-Bird. New York: Pearson Education, 2000. 223–239.

Coulter, Ellis Merton. "Nancy Hart, Georgia Heroine of the Revolution: The Story of the Growth of a Tradition." *Georgia Historical Quarterly* 39 (1955): 118–151.

Cousin, Victor. *Madame de Chevreuse*. Paris: Pernin, 1886.

————. *Madame de Longueville pendant la Fronde*. 7th ed. Paris: Pernin, 1891.

Cowdrey, H.E.J. *Pope Gregory VII, 1073–1085*. London: 1998.

Crankshaw, Edward. *Maria Theresa*. New York: Viking, 1970.

Crim, Brian. "Silent Partners: Women and Warfare in Early Modern Europe." *A Soldier and a Woman: Sexual Integration in the Military*. Ed. Gerard J. DeGroot and Corinna Peniston-Bird. New York: Pearson Education, 2000. 18–32.

Cuénin, Micheline. *La derniére des Amazones, Madame de Saint-Baslemont*. Nancy: 1992.

Cuevas, Tomasa. *Cárcel de mujeres (1939–1945)*. Barcelona: Edicimes Sirocco, 1985.

Cunliffe, Barry. *Wessex to AD 1000*. London: Longman, 1993.

Curtis, Lettice. *The Forgotten Pilots: A Story of the Air Transport Auxiliary, 1939–45*. 3rd ed. Olney, Buckinghamshire: Nelson and Saunders, 1985.

Dadeshkeliani, Princess Kati. *Princess in Uniform*. London: G. Bell and Sons, 1934.

Dandeker, Christopher, and Mady Wechsler Segal. "Gender Integration in Armed Forces: Recent Policy Developments in the United Kingdom." *Armed Forces & Society* 23.1 (1996): 29–47.

Daniel, David P. "Piety, Politics, and Perversion: Noblewomen in Reformation Hungary." *Women in Reformation and Counter-Reformation Europe: Public and Private Worlds*. Ed. Sherrin Marshall. Bloomington: Indiana University Press, 1989. 68–88.

Danner, Dorothy S. *What a Way to Spend a War: Navy Nurse POWs in the Philippines*. Annapolis, MD: Naval Institute Press, 1995.

Dannett, Sylvia, ed. *Noble Women of the North*. New York: Sagamore Press, 1959.

Darrach, Henry. "Lydia Darragh, of the Revolution." *Pennsylvania Magazine of History and Biography* 23 (1899): Women of the American Revolution.

David, Katherine. "The First in Austria: Czech Feminists and Nationalism in the Late Habsburg Monarchy." *Journal of Women's History* 3.2 (1991): 26–45.

Davis, Curtis Carroll. "A 'Gallantress' Gets Her Due: The Earliest Published Notice of Deborah Sampson." *Proceedings of the American Antiquarian Society* 91.2 (1981): 319–323.

Davis, Mary B., ed. *Native America in the Twentieth Century*. New York: Garland Publishing, 1994.

Davis, R.H.C. *King Stephen, 1135–1154*. 3rd ed. London: Longman, 1990.

Davis, Rodney O. "Private Albert Cashier as Regarded by His/Her Comrades." *Illinois Historical Journal* 82.2 (1989): 108–112.

Davis-Kimball, Jeannine. "Warrior Women of the Eurasian Steppes." *Archaeology* January/February 1997: 44–48.

———. *Warrior Women: An Archaeologist's Search for History's Hidden Heroines*. New York: Warner Books, 2002.

Day, John, Bruno Anatra, and Lucetta Scaraffia. *La Sardegna medioevale e moderna*. Turin: UTET, 1984.

De Madariaga, Isabel. *Russia in the Age of Catherine the Great*. New Haven: Yale University Press, 1981.

———. *Catherine the Great*. New Haven: Yale University Press, 1990.

De Pauw, Linda Grant. *Founding Mothers: Women in America in the Revolutionary Era*. Boston: Houghton Mifflin, 1975.

———. "Women in Combat: The Revolutionary War Experience." *Armed Forces and Society* 7.2 (1980): 209–226.

De Pauw, Linda Grant, and Conover Hunt. *Remember the Ladies: Women in America, 1750–1815*. New York: Viking, 1976.

Debû-Bridel, Jacques. *Anne-Geneviève de Bourbon, duchesse de Longueville*. Paris: Gallimard, 1938.

Defoe, Daniel. *The Life and Adventures of Mrs. Christian Davies, Commonly Called Mother Ross*. London: Peter Davies, 1928.

DeGroot, Gerard. "I Love the Scent of Cordite in Your Hair: Gender Dynamics in Mixed

Anti-Aircraft Batteries during the Second World War." *History* 265 (1997): 73–92.

DeGroot, Gerard J., and Corinna Peniston-Bird, eds. *A Soldier and a Woman: Sexual Integration in the Military.* New York: Pearson Education, 2000.

Dekker, Rudolf M., and Lotte C. van de Pol. "Republican Heroines: Cross-Dressing Women in the French Revolutionary Armies." *History of European Ideas* 10.3 (1989): 353–364.

———. *The Tradition of Female Transvestism in Early Modern Europe.* Trans. Judy Marcure and Lotte van de Pol. New York: St. Martin's Press, 1989.

Demosthenes. *Demosthenes' Public Orations.* Trans. A.W. Pickard-Cambridge. Oxford: Clarendon Press, 1963.

Denig, Edwin Thompson. *Five Indian Tribes of the Upper Missouri.* Norman: University of Oklahoma Press, 1961.

Dennis, P., ed. *The Oxford Companion to Australian Military History.* Melbourne: Oxford University Press, 1995.

Denti, Giannina. *Storia di Cremona.* Cremona: Turris, 1985.

Dever, John P., and Maria C. Dever. *Women and the Military: Over 100 Notable Contributors, Historic to Contemporary.* Jefferson, NC: McFarland, 1995.

DeVries, Kelly. *Joan of Arc: A Military Leader.* Stroud: Sutton, 1999.

Dewald, Carolyn. "Women and Culture in Herodotus' Histories." *Reflections on Women in Antiquity.* Ed. Helene P. Foley. New York: Gordon and Breach, 1981. 91–125.

Dexter, Elisabeth Anthony. *Colonial Women of Affairs.* 2nd ed. Boston: Houghton Mifflin, 1931.

Dill, Samuel. *Roman Society in Gaul in the Merovingian Age.* London: Macmillan, 1926.

Diodorus Siculus. *Diodorus of Sicily.* Trans. C.H. Oldfather. 12 vols. New York: G.P. Putnam's Sons, 1933–1967.

Director of Women Personnel, Canadian Forces. *Women in the Canadian Forces.* Ottawa: Department of National Defence, 1986.

Długosz, John. *Historiae Polonicae.* Book 13. Cracow: Ephemeridum, 1878.

Dmitrieva, T.V. "Rol' zhenshchin Urala v Bor'be protiv Interventov i Belogvardeitsev i Okazanii Pomoshchi Fronty (mai 1918–1920gg)" [The Role of Women of the Urals in the Fight against the Intervention and White Guards and their Assistance to the Front (May 1918–1920)]. Avtoreferat: Dissertation abstract. University of Sverdlovsk, 1985.

Dodgeon, M.H., and S.N.C. Lieu, eds. *The Roman Eastern Frontier and the Persian Wars (AD 226–363): A Documentary History.* London: Routledge, 1991.

Donzel, E.J. van. *The Encyclopaedia of Islam.* New edition. vol 1. Leiden: E.J. Brill, 1993.

Douglas, David C. *William the Conqueror: The Norman Impact on England.* Berkeley: University of California Press, 1964.

Douglas, Deborah G. *United States Women in Aviation, 1940–1985.* Washington, DC: Smithsonian Institution Press, 1990.

Downey, G. "Aurelian's Victory over Zenobia at Immae, A.D. 272." TAPA: *Transactions and Proceedings of the American Philological Association* 81 (1950): 57–68.

Drokov, Sergei Vladimirovich. "Organizator Zhenskogo Batal'ona Smerti" [The Organizer of the Women's Battalion of Death]. *Voprosy Istorii* 7 (1993): 164.

Dudley, Donald Reynolds, and Graham Webster. *The Rebellion of Boudicca.* New York: Barnes & Noble, 1962.

———. *The Roman Conquest of Britain, A.D. 43–57.* London: B.T. Batsford, 1965.

Duff, Nora. *Matilda of Tuscany, la Gran Donna d'Italia.* London: Methuen, 1909.

Duffy, Christopher. *The Military Life of Frederick the Great.* New York: Atheneum, 1986.

———. *Siege Warfare: The Fortress in the Early Modern World, 1494–1660.* Reprint ed. London: Routledge, 1987.

Dugaw, Dianne. *Warrior Women and Popular Balladry, 1650–1850*. Cambridge: Cambridge University Press, 1989.

Duiker, William J. "Vietnam: War of Insurgency." *Female Soldiers—Combatants or Noncombatants? Historical and Contemporary Perspectives*. Ed. Nancy Loring Goldman. Westport, CT: Greenwood Press, 1982. 107–122.

Duncan, John. *Travels in Western Africa, in 1845 and 1846*. Vol. 1. London: Richard Bentley, 1847.

Durant, Will. *The Renaissance: A History of Civilization in Italy from 1304–1576*. Vol. 5. New York: Simon and Schuster, 1953.

Durova, Nadezhda. *Zapiski Aleksandrova (Durovoi): Dobavlenie k Devitse-kavalerist* [Notes of Aleksandrov-Durova: Addendum to *The Cavalry Maiden*]. Moscow: 1839.

———. *The Cavalry Maiden: Journals of a Female Russian Officer in the Napoleonic Wars*. Trans. Mary Fleming Zirin. London: Angel, 1988.

Eads, Valerie. "Mighty in War: The Role of Matilda of Tuscany in the War between Pope Gregory VII and Emperor Henry IV." Ph.D. dissertation, City University of New York, 2000.

———. "The Geography of Power: Matilda of Tuscany and the Strategy of Active Defense." *Crusaders, Condottieri, and Cannon: Medieval Warfare in Societies around the Mediterranean*. Ed. Kagay, Donald J. and L.J. Andrew Villalon. Leiden: Brill, 2002.

Eales, Jacqueline. *Puritans and Roundheads: The Harleys of Brampton Bryan and the Outbreak of the English Civil War*. Cambridge: Cambridge University Press, 1990.

Earley, Charity Adams. *One Woman's Army: A Black Officer Remembers the WAC*. College Station: Texas A&M University Press, 1989.

Ebbert, Jean, and Marie-Beth Hall. *Crossed Currents: Navy Women from WWI to Tailhook*. Washington, DC: Brassey's, 1993.

Echols, Anne, and Marty Williams. *An Annotated Index of Medieval Women*. New York: Markus Wiener, 1992.

Edgerton, Robert B. *Warrior Women: The Amazons of Dahomey and the Nature of War*. Boulder, CO: Westview, 2000.

Edmonds, S. Emma E. *Unsexed; or, The Female Soldier*. Philadelphia: Philadelphia Publishing Co., 1864.

———. *Nurse and Spy in the Union Army, Comprising the Adventures and Experiences of a Woman in Hospitals, Camps, and Battle-fields*. Hartford: W.S Williams and Co., 1865.

———. *Memoirs of a Soldier, Nurse, and Spy*. Ed. Elizabeth Leonard. Dekalb: Northern Illinois University Press, 1999.

Ellet, Elizabeth F. *The Women of the American Revolution*. 3 vols. New York: Baker and Scribner, 1848–1850.

Elshtain, Jean Bethke. *Women and War*. New York: Basic Books, 1987.

Elting, John R. *Swords around a Throne: Napoleon's Grande Armée*. New York: Free Press, 1988.

England, J. Merton. *Women Pilots of the AAF, 1941–1944*. March 1946. AAF Historical Office, Headquarters, Army Air Forces. USAAF Historical Study No. 55.

Engle, Paul. *Women in the American Revolution*. Chicago: Follett, 1976.

Engle, Regula. *L'amazone de Napoléon*. Paris: Oliver Orban, 1985.

Enloe, Cynthia. "The Politics of Constructing the American Woman Soldier." *Women Soldiers: Images and Realities*. Ed. Elisabetta Addis, Valeria E. Russo, and Lorenza Sebesta. New York: St. Martin's Press, 1994. 81–110.

Erauso, Catalina de. *Lieutenant Nun: Memoir of a Basque Transvestite in the New World*. Trans. Michele Stepto and Gabriel Stepto. Boston: Beacon Press, 1996.

Erauso, Catalina de, and Rima de Vallbona. *Vida I Sucesos De La Monja Alférez*. Tempe, AZ: Arizona State University, 1992.

Erdmann, Carl. *The Origin of the Idea of Crusade*. Princeton: Princeton University Press, 1977.

Eremin, Boris. *Vozdushnye boitsy* [Air warriors]. Moscow: Voenizdat, 1987.

Eremin, V.I., and P.F. Isakov. *Molodezh v gody Velikoi Otechestvennoi voiny* [Young people during the Great Patriotic War]. Rev. ed. Moscow: Mysl', 1984.

Erickson, John. "Soviet Women at War." *World War 2 and the Soviet People*. Ed. John Garrard, Carol Garrard, and Stephen White. New York: St. Martin's Press, 1993. 50–76.

Erlanger, Philippe. *Madame de Longueville, de la révolte au mysticisme*. Paris: Perrin, 1977.

Escher, Max. "Melitta Schiller-Stauffenberg: Eine Begegnung." *Kulturwarte* 4 February 1972.

Escobedo, Raquel. *Galeria de mujeres ilustres*. N.p.: Editores Mexicanos Unidos, S.A., 1967.

Escott, Beryl E. *Our Wartime Days: The WAAF in World War II*. Stroud: Alan Sutton, 1995.

Etchebéhère, Mika. *Ma guerre d'Espagne à moi*. Paris: Editions Denoël, 1976.

Evans, Elizabeth. *Weathering the Storm: Women of the American Revolution*. New York: Paragon House, 1989.

Everett, Dick. *The Dixie Frontier*. New York: Knopf, 1948.

Ewers, John C. "Deadlier than the Male." *American Heritage* 26.4 (1965): 10–13.

Ewing, Elizabeth. *Women in Uniform: Through the Centuries*. London: B.T. Batsford, 1975.

Expilly, Jean-Joseph. *Dictionnaire géographique, historique, et politique des Gaules et de la France*. Vol. 4. Amsterdam: 1766.

Fage, J.D., ed. *The Cambridge History of Africa*. Vol. 2. Cambridge: Cambridge University Press, 1978.

Fang, Xuanling, and Baoyuan Du, eds. *Jin shu* [The history of the Jin Dynasty (265–420)]. Beijing: Zhonghua shuju, 1974.

Faraglia, Nunzio Federigo. *Storia della Regina Giovanna II d'Angiò*. Lanciano: Carabba, 1904.

Fenelon, Fania. *Playing for Time*. Trans. Judith Landry. Syracuse, NY: Syracuse University Press, 1997.

Finucane, Ronald C. *Soldiers of the Faith: Crusaders and Moslems at War*. London: Dent, 1983.

Firth, C.H. *Cromwell's Army: A History of the English Soldier during the Civil Wars, the Commonwealth, and the Protectorate*. London: Methuen, 1902.

Fischer, David Hackett. *Paul Revere's Ride*. New York: Oxford University Press, 1994.

Fishel, Edwin C. *The Secret War for the Union: The Untold Story of Military Intelligence in the Civil War*. Boston: Houghton Mifflin, 1996.

Fittis, Robert Scott. *Heroines of Scotland*. London: Alexander Gardner, 1889.

Fladeland, Betty. "Alias Franklin Thompson." *Michigan History* 42.3 (1958): 435–462.

———. "New Light on Sarah Emma Edmonds, alias Frank Thompson." *Michigan History* 48.4 (1963): 357–362.

Fletcher, Anthony. *Tudor Rebellions*. 3rd ed. London: Longman, 1983.

Flodoard of Rheims. *Les Annales de Flodoard*. Paris: A. Picard, 1905.

Florence of Worcester. *Chronicon ex chronicis*. 2 vols. 3rd ed. London: Sumptibus Societatis, 1848–1849.

Foot, M.R.D. *SOE in France: An Account of the Work of the British Special Operations Executive in France, 1940–1944*. London: Her Majesty's Stationery Office, 1966.

Forbes, Frederick E. *Dahomey and the Dahomans; Being the Journals of Two Missions to the*

King of Dahomey, and Residence at His Capital, in the Year 1849 and 1850. London: Longman, Brown, Green, and Longmans, 1851.

Foreman, Carolyn Thomas. *Indian Women Chiefs.* Washington, DC: Zenger, 1976.

Foster, Thomas A. " 'In Defense of All That Is Dear and Lovely': Revolutionary War Soldier Deborah Sampson and the Permeability of War-Time Gender Norms." Master's thesis, North Carolina State University at Raleigh, 1995.

Foucher de Chartres. *A History of the Expedition to Jerusalem, 1095–1127.* New York: W.W. Norton, 1972.

Franceschi, Lydia, and Isotta Gaetá, eds. *L'altra metà della Resistenza* [The other half of the Resistance]. Milan: Mazzotta, 1978.

Francke, Linda Bird. *Ground Zero: The Gender Wars in the Military.* New York: Simon and Schuster, 1997.

Fraser, Antonia. *The Weaker Vessel: Woman's Lot in Seventeenth-Century England.* London: Weidenfeld and Nicolson, 1984.

———. *The Warrior Queens.* New York: Knopf, 1989.

Freedman, Lawrence, and Virginia Gamba-Stonehouse. *Signals of War: The Falklands Conflict of 1982.* Princeton: Princeton University Press, 1991.

Friedl, Vicki L. *Women in the United States Military, 1901–1995: A Research Guide and Annotated Bibliography.* Westport, CT: Greenwood, 1996.

Froissart, Jean. *The Chronicle of Froissart.* New York: AMS Press, 1967.

Fryde, Natalie. *The Tyranny and Fall of Edward II, 1321–1326.* Cambridge: Cambridge University Press, 1979.

Fuller, Jean Overton. *Noor-un-nisa Inayat Khan (Madeleine).* London: Barrie and Jenkins, 1971.

Fuyola, Encarnación. *Mujeres antifascistas: Su trabajo y su organización.* Valencia: Ediciones de las Mujeres Antifascistas, 1936.

Gabrieli, Francesco. *Arab Historians of the Crusades.* Trans. from the Italian by E.J. Costello. Berkeley: University of California Press, 1969.

Gal, R. *A Portrait of the Israeli Soldier.* Westport, CT: Greenwood Press, 1986.

Galagan, Valentina Yakovlevna. *Ratnyipodvig zhenshchin v gody Velikoi Otechestvennoi voiny* [Military feats of women during the Great Patriotic War]. Kiev: Vysshaia shkola, 1986.

Ganson, Barbara. "Following Their Children into Battle: Women at War in Paraguay, 1864–1870." *Americas* 46 (1990): 335–371.

Gantier, Joaquin. *Doña Juana Azurduy De Padilla.* Buenos Aires: Imprenta Lopez, 1946.

García Granados, Miguel. *Memorias del General don Miguel García Granados.* 2nd ed. 2 vols. Guatemala: El Progreso, Tipografía Nacional, 1877–1893.

Gardiner, Samuel Rawson. *History of the Great Civil War, 1642–1649.* Vol. I, *(1642–1644).* London: Longmans, Green and Co., 1904.

Garraty, John Arthur, Mark C. Carnes, and American Council of Learned Societies., eds. *American National Biography.* New York: Oxford University Press, 1999.

Gatti, Luigi. *Bertinoro: Notizie storiche.* 2nd ed. Bertinoro: Pro Loco, 1968–1971.

George, Carol V.R., ed. *"Remember the Ladies": New Perspectives on Women in American History: Essays in Honor of Nelson Manfred Blake.* Syracuse, NY: Syracuse University Press, 1975.

The Georgian Chronicle. Trans. Katharine Vivian. Amsterdam: Adolph M. Hakkert, 1991.

Gera, Deborah. *Warrior Women: The Anonymous Tractatus de Mulieribus.* Mnemosyne, Bibliotheca Classica Batava, Supplementum, No. 162. New York: E.J. Brill, 1997.

Gesta Stephani. 3rd ed. 2 vols. Oxford: Clarendon Press, 1976.

Gherner, Ugo. "La contessa Adelaide e la società del secolo XI." *Bollettino storico-bibliografico subalpino* 90.2 (1992): 691–698.

Gilbert, Charles. *Brave l'Angevin; ou, La véritable histoire de Renée Bordereau*. Les Sables d'Olonne: Le Cercle d'or, 1976.

Gillingham, John. *The Wars of the Roses: Peace and Conflict in Fifteenth-Century England*. London: Weidenfeld and Nicolson, 1981.

Ginzburg, Evgeniia Semenovna. *Journey into the Whirlwind*. New York: Harcourt Brace Jovanovich, 1975.

Glaber, Ralph. *Historiarum libri quinti*. Paris: A. Picard, 1886.

Glaesener, Henri. "Un mariage fertile en conséquences (Godefroid le Barbu et Béatrice de Toscane)." *Revue d'Histoire Ecclésiastique* 42 (1947): 379–416.

Goez, Elke. *Beatrix von Canossa und Tuszien: Eine Untersuching zur Geschichte des II. Jahrhunderts*. Sigmaringen: J. Thorbecke, 1995.

Goez, Werner. "Markgräfin Mathilde von Canossa." *Gestalten des Hochmittelalters: personengeschichtliche Essays im allgemeinhistorischen Kontext*. Darmstadt: Wissenschaftliche Buchgesellschaft, 1983.

Gollaher, David. *Voice for the Mad: The Life of Dorothea Dix*. New York: Free Press, 1995.

Gould, Jenny. "Women's Military Service in First World War Britain." *Behind the Lines: Gender and the Two World Wars*. Ed. Margaret Higonnet, Jane Jensen, Sonya Michel, and Margaret Weitz. New Haven: Yale University Press, 1987. 114–125.

Gower, Pauline. "A.T.A. Girls: Britain's Women Flyers Take Their Place with the Men in Ferrying England's Aircraft." *Flying* August 1943: 30–32ff.

Graeff-Wassink, Maria. *Women at Arms: Is Ghadafi a Feminist?* Trans. Elio Bracuti. London: Darf Publishers, 1993.

Graham, Harry. *A Group of Scottish Women*. 2nd ed. London: Methuen, 1908.

Graham, Maria Dundas. *Journal of a Voyage to Brazil and Residence There, during Part of the Years 1821, 1822, 1823*. London: Longman, Hurst, Rees, Orme, Brown, and Green, 1824. Reprint, New York: Praeger, 1969.

Graham, Ruth. "Loaves and Liberty: Women in the French Revolution." *Becoming Visible: Women in European History*. Ed. Renate Bridenthal and Claudia Koonz. Boston: Houghton Mifflin, 1977. 236–254.

Grant, Michael. *History of Rome*. New York: History Book Club, 1997.

Grasselli, Giuseppe. *Abecedario biografico dei pittori, scultori, ed architetti cremonesi*. Milan: Manini, 1827.

Grechko, A.A., ed. *Sovetskaiia voennaiia entsiklopediia*. 8 vols. Moskva: Voenizdat, 1976.

Green, David S. "The Household of Edward, the Black Prince." Ph.D. dissertation, University of Nottingham, 1997.

Green, H. *The Battlefields of Britain and Ireland*. 2nd ed. London: Constable, 1983.

Green, Mary Anne Everett, ed. *Letters of Queen Henrietta Maria, Including Her Private Correspondence with Charles the First*. London: R. Bentley, 1857. Microform History of Women no. 1794.1. New Haven, CT: Research Publications, 1975.

Green, Peter. *Alexander to Actium: The Historical Evolution of the Hellenistic Age*. Berkeley: University of California Press, 1990.

Greer, Germaine. *The Obstacle Race: The Fortunes of Women Painters and Their Work*. New York: Farrar, Straus, Ginoux, 1979.

Gribble, Francis. *Women in War*. New York: Dutton, 1917.

Griesse, Anne Eliot, and Richard Stites. "Russia: Revolution and War." *Female Soldiers—Combatants or Noncombatants?: Historical and Contemporary Perspectives*. Ed. Nancy Loring Goldman. Westport, CT: Greenwood Press, 1982. 61–84.

Grinnell, George Bird. *The Fighting Cheyennes*. Norman: University of Oklahoma Press, 1915.

———. *The Cheyenne Indians: Their History and Ways of Life*. 2 vols. New Haven, CT: Yale University Press, 1923.

Gruhzit-Hoyt, Olga. *They Also Served: American Women in World War II*. Secaucus, NJ: Birch Lane Press, 1995.

Gruner, Elliot. "Women as POWs: Forgetting the Rhonda Cornum Story." *Minerva: Quarterly Report on Women and the Military* 14.1 (1996): 1–14.

Guba, Emil F. *Deborah Samson alias Robert Shurtliff: Revolutionary War Soldier*. New York: Paragon House, 1992.

Gugliotta, Bobette. *Women of Mexico: The Consecrated and the Commoners, 1519–1900*. Encino, CA: Floricanto Press, 1989.

Guillaume de Pouille (William of Apulia). *La Geste de Robert Guiscard*. Trans. and ed. Marguerite Mathieu. Palermo: Istituto siciliano di studi bizantini e neoellenici, 1961.

Guizot de Witt, Madam. *The Lady of Lathom: Being the Life and Original Letters of Charlotte de la Trémoille, Countess of Derby*. London: Smith, Elder and Co., 1869.

Gullickson, Gay. *Unruly Women of Paris: Images of the Commune*. Ithaca: Cornell University Press, 1996.

Gurewitsch, Brana. *Mothers, Sisters, Resisters: Oral Histories of Women Who Survived the Holocaust*. Tuscaloosa: University of Alabama Press, 1998.

Gwynne-Vaughan, Helen. *Service with the Army*. London: Hutchinson, 1942.

Hacker, Barton C. "Women and Military Institutions in Early Modern Europe: A Reconnaissance." *Signs: Journal of Women in Culture and Society* 6.4 (1981): 643–671.

———. "Where Have All the Women Gone? The Pre-Twentieth Century Sexual Division of Labor in Armies." *Minerva: Quarterly Report on Women and the Military* 3.1 (1985): 107–148.

Hagist, Don N. "The Women of the British Army: A General Overview, Part 1: Who and How Many." *Brigade Dispatch* 24.3 (1993): 2–10; "The Women of the British Army: A General Overview, Part 2: Sober, Industrious Women." *Brigade Dispatch* 24.4 (1993): 9–17; "The Women of the British Army: A General Overview, Part 3: Living Conditions." *Brigade Dispatch* 25.1 (1995): 11–16; "The Women of the British Army: A General Overview, Part 4: Miscellaneous Notes." *Brigade Dispatch* 25.2 (1995): 8–14.

Hall, Edward H. *Margaret Corbin, Heroine of the Battle of Fort Washington, 16 November 1776*. New York: American Scenic and Historic Preservation Society, 1932.

Hall, Richard. *Patriots in Disguise: Women Warriors of the Civil War*. New York: Paragon House, 1993.

———. "They All Fought at Bull Run." *Minerva: Quarterly Report on Women and the Military* 9.3 (1991): 48–54.

Hamel, Frank. *A Woman of the Revolution: Théroigne de Méricourt*. New York: Brentano's, 1911.

Hammack, Bill. "Cherokee Phoenix." *Outdoors in Georgia* February 1978: 18–22.

Hancock, Joy B. *Lady in the Navy: A Personal Reminiscence*. Annapolis, MD: Naval Institute Press, 1972.

Hanson, Elizabeth. *God's Mercy Surmounting Man's Cruelty Exemplified in the Captivity of Elizabeth Hanson*. Philadelphia: n p , 1728.

Hanson, W.S., and D.B. Campbell. "The Brigantes: From Clientage to Conquest." *Britannia* 17 (1986): 73–89.

Hardy, B.C. *Philippa of Hainault and Her Times*. London: John Long, 1910.

Hartmann, Susan M. *The Home Front and Beyond: American Women in the 1940s*. Boston: Twayne, 1982.

Harvey, John Hooper. *The Black Prince and His Age*. London: Batsford, 1976.

Haselholdt-Stockheim, F., ed. *Herzog Albrecht IV. von Bayern und seine Zeit*. Vol. I, part 1. Leipzig: Franz Wagner, 1865.

Hayton-Keeva, Sally, ed. *Valiant Women in War and Exile: Thirty-eight True Stories.* San Francisco: City Light Books, 1987.

Haywood, John. *Encyclopedia of the Viking Age.* New York: Thames & Hudson, 2000.

Helie-Lucas, Marie-Aimee. "Women, Nationalism, and Religion in the Algerian Liberation Struggle." *Opening the Gates.* Ed. Margot Badran and Miriam Cooke. Bloomington: Indiana University Press, 1990.

Henderson, James D., and Linda Roddy Henderson. *Ten Notable Women of Latin America.* Chicago: Nelson-Hall, 1978.

Hendrix, Scott N. "In the Army: Women, Camp Followers and Gender Roles in the British Army in the French and Indian Wars, 1755–1765." *A Soldier and a Woman: Sexual Integration in the Military.* Ed. Gerard J. DeGroot and Corinna Peniston-Bird. New York: Longman, 2000. 33–48.

Hennet, Léon. "Rose Barreau de Sémalens, Tarn, volontaire de la République en 1793." *Revue de Tarn*: 1–22.

Herodotus. *The Histories.* Trans. Aubrey de Selincourt. London: Penguin, 1972.

Herrera-Sobek, María. *The Mexican Corrido: A Feminist Analysis.* Bloomington: Indiana University Press, 1990.

Herrington, Walter Stevens. *Heroines of Canadian History.* Toronto: William Briggs, 1910.

Hewitt, Linda L. *Women Marines in World War I.* Washington, DC: History and Museums Division, HQ USMC, 1974.

Heymann, Frederick. *John Zizka and the Hussite Revolution.* Princeton: Princeton University Press, 1955.

Hicks, George L. *The Comfort Women: Japan's Brutal Regime of Enforced Prostitution in the Second World War.* 1st American ed. New York: W.W. Norton, 1995.

Higgins, P.M. "Women in the English Civil War." M.A thesis, University of Manchester, 1965.

Higonnet, Margaret, and Patrice Higonnet. "The Double Helix." *Behind the Lines: Gender and the Two World Wars.* Ed. Margaret Higonnet, Jane Jensen, Sonya Michel, and Margaret Weitz. New Haven and London: Yale University Press, 1987. 31–47.

Higonnet, Margaret Randolph, Jane Jenson, Sonya Michel, and Margaret Collins Weitz, eds. *Behind the Lines: Gender and the Two World Wars.* New Haven and London: Yale University Press, 1987.

Hitti, Philip Khuri. *History of the Arabs from the Earliest Times to the Present.* 10th ed. London: Macmillan, 1970.

Hochedlinger, Michael. "Mars Ennobled: The Ascent of the Military and the Creation of a Military Nobility in Mid-Eighteenth Century Austria." *German History* 17.2 (1999): 141–176.

Hodgson, Marion Stegeman. *Winning My Wings: A Woman Airforce Service Pilot in World War II.* Annapolis, MD: Naval Institute Press, 1996.

Hoefer, Jean Chrétien Ferdinand. *Nouvelle biographie générale.* Paris: Firmin Didot Frères, fils et cie, 1858.

Hoefer, Jean M. "Harriet Tubman: A Heroine of the Underground Goes to War." *Civil War Times Illustrated* February 1988: 37–41.

Hoffert, Sylvia D. "Madame Loreta Velazquez: Heroine or Hoaxer?" *Civil War Times Illustrated* June 1978: 24–31.

Hoffmann, Peter. *Stauffenberg: A Family History, 1905–1944.* Cambridge: Cambridge University Press, 1995.

Holm, Jeanne. *Women in the Military: An Unfinished Revolution.* Rev. ed. Novato, CA: Presidio Press, 1992.

Holman, Dennis. *Sikander Sahib: The Life of Colonel James Skinner, 1778–1841.* London: Heinemann, 1961.

Hornblower, Simon. *Mausolus.* Oxford: Clarendon Press, 1982.

Howard, Keith, Han'guk Chongsindae Munje Taech'aek Hyobuihoe, and Chongsindae Yon'guhoe (Korea). *True Stories of the Korean Comfort Women: Testimonies*. London and New York: Cassell, 1995.

Howes, Ruth, and Michael Stevenson, eds. *Women and the Use of Military Force*. Boulder, CO: Lynne Rienner, 1993.

Howlett, Richard, ed. *Chronicles of the Reigns of Stephen, Henry II, and Richard I*. 4 vols. London: Her Majesty's Stationery Office, 1884–1889.

Huey, Lois M., and Bonnie Pulis. *Molly Brant: A Legacy of Her Own*. Old Fort Niagara Association, 1997.

Hummel, Arthur W., ed. *Eminent Chinese of the Ch'ing Period*. 2 vols. Washington, DC: GPO, 1943–1944.

Hutchins, John. *The History and Antiquities of the County of Dorset*. 3rd ed. Vol. 1. EP Publishing, 1973.

Imparato, Edward T. *Rescue from Shangri-La*. Paducah, KY: Turner, 1997.

Iongh, Jane de. *Mary of Hungary, Second Regent of the Netherlands*. New York: Norton, 1958.

Isaac, B. *The Limits of Empire: The Roman Army in the East*. Rev. ed. Oxford: Oxford University Press, 1992.

Ivanova, Iu. "I na Rusi byli Amazonki" [There were Amazons in Russia, too]. *Armiia* 5 (1992): 44–49.

———. "Zhenshchiny v istorii Rossiiskoi Armii" [Women in the history of the Russian army]. *Voenno-istoricheskii zhurnal* 3 (1992): 86–89.

———. "Prekrasneishie iz khrabrykh" [The fairest of the brave]. *Voenno-istoricheskii zhurnal* 3 (1994): 93–96.

Izraeli, Dafna N. "Gendering Military Service in the Israel Defence Forces." *A Soldier and a Woman: Sexual Integration in the Military*. Ed. Gerard J. DeGroot and Corinna Peniston-Bird. New York: Pearson Education, 2000. 256–274.

Izzard, Molly. *A Heroine in Her Time: A Life of Dame Helen Gwynne-Vaughan, 1879–1967*. London: Macmillan, 1969.

Jaiven, Ana Lau, and Carmen Ramos Escandon. *Mujeres y revolución, 1910–1917*. Mexico City: Instituto nacional de Estudios Históricos de la Revolución Mexicana, 1993.

James, Edward. *The Origins of France: From Clovis to the Capetians, 500–1000*. New Studies in Medieval History. London: MacMillan, 1982.

James, Edward T., Janet Wilson James, and Paul S. Boyer, eds. *Notable American Women 1607–1950: A Biographical Dictionary*. Cambridge, MA: Harvard University Press, 1971.

Jancar, Barbara. "Yugoslavia: War of Resistance." *Female Soldiers—Combatants or Noncombatants? Historical and Contemporary Perspectives*. Ed. Nancy Loring Goldman. Westport, CT: Greenwood Press, 1982. 85–105.

Jancar-Webster, Barbara. *Women and Revolution in Yugoslavia, 1941–1945*. Denver: Arden Press, 1990.

Janda, Lance. " 'A Simple Matter of Equality': The Admission of Women to West Point." *A Soldier and a Woman: Sexual Integration in the Military*. Ed. Gerard J. DeGroot and Corinna Peniston-Bird. New York: Pearson Education, 2000. 305–319.

Jesch, Judith. *Women in the Viking Age*. Woodbridge: Boydell Press, 1991.

Jirásek, Alois. *Old Czech Legends*. Trans. Marie K. Holecek. London: Forest Books, 1992.

Johannsen, Robert W. *To the Halls of the Montezumas: The Mexican War in the American Imagination*. New York: Oxford University Press, 1985.

Johnson, Jesse. *Black Women in the Armed Forces, 1942–1974*. New York: Hampton J. Johnson, 1974.

Johnson, Louanne. *Making Waves*. New York: St. Martin's, 1986.

Johnson, Martin Phillip. "Citizenship and Gender: The Légion des Fédérées in the Paris Communie of 1871." *French History* 8.3 (1994): 276–295.

Johnson, Richard. "The Role of Women in the Russian Civil War (1917–1921)." *Conflict* 2.2 (1980): 201–217.

Johnson, Stephen P.L. *A Kriegie's Log*. Tunbridge Wells: Parapress, 1995.

Johnstone, H. "Isabella, the She-Wolf of France." *History* 21 (1936): 208–218.

Jones, A.H.M., J.R. Martindale, and J. Morris. *The Prosopography of the Later Roman Empire*. Cambridge: Cambridge University Press, 1971.

Jones, Gwyn. *A History of the Vikings*. Oxford: Oxford University Press, 1984.

Jones, Michael. *Ducal Brittany, 1364–1399*. Oxford: Oxford University Press, 1970.

———. "The Breton Civil War." *Froissart: Historian*. Ed. J.J.N. Palmer. Woodbridge: Boydell and Brewer, 1981. 64–81, 169–72.

———. *The Creation of Brittany: A Late Medieval State*. London: Hambledon, 1988.

———. *Recueil des actes de Charles de Blois et Jeanne de Penthièvre, duc et duchesse de Bretagne*. Rennes: Presses Universitaires de Rennes, 1996.

Kamath, K.V., and V.B. Kher. *Devi Ahalyabai Holkar: The Philosopher Queen*. Bombay: Bharatiya Vidya Bhavan, 1995.

Kaminski, Theresa. *Prisoners in Paradise: American Women in the Wartime South Pacific*. Lawrence: University Press of Kansas, 2000.

"Kanehira." *Twenty Plays of the No Theatre*. Ed. Donald Keene. New York: Columbia University Press, 1970. 265–280.

Karski, Jan. *Story of a Secret State*. Boston: Houghton Mifflin, 1944.

Kates, Gary. *Monsieur d'Eon Is a Woman*. New York: Basic Books, 1995.

———. "The Transgendered World of the Chevalier/Chevaliere d' Eon." *Journal of Modern History* 67.3 (1995): 558–595.

Katz, Doris. *The Lady Was a Terrorist, during Israel's War of Liberation*. New York: Shiloni Publishers, 1953.

Katz, Samuel. "Heyl Nashim: The Israel Defence Forces Women's Corps, 1948–1988." *Military Illustrated: Past and Present* April/May (1988): 8–15.

Kazarinova, M.A., N.F. Kravtsova, and A.A. Poliantseva, eds. *V nebe frontovom: sbornik vospominanii sovetskikh letchits-uchastnits Velikoi Otechestvennoi voiny* [In the Sky Above the Front: A Collection of Memoirs of Soviet Women Pilots/Who Participated in the Great Patriotic War]. 1st ed. Moscow: Molodaia Gvardiia, 1962.

———. *V nebe frontovom: sbornik vospominanii sovetskikh letchits-uchastnits Velikoi Otechestvennoi voiny*. 2nd ed. Moscow: Molodaia Gvardiia, 1971.

Keene, Judith. " 'No More than Brothers and Sister': Women in Frontline Combat in the Spanish Civil War." *Modern Europe: Histories and Identities*. Ed. Peter Monteath and Frederic Zukerman. Adelaide: Australian Humanities Press, 1998. 121–132.

Keil, Sally van Wagenen. "Those Magnificent Women in Their Flying Machines." *Viva* May 1977: 44–47, 100–102.

———. *Those Wonderful Women in Their Flying Machines*. New York: Rawson, Wade, 1979.

Keith, Agnes Newton. *Three Came Home*. Boston: Little, Brown, 1947.

Kelly, Amy. *Eleanor of Aquitaine and the Four Kings*. London: 1952.

Kendall, Paul Murray. *The Yorkist Age: Daily Life during the Wars of the Roses*. New York: Norton, 1962.

Kennett, Lee. *The French Armies in the Seven Years' War: A Study in Military Organization and Administration*. Durham, NC: Duke University Press, 1967.

Kenny, Catherine. *Captives: Australian Army Nurses in Japanese Prison Camps*. St. Lucia and New York: University of Queensland Press, 1986.

Kentner, Janet R. "The Socio-Political Role of Women in the Mexican Wars of Independence." Ph.D. dissertation, Loyola University, 1974.

Kerkhoff, Jacqueline, and Bob van den Boogert, eds. *Maria von Hongarije, 1505–1558*. Utrecht: Rijksmuseum het Catharijneconvent, 1993.

Khristinin, Iu. N. "Ne radi nagrad, no radi tokmo rodnogo narodu" [Seeking no reward, only to serve her country]. *Voenno-istoricheskii zhurnal* 1 (1994): 92–95.

Kibler, William W., ed. *Eleanor of Aquitaine: Patron and Politician*. Austin: University of Texas Press, 1976.

Kibler, William W., and Grover A. Zinns, eds. *Medieval France: An Encyclopedia*. New York: Garland, 1995.

Kincaid, C.A. *Lakshmibai, Rani of Jhansi, and Other Essays*. London: Kincaid, 1943.

King, Alison. *Golden Wings: The Story of Some of the Women Ferry Pilots of the Air Transport Auxiliary*. London: C. Arthur Pearson, 1956.

King, Margaret L. *Women of the Renaissance*. Chicago: University of Chicago Press, 1991.

King, Stella. *"Jacqueline": Pioneer Heroine of the Resistance*. London: Arms and Armour Press, 1989.

Kittle, Laurie L. "A Female Marine aboard the Constitution." *Marine Corps Gazette* February 1980: 53–56.

Klassen, John. "Women and Religious Reform in Late Medieval Bohemia." *Renaissance and Reformation* 5 (1981).

Klein, Yvonne, ed. *Beyond the Home Front: Women's Autobiographical Writing of the Two World Wars*. New York: New York University Press, 1997.

Kleinbaum, Abby Wettan. *The War against the Amazons*. New York: New Press, 1983.

Kolárová-Císarová. *Zena v hnutí husitském* [Woman in the Hussite movement]. Praha-Nusle: Nákladem "Sokolice," 1915.

Kolomiets, T.K. "Chapaevtsy stoiali na smert" [Soldiers of the Chapaev Division Stood to the Death]. *U chernomorskikh tverdyn*. Moscow: Voenizdat, 1967. 216–217.

Kordatos, Yannis. *History of Greece, 2500 BC–1924 AD*. Athens, Greece: 20th Century Publications, 1956.

Kotelenets, A.I., ed. *Zhenshchiny Strany Sovetov: Kratkii istoricheskii ocherk* [Women of the Soviet Land: Short historical essay]. Moscow: Politizdat, 1977.

Krivich, G.D. *Zhenshchiny-snaipery Leningrada* [Women Snipers of Leningrad]. Leningrad: Znanie, 1966.

Kurz, Rudolph Friederic. *Journals of Rudolph Friederic Kurz*. 1937. Smithsonian Institution, Bureau of American Ethnology, Bulletin 115.

La Bédollière, Emile de. *Beautés des victoires et conquêtes des français: Fastes militaires de la France depuis 1792 jusqu'en 1815*. Paris: Georges, 1839.

La Guette, Madame de. *Mémoires*. Editions avec introduction et notes par Célestin Moreau. Paris: Jannet, 1856.

Labarge, Margaret Wade. *A Small Sound of the Trumpet*. Boston: Beacon Press, 1986.

Lacocque, André. *The Feminine Unconventional: Four Subversive Figures in Israel's Tradition*. Minneapolis: Fortress Press, 1990.

Ladewig, Nicole F. "Between Worlds: Algerian Women in Conflict." *A Soldier and a Woman: Sexual Integration in the Military*. Ed. Gerard J. DeGroot and Corinna Peniston-Bird. New York: Pearson Education, 2000. 240–251.

Laffin, John. *Women in Battle*. New York: Abelard-Schuman, 1967.

Lalanne, Ludovic, ed. *Dictionnaire historique de la France*. 2nd ed. New York: Burt Franklin, 1877.

Lan, D. *Guns and Rain: Guerrillas and Spirit Mediums in Zimbabwe*. London: James Currey, 1985.

Landes, Ruth. *The Mystic Lake Sioux: Sociology of the Mdewakantonwan Santee*. Madison: University of Wisconsin Press, 1968.

Landis, John B. "Investigation into American Tradition of [the] Woman Known as Molly Pitcher." *Journal of American History* 5 (1911): 80–96.

Lang, David Marshall. *The Georgians*. London: Thames and Hudson, 1966.

Lannon, Frances. "Women and Images of Woman in the Spanish Civil War." *Transactions of the Royal Historical Society* Series 6. Vol. 41 (1991): 213–228.

Lapchick, Richard Edward, and Stephanie Urdang. *Oppression and Resistance: The Struggle of Women in Southern Africa*. Contributions in Women's Studies, no. 29. Westport, CT: Greenwood Press, 1982.

Laqueur, Thomas. *Making Sex: Body and Gender from the Greeks to Freud*. Cambridge, MA: Harvard University Press, 1990.

Larimer, Sarah L. (Mrs.). *The Capture and Escape; or, Life among the Sioux*. Philadelphia: Claxton, Ramsen, and Haffelfinger, 1870.

Larson, C. Kay. "Bonny Yank and Ginny Reb." *Minerva: Quarterly Report on Women and the Military* 8.1 (1990): 33–48.

———. "Bonny Yank and Ginny Reb Revisited." Minerva: Quarterly Report on Women and the Military 10.2 (1992): 35–61.

———. *'Til I Come Marching Home: A Brief History of American Women in World War II*. Pasadena, MD: Minerva Center, 1995.

Laska, Vera. *Women in the Resistance and in the Holocaust: The Voices of Eyewitnesses*. Westport, CT: Greenwood Press, 1983.

Laurence of Březová. "Laurence of Březová's Hussite Chronicle." *Fontes rerum Bohemicarum*. Vol. 5. Ed. Jaroslav Goll. Prague: Nadání F. Palackého, 1873.

Lavrinenkov, Vladimir Dmitrievich. *Vozvrashchenie v nebo* (Return to the sky). 2nd ed. Moscow: Voenizdat, 1983.

Law, Robin. "The 'Amazons' of Dahomey." *Paideuma* 39 (1993): 245–260.

Le Moël, Michel. *La Grande Mademoiselle*. Paris: Éditions de Fallois, 1994.

Lebedev, Z. "Znak osobogo otlichiia" [An award of special distinction]. *Voenno-istoricheskii zhurnal* 10 (1979): 84–87.

Lebra-Chapman, Joyce. *The Rani of Jhansi: A Study in Female Heroism in India*. Honolulu: University of Hawaii Press, 1986.

Leduc, Saint-Germain, ed. *Les campagnes de Mlle Thérèse Figueur, aujourd'hui Madame veuve Sutter*. Paris: Dauvin et Fontaine, 1842.

Lehmann, A. *Le rôle de la femme dans l'histoire de France au Moyen Age*. Paris: 1952.

Lentin, Ronit, ed. *Gender and Catastrophe*. New York: Zed Books, 1997.

León, Nicolás. *Aventuras de la Monja Alférez*. Mexico, DF: Complejo Editorial Mexicano, 1973.

Leonard, Elizabeth D. *Yankee Women: Gender Battles in the Civil War*. New York: Norton, 1994.

———. *All the Daring of the Soldier: Women of the Civil War Armies*. New York: Norton, 1999.

Leonard, Patrick J. "Ann Bailey: Mystery Woman of 1777." *Minerva: Quarterly Report on Women and the Military* 11.3–4 (1993): 1–4.

Levchenko, Irina. *V gody Velikoi voiny: frontovye zapiski* [During the Great War: Frontline notes]. 2nd ed. Moscow: Voenizdat, 1955.

———. *Povest' o voennykh godakh* [The story of the war years]. 2nd ed. Moscow: Moskovskii rabochii, 1965.

Levkovich, M.O., ed. *Bez nikh my ne pobedili by* [Without them victory would not have been possible]. Moscow: Politizdat, 1975.

Lewis, Archibald R. *The Development of Southern French and Catalan Society, 718–1050*. Austin: University of Texas Press, 1965.

Lewis, Thomas Taylor, ed. *Letters of the Lady Brilliana Harley*. Camden Society Publications, 1st ser., vol. 58. London: Camden Society, 1854.

Li Yanshou. *Bei shi* [The history of the Northern dynasties (386–581)]. Beijing: Zhonghua shuju, 1974.

Liber Pluscardensis. The Historians of Scotland. Edinburgh: Edmonston and Douglas, 1876.

"Lincoln's Russian General." *Illinois State Historical Society Journal* (1959): 106.

Linderman, Frank B. *Pretty Shield, Medicine Woman of the Crows*. New York: John Day Company, 1972.

Litoff, Judy Barrett, and David C. Smith, eds. *American Women in a World at War: Contemporary Accounts from World War II*. Wilmington, DE: SR Books, 1996.

———, eds. *We're in This War, Too: World War II Letters from American Women in Uniform*. New York: Oxford University Press, 1994.

Litvinova, Larisa Nikolaevna. *Letiat skvoz' gody* [They fly through the years]. Moscow: Voenizdat, 1983.

Liu Xu. *Jiu Tang shu* [The old history of the Tang dynasty (618–907)]. Beijing: Zhonghua shuju, 1975.

Livermore, Mary A. *My Story of the War: A Woman's Narrative of Four Years Personal Experience in the Union Army*. Hartford, CT: Worthington, 1888.

Loades, David. *Mary Tudor*. Oxford: Blackwell, 1989.

Lomax, Judy. *Hanna Reitsch: Flying for the Fatherland*. London: John Murray, 1988.

Lossing, Benson. *Harper's Encyclopaedia of United States History*. Vol. 6. New York: Harper's, 1901.

Low, Mary. *Red Spanish Notebook: The First Six Months of the Revolution and the Civil War*. London: Martin Secker and Warburg, 1937.

Lynn, John A. *The Bayonets of the Republic: Motivation and Tactics in the Army of Revolutionary France, 1791–94*. Urbana: University of Illinois Press, 1984.

———. "The Strange Case of the Maiden Soldier of Picardy." *MHQ: The Quarterly Journal of Military History* 2.3 (1990): 54–56.

———. *Giant of the Grand Siècle: The French Army, 1610–1715*. Cambridge: Cambridge University Press, 1997.

Lynn, Mary C., and Kay Arthur. *Three Years behind the Mast: The Story of the United States Coast Guard SPARs*. Washington, DC: U.S. Naval Office, 1946.

Lyons, T., and D. Moore. *Written in the Revolutions: (Mis)Representations, the Politics of Gender, and the Zimbabwean National Liberation War*. African Studies Association of Australasia and the Pacific, Annual Conference Proceedings. 1995.

MacCaffrey, Wallace. *Elizabeth I: War and Politics, 1588–1603*. Princeton: Princeton University Press, 1992.

Macchiavelli, Niccolò. *The Discourses of Niccolò Macchiavelli*. Trans. Leslie J. Walker. Vol. 1. London: Routledge & Kegan Paul, 1975. 2 vols.

———. *The Prince and Other Works*. Trans. Allan H. Gilbert. New York: Hendricks House, 1964.

Macdonald, Sharon. "Boadicea: Warrior, Mother and Myth." *Images of Women in Peace and War*. Ed. Sharon Macdonald, Pat Holden, and Shirley Ardener. London: Macmillan, 1987. 40–61.

Macías, Anna. *Against All Odds: The Feminist Movement in Mexico to 1940*. Westport, CT: Greenwood Press, 1982.

Mackenzie, Mary L. *Dame Christian Colet: Her Life and Family*. Cambridge: Cambridge University Press, 1923.

Macurdy, Grace Harriet. *Hellenistic Queens: A Study of Woman-Power in Macedonia, Seleucid Syria, and Ptolemaic Egypt*. Westport, CT: Greenwood Press, 1975.

Maddicott, J.R. *Thomas of Lancaster, 1307–22: A Study in the Reign of Edward II*. London: Oxford University Press, 1970.

Mahasveta, Debi, Mandira Sengupta, and Sagaree Sengupta. *The Queen of Jhansi*. Calcutta: Seagull Books, 2000.

Mainzer, Ferdinand. *Caesar's Mantle: The End of the Roman Republic*. Trans. Eden Paul and Cedar Paul. New York: Viking, 1936.

Major, Albany F. *Early Wars of Wessex*. Cambridge: Cambridge University Press, 1913.

Malone, Henry T. *Cherokees of the Old South*. Athens: 1956.

Mangini, Shirley. *Memories of Resistance: Women's Voices from the Spanish Civil War*. New Haven: Yale University Press, 1995.

Mann, Herman. *The Female Review: Life of Deborah Sampson, the Female Soldier in the War of Revolution*. Reprint of 1866 ed. New York: Arno, 1972.

Mant, Joan. *All Muck, No Medals: Land Girls by Land Girls*. Sussex: Book Guild, 1994.

Marcellin, Berthelot. *La Grande encyclopédie*. Vol. 19. Paris: Lamirault, n.d.

Markova, Galina I. "Youth under Fire: The Story of Klavdiya Fomicheva, a Woman Dive Bomber Pilot." *Soviet Airwomen in Combat in World War II*. Ed. K.J. Cottam. Manhattan, KS: Sunflower, 1983.

Marks, Claude. *Pilgrims, Heretics, and Lovers: A Medieval Journey*. New York: Macmillan, 1975.

Marshall, Rosalind K. *Virgins and Viragos: A History of Women in Scotland from 1080 to 1980*. Chicago: Academy Chicago, 1983.

Martin, D., and P. Johnson. *The Struggle for Zimbabwe: The Chimurenga War*. London: Faber and Faber, 1981.

Martin, Jean-Clément. *La Vendée et la France*. Paris: Seuil, 1987.

Martinsen, Jan. "Canada's First Women Fighter Pilots." *Airforce (Canada)* 13.3 (1989): 2.

———. "Through Adversity to the Stars." *Sentinel (Canada)* 30.2 (1994): 15.

Marx, Walter J. "Women Pilots in the Air Transport Command (Revised)." Historical Branch, Intelligence and Security Division, Headquarters, Air Transport Command. Air Force Historical Research Agency, Maxwell AFB, Alabama, AFHRA 300.0721-1. 1945.

Massare de Kostianovsky, Olinda. *La mujer paraguaya: Su participación en la Guerra Grande*. Asunción: Tallares Gráficos de la Escuela Salesiano, 1970.

Massey, Mary E. *Bonnet Brigades*. New York: Knopf, 1966.

Massey, Mary Elizabeth. *Women in the Civil War*. Lincoln: University of Nebraska Press, 1994.

Mathes, Valerie Sherer. "Native American Women in Medicine and the Military." *Journal of the West* 21.2 (1982): 41–48.

Matilde, Elke Goez, and Werner Goez. *Die Urkunden und Briefe der Markgrèafin Mathilde von Tuszien*. Hannover: Hahnsche Buchhandlung, 1998.

Mattingly, Garrett. *Catherine of Aragon*. Boston: Little Brown, 1941.

May, Steven W. "Recent Studies in Elizabeth I." *English Literary Renaissance* 23.2 (1993): 345–354.

Mayer, Holly A. *Belonging to the Army: Camp Followers and Community during the American Revolution*. Columbia: University of South Carolina Press, 1996.

McCullough, Helen Craig. *The Tale of the Heike*. Stanford: Stanford University Press, 1988.

McElligott, Mary Ellen. "A Monotony Full of Sadness: The Diary of Nadine Turchin." *Journal of the Illinois State Historical Society* 52 (1977): 27–89.

McKenzie, Ruth. *Laura Secord: The Legend and the Lady*. Toronto: McClelland and Stewart, 1972.

McKernan, M. *All In! Australia during the Second World War*. Melbourne: Thomas Nelson, 1983.

McKisack, M. *The Fourteenth Century, 1307–1399*. Oxford: Oxford University Press, 1959.

McLaughlin, Megan. "The Woman Warrior: Gender, Warfare, and Society in Medieval Europe." *Women's Studies* 17 (1990): 193–209.

McNamara, JoAnn, and Suzanne F. Wemple. "The Power of Women through the Family in Medieval Europe, 500–1100." *Clio's Consciousness Raised: New Perspectives on the History of Women.* Ed. Mary S. Hartman and Lois Banner. New York: Harper and Row, 1974. 103–118.

———. "Sanctity and Power: The Dual Pursuit of Medieval Women." *Becoming Visible: Women in European History.* Ed. Renate Bridenthal and Claudia Koonz. Boston: Houghton Mifflin, 1977. 90–118.

Medicine, Beatrice. " 'Warrior Women'—Sex Role Alternatives for Plains Indian Women." *The Hidden Half: Studies of Plains Indian Women.* Ed. Beatrice Medicine and Patricia Albers. Washington, DC: University Press of America, 1983. 267–280.

Medlicott, Alexander, Jr. "The Legend of Lucy Brewer: An Early American Novel." *New England Quarterly* 39 (1966): 465–467.

Meeker, Josephine. *The Ute Massacre! Brave Miss Meeker's Captivity! Her Own Account of It, Also the Narratives of Her Mother and Mrs. Price.* Philadelphia: n.p., 1879.

Meid, Pat. *Marine Corps Women's Reserve in World War II.* Washington, DC: Historical Branch, G-3 Division, HQ USMC, 1968.

Meir, Golda. *My Life.* London: Weidenfeld and Nicolson, 1975.

Mendieta Alatorre, Angeles. *La mujer en la Revolución Mexicana.* Mexico City: Talleres Graficos de la nacion, 1961.

Mernissi, Fatima, and Mary Jo Lakeland. *The Forgotten Queens of Islam.* Cambridge: Polity Press, 1993.

Merrim, Stephanie. "Catalina de Erauso: From Anomaly to Icon." *Coded Encounters.* Ed. Francisco Javier Ceballos-Candau. Amherst: University of Massachusetts Press, 1994. 177–205.

Merryman, Molly. *Clipped Wings: The Rise and Fall of the Women Airforce Service Pilots (WASPs) of World War II.* New York: New York University Press, 1998.

Meyer, Alfred G. "The Impact of World War I on Russian Women's Lives." *Russia's Women: Accommodation, Resistance, Transformation.* Ed. Barbara Evans Clements, Barbara Alpern Engel, and Christine D. Worobec. Berkeley: University California Press, 1991. 208–224.

Meyer, Eugene L. "The Soldier Left a Portrait and Her Eyewitness Account." *Smithsonian* 1995: 96–104.

Meyer, Leisa D. *Creating G.I. Jane: Sexuality and Power in the Women's Army Corps during World War II.* New York: Columbia University Press, 1996.

Meyer von Knonau, Gerold. *Jahrbücher des Deutschen Reichs unter Heinrich IV. und Heinrich V.* 7 vols. Leipzig: 1890–1907.

Michaud, Joseph. *Biographie universelle, ancienne et moderne.* Vol. 7. Paris: Michaud, 1813.

Michel, Louise, ed. *The Memoirs of Louise Michel: The Red Virgin.* University: University of Alabama Press, 1981.

Migunova, E.A. *Prodolzheniie podviga* [Continuation of an achievement]. Moscow: DOSAAF, 1976.

Mikora, V. "Zhenshchiny kavalery ordena Slavy" ["Women recipients of the Order of Glory"]. *Voyenno-istoricheskii zhurnal* 3 (1976): 51–56.

Milberry, Larry, ed. *Sixty Years: The RCAF and CF Air Command, 1924–1984.* Toronto: CANAV Books, 1984.

Miles, Rosalind. *The Women's History of the World.* Topsfield, MA.: Salem House, 1989.

Millar, F. *The Roman Near East, 31 BC–AD 337.* Cambridge, MA: Harvard University Press, 1993.

Minhaj-us-Siraj. *Tabaqat-i-Nasiri.* Tihran, Iran: Dunya-yi Kitab, 1984.

Minaeva, I.N., ed. *Srazhalas' za rodinu: Pisma i dokumenty geroin' Velikoi Otechestvennoi voiny* [She fought in battle for the motherland: Letters and documents of the heroines of the Great Patriotic War]. Moscow: Mysl', 1964.

Mitre, Bartolomé. *Historia De Belgrano*. Vol. 2. Buenos Aires: 1902.

Mitrofanova, A.V. *Rabochy klass SSSR v gody Velikoi Otechestvennoi voiny* [The working class of the USSR during the Great Patriotic War]. Moscow: Nauka, 1971.

Mizin, V.M. *Snaiper Petrova*. Leningrad: Lenizdat, 1988.

Montpensier, Mademoiselle de. *Mémoires*. Ed. Adolphe Chéruel. Vol. 4. Paris: Charpentier, 1858–1859.

Moolman, Valerie. *Women Aloft: The Epic of Flight*. Epic of Flight. Alexandria, VA: Time-Life Books, 1981.

Moore, Brenda L. "African-American Women in the US Military." *Armed Forces & Society* 17.3 (1991): 363–384.

———. "Black, Female and in Uniform: An African-American Woman in the United States Army 1973–1979." *Minerva: Quarterly Report on Women and the Military* 8.2 (1990): 62–66.

———. *To Serve My Country, to Serve My Race: The Story of the Only African American WACs Stationed Overseas during World War II*. New York: New York University Press, 1996.

Moore, Frank. *Women of the War: Their Heroism and Self-Sacrifice*. Hartford, CT: S.S. Scranton & Co., 1866.

Morden, Bettie J. *The Women's Army Corps, 1945–1978*. Washington, DC: GPO, 1990.

Murmantseva, Vera Semenova. *Zhenshchiny v soldatskikh shineliakh* [Women in soldiers' overcoats]. Moscow: Voenizdat, 1971.

———. *Sovetskie zhenshchiny v Velikoi Otechestvennoi voine, 1941–1945* [Soviet women in the Great Patriotic War, 1941–1945]. Moscow: Mysl', 1974.

Murphy, Frances. *Desert, Bamboo, and Barbed Wire: The 1939–45 Story of a Special Detachment of Australian Army Nursing Sisters, Fondly Known as the "Angels in Grey", and Their Fate in War and Captivity*. Hornsby, N.S.W.: Ollif, 1983.

Nagrale, N.N. *Peshwa Maratha Relations and Malhar Rao Holkar*. Jaipur: Publication Scheme, 1989.

Nash, June. "The Aztecs and the Ideology of Male Dominance." *Signs: Journal of Women in Culture and Society* 4 (1978): 349–362.

Nash, Mary. "'Milicianas' and Homefront Heroines: Images of Women in Revolutionary Spain (1936–1939)." *History of European Ideas* 11 (1989): 235–244.

———. "Women in War: Milicianas and Armed Combat in Revolutionary Spain, 1936–1939." *International History Review* 15.2 (1993): 269–282.

———. *Defying Male Civilization: Women in the Spanish Civil War*. 1995.

Naumova, A.I. "Zhenshchina s barrikady." *Leningradki: Vospominanie, ocherki, dokumenty*. Leningrad: Lenizdat, 1968.

Neale, J.E. *Queen Elizabeth*. New York: Harcourt, Brace, 1934.

Nemirov, N.G., ed. *Kniga o geroiakh* [Book about heroes]. Vol. 2. Moscow: Voenizdat, 1963.

Neville, Cynthia J. "Widows of War: Edward I and the Women of Scotland during the War of Independence." *Wife and Widow in Medieval England*. Ed. Sue Sheridan Walker. Ann Arbor: University of Michigan Press, 1993.

Newark, Tim. *Women Warlords*. London: Blandford/Cassell Artillery House, 1989.

Newman, Debra L. "The Propaganda and the Truth: Black Women and World War II." *Minerva: Quarterly Report on Women and the Military* 4.4 (1986): 72–92.

Nguyen Thi Dinh. *No Other Road to Take: Memoir of Mrs. Nguyen Thi Dinh*. Trans. Mai Elliott. Ithaca, NY: Cornell University, 1976.

Nicholson, Helen. "Women on the Third Crusade." *Journal of Medieval History* 23.4 (1997): 335–349.

Nicholson, Ranald. *Edward III and the Scots*. Oxford: 1965.

Niethammer, Carolyn. *Daughters of the Earth: The Lives and Legends of American Indian Women.* New York: Collier, 1977.

Nikiforova, E., ed. *Rozhdennaia voinoi* [Destined for war]. Moscow: Molodaia gvardiia, 1985.

Noggle, Anne. *A Dance with Death: Soviet Airwomen in World War II.* College Station: Texas A&M University Press, 1994.

Norgate, Kate. *The Minority of Henry III.* London: Macmillan, 1912.

Norman, Elizabeth. *We Band of Angels: The Untold Story of American Nurses Trapped on Bataan by the Japanese.* New York: Random House, 1999.

Norwich, John Julius. *The Kingdom in the Sun, 1130–1194.* New York: Harper and Row, 1970.

———. *The Normans in the South, 1016–1130.* New York: Solitaire, 1981.

Odložilik, O. *The Hussite King.* New Brunswick, NJ: Rutgers University Press, 1965.

Odom, William E. *The Soviet Volunteers: Modernization and Bureaucracy in a Public Mass Organization.* Princeton: Princeton University Press, 1973.

O'Donnell, James H. *Southern Indians in the American Revolution.* Knoxville: University of Tennessee Press, 1973.

O'Donnell, Pacho. *Juana Azurduy, La Teniente Coronela.* Buenos Aires: Planeta, 1994.

Ofer, Dalia, and Lenore J. Weitzman. *Women in the Holocaust.* New Haven, CT: Yale University Press, 1998.

Ol'khovskaia, Galina. "Otvazhnaia eskadril'ia." *V nebe frontovom.* Ed. M.A. Kazarinova, N.F. Kravtsova, and A.A. Poliantseva. 2nd ed. Moscow: Molodaia gvardiia, 1971. 37–43.

Olmstead, A.T. *History of Assyria.* Chicago: University of Chicago Press, 1923.

Orderic Vitalis. *The Ecclesiastical History of Orderic Vitalis.* Trans. Thomas Forester. London: Henry G. Bohn, 1854.

Ortalli, Gherardo. "Ezzelino: Genesi e sviluppi di un mito." *Nuovi studi ezzeliniani.* Ed. Giorgio Cracco. Vol. 2. Rome: Istituto Storico Italiano per il Medio Evo, 1992.

Ou-yang Xiu. *Tang shu* [The history of the Tang dynasty (618–907)]. Beijing: Zhonghua shuju, 1975.

Ou-yang Xiu. *Xin Tang shu* [The new history of the Tang Dynasty (618–907)]. Beijing: Zhonghua shuju, 1975.

Owen, D.D.R. *Eleanor of Aquitaine.* Oxford: Blackwell, 1993.

Page, W., ed. *Victoria County History, Kent.* Vol. 3. London: St. Catherine's Press, 1908–1932.

Painter, Sidney. *French Chivalry: Chivalric Ideas and Practices in Mediaeval France.* Ithaca: Great Seal, 1957.

Paparrigopoulos, Konstantinos. *History of the Greek Nation.* Updated 7th ed. Athens, Greece: Seferlis Publications, 1955.

Parker, Geoffrey. *The Military Revolution: Military Innovation and the Rise of the West, 1500–1800.* Cambridge: Cambridge University Press, 1988.

———, ed. *The Thirty Years' War.* New York: Routledge, 1987.

Parker, S. Thomas. *Romans and Saracens: A History of the Arabian Frontier.* Winona Lake, IN: American Schools of Oriental Research, 1986.

Parks, Annette. "Prisoners of Love: Medieval Wives as Hostages." *Journal of the GAH* 16 (1996): 61–83.

Pausanias. *Description of Greece.* Trans. W.H.S. Jones. Vol. 1. Cambridge, MA: Harvard University Press, 1918.

Pavlichenko, Liudmila Mikhailovna. *Geroicheskaia byl: Oborona Sevastopolia, 1941–1942 gg.* [A heroic true story: The defense of Sevastopol, 1941–1942]. Moscow: Politizdat, 1960.

———. "I Was a Sniper." *The Road of Battle and Glory*. Ed. I.M. Danishevskii and trans. David Skvirsky. Moscow: Politizdat, 1977.

Pennington, Reina. "Offensive Women: Women in Combat in the Red Army." *Time to Kill: The Soldier's Experience of War in the West, 1939–1945*. Ed. Paul Addison and Angus Calder. London: Pimlico Press, 1997. 249–262.

———. " 'Do not speak of the services you rendered': Women Veterans of Aviation in the Soviet Union." *A Soldier and a Woman: Sexual Integration in the Military*. Ed. Gerard J. DeGroot and Corinna Peniston-Bird. New York: Pearson Education, 2000. 152–174.

———. "Stalin's Falcons: The 586th Fighter Aviation Regiment." *MINERVA: Quarterly Report on Women and the Military* XVIII.3–4 (2000): 76–108.

———. "Women and Military Aviation in the Second World War: A Comparative Study of the USA and USSR, 1941–1945." Ph.D. dissertation, University of South Carolina, 2000.

———. *Wings, Women, and War: Soviet Airwomen in World War II Combat*. Lawrence: University Press of Kansas, 2001.

Perez, Esther R., James Kallas, and Nina Kallas. *Those Years of the Revolution, 1910–1920: Authentic Bilingual Life Experiences as Told by Veterans of the War*. San Jose: Aztlan Today, 1974.

Pernoud, Régine. *Joan of Arc by Herself and Her Witnesses*. New York: Stein and Day, 1966.

Pernoud, Régine, and Marie-Veronique Clin. *Joan of Arc: Her Story*. 1st ed. New York: St. Martin's Press, 1998.

Peters, Edward, ed. *The First Crusade: The Chronicle of Fulcher of Chartres and Other Source Materials*. 2nd ed. Philadelphia: University of Pennsylvania Press, 1998.

Petersen, Karen, and J.J. Wilson. *Women Artists: Recognition and Reappraisal from the Early Middle Ages to the Twentieth Century*. New York: New York University Press, 1976.

Petrarca, Francesco. *Rerum familiarium libri I–VIII*. Trans. Aldo S. Bernardo. Albany: State University of New York Press, 1975.

Pierce, Grace M. "Three American Women Pensioned for Military Service." *Daughters of the American Revolution Magazine* September 1975: 140–145; October: 222–228.

Pile, Sir Frederick. *Ack-Ack*. London: Harrap, 1949.

Pillorget, René, and Suzanne Pillorget. *France baroque, France classique*. Vol. 2, *Dictionnaire*. Paris: Robert Laffont, 1995.

Piszkiewicz, Dennis. *From Nazi Test Pilot to Hitler's Bunker: The Fantastic Flights of Hanna Reitsch*. Westport, CT: Praeger, 1997.

Pizzagalli, Daniela. *Tra due dinastie: Bianca Maria Visconti e il ducato di Milano*. Milan: Camunia, 1988.

Plutarch. *Plutarch's Lives in Eleven Volumes*. Trans. Bernadotte Perrin. Cambridge, MA: Harvard University Press; W. Heinemann, 1967.

———. *Moralia*. Trans. Frank Cole Babbit. Cambridge, MA: Harvard University Press, 1983.

Polivanov, A.N. "Voiteli iz roda Polivanovykh" [Warriors of the Polivanov family]. *Voenno-istoricheskii zhurnal* 1–2 (1994): 60–69; 2 (1994) 57–64.

Pollard, A.J. *The Wars of the Roses*. London: Macmillan, 1988.

Pollock, Frederick, and Frederic William Maitland. *The History of English Law before the Time of Edward I*. 2nd ed. Vol. 1. Cambridge: Cambridge University Press, 1968.

Polverari, Michele. *Ancona e Bisanzio*. Ancona: Comune di Ancona, Assessorato ai Beni e Attività Culturali, 1992.

Polyaenus. *Polyaeni Strategematon libri VIII*.

Polybius. *The Histories*. Newly translated by Mortimer Chambers; revised and abridged with an introduction by E. Badian. New York: Twayne, 1966.

Poniatowska, Elena. *Hasta no verte Jesús mio*. Mexico City: Ediciones Era, 1969.

Ponomarenko, P.K. *Vsenarodnaia bor'ba v tylu nemetsko-fashistskikh zakhvatchikov, 1941–1944* (The all-popular struggle in the rear of the German-Fascist invaders). Moscow: Nauka, 1986.

Popham, Hugh. *FANY: The Story of the Women's Transport Service, 1907–1984*. London: Leo Cooper, 1984.

Postan, M.M., ed. *Medieval Women*. London: Weidenfeld and Nicolson, 1975.

Potter-MacKinnon, Janice. *While the Women Only Wept: Loyalist Refugee Women in Eastern Ontario*. Montreal: McGill-Queens University Press, 1993.

Potthast-Jutkeit, Barbara. *Paradies Mohammeds oder Land der Frauen? Zur Rolle von Frau und Familie in Paraguay im 19. Jahrhundert*. Köln: Böhlau Verlag, 1994.

Powell, Father Peter John. *People of the Sacred Mountain: A History of the Northern Cheyenne Chiefs and Warrior Societies, 1830–1879, with an Epilogue, 1969–1974*. 2 vols. San Francisco: Harper and Row, 1981.

Powicke, Sir Maurice. *The Thirteenth Century*. 2nd ed. Oxford: Oxford University Press, 1991.

Poynter, Lida. "Dr. Mary Walker, M.D.: Pioneer Woman Physician." *Medical Woman's Journal* (1946): 43–51.

Prentice, Alison, Paula Bourne, Gail Cuthbert Brandt, Beth Light, Wendy Mitchinson, and Naomi Black. *Canadian Women: A History*. Toronto: Harcourt Brace Jovanovich, 1988.

Prescott, H.F.M. *Mary Tudor*. New York: Macmillan, 1962.

Pushkareva, Natalia. *Women in Russian History: From the Tenth to the Twentieth Century*. Armonk, NY: M.E. Sharpe, 1997.

Putney, Martha S. *When the Nation Was in Need: Blacks in the Women's Army Corps during World War II*. Metuchen, NJ: Scarecrow, 1992.

Qin Liangyu shi yanjiu bianji weiyuanhui, ed. *Qin Liangyu shiliao jicheng* [Collection of Historical Materials on Qin Liangyu]. Chengdu, China: Sichuan daxue chubanshe, 1987.

Qunta, Christine, ed. *Women in Southern Africa*. London: Allison and Busby, 1987.

Rabb, Theodore K. "Artemisia Gentileschi: Judith and Holofernes." *MHQ: The Quarterly Journal of Military History* 10.1 (1997): 82–85.

Rachewiltz, Igor de, ed. *In the Service of the Khan: Eminent Personalities of the Early Mongol-Yüan Period (1200–1300)*. Wiesbaden: Harrassowitz, 1993.

Radner, Joan Newlon, ed. *Fragmentary Annals of Ireland*. Dublin: Dublin Institute for Advanced Studies, 1978.

Ranger, T. *Revolt in Southern Rhodesia, 1896–7: A Study in African Resistance*. London: Heinemann, 1967.

———. *Peasant Consciousness and Guerrilla War in Zimbabwe: A Comparative Study*. London: James Currey, 1985.

Rappoport, S. *History of Egypt from 330 B.C. to the Present Time*. Vol. 10. London: Grolier, 1904.

Raskova, Marina. *Zapiski shturmana* [Notes of a navigator]. Moscow: DOSAAF, 1976.

Rawicz, Slavomir. *The Long Walk: A Gamble for Life*. New York: Harper, 1956.

Reed, Mary E. "The Anti-Fascist Front of Women and the Communist Party in Croatia: Conflicts within the Resistance." *Women in Eastern Europe and the Soviet Union*. Ed. Tova Yedlin. New York: Praeger, 1980. 128–139.

Reed, T. Dayrell. *The Rise of Wessex*. London: Methuen, 1947.

Rees, John. " 'The Multitude of Women': An Examination of the Numbers of Female Camp Followers with the Continental Army, Part 1." *Brigade Dispatch* 23.4 (1992):

5–17; " 'The Multitude of Women': An Examination of the Numbers of Female Camp Followers with the Continental Army, Part 2." *Brigade Dispatch* 24.1 (1992): 6–16; " 'The Multitude of Women': An Examination of the Numbers of Female Camp Followers with the Continental Army, Part 3." *Brigade Dispatch* 24.2 (1993): 2–6.

Reinharz, Shulamit. "Toward a Model of Female Political Action: The Case of Manya Shochat, Founder of the First Kibbutz." *Women's Studies International Forum* 7.4 (1984): 275–287.

Reis Júnior, Pereira. *Maria Quitéria*. Rio de Janeiro: Imprensa Nacional, 1953.

Reisner, L.M. *Svyazhsk: An Epic of the Russian Civil War, 1918*. Trans. John G. Wright and Amy Jensen. Maradana: Hashim Press, 1948.

Reitsch, Hanna. *Flying Is My Life*. Trans. Lawrence Wilson. New York: Putnam, 1954 (also published as *The Sky My Kingdom*).

Render, Shirley. *No Place for a Lady: The Story of Canadian Women Pilots, 1928–1992*. Winnipeg: Portage and Main Press, 1992.

Reynolds, Henry. *Frontier: Aborigines, Settlers, and Land*. Sydney and Boston: Allen and Unwin, 1987.

Richard, Jules-Marie. "Les livres de Mahaut, comtesse d'Artois et de Bourgogne, 1302–29." *Revue des Questions Historiques* 40 (1886): 135–141.

———. *Une petit-nièce de Saint Louis: Mahaut, comtesse d'Artois et de Bourgogne*. 1887.

Richardson, H.G. "The Letters and Charters of Eleanor of Aquitaine." *English Historical Review* 74 (1974): 193–213.

Riché, Pierre. *The Carolingians: A Family Who Forged Europe*. Trans. Michael Idomir Allen. Philadelphia: University of Pennsylvania Press, 1993.

Richmond, I.A. "Queen Cartimandua." *Journal of Roman Studies* 44 (1954): 43–52.

Rigdon, Susan M. "Women in China's Changing Military Ethic." *A Soldier and a Woman: Sexual Integration in the Military*. Ed. Gerard J. DeGroot and Corinna Peniston-Bird. New York: Pearson Education, 2000. 275–293.

Robins, Gay. *Women in Ancient Egypt*. London: British Museum Publications, 1993.

Robinson, Helen Caister. *Mistress Molly, the Brown Lady*. Toronto and Charlottetown: Dundurn Press, 1980.

———. "Molly Brant: Mohawk Heroine." *Eleven Exiles: Accounts of Loyalists of the American Revolution*. Ed. Phyllis R. Blakely and John N. Grant. Toronto: Dundurn Press, 1982.

Rochejaquelein, Marie-Louise-Victoire, marquise de La. *Memoirs of the Marquise de La Rochejaquelein*. Trans. Cecil Biggane. London: George Routledge and Sons, 1933.

Rodney, Walter. "A Reconsideration of the Mane Invasions of Sierra Leone." *Journal of African History* 7 (1967): 219–246.

Roider, Karl A., ed. *Maria Theresa*. Great Lives Observed. Englewood Cliffs, NJ: Prentice-Hall, 1973.

Romain, Charles Armand (pseud. for Armand Charmain). *Les guerrières*. Paris: 1931.

Roman d'Amat, Charles. *Dictionnaire de biographie française*. Paris: Letouzey et Ané, 1959.

Romero Aceves, Ricardo. *La Mujer en la Historia de Mexico*. Mexico City: Costa-Amic, 1982.

Rossiter, Margaret. *Women in the Resistance*. New York: Praeger, 1986.

Roudinesco, Elisabeth. *Théroigne de Méricourt: A Melancholic Woman during the French Revolution*. Trans. Martin Thom. London: Verso, 1991.

Roux, Georges, ed. *Ancient Iraq*. 2nd ed. New York: Penguin, 1992.

Rudershausen, Jutta. "Taeglich fuenfzehn Sturzfluege—Zu Unrecht vergessen: Flugkapitaen Melitta Schiller-Stauffenberg war vor vierzig Jahren ein Pionier der Luftfahrt." *Die Zeit* 5 January 1973.

Runciman, Sir Stephen. *A History of the Crusades*. Vol. 3, *The Kingdom of Acre and the Later Crusades*. Cambridge: Cambridge University Press, 1954.

Rustad, Michael. *Women in Khaki: The American Enlisted Woman*. New York: Praeger, 1982.

Ryder, Alan. *Alfonso the Magnanimous*. Oxford: Clarendon Press, 1990.

Sackville-West, Vita. *The Women's Land Army*. London: Michael Joseph, 1944.

Salas, Elizabeth. *Soldaderas in the Mexican Military: Myth and History*. Austin: University of Texas Press, 1990.

———. "Soldaderas: New Questions, New Sources." *Women's Studies Quarterly* 23.3 and 4 (1995): 112–116.

Salem, Dorothy C. *African American Women: A Biographical Dictionary*. New York: Garland, 1993.

Salvatorelli, Luigi. *L'Italia comunale dal secolo XI alla metà del secolo XIV*. Milan: Mondadori, 1940.

Sams, Margaret, and Lynn Z. Bloom. *Forbidden Family: A Wartime Memoir of the Philippines, 1941–1945*. Madison: University of Wisconsin Press, 1989.

Samuelson, Nancy B. "The Fate Worse than Death: Women Captives of the Indian Wars." *Minerva: Quarterly Report on Women and the Military* 3.4 (1985): 117–137.

Sandes, Flora. *An English Woman-Sergeant in the Serbian Army*. London: Hodder and Stoughton, 1916.

———. *The Autobiography of a Woman Soldier: A Brief Record of Adventure with the Serbian Army, 1916–1919*. London: Witherby, 1927.

Saracini, Giuliano. *Notitie historiche della città d'Ancona . . .* Rome, 1675. Bologna: Forni, 1968.

Sarma, Hira Lal. *Ahilyabai*. New Delhi: National Book Trust of India, 1969.

Sartorti, Rosalinde. "On the Making of Heroes, Heroines, and Saints." *Culture and Entertainment in Wartime Russia*. Ed. Richard Stites. Bloomington: Indiana University Press, 1995.

Savi Lopez, Maria. *La donna italiana del trecento*. Napoli: Bideri, 1891.

Saxo Grammaticus. *The History of the Danes*. Trans. Peter Fisher. Suffolk: Brewer, 1979.

Saywell, Shelley. *Women in War*. Markham, Ontario: Viking, 1985.

Sbornik instruktsii Otdela TsKRKP Po Rabote Sredi Zhenshchin [Collection of instructions of the Office of the Central Committee of the Russian Communist Party for Work among Women]. St. Petersburg: Government Publishing House, 1920.

Scarisbrick, J.J. *Henry VIII*. London: Eyre and Spottiswoode, 1968.

Schama, Simon. *Citizens: A Chronicle of the French Revolution*. New York: Knopf, 1989.

Scharr, Adela Riek. *Sisters in the Sky*. Vol. 1, *The WAFS*. Gerald, MO: Patrice Press, 1986.

———. *Sisters in the Sky*. Vol. 1, *The WASP*. Gerald, MO: Patrice Press, 1986.

Schellstede, Sangmie Choi, and Soon Mi Yu. *Comfort Women Speak: Testimony by Sex Slaves of the Japanese Military (Includes New United Nations Human Rights Report)*. New York: Holmes and Meier, 2000.

Schiller, K. "Melitta Graefin Schenk von Stauffenberg, geb. Schiller (1903–1945)." *Schlesische Flieger Nachrichten* 6.5 (1988): 2–6.

Schmidt, Minna Moshcherosch. *400 Outstanding Women of the World and Costumology of Their Time*. Chicago: Schmidt, 1933.

Schmitz, Leonhard. *Ancient History*. New York: Peter Fenelon Collier, 1898.

Schneider, Carl J., and Dorothy Schneider. *Into the Breach: American Women Overseas in World War I*. New York: Viking, 1991.

Schulkind, Eugene. "Socialist Women during the 1871 Paris Commune." *Past and Present* 106 (1985): 124–163.

Schwartz, Paula. "Redefining Resistance: Women's Activism in Wartime France." *Be-

hind the Lines: Gender and the Two World Wars. Ed. Margaret Higonnet, Jane Jensen, Sonya Michel, and Margaret Weitz. New Haven, CT: Yale University Press, 1987. 141–153.

———. "*Partisanes* and Gender Politics in Vichy France." *French Historical Studies* 16 (1989): 126–150.

Schwertfeger, Ruth. *Women of Theresienstadt: Voices from a Concentration Camp*. New York: Berg, 1989.

Schwinn, Monika, and Bernhard Diehl. *We Came to Help*. Trans. Jan van Heurck. 1st ed. New York: Harcourt Brace Jovanovich, 1976.

Scott, Hamish M. "Verteidigung und Bewahrung: Österreich und die europäischen Mächte, 1740–1780." *Maria Theresia und ihre Zeit*. Ed. Walter Koschatzky. Salzburg: Residenz Verlag, 1980.

Seeley, Charlotte Palmer, ed. *American Women and the U.S. Armed Forces: A Guide to the Records of Military Agencies in the National Archives Relating to American Women*. Washington, DC: National Archives and Records Administration, 1992.

Segal, Mady Wechsler. "The Argument for Female Combatants." *Female Soldiers—Combatants or Noncombatants? Historical and Contemporary Perspectives*. Ed. Nancy Loring Goldman. Westport, CT: Greenwood Press, 1982. 267–290.

———. "Women in the Armed Forces." *Women and the Use of Military Force*. Ed. Ruth Howes and Michael Stevenson. Boulder, CO: Lynne Rienner, 1993. 81–93.

Seidler, Franz Wilhelm. *Blitzmädchen: Die Geschichte der Helferinnen der deutschen Wehrmacht im Zweiten Weltkrieg*. Bonn: Wehr und Wissen, 1979.

Senin, A.S. "Zhenskie batal'ony i voennye komandy v 1917 godu." *Voprosy Istorii* 10 (1987): 176–182.

Serruys, Henry A. "Two Remarkable Women in Mongolia: The Third Lady Erketü Qatun and Dayičing-beyiji." *Asia Major* 19 (1975): 191–245.

Shahar, Shulamith. *The Fourth Estate: A History of Women in the Middle Ages*. Trans. Chaya Galai. New York: Routledge, forthcoming.

Shamiakin, I.P., ed. *Navechno v serdtse narodnom* [Forever in people's hearts]. 3rd ed. Minsk: Belorusskaia Sovetskaia entsiklopediia, 1984.

Shaomin, Ke. "Xin Yuan shi." *Ershiwu shi*. Hong Kong: Wenxue yanjiushe, 1959.

Sharma, Mahendra Narain. *The Life and Times of Begam Samru of Sardhana, A.D. 1750–1836*. Sahibabad: Vibhu Prakashan, 1985.

Shattuck, H.R. "Anna Ella Carroll: The Originator of the Tennessee Campaign." *Outing* 6 (1885): 403–409.

Shattuck, Mary L.P. *The Story of Jewett's Bridge*. Ayer, MA: H.S. Turner, 1912.

Shell, Cheryl. "Making Sense of Vietnam and Telling the Real Story: Military Women in the_Combat Zone_." *Vietnam Generation* 1.3–4 (1989).

Shephard, A. *A Compendium of Australian Defence Statistics*. Canberra: Australian Defence Studies Centre, 1995.

Shirer, William. *End of a Berlin Diary*. New York: Alfred A. Knopf, 1947.

Shkadov, I.N., ed. *Geroi Sovetskogo Soiuza: Kratkii biograficheskii slovar* [Hero of the Soviet Union: A short biographical dictionary]. 2 vols. Vol. 2 (Liubov–Yashchuk). Moscow: Voenizdat, 1988.

Shneidman, J. Lee. *The Rise of the Aragonese-Catalan Empire, 1200–1350*. New York: New York University Press, 1970.

Shochat, Manya. "The Guarding of the Land." *Kovetz Hashomer*. Ed. Rachel Katznelson Shazar (Rubashow). Tel Aviv: Archion Ha'avodah, 1937. 51–56.

———. "My Path in Hashomer." *Sefer Hashomer*. Tel Aviv: Devir, 1957. 385–394.

———. "The Collective." *The Plough Woman: Memoirs of the Pioneer Women of Palestine*. Ed. Rachel Katznelson Shazar (Rubashow). New York: Herzl Press, 1975.

Shreeve, Nicholas. *Dark Legacy*. Crossbush, England: Bookwright, 1996.

Simons, Jessie Elizabeth. *In Japanese Hands: Australian Nurses as POWS*. Melbourne: W. Heinemann, 1985.

Sinitsyn, A.M. "Put' muzhestva i otvagi." *Geroi ognennykh let*. Ed. A.M. Sinitsyn, Moscow: Moskovskii rabochii, 1983. 704–710.

Slaughter, Jane. *Women and the Italian Resistance, 1943–45*. Denver, CO: Arden Press, 1997.

Slepyan, Kenneth D. "The Limits of Mobilisation: Party, State, and the 1927 Civil Defence Campaign." *Europe-Asia Studies* 45.5 (1993): 851–868.

———. " 'The People's Avengers': Soviet Partisans, Stalinist Society and the Politics of Resistance, 1941–1944." Ph.D. dissertation. University of Michigan, 1994.

Smirnov, P.P., and E.V. Chistiakova, eds. *Alena Arzamasskaia-Temnikovskaia*. Saransk: 1986.

Smirnova-Medvedeva, Z.M. *On the Road to Stalingrad: Memoirs of a Woman Machine Gunner*. Trans. Kazimiera J. Cottam. Nepean, Ontario: New Military Publishing, 1997.

Smyth, Sir John George. *The Rebellious Rani*. London: Muller, 1966.

Snaipery. [Snipers]. Moscow: Molodaia gvardiia, 1976.

Snyder, Charles McCool. "Political Strategist and Gadfly to President Fillmore." *Maryland Historical Magazine* 68 (1973): 36–63.

Snyder, Charles McCool. *Dr. Mary Walker: The Little Lady in Pants*. Women in America: From Colonial Times to the 20th Century. New York: Arno Press, 1974.

———, ed. *The Lady and the President: The Letters of Dorothea Dix and Millard Fillmore*. Lexington: University Press of Kentucky, 1975.

Snyder, Jane McIntosh. *The Woman and the Lyre: Women Writers in Classical Greece and Rome*. Carbondale: Southern Illinois University Press, 1989.

Soderbergh, Peter A. *Women Marines: The World War II Era*. Westport, CT: Praeger, 1992.

———. *Women Marines in the Korean War Era*. Westport, CT: Praeger, 1994.

Solterer, H. "Female Militancy in Medieval France." *Signs* (1991): 522–549.

Somerset, Anne. *Elizabeth I*. New York: St. Martin's Press, 1991.

Soto, Shirlene Ann. "The Mexican Woman: A Study of Her Participation in the Revolution, 1910–1940." Ph.D. dissertation, University of New Mexico, 1977.

Souza, Antonio Loureiro de. "Maria Quitéria." *Baianos ilustres, 1567–1925*. 3rd ed. Brasília: INL, 1979.

Spears, Sally. *Call Sign Revlon: The Life and Death of Navy Fighter Pilot Kara Hultgreen*. Annapolis: Naval Institute Press, 1998.

Spiegel, Allen D., and Andrea M. Spiegel. "Civil War Doctress Mary: Only Woman to Win Congressional Medal of Honor." *Minerva: Quarterly Report on Women and the Military* 12 (Fall 1994).

Stafford, Pauline. *Queens, Concubines, and Dowagers: The King's Wife in the Early Middle Ages*. Athens: University of Georgia Press, 1983.

———. *Unification and Conquest: A Political and Social History of England in the Tenth and Eleventh Centuries*. London: Arnold, 1989.

Stanley, Jo, ed. *Bold in Her Breeches: Women Pirates across the Ages*. San Francisco: Pandora, 1996.

Stark, Suzanne J. *Female Tars: Women aboard Ship in the Age of Sail*. Annapolis, MD: Naval Institute Press, 1996.

Staunton, Irene, ed. *Mothers of the Revolution: The War Experiences of Thirty Zimbabwean Women*. Bloomington: Indiana University Press, 1991.

Steindorff, Ernst. *Jahrbücher des Deutschen Reichs unter Heinrich III*. 2 vols. Leipzig: 1881.

Sten, Maria. *The Mexican Codices and Their Extraordinary History*. Mexico City: Editorial Joaquin Mortiz, 1972.

Stetz, Margaret D., and Bonnie B.C. Oh. *Legacies of the Comfort Women of World War II.* Armonk, NY: M.E. Sharpe, 2001.

Stickley, Julia Ward. "The Records of Deborah Sampson Gannett, Woman Soldier of the Revolution." *Prologue: The Journal of the National Archives* 4 (1972): 233–241.

Stiehm, Judith Hicks, ed. *It's Our Military, Too! Women and the U.S. Military.* Philadelphia: Temple University Press, 1996.

Stites, Richard. *The Women's Liberation Movement in Russia: Feminism, Nihilism, and Bolshevism, 1860–1930.* Princeton: Princeton University Press, 1978.

Stockel, H. Henrietta. *Women of the Apache Nation: Voices of Truth.* Reno: University of Nevada Press, 1991.

———. *Survival of the Spirit: Chiricahua Apaches in Captivity.* Reno: University of Nevada Press, 1993.

Stoff, Laurie. "They Fought for Russia: Female Soldiers of the First World War." *A Soldier and a Woman: Sexual Integration in the Military.* Ed. Gerard J. DeGroot and Corinna Peniston-Bird. New York: Pearson Education, 2000. 66–82.

Stoneman, Richard. *Palmyra and Its Empire: Zenobia's Revolt against Rome.* Ann Arbor: University of Michigan Press, 1994.

Stott, Leda. *Women and the Armed Struggle for Independence in Zimbabwe (1964–1979).* Edinburgh: Centre of African Studies, 1989.

Strabo. *Geography.* Trans. H.L. Jones. Cambridge, MA: Harvard University Press, 1966.

Streeter, Ruth Cheney. "History of the Marine Corps Women's Reserve: A Critical Analysis of Its Development and Operation, 1943–1945." 5 December 1945. Radcliffe College, Schlesinger Library.

———. "Oral History Transcript." n.d. Marine Corps Historical Center, Oral History Collection, interviews conducted with Mr. John T. Mason, Jr., in 1979.

Stremlow, Colonel Mary V. *A History of the Women Marines, 1946–1977.* Washington, DC: History and Museums Division, HQ USMC, 1986.

———. *Free a Marine to Fight: Women Marines in World War II.* Washington, DC: History and Museums Division, HQ USMC, 1994.

Sulimirski, Tadeusz. *The Sarmatians.* New York: Praeger, 1970.

Sumption, Jonathan. *The Albigensian Crusade.* London: Faber and Faber, 1978.

———. *The Hundred Years War: Trial by Battle.* London: Faber and Faber, 1990.

Sutin, Jack, Rochelle Sutin, and Lawrence Sutin. *Jack and Rochelle: A Holocaust Story of Love and Resistance.* Saint Paul, MN: Graywolf Press, 1995.

Swirski, Barbara, and Marilyn P. Safir, eds. *Calling the Equality Bluff: Women in Israel.* New York: Pergamon Press, 1991.

Tacitus. *The Annals.* Trans. Alfred John Church Brodribb and William Jackson. Chicago: Encyclopaedia Britannica's Great Books, 1952.

———. *The Agricola and the Germania.* Trans. S.A. Handford. London: Penguin, 1970.

Tallett, Frank. *War and Society in Early-Modern Europe, 1495–1715.* London: Routledge, 1992.

Tanner, J.R., C.W. Previté-Orton, and Z.N. Brooke, eds. *Contest of Empire and Papacy.* Vol. 5 of *The Cambridge Medieval History.* New York: Macmillan, 1926.

Tarble, Helen Mar. *The Story of My Capture and Escape during the Minnesota Indian Massacre of 1862.* St. Paul, MN: n.p., 1904.

Taylor, Keith. *The Birth of Vietnam.* Berkeley: University of California Press, 1983.

Taylor, Sandra C. *Vietnamese Women at War: Fighting for Ho Chi Minh and the Revolution.* Lawrence: University Press of Kansas, 1998.

Taylor, Susie King. *Reminiscences of My Life in Camp.* New York: Arno, 1968.

Terni de Gregorj, W[inifred]. *Bianca Maria Visconti, duchessa di Milano.* Bergamo: Istituto Italiano d'Arti Grafiche, 1940.

Terry, Roy. *Women in Khaki: The Story of the British Women Soldier, 1914–1988*. London: Columbia, 1988.

Tétreult, Mary Ann. "Women and Revolution in Vietnam." *Vietnam's Women in Transition*. Ed. Kathleen Barry. New York: St. Martin's Press, 1996: 38–53.

Thatcher, Margaret. *In Defence of Freedom: Speeches on Britain's Relations with the World, 1976–1986*. Buffalo: Prometheus Books, 1987.

———. *The Downing Street Years*. New York: HarperCollins, 1993.

Thomas, Edith. *The Women Incendiaries*. Trans. James Atkinson and Starr Atkinson. New York: George Braziller, 1966.

———. *Louise Michel*. Montreal: Black Rose Books, 1980.

Thomas, Patricia J. "Women in the Military: American and the British Commonwealth." *Armed Forces & Society* 4.4 (1978): 623–645.

Thompson, Kathleen. "Family and Influence to the South of Normandy in the Eleventh Century." *Journal of Medieval History* 11.3 (1985): 215–226.

Thomson, Joyce A. *The WAAAF in Wartime Australia*. Melbourne: Melbourne University Press, 1991.

Thomson, Robin J. *The Coast Guard and the Women's Reserve in World War II*. Washington: Coast Guard Historical Office, 1992.

Tilley, John A. *A History of Women in the Coast Guard*. Washington: U.S. Coast Guard, 1996.

Timofeeva-Egorova, Anna Aleksandrovna. *Derzhis', sestrenka!* [Hold on, Sisters!]. Moscow: Voenizdat, 1983.

Tone, John Lawrence. "Women in the Resistance to Napoleon." *Constructing Spanish Womanhood: Female Identity in Modern Spain*. Ed. Pamela Radcliff and Victoria Enders. Albany, NY: State University of New York Press, 1999.

Toreno, José María. *Historia del levantamiento, guerra, y revolución de España*. 3 vols. Paris: 1851.

Toropov, L.F., ed. *Geroini: Ocherki o zhenshchinakh—Geroiakh Sovetskogo Soiuza* [Heroines: Biographical sketches of women heroes of the Soviet Union]. Vol. 2. Moscow: Politizdat, 1969.

Tracy, James D. "Herring Wars: The Habsburg Netherlands and the Struggle for Control of the North Sea, ca. 1520–1560." *Sixteenth Century Journal* 24 (1993): 249–272.

Tranchant, Alfred, and Jules Ladimir. *Les femmes militaires de la France*. Paris: 1866.

Treadway, Sandra Gioia. "Anna Maria Lane: An Uncommon Common Soldier of the American Revolution." *Virginia Cavalcade* 37.3 (1988): 134–147.

Treadwell, Mattie E. *The Women's Army Corps*. Washington, DC: Office of the Chief of Military History, Department of the Army, 1954.

Trease, Geoffrey. *The Condottieri: Soldiers of Fortune*. New York: Holt, Rinehart and Winston, 1971.

Trevor-Roper, H.R. *The Last Days of Hitler*. 4th ed. Macmillan, 1971.

Trikoupis, Spyridon. *History of the Greek Revolution*. Athens, Greece: Christos Yovannis Publications, 1968.

Trotsky, Leon. *My Life: An Attempt at an Autobiography*. New York: Scribner's, 1930.

Tuchman, Barbara W. *A Distant Mirror: The Calamitous 14th Century*. New York: Knopf, 1978.

Tuotuo et al., ed. *Jin shi* [The history of the Jin dynasty (1115–1234)]. Beijing: Zhonghua shuju, 1975.

Tuotuo et al. *Song shi* [The history of the Song dynasty (960–1279)]. Beijing: Zhonghua shuju, 1977.

Turley, William S. "Women in the Communist Revolution in Vietnam." *Asian Survey* (1972).

Turner, Karen G., and Thanh Hao Phan. *Even the Women Must Fight: Memories of War from North Vietnam*. New York: Wiley, 1998.

Turney-High, Harry Holbert. *Primitive War: Its Practice and Concepts*. Columbia: University of South Carolina Press, 1991.

Twinch, Carol A. *Women on the Land: Their Story during Two World Wars*. Cambridge: Lutterworth Press, 1990.

Tyldesley, Joyce. *Hatchepsut: The Female Pharaoh*. New York: Viking, 1996.

Tyler, Royall. "Tomoe: The Woman Warrior." *Heroic with Grace: Legendary Women of Japan*. Ed. Chieko Irie Mulhern. Armonk, NY: M.E. Sharpe, 1991. 129–150.

Tyrrell, William Blake. *Amazons: A Study in Athenian Mythmaking*. Baltimore: Johns Hopkins University Press, 1984.

Uglow, Jennifer S., ed. *The Continuum Dictionary of Women's Biography*. New and expanded ed. New York: Continuum, 1989.

United States Marine Corps, History and Museums Division. *The Legend of Lucy Brewer*. Washington, DC: The Division, 1957.

Urry, K., and C. Wilcox. *Women and the Australian Armed Forces since the Second World War*. Canberra: Australian War Memorial, 1994.

Urzureau, Chanoine. "Une amazone vendéenne, Renée Bordereau." *Anjou Historique* 47 (1947): 63–65.

Vaissete, Joseph. *Histoire générale de Languedoc*. 2nd ed. Vol. 11. Toulouse: Privat, 1889.

Valencia Vega, Alipio. *Manuel Ascencio Padilla Y Juana Azurduy: Los Esposos Que Sacrificaron Vida Y Hogar a La Obra De Creaciôn De Patria*. La Paz, Bolivia: Librerâia Editorial Juventud, 1981.

Valeri, Nino, ed. *Storia d'Italia*. Vol. 1, *Il Medioevo*. Turin: UTET, 1965.

Van Creveld, Martin. "Women of Valor: Why Israel Doesn't Send Women into Combat." *Policy Review* Fall 1991: 65–67.

Vann, Richard T. "Women in Preindustrial Capitalism." *Becoming Visible: Women in European History*. Ed. Renate Bridenthal and Claudia Koonz. Boston: Houghton Mifflin, 1977. 192–216.

Vaughan, Elizabeth. *The Ordeal of Elizabeth Vaughan: A Wartime Diary of the Philippines*. Ed. by Carol M. Petillo. Athens: University of Georgia Press, 1985.

Vaughn, J.W. *With Crook at the Rosebud*. Harrisburg, PA: Stackpole, 1956.

Vaux-de-Cernay, Peter. *Histoire albigeoise*. Trans. Pascal Guébin and Henri Maisonneuve. Paris: Librairie Philosophique, 1951.

Velazquez, Loreta Janeta. *The Woman in Battle: A Narrative of the Exploits, Adventures, and Travels of Madame Loreta Janeta Velazquez, Otherwise Known as Lieutenant Harry T. Buford, Confederate States Army*. Reprint of 1876 ed. New York: Arno, 1972.

Verkhozin, A. "Polkom komanduet zhenshchina." *Kryl'ia Rodiny* 1966: 7–9.

———. "Komandir polka." *Geroini: Ocherki o zhenshchinakh—Geroiakh Sovetskogo Soiuza*. Ed. L.F. Toropov. Moscow: Politizdat, 1969. 1:133–142.

Vershinin, Konstantin Andreevich. *Chetvertaia Vozdushnaia* [Fourth Air (Army)]. Moscow: Voenizdat, 1975.

Vilenskii, Semen Samuilovich, John Crowfoot, and Zaiara Veselaia. *Till My Tale Is Told: Women's Memoirs of the Gulag*. Bloomington: Indiana University Press, 1999.

Vitruvius Pollio. *On Architecture*. Trans. Frank Granger. 2 vols. New York: Putnam, 1931–1934.

Volkmann, Hans. *Cleopatra: A Study in Politics and Propaganda*. New York: Sagamore Press, 1958.

Wade, Rex. *Red Guards and Workers' Militias in the Russian Revolution*. Stanford: Stanford University Press, 1984.

Wagner, Anton, ed. *Women Pioneers: Canada's Lost Plays*. Vol. 1. Toronto: Canadian Theatre Review Publications, 1979.

Wainwright, F.T. "Aethelflaed, Lady of the Mercians." *The Anglo-Saxons.* Ed. Peter Clemoes. London: Bowes, 1959. 53–69.

Wakefield, Walter L. *Heresy, Crusade, and Inquisition in Southern France, 1100–1250.* London: Allen and Unwin, 1974.

Wallace-Hadrille, J.M. *The Long-Haired Kings.* London: Methuen, 1962.

Wandruszka, Adam. *The House of Habsburg: Six Hundred Years of a European Dynasty.* Trans. Cathleen Epstein and Hans Epstein. Garden City, NY: Anchor Books, 1965.

Ward, Irene. *F.A.N.Y. Invicta.* London: Hutchinson, 1955.

Warner, Lavinia, and John Sandilands. *Women beyond the Wire: A Story of Prisoners of the Japanese, 1942–1945.* London: Joseph, 1982.

Weatherford, Doris. *American Women and World War II.* New York: Facts on File, 1990.

Webb, Kate. *On the Other Side; 23 Days with the Viet Cong.* New York: Quadrangle Books, 1972.

Webster, Graham. *Rome against Caratacus: The Roman Campaigns in Britain, AD 48–58.* Totowa, NJ: Barnes and Noble, 1982.

Wedgwood, C.V. *The Thirty Years War.* London: Jonathan Cape, 1938. Reprint, London: Jonathan Cape, 1971.

Wei Shou, ed. *Wei shu* [The history of the Northern Wei dynasty (386–543)]. Beijing: Zhonghua shuju, 1974.

Weiser, Marjorie P.K., and Jean S. Arbeiter. *Womanlist.* Saddle Brook, NJ: Stratford, 1981.

Weiss, Ruth. *The Women of Zimbabwe.* Harare: Nehanda Publishers, 1986.

Weitz, Margaret C. *Sisters in the Resistance: How Women Fought to Free France, 1940–1945.* New York: John Wiley, 1995.

Weitz, Margaret C. "Soldiers in the Shadows: Women of the French Resistance." *A Soldier and a Woman: Sexual Integration in the Military.* Ed. Gerard J. DeGroot and Corinna Peniston-Bird. New York: Pearson Education, 2000. 135–151.

Wernham, R.B. *Before the Armada.* New York: Norton, 1972.

West, Lucy Brewer. *The Female Marine; or, Adventures of Miss Lucy Brewer.* New York: Da Capo Press, 1966.

Whateley, Leslie. *As Thoughts Survive: An Account of Service with the Auxiliary Territorial Service.* London: Hutchinson, 1949.

Wheelwright, Julie. *Amazons and Military Maids: Women Who Dressed as Men in the Pursuit of Life, Liberty, and Happiness.* London: Pandora, 1989.

———. "Tarts, Tars, and Swashbucklers." *Bold in Her Breeches: Women Pirates across the Ages.* Ed. Jo Stanley. San Francisco: Harper, 1996.

White, Christine A. "Gossamer Wings: Women in Early Russian Aviation, 1910–1920." *Women in Aviation.* Ed. Barbara Lynch. Parks College of Saint Louis University, 1991.

White, John Todd. "The Truth about Molly Pitcher." *The American Revolution: Whose Revolution?* Ed. James Kirby Martin and Karen R. Stubaus. Huntington, NY: R.E. Krieger, 1977. 99–105.

Willard, C.C. "Christine de Pisan's Treatise on the Art of Medieval Warfare." *Essays in Honor of Louis Franis Solano.* Ed. R.J. Cormier and U.T. Holmes. Chapel Hill: 1970. 179–191.

Willenz, June A. *Women Veterans: America's Forgotten Heroines.* New York: Continuum, 1983.

William of Malmesbury. *De gestis regum Anglorum.* London: HMSO, 1887.

———. *Historia Novella.* London: Thomas Nelson, 1955.

William of Puylaurens. *Chronique, 1203–1275.* Trans. Jean Duvernoy. Paris: Centre National de la Recherche Scientifique, 1976.

William of Tudela and Anonymous. *The Song of the Cathar Wars: A History of the Albigensian Crusade.* Trans. Janet Shirley. Great Britain: Scolar Press, 1996.

William of Tyre. *A Middle English Chronicle of the First Crusade: The Caxton Eracles.* Trans. Dana Cushing. Lewiston, NY: Mellen Press, 2001.

Williams, Kenneth. "The Tennessee River Campaign and Anna Ella Carroll." *Indiana Magazine of History* 46 (1950): 221–248.

Williams, Louis. *The Israel Defense Forces: A People's Army.* Tel Aviv: Ministry of Defense, 1989.

Williams, Walter L. *The Spirit and the Flesh: Sexual Diversity in American Indian Culture.* Boston: Beacon Press, 1986.

Williamson, G.W. "The Air Transport Auxiliary." *RUSI (Journal of the Royal United Service Institution)* 88 (1943): 107–120.

Wills, Philip. *Free as a Bird.* New York: Barnes and Noble, 1974.

Woodward, Helen Beal. *The Bold Women.* Freeport, NY: Books for Libraries Press, 1956.

Woodward, Ralph Lee, Jr. *Rafael Carrera and the Emergence of the Republic of Guatemala, 1821–1871.* Athens: University of Georgia Press, 1993.

Yalom, Marilyn. *Blood Sisters: The French Revolution in Women's Memory.* New York: Basic Books, 1993.

Yanait, Rachel, Itzhak Avrahami, and Yerach Etzion, eds. *Hahaganah Biyerushalaim* [The defense in Jerusalem]. 2 vols. Jerusalem: Kiryat-Sefer, 1973–1975.

Young, Hugo. *The Iron Lady: A Biography of Margaret Thatcher.* New York: Farrar Straus Giroux, 1989.

Young, Helen Praeger. "Women at Work: Chinese Soldiers on the Long March, 1934–1936." *A Soldier and a Woman: Sexual Integration in the Military.* Ed. Gerard J. DeGroot and Corinna Peniston-Bird. New York: Pearson Education, 2000. 83–99.

Yurlova, Marina. *Cossack Girl.* New York: Macaulay Company, 1934.

Zarandi, Nabil. *The Dawn-Breakers: Nabil's Narrative of the Early Days of the Baha'i Revelation.* Trans. Shoghi Effendi. Wilmette, IL: Baha'i Publishing Trust, 1932.

Zeide, Alla. "Larisa Reisner: Myth as Justification for Life." *Russian Review* 51 (1992): 172–187.

Zerner, Monique. "L'épouse de Simon de Monfort et la croisade albigeoise." *Femmes, Mariages-Lignages, XIIe–XIVe siècles: Mélanges offerts à Georges Duby.* Ed. J. Dufournet, A. Joris, and P. Toubert. Brussels: De Boeck, 1992. 449–470.

Zhang, Tingyu. *Ming shi* (The history of the Ming dynasty [1368–1644]). Beijing: Zhonghua shuju, 1974.

Zimonti, Gino. *Vicende storiche vigevanesi.* 1st ed. Corscio, 1983.

Zirin, Mary F. "Nadezhda Andreevna Durova." *Dictionary of Russian Women Writers.* Ed. Marina Ledkovsky et al. Westport, CT: Greenwood, 1994. 163–166.

Index

The indexed portions of the book include the Introduction (volume I, in Roman numerals), the entries, and the Timeline. **Bold** type indicates an entry on the topic.

About the Contributors

JOHN T. ALEXANDER, PhD is professor of history and Russian and East European studies at the University of Kansas. He has published extensively on early modern Russia, especially the reign of Catherine the Great. His *Catherine the Great: Life and Legend* was chosen as a main selection of the History Book Club and several other book clubs. His translation of Evgenii V. Anisimov, *The Reforms of Peter the Great*, was also a selection of the History Book Club. He is currently working on a study of the four Russian empresses of the eighteenth century tentatively entitled *Amazon Autocratrixes*.

GLORIA ALLAIRE, PhD teaches at the University of Kentucky. She has published extensively on the chivalric literature and culture of late medieval Italy. She has contributed numerous entries to *Travel, Trade and Exploration in the Middle Ages: An Encyclopedia*, edited by John B. Friedman, and to *Medieval Italy: An Encyclopedia*, edited by Christopher Kleinhenz. Her books include *Andrea da Barberino and the Language of Chivalry*, the edited collection of articles *Modern Retellings of Chivalric Texts*, and *Il Tristano panciatichiano*, a forthcoming edition with translation.

MARY ALLEN is ABD writing her dissertation in history at the University of Toronto, Canada. Her dissertation topic is "Soviet Amazons? Women's Participation in the Red Army, 1918–1945."

DAVID BALFOUR, PhD is associate professor of history at the College of St. Joseph in Vermont. His research focuses on twelfth-century England, and his article "The Origins of the Longchamp Family" appeared in *Medieval Prosopography*.

JAN BASSETT, PhD (deceased) was born in Melbourne, Australia, and was educated at the University of Melbourne. She was the author of several books, including *Guns and Brooches: Australian Army Nursing from the Boer War to the Gulf War* and *The Home Front, 1914–1918*.

JAMES S. BAUGESS received his MA at the Ohio State University and his master of divinity degree at Southeastern Baptist Theological Seminary. His research interests are southern evangelicalism and Confederate military history. His publications include contributions to the *Encyclopedia of the American Civil War*. He is an instructor at Columbus State Community College, where he teaches American civilization in the Humanities Department.

DOUGLAS CLARK BAXTER, PhD is an associate professor of history at Ohio University, Athens, Ohio. He is the author of *Servants of the Sword: French Intendants of the Army, 1630–1670* and several articles on military administration.

EDNA G. BAY, PhD is associate professor in the Graduate Institute of the Liberal Arts, Emory University. She is the author of *Wives of the Leopard: Gender, Politics, and Culture in the Kingdom of Dahomey*.

PATRICIA BOWLEY obtained her MA in history from the University of Guelph and currently works as a freelance researcher and writer in Guelph, Ontario.

MARVIN A. BRESLOW, PhD is an associate professor emeritus of history at the University of Maryland, College Park. His works include *A Mirror of England: English Puritan Views of Foreign Nations, 1618–1640* and *The Political Writings of John Knox*.

ROBERT BRUCE, PhD is assistant professor of military history at Sam Houston State University in Huntsville, Texas. He is the author of *A Fraternity of Arms: America's Military Relationship with France during the First World War* and editor of *France in the Era of the Great War, 1911–1919: A Historical Dictionary*.

SUSANNAH U. BRUCE, PhD is an assistant professor of history in the Department of History at Sam Houston State University, Huntsville, Texas. She is working on a book that examines the experience of Irish-American military service in the American Civil War.

SUSANNA CALKINS, PhD is assistant professor of history at the University of Louisville. Her dissertation examined Quaker women and English political culture in late Stuart England. Her research interests include female prisoners and Quaker women in England in the seventeenth to the nineteenth centuries.

TIM CLARKSON is pursuing a PhD at the University of Manchester; his research topic is warfare in northern Britain from ca. 500 to ca. 750. His publications include "Richmond and Catraeth," *Cambrian Medieval Celtic Studies* 26 (1993): 15–20, and "Local Folklore and the Battle of Arthuret," *Transactions of the Cumberland and Westmorland Antiquarian and Archaeological Society* 95 (1995): 282–284.

COLIN COATES is director of the Centre of Canadian Studies, University of Edinburgh. His coauthored study *Heroines and History: The Commemoration of Madeleine de Verchères and Laura Secord* appeared in 2001.

S.P. CONNER, PhD is professor of history, vice-president for academic affairs, and dean of Florida Southern College. She is the author of a number of articles on issues of gender during the French Revolution and Napoleonic era, published in *Eighteenth-Century Studies, Eighteenth Century Life, Journal of Women's History,* and *Journal of Social History.*

CHRISTOPHER CORLEY, PhD is assistant professor of history at Minnesota State University at Moorhead. He teaches women's history and European history and is working on a book entitled *The King's Families: Parenting and Adolescence in Early Modern France.*

JANET L. CORYELL, PhD is professor of history at Western Michigan University. She is the author of *Neither Heroine nor Fool: Anna Ella Carroll of Maryland* and coeditor of *A Surgeon's Civil War: The Letters and Diary of Daniel M. Holt, M.D.* She won the Walter Prescott Webb Essay Prize with "Superseding Gender: The Role of the Woman Politico in Antebellum Partisan Politics," in *Women and the Unstable State in Nineteenth-Century America.*

KAZIMIERA J. COTTAM, PhD, is a former part-time history professor, military translator, and intelligence support analyst. She is a published author since 1972. Her recent publications include *Women in War and Resistance* and three edited and translated collections: *Women in Air War; On the Road to Stalingrad: Memoirs of a Woman Machine Gunner;* and *Defending Leningrad: Women behind Enemy Lines.* In 1999 she was awarded the Mary Zirin Prize by the Association for Women in Slavic Studies.

JOSEPHINE CRAWLEY is a doctoral student at the University of California, Berkeley.

DONNA DEFABIO CURTIN is a graduate student in the Department of History, Brown University.

PAUL K. DAVIS, PhD teaches at Texas Military Institute in San Antonio. His most recent publications include *An Encyclopedia of Invasions and Conquests, Encyclopedia of Warrior Peoples and Famous Fighting Units, 100 Decisive Battles,* and *Besieged: Great Sieges through History.*

W. JAMES DIXON, PhD is conducting research on issues concerning nationalism in central Europe in the nineteenth and twentieth centuries; his dissertation focused on the development and consolidation of the underground resistance movement in Poland during the German occupation (1939–1945). He has given presentations concerning women in the Polish resistance at national and international conferences.

KEVIN M. DOAK, PhD is associate professor of Japanese history at the University of Illinois at Urbana-Champaign. He is the author of *Dreams of Difference: The Japan Romantic School and the Crisis of Modernity* and coeditor of *Constructing Nationhood in Modern East Asia* and has written widely on Japanese history in journals such as *American Historical Review, Journal of Japanese Studies*, and *East Asian History*.

WILLIAM J. DUIKER, PhD is professor of history at Pennsylvania State University. He served as a foreign service officer in Taiwan and South Vietnam. His books include *Sacred War: Nationalism and Revolution in a Divided Vietnam* and *China and Vietnam: The Roots of Conflict*.

VALERIE EADS, PhD published "The Geography of Power: Matilda of Tuscany and the Strategy of Active Defense" in *Crusaders, Condottieri, and Cannon: Medieval Warfare in Societies around the Mediterranean*. Her dissertation was entitled "Mighty in War: The Role of Matilda of Tuscany in the War between Pope Gregory VII and Emperor Henry IV" (City University of New York, 2000).

KONRAD EISENBICHLER is professor of Renaissance studies/Italian and past director of the Centre for Reformation and Renaissance Studies at the University of Toronto. He has published on premodern Italian theatre, on confraternities, and on such figures as Lorenzo de' Medici, Savonarola, Michelangelo, Della Casa, and Bronzino. His volume *The Boys of the Archangel Raphael: A Youth Confraternity in Florence, 1411–1785* won the 2000 Howard R. Marraro Prize from the American Catholic Historical Association.

MICHAEL EVANS, PhD is lecturer in medieval history at Canterbury Christ Church University College. He has recently published on poor crusaders and on the Robin Hood legend in English place names and is currently carrying out research on the death of kings in medieval England and on gender and the crusades.

ELIZABETH EWAN, PhD is associate professor of history at the University of Guelph in Canada. Her publications include *Townlife in Fourteenth-Century Scotland, Women in Scotland, c. 1100–c. 1170* (coedited with Maureen Meikle), and articles in *Canadian Journal of History, Innes Review*, and various collections of essays.

DINA RIPSMAN EYLON is a scholar, writer, poet, translator, and former instructor of Jewish studies at the Department of Near and Middle Eastern Civilizations, University of Toronto. She received her BA from Haifa University and a PhD from the University of Toronto. She is editor and publisher of *Women in Judaism: A Multidisciplinary Journal* and its related publications.

GAYLE VERONICA FISCHER, PhD is assistant professor of history at Salem State College in Salem, Massachusetts. She has published extensively in the field of dress history, including *Pantaloons and Power: A Nineteenth-Century Dress Reform in the United States*.

NATALIE FORGET is a graduate student at the University of Guelph in Ontario. Her master's thesis was entitled "The Restructuring of the Gender System: A Case Study of Eleanor of Aquitaine and Matilda, Duchess of Normandy."

THOMAS ALAN FOSTER is completing his doctoral dissertation on eighteenth-century male sexuality and masculinity at the Johns Hopkins University. He is the author of an award-winning article on impotence and manhood in seventeenth-century New England.

WILLIAM HENRY FOSTER is a PhD candidate in the Department of History at Cornell University. He is currently researching American legal and constitutional history.

KARL FRIDAY, PhD is professor of Japanese history at the University of Georgia. His publications include *Hired Swords: The Rise of Private Warrior Power in Early Japan*, "Pushing beyond the Pale: The Yamato Conquest of the Emishi and Northern Japan" (*Journal of Japanese Studies*, 1997), and *Legacies of the Sword: The Kashima-Shinryu and Samurai Martial Culture*.

VICKI L. FRIEDL is the author of *Women in the United States Military, 1901–1995: A Research Guide and Annotated Bibliography*. She served on active duty in the United States Army Transportation Corps from 1980 to 1984. She is a librarian and writer whose research interests include twentieth-century military women.

RALPH F. GALLUCCI, PhD is a lecturer at the University of California, Santa Barbara. His research interests include mythology and legend in early Greece, Athenian democracy, and women in antiquity. He is presently working on a book, *The Myth of the Hoplite Oligarchy: Problems in Late Fifth-Century Athenian Politics, Ideology, and Constitutional History*.

BARBARA GANSON, PhD is associate professor of history at Florida Atlantic University. Her book *The Guaraní under Spanish Rule* has been accepted for publication. She is vice president of the Southwestern Historical Association. Ganson is currently conducting research on native herbal medicine and is revising her earlier publication on the history of Paraguayan women in the War of the Triple Alliance for a new edited volume on the Paraguayan War.

ROBERT W. GEE received his MA from the University of Toledo; his thesis examined the religious beliefs of the Levellers during the English Civil War. His current research interests revolve around social and cultural history of American radio broadcasting, and he is completing a study on the use of small-town ideals and imagery in certain American radio comedies from the 1930s to the 1950s. He has most recently taught history at Newberry College, South Carolina.

MARK W. GRAHAM, PhD is a lecturer in the humanities at Stanford University. He completed his doctoral dissertation, " 'World with Limits': News and Frontier Consciousness in the Late Roman Empire," at Michigan State University. His research interests include late Roman frontiers, intellectual and cultural approaches to late antiquity, and comparative ancient history.

DAVID S. GREEN teaches at the University of St. Andrew's. His research interests include chivalry, the religious and secular concerns of the medieval aristocracy, bastard feudal associations, and prosopography. He has written a number of articles on the household and military retinue of Edward the Black Prince and a biography of Edward of Woodstock.

DAVID HAY, PhD is assistant professor of history at the University of Lethbridge. He defended his doctoral thesis on the military career of Matilda of Tuscany at the University of Toronto's Centre for Medieval Studies in 2000. He has recently published "Gender Bias and Religious Intolerance in Accounts of the 'Massacres' of the First Crusade" in *Tolerance and Intolerance: Social Conflict in the Age of the Crusades*. His research interests include the history of warfare, gender, and canon law.

ELIZABETH LUTES HILLMAN is pursuing a JD/PhD in history at Yale University. She spent seven years in the United States Air Force as a space operations officer and instructor of history at the Air Force Academy; her primary research interests are gender, sexuality, and race in American military law and culture.

C.A. HOFFMAN completed master's degrees in classics and Near East studies at the University of California at Berkeley; he is currently translating the *Restitutio Christianismi* of Michael Servetus into English and writing a dissertation on the legal status of magic at Rome.

PETER HOFFMANN, PhD is William Kingsford Professor of History at McGill University, Montreal, Canada. He is the author of *Stauffenberg: A Family History, 1905–1944* and *The History of the German Resistance 1933–1945*.

STEPHANIE HOLLIS, PhD is associate professor in the Department of English, University of Auckland, New Zealand, and the author of *Anglo-Saxon Women and the Church: Sharing a Common Fate*.

JAMES W. HOOVER is a PhD candidate at the University of Wisconsin, Madison.

C.H.N. HULL is a doctoral student at the University of Toronto, working on the place of the army in British society in the 1930s. His publications include "The Crisis in British Army Recruiting in the 1930's," *Journal of the Canadian Historical Association* (1994): 125–146.

ALEXANDER INGLE is currently completing his doctoral dissertation at Boston University on the uses of agricultural profit in the Roman Empire. He has published articles on Roman women and Roman slavery.

M. ELEANOR IRWIN, PhD is retired from the Division of Humanities at the University of Toronto at Scarborough. She continues to teach a graduate course in the Department of Classics. Her article "Evadne, Iamos, and Violets in Pindar's Sixth Olympian" appeared in *Hermes*.

MARTIN P. JOHNSON, PhD has published on a variety of topics in French history. His publications include *The Paradise of Association: Political Culture and Popular Organizations in the Paris Commune of 1871*. He is currently writing a book on the Dreyfus affair.

JUDITH KEENE is the director of the European Studies Centre, Department of History, at the University of Sydney, Australia, where she teaches twentieth-century European political and cultural history. She completed her graduate studies at the University of California, San Diego, and has published on the Spanish Republic and the civil war and on European cinema. Her latest book is *Fighting for Franco: International Volunteers in Nationalist Spain during the Spanish Civil War, 1936–1939*.

DORIS KEHRY-KURZ teaches in the Department of Chinese Studies, University of Kiel, Germany. Her MA thesis for the University of Heidelberg, 1996, was a study of Qin Liangyü.

JOHN KLASSEN, PhD is professor of history at Trinity Western University in British Columbia. His publications include *The Letters of the Rozmberk Sisters: Noblewomen in Fifteenth-Century Bohemia* and *Warring Maidens, Captive Wives, and Hussite Queens*.

HENDRIK KRAAY, PhD is assistant professor of history and political science at the University of Calgary. He is the author of *Race, State, and Armed Forces in Independence-Era, Brazil*, has published articles in *Hispanic American Historical Review, Journal of Social History*, and *Slavery and Abolition*, and is completing a book-length social history of the military institutions of Bahia, Brazil, in the era of independence.

MARIE-THÉRÈSE LALAGUË-GUILHEMSANS is archivist and curator in the national archives in Paris. Her most recent publications include contributions to the *Dictionnaire de la musique en France aux XVIIe et XVIIIe siècles* and the *Histoire du notariat en Belgique*.

ANTAL LEISEN, PhD is the director of Kreorg Educational Center Ltd., running Grid Od and Edward de Bono creativity seminars in Budapest, Hungary.

NICOLAS LEMIRE is a graduate student in medieval history at the University of Toronto with research interests in gender and the English criminal justice system ca. 1300–1600.

ELIZABETH D. LEONARD, PhD is assistant professor of history at Colby College and teaches American history from the Revolution through the Civil War and American women's history from colonial times to the present. She is the author of *Yankee Women: Gender Battles in the Civil War* and *All The Daring of the Soldier: Women of the Civil War Armies*.

JOHN A. LYNN, PhD is professor of history at the University of Illinois at Urbana-Champaign. He is author of *The Bayonets of the Republic: Motivation and Tactics in the Army of Revolutionary France, 1791–1794* and *Giant of the Grand Siècle: The French Army, 1610–1715*.

TANYA LYONS is a PhD candidate in the Department of Politics at the University of Adelaide, South Australia. Her thesis is entitled "Guns and Guerrilla Girls: Zimbabwean Women in the National Struggle for Independence."

JEAN-CLÉMENT MARTIN is professor of history at the University of Nantes, France. He is the author of *La Vendée et la France* and *Révolution et Contre-Révolution en France, 1789–1989*.

LAURENCE W. MARVIN, PhD is assistant professor of history at Berry College; his research interests include the military history of the High Middle Ages, especially work on common soldiers, and the Albigensian Crusade. His article "Men Famous in Combat and Battle: Common Soldiers and the Siege of Bruges, 1127" appeared in the *Journal of Medieval History*.

CURTIS F. MORGAN, PhD is associate professor of history at Lord Fairfax Community College in Middletown, Virginia. His research interests include twentieth-century Germany and American diplomatic history.

SHERRY J. MOU, PhD is associate professor of history and assistant professor in the Chinese Department at Wellesley College, Massachusetts. Her interests are mainly in classical Chinese women's history and literature. She is currently working on a collection of articles on medieval Chinese women and a book on the tradition of "biographies of women" in Chinese official histories.

VAN THANH NGUYEN-MARSHALL is a PhD candidate at the University of British Columbia, Vancouver, Canada. Her dissertation examines the Vietnamese elite's thinking on issues of poverty and charity in North Vietnam under French colonialism. Her teaching interests include modern Southeast Asian, modern Chinese, and world histories.

PATRICK J. O'CONNOR is a PhD candidate at West Virginia University.

BOBBIE OLIVER, PhD is a research fellow at the Research Institute for Cultural Heritage, Curtin University of Technology, Perth, Western Australia. She was educated at the University of Western Australia, has taught in several Australian universities, and worked for two years as a research officer at the Australian War Memorial. She is the author of several books, including *War and Peace in Western Australia: The Social and Political Impact of the Great War, 1914–1926* and *Peacemongers: Australian Conscientious Objectors to Military Service, 1911 to 1945*. She is presently researching and writing a history of the organized-labor movement in Western Australia.

CYNTHIA PACES is a PhD candidate at Columbia University. Her dissertation is entitled "Monumental Crusade: The Jan Hus Memorial and the Battle for Public Space in Prague's Old Town Square, 1890–1925."

ANNETTE PARKS, PhD is an assistant professor at the University of Evansville. Her dissertation is entitled "Living Pledges: Hostageship in the Middle Ages, 1050–1300." Her most recent publication was "Prisoners of Love: Medieval Wives as Hostages," *Journal of the Georgia Association of Historians*.

JOSEPH F. PATROUCH, PhD is associate professor in the Department of History at Florida International University. He is currently researching a biography of the Habsburg archduchess Isabell (1554–1592), and his publications include *A Negotiated Settlement: The Counter-Reformation in Upper Austria under the Habsburgs*.

HAYDEN PEAKE is an adjunct professor of intelligence history at the Joint Military Intelligence College, Washington, D.C.

REINA PENNINGTON, PhD is director of the Peace, War, and Diplomacy Studies program at Norwich University in Vermont. Her publications include *Wings, Women, and War: Soviet Airwomen in World War II Combat* and numerous scholarly and popular articles. She serves as the U.S. editor for *Minerva: Quarterly Report on Women and the Military*.

JANE MARIE PINZINO, PhD is assistant professor of religion at the University of Puget Sound. Her research focus is Joan of Arc; she recently published "Speaking of Angels: A Fifteenth Century Bishop in Defense of Joan of Arc's Mystical Experiences" in *Fresh Verdicts on Joan of Arc*.

ROBERT PONICHTERA, PhD is deputy director of grants development for the Vietnam Veterans of America Foundation. His publications include "Feminists, Nationalists, and Soldiers: Women in the Fight for Polish Independence" in *International History Review*.

J.M.B. PORTER, PhD studied with Bernard Hamilton at the University of Nottingham. His thesis examined monastic reform movements in England and France during the twelfth century. His research interests include monastic reform, popular preaching, heresy, and the role of women in the medieval church. He is currently teaching in the Change and Tradition program at Butler University in Indianapolis, Indiana.

SARAH J. PURCELL, PhD is assistant professor of history at Grinnell College. She is the author of *Sealed with Blood: National Identity and Public Memory of the Revolutionary War, 1775–1825* and coauthor of *Out of the Ordinary: A Biographical Dictionary of Women Travelers and Explorers* and *Encyclopedia of Battles in North America, 1517–1916.*

CONNIE L. REEVES, MA is currently writing the history of the Air Force Nurse Corps and has written several articles and chapters on military nursing. She wrote the history of the Department of the Army for the fiscal years 1996 and 1997, which will be published by the U.S. army Center of Military History. She is a retired Army officer and served as a helicopter pilot, intelligence officer, imagery analyst, and Western European specialist.

ELIZABETH SALAS, PhD is associate professor in the Department of American Ethnic Studies, University of Washington, and the author of *Soldaderas in the Mexican Military: Myth and History.* Her latest book chapter is about three New Mexican politicians.

ALEXA SAMUELS, MA says that having completed degrees in Latin American studies from McGill and Tulane Universities, she now resides in her hometown of Toronto, spending her days wrapped in dreamy irreverence, awaiting epiphany.

ALAN SHEPARD, PhD is associate professor of English at Texas Christian University. He has published on the links between militarism, nationalism, and literature (especially dramas and military conduct books) in England, Scotland, and Ireland in the sixteenth and seventeenth centuries. He is the author of *Marlowe's Soldiers: Rhetorics of Masculinity in the Age of the Armada.*

JANE SLAUGHTER, PhD is associate professor of history at the University of New Mexico. Her publications include *Women and the Italian Resistance, 1943–45,* and her latest project is "Gender and the Reconstruction of Italy, 1945–60."

KENNETH SLEPYAN, PhD is associate professor of history at Transylvania University. His publications include *"The People's Avengers": Soviet Partisans, Stalinist Society, and the Politics of Resistance, 1941–1945.*

HENRIETTA STOCKEL has published five books, four of which are about the Chiricahua Apaches. She has appeared in television documentaries discussing the topic, lectures widely, and is a recognized national expert on Chiricahua Apache women and children.

LAURIE STOFF received her PhD in history from the University of Kansas. She is currently revising her dissertation, focusing on Russian women in combat during the First World War, for publication. She is the author of "They Fought for Russia: Female Soldiers of the First World War," in Gerard De-Groot and Corinna Peniston-Bird, eds., *A Soldier and a Woman: Sexual Integration in the Military* (2000) and has served as historical consultant on several film projects, including the PBS/BBC documentary series *The Great War* and a feature film on the life of Mariia Bochkareva, commander of the First Russian Women's Battalion of Death.

CLAIRE TAYLOR is pursuing a PhD at the University of Nottingham; her research topic is "Dualist Heresy in Aquitaine and the Agenais, c. 1000–c. 1249." She is interested in the political and military role of women in the Crusader States.

DAVID G.K. TAYLOR, PhD is a lecturer in the Theology Department of the University of Birmingham, England, where he is responsible for postgraduate supervision in Syriac, Aramaic, and Hebrew and lectures to undergraduates on the Hebrew Bible, patristics, and Middle Eastern Christianity. He is currently producing the editio princeps of the earliest Syriac commentary on the Psalter.

HEATHER THIESSEN-REILY, PhD is assistant professor of history at Western State College in Gunnison, Colorado.

RODNEY G. THOMAS, Colonel, United States Army (retired), is working on an analytical history of the Battle of the Little Big Horn from the Native American point of view, making extensive use of both published and unpublished testimony as well as pictographs or ledger art. He holds an MS in transportation management and an MA in strategic studies.

JOYCE A. THOMSON, MA, is a freelance researcher and author of *The WAAAF in Wartime Australia.*

JOHN LAWRENCE TONE, PhD is associate professor in the School of History, Technology, and Society at the Georgia Institute of Technology. His publications include "Women in the Resistance to Napoleon" in *Constructing Spanish Womanhood,* edited by Pamela Radcliff and Victoria Enders.

JOYCE TYLDESLEY is Honorary Research Fellow at the School of Archaeology, Classics, and Oriental Studies, Liverpool University, England. Her recent publications include *Daughters of Isis: Women of Ancient Egypt* and *Hatchepsut: The Female Pharaoh.* She is now writing a biography of Queen Nefertiti.

MARK D. VAN ELLS is a doctoral candidate in the Department of History at the University of Wisconsin at Madison, writing his dissertation on the readjustment of Second World War veterans to civilian life. His research and teaching interests include social and cultural perspectives on the U.S. military.

JOHN WALBRIDGE, PhD teaches in the department of Near Eastern Languages at Indiana University. He is the author of "The Babi Uprising in Zanjan," *Iranian Studies*.

TIM J. WATTS is humanities bibliographer at Hale Library, Kansas State University. His research interests include American military history, nineteenth century legal history, and the significance of gender in library science.

MAURICE WEBB, PhD is associate professor of history at the University of Central Arkansas. His research interests include nineteenth century Germany, France, and Italy.

PAUL WESTERMEYER served as a rifleman in the United States Marine Corps. He is currently an instructor at Columbus State Community College and a PhD candidate in history at the Ohio State University.

JULIE WHEELWRIGHT is the author of *Amazons and Military Maids: Women Who Dressed as Men in the Pursuit of Life, Liberty, and Happiness*. She is currently working on a book about the history of the fur trade.

CHRISTINE WHITE, PhD is Professor of History at Pennsylvania State University. She is the author of the award-winning *British and American Commercial Relations with Soviet Russia, 1918–1924* as well as several articles on women in aviation.

J. KEITH WIKELEY recently retired as Western European studies librarian, Humanities and Social Sciences Library, University of Alberta. He is working on a historical dictionary of Tyrol and the Trentino, as a translator into English from German and Italian, and on his swimming technique.

RALPH LEE WOODWARD, JR., PhD, is professor emeritus of History at Tulane University. He is the author of *Central America, a Nation Divided* and *Rafael Carrera and the Emergence of the Republic of Guatemala, 1821–1871*, as well as many other books and articles.

ROBERT J. ZALIMAS, JR., is a doctoral candidate at The Ohio State University. His dissertation focuses on black Union troops as a garrison force in the postwar South and trans-Mississippi West. He is a writer/researcher for "This Day in Civil War History" on HistoryChannel.com.

MARY F. ZIRIN of Altadena, California, is an independent researcher-translator concentrating on the works and lives of prerevolutionary Russian women writers. She is coeditor of the forthcoming *Women and Gender in Russia and Eastern Europe: A Comprehensive Bibliography*.